Woodworking: The Right Technique

Three Practical Ways to Do Every Job— and How to Choose the One That's Right for You

Bob Moran

Rodale Press, Inc.
Emmaus, Pennsylvania

Contributing Writers
Kenneth S. Burton, Jr.
Tony O'Malley
Robert A. Yoder

Woodworking: The Right Technique
Editorial and Design Staff
Editor: Kevin Ireland
Interior Book Designer: Frank Milloni
Cover Designer: Kitty Pierce Mace
Interior Layout: Jerry O'Brien
Illustrators: Sally Onopa and Frank Rohrbach
Photographers: John Hamel and Mitch Mandel
Senior Copy Editor: Barbara McIntosh Webb
Project Copy Editor: Candace B. Levy
Editorial Assistance: Gloria Krupa Andrew,
Nancy Kutches, and Stephanie Wenner
Production Coordinator: Patrick T. Smith
Indexer: Lucia Read

Rodale Press Home and Garden Books
Vice President and Editorial Director:
Margaret Lydic Balitas
Managing Editor, Woodworking/DIY Books:
Kevin Ireland
Art Director: Michael Mandarano
Associate Art Director: Mary Ellen Fanelli
Studio Manager: Leslie Keefe
Copy Director: Dolores Plikaitis
Office Manager: Karen Earl-Braymer
Production Manager: Helen Clogston

Photo Credits
The photos on pages 94 and 97 were provided by the
manufacturers of the machines shown:
Delta International Machinery Corporation
Porter-Cable Corporation
Powermatic Incorporated
Sears, Roebuck and Company
Tools and supplies used in other photographs were
provided by:
Garrett Wade Company (page 2)
The St. James Bay Tool Company (page 115)
Wentz Hardware (page 36)
Woodcraft Supply Corporation (pages 108, 110,
and 120)

If you have any questions or comments concerning this
book, please write to:
Rodale Press, Inc.
Book Readers' Service
33 East Minor Street
Emmaus, PA 18098

Library of Congress Cataloging-in-Publication Data

Moran, Bob (Robert J.)
Woodworking : the right technique : three practical
ways to do every job—and how to choose the one that's
right for you / by Bob Moran.
p.   cm.
Includes index.
ISBN 0–87596–712–4 (hc : alk. paper)
1. Woodwork.   2. Woodworking tools.   I. Title.
TT180.M65   1996
684'.08—dc20   95–46500

Distributed in the book trade by St. Martin's Press

2 4 6 8 10 9 7 5 3 1   hardcover

To my father, who, as Santa Claus, built my first workbench.

CONTENTS

INTRODUCTION

Woodworking has its fair share of evangelists, members of the fraternity who will try to convert you to this technique or that kind of wood, this tool or that finish, this machine or that kind of glue. I count myself among them. With little excuse and no encouragement, I'll argue whole-heartedly for having fun at woodworking and I'll brook no dissent. If you're not going to enjoy woodworking, give it up.

But beyond having fun, the straight and narrow begins to meander, for me anyway. The right technique for resawing today may not be the best technique after I sneak my latest tool purchase past my wife. The right technique for dovetailing the 4 highly visible corner joints of a blanket chest may not be the best technique for dovetailing the 44 hidden corner joints in a set of kitchen cabinet drawers. And the right technique for preparing the edge of a board for gluing may change after I have another 50 hours of experience with hand planes. I just can't get into the attitude that some one technique is always right. So this book presents a variety of techniques for you to choose from.

I've tried to include at least three different methods for every major woodworking task. You'll find that in some cases those three methods involve three different tools—in other cases the methods are three ways to use the same tool. The alternatives are *not* good, better, and best, or good, bad, and indifferent. Each choice is the best choice under appropriate circumstances. If there aren't three best methods for a particular job, I'll say so. Weigh the alternatives and choose what works for you.

Choosing the right technique is part of the fun of woodworking—but there's more. There's a certain smile that creeps across the face of woodworkers when they discover a new technique, a smile that says, "Hey, I can do that!" It's the smile that crosses the face of a beginner when he first discovers that he can joint the edge of a board with a router mounted in a table, or the smile that crosses the face of a professional when he first discovers that he can cut both cheeks of a tenon at once with a pair of spaced saw blades. It's the smile that says, "I'm really getting good at this." I hope that smile creeps across your face as you go through this book.

Woodworking is fun for so many because there are so many ways to go about it. If you're a highly intuitive kind of person, one who likes to mold and massage things to your liking, sneaking up on the final result, you may get the most pleasure from working wood with hand tools, like planes and chisels. On the other hand, if you're the sort who figures out all the nitty-gritty details ahead of time and then executes your idea in one bold, precise, perfect stroke, you may get more pleasure from working wood with machines, like table saws and routers. In either case, you can learn and expand your horizons by becoming familiar with the alternatives. In both the long run and the short run, you'll have more fun if you're familiar with the choices available to you. And if you spend a little time messin' around with the other guy's technique, you could wind up discovering talents you never dreamed you had. That discovery can be the most fun of all.

Using This Book

Just as woodworkers get a thrill when their projects get well used, book writers get a thrill when folks read their books. But if you're in such a hurry to get to your shop that you can't sit down and read this book cover to cover, I won't take offense. In fact, I've tried to arrange things so the book will be useful to you anyway.

If you're building a project using plans from another book or a magazine and the instructions tell you to use a tool that you don't have, page through the relevant chapter in this book for some solutions. You'll find alternative techniques that are fully illustrated so you can get the main idea without wading through the text. And you'll usually find a chart near the end of the chapter or section that sums up the pros and cons of each of the alternatives. If you're an experienced woodworker and you're considering skipping a chapter because you have the techniques down pat, flip through it anyway and read the tips. You may pick up a handy detail that you weren't familiar with. If you spot an intriguing technique in the drawings but wonder about how practical it really is, read the associated text. I've tried to provide both even-handed evaluations and frank, personal opinions. You can disagree with both if you like—just be sure to have fun doing it your own way.

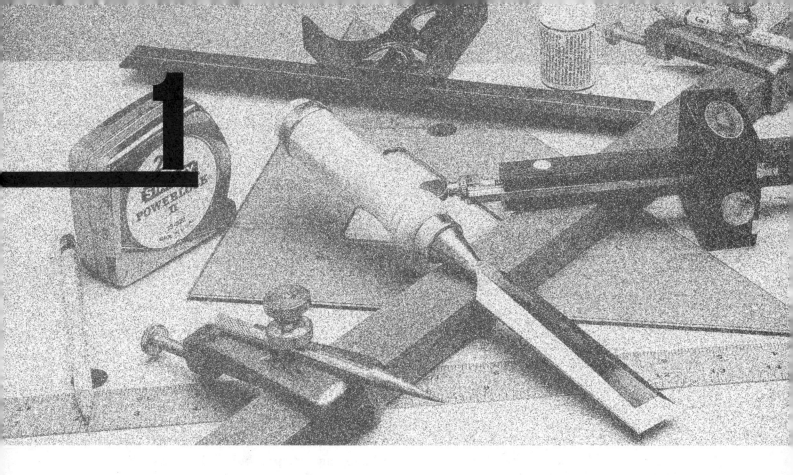

ESSENTIAL

SHOP

TECHNIQUES

I once thought that I had mastered walking by the time I turned two, certainly by the time I earned the Boy Scout Merit Badge in Hiking. Then, in my late twenties, a veteran hiker in the Hawaiian Trail and Mountain Club, Joe Nielson, taught me how to pace myself, fine-tune my stride, and place my feet. Without intending to, Joe also taught me to question how much I really know about simple, ordinary skills. And he taught me that the most important skills are the ones you use most often.

These lessons apply to woodworking as well. Common tasks like measuring; sharpening; drawing lines, shapes, and curves; and gluing may seem simple; but doing them right is as important to good woodworking as walking is to getting across the street. In questioning how I've performed basic woodworking tasks over the years, I've chucked out some conventional wisdom—like the advice that you should always measure precisely—and embraced other, out-of-favor practices like using glue that you can unglue.

If you're new to woodworking, you'll find that this kind of attention to basic techniques has a double payback. It not only increases your pleasure in every project you undertake, it also makes the more specialized woodworking skills easier and more enjoyable to learn.

MEASURING, LAYING OUT, AND SETTING UP

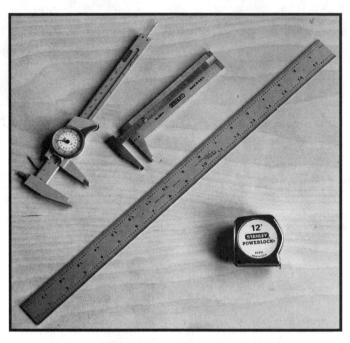

The most useful measuring tools for the woodworking shop are a small tape measure, a steel ruler with scales reading from both ends, and calipers.

Ask a woodworker what tools he has, and he'll tell you about his planes and chisels. But watch him get down to work, and the first tools he picks up will be rulers and pencils and squares. The only time you're likely to cut wood without first measuring is when you're trying out the saw.

This is a book about choosing among alternatives, and choices start even at the level of measuring. Every time you mark a piece of wood or adjust a machine, you're choosing a degree of accuracy. If you're rough-cutting lumber, there's no point in measuring a part exactly; since your purpose is to make the stock manageable, all you need to do is cut the piece a bit oversized. Even if you're cutting a tabletop to final width, you don't need to work from precise marks; no one will ever notice if the width differs a little from one end to the other. But if you're cutting a tenon, your layout or setup must be precise or else your joint will fail.

Keep in mind the purpose of your measurements. If you intend to cut a joint with hand tools, then you need to choose accurate methods of laying out the joint because only your hand and your eye guide the cut. If you intend to cut the joint with machines, the layout is little more than your notes to yourself about where the joint must go. In this case you need to choose accurate methods of setting up, because machine adjustments determine where the cut will go.

A friend of mine once observed, "Some jobs are well worth doing poorly." Save your energy and concentration for the jobs that benefit from it, and then be as precise as you can.

MEASURING TOOLS

When you think of measurement, the first tools that come to mind are scales, such as tape measures and rulers. If you have a background in engineering or mechanics, micrometers might also occur to you. But in the woodworking shop, scales are appropriate, micrometers are not. This is because as a craftsman you're building one-of-a-kind projects, not interchangeable parts for mass production. If a cabinet door is a wee bit too tight you can always take another plane shaving off of it.

Scales

Scales are available in a variety of calibrations, including fractional inches, decimal inches, and metric. Stay away from scales with one calibration along one edge and another along the opposite edge. A better use for the second edge is a scale reading from right to left. A ruler reading from both directions is convenient because you can read the scale no matter how you pick it up, and regardless of the direction you need to measure. Narrow scales like most tape measures are quick and easy to read if they're divided into sixteenths along one edge and eighths along the other.

Calipers

While scales are indispensable for a lot of shop work, their accuracy is limited by your eyesight. Those of you still on the uphill side of life may have no difficulty reading a scale to ¹⁄₆₄ inch in poor lighting but some of us who are picking up speed on the downhill side have more trouble. For us, calipers are essential.

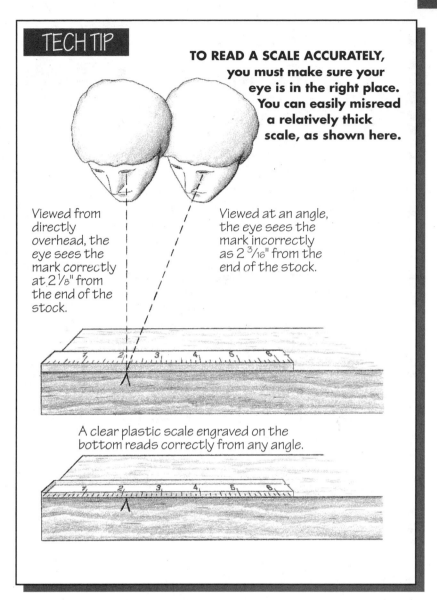

TECH TIP

TO READ A SCALE ACCURATELY, you must make sure your eye is in the right place. You can easily misread a relatively thick scale, as shown here.

Viewed from directly overhead, the eye sees the mark correctly at 2⅛" from the end of the stock.

Viewed at an angle, the eye sees the mark incorrectly as 2 ³⁄₁₆" from the end of the stock.

A clear plastic scale engraved on the bottom reads correctly from any angle.

The needle movement in dial calipers makes measurements to a sixty-fourth or a hundredth of an inch easy to read. Some calipers can read to a few thousandths. Modern high-tech plastics have brought dial calipers, as shown in the photo on the opposite page, within the price range of most woodworkers. They combine conventional outside calipers with inside calipers and a depth gauge. All three measures will read the same at the same time.

Plain calipers, as shown in the photo, are convenient for measuring thickness but are no more readable than tapes and scales.

When setting up machines, your best measuring tool may be neither a scale *nor* calipers. "Setup Tools" on page 8 explains how to measure with screws and standard references.

THREE RULES FOR MEASURING

You can avoid a lot of unpleasant surprises by becoming a creature of habit. I've found the following three rules of measurement to be well worth making into regular habits. Follow them as rules until they become second nature.

Rule 1: Always make your measurements from as few surfaces as possible. The surfaces that you measure from are called "reference surfaces." By keeping them to a minimum, you avoid cumulative errors. For example, if you are laying out dadoes for shelves on the sides of a bookcase, measure them all from one end of the workpiece, as shown in the bottom half of the drawing, rather than measuring between them, as shown in the top half of the drawing. If you measure each dado and each space separately and each one is off by a hair, you could be off by several hairs by the time you get to the last one. If you measure them all from one end of the board, none of your marks will be off by more than a single hair.

Rule 2: Think twice, measure once. Everybody who owns both a saw and a tape measure has heard the addage "measure twice, cut once." Forget it. Think twice and measure once. Think about what you are measuring. When measuring the correct length for the shelves in our bookcase example, you can measure the distance between the sides a dozen times and the shelves will still be too short. But just one accurate measurement from dado bottom to dado bottom will get it right.

Rule 3: Whenever possible, use the actual workpiece as your gauge instead of measuring the piece and working from the measurement. This saves time and reduces the chances of error. For example, if you are setting up your router to rabbet the back edges of your bookcase sides for a ¼-inch plywood back panel, don't measure the actual plywood thickness; use a scrap of the plywood to gauge the router setting.

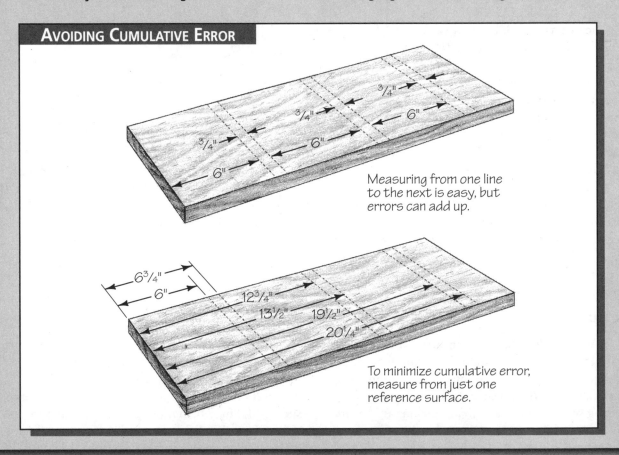

AVOIDING CUMULATIVE ERROR

¾"   ¾"
6"   6"   6"
¾"
6"

Measuring from one line to the next is easy, but errors can add up.

6¾"
6"
12¾"
13½"   19½"
20¼"

To minimize cumulative error, measure from just one reference surface.

Marking Tools

Many woodworkers give little thought to marking tools. They stick a sharp pencil in their pocket and never use anything else. It's too bad, because marking tools are inexpensive and choosing the right one for the job makes the job a lot easier.

Big, fat **lumber crayons** are my favorite marking tools for rough layouts. I circle faults in the stock with a red crayon before deciding where to lay out each part. Then I mark my cut lines with a black crayon. A pencil mark on a rough oak plank is hard to see without getting a splinter in your nose, but a crayon mark is visible from across the room.

I use a mechanical **drafting pencil** loaded with soft lead, say 2B, for noncritical layouts for machine work. It makes an easily seen mark

Useful marking tools, in order from the least precise to the most precise, are a lumber crayon, a soft-lead pencil, a hard carpenter's pencil sharpened to a single-bevel skew tip, and a layout knife.

without scratching the wood. You can really be quite free and easy with 2B lead. As long as you don't bear down heavily on soft woods, your penciled lines will disappear when you scrape or sand the wood after assembly.

A **carpenter's pencil** is my choice for critical layouts that I need to see easily. Properly sharpened, its mark is much more precise than one made with a 2B pencil, but it's more easily seen than one made with a knife. Buy carpenter's pencils with "hard" lead, and sharpen them as shown in *Sharpening a Carpenter's Pencil* to make precision tools out of them. The hard lead will take and hold a

SHARPENING A CARPENTER'S PENCIL

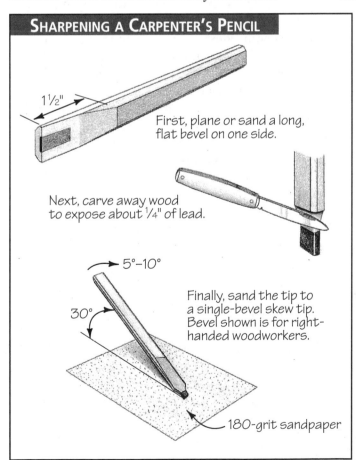

1½"

First, plane or sand a long, flat bevel on one side.

Next, carve away wood to expose about ¼" of lead.

5°–10°

30°

Finally, sand the tip to a single-bevel skew tip. Bevel shown is for right-handed woodworkers.

180-grit sandpaper

MARKING WITH A CARPENTER'S PENCIL

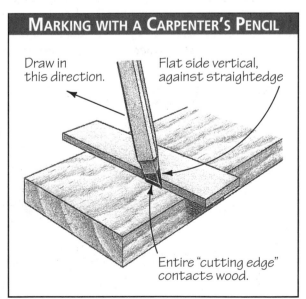

Draw in this direction.

Flat side vertical, against straightedge

Entire "cutting edge" contacts wood.

sharper edge than a standard pencil, will produce a fine line several feet in length before you need to resharpen it, and will even sever the fibers of softer woods. But producing these precise, black, knife-like lines with a fragile lead requires that you frequently touch up the lead's edge.

To use the pencil, keep the flat side vertical, against a straightedge, and the entire "cutting" edge in contact with the stock. Pull the pencil in the direction that it's tilted, as shown in *Marking with a Carpenter's Pencil* on page 5. Apply only enough pressure to leave a clear mark. Too much pressure will just dull the pencil prematurely.

The **layout knife** is the traditional tool for precise layout. It does more than just show you where to cut: It scores the wood fibers, which minimizes tear-out when you cut the stock, and it provides a groove that allows you to position a chisel by feel instead of by eye. Unfortunately, layout knife marks are often difficult to see without strong illumination from the side. They also mar the stock rather permanently. A good number of commercially available layout knives are no better than your pocketknife, but I find one particular design to be a cut above the rest. It has a thin, skew tip blade with a single bevel, as shown in *Single- and Double-Bevel Layout Knives*. The advantage of the single bevel is that you know the cutting edge is right up against the guiding straightedge when the knife is perpendicular to the surface of the stock. To make your own, see the "Marking Knife" chapter on page 244.

Gauges

Think of the marking gauge, cutting gauge, and mortise gauge as self-guiding layout knives. The marking gauge, shown at left in *Layout Gauges*, marks with a pin sharpened to a conical point. Use

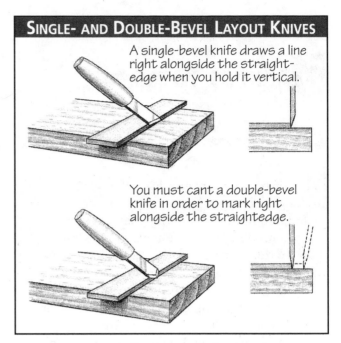

SINGLE- AND DOUBLE-BEVEL LAYOUT KNIVES

A single-bevel knife draws a line right alongside the straightedge when you hold it vertical.

You must cant a double-bevel knife in order to mark right alongside the straightedge.

it when marking end grain and when working parallel to the grain. It will tear out the fibers of the wood if you try to use it across the grain. The cutting gauge, shown at center in the drawing, marks with a knife sharpened to a rounded single-bevel edge. Use it when marking across the grain. The mortise gauge, shown at right in the drawing, is a sophisticated marking gauge with two pins for marking both sides of a mortise or tenon at once. This is not simply a timesaving feature; it ensures that both the mortise and tenon are laid out to exactly the same dimensions.

The usefulness of each of the gauges depends entirely on the kind of work you do. Since the cutting gauge severs the wood fibers, it helps prevent splintering along a crosscut, whether you make the cut with a handsaw or a machine. If you do your joinery with machines, the cutting gauge may be the only gauge you have real use for. Use it to sever

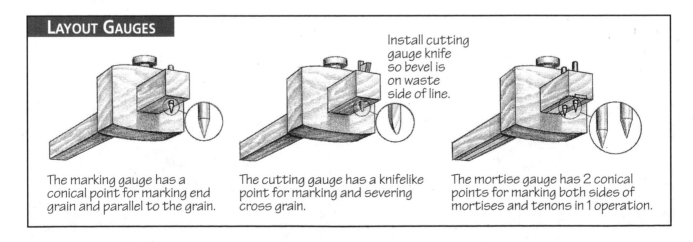

LAYOUT GAUGES

Install cutting gauge knife so bevel is on waste side of line.

The marking gauge has a conical point for marking end grain and parallel to the grain.

The cutting gauge has a knifelike point for marking and severing cross grain.

The mortise gauge has 2 conical points for marking both sides of mortises and tenons in 1 operation.

the grain and prevent splintering on tenon shoulders and similar cuts. The marking and mortise gauges are useful primarily for laying out hand cuts.

If you cut joints with hand tools, you will eventually want all three gauges. You'll use them all just in laying out a tenon—the mortise gauge for the cheeks, the marking gauge for the edges, and the cutting gauge for the shoulders. Buy the marking gauge and cutting gauge first. The two together cost much less than a mortise gauge and can mark all of the possible grain orientations. Then save up for the more expensive mortise gauge. Don't be tempted by mortise gauges with a single marking gauge pin opposite the mortise pins. They're a pain, literally: You'll invariably prick your fingers on the pins that you're not using at the moment. The marking gauge pin is pretty useless anyway; you have to lose the fence adjustment that positions the tenon cheeks in order to mark the edges. (See the chapter "Mortise-and-Tenon Joints" on page 152 for laying out mortises and tenons.) If you own one of these ill-conceived hybrid gauges, pull out the marking gauge pin and buy yourself a proper marking gauge.

TECH TIP

IF YOU DON'T HAVE ENOUGH USE FOR A MORTISE GAUGE to warrant buying one but have a significant number of identical mortises to lay out, you can speed things up with a shim. Set the gauge to mark the sides of the mortises farthest from the reference surfaces. To mark the nearer sides of the mortises, make a shim the same thickness as the tenons and put it between the gauge fence and the reference surface. Then use the same shim when laying out the tenons.

Gauges leave a rather permanent mark on the stock, and this bothers some woodworkers. When using a gauge, stop when you've gone as far as you need to go but don't worry if you overshoot a bit. Gauge marks left on your work stamp it as handcrafted; some of the finest antiques show gauge marks longer than they needed to be.

Other Layout Tools

Choosing among the available squares, straightedges, and drafting triangles is a matter of personal preference. I'd rather spend my money on the best available combination square and forego engineer's squares and fancy rosewood-handled try squares—but I can't claim that my preference has any practical advantages.

STEP-BY-STEP MARKING WITH A GAUGE

1 Set gauge fence to proper distance.

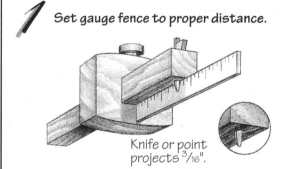

Knife or point projects ³⁄₁₆".

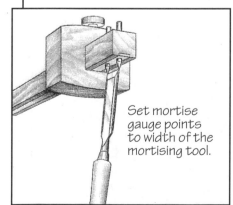

Set mortise gauge points to width of the mortising tool.

2 Begin a mark with both the gauge beam and the point touching the stock.

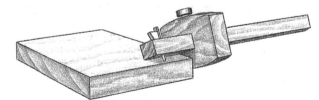

3 Roll the gauge slightly toward you and push it away from you to make your mark.

SETUP TOOLS

We use the same measuring tools when setting up a machine as we do when laying out hand cuts, but there are also some specialized tools that make setups more convenient or more accurate. These include screws, standard references, and paired sticks.

Screws

A stop for positioning stock on a machine is much more convenient to use if the actual contact point is adjustable. If the contact is a ⅜-inch-diameter machine screw with 16 threads per inch, it will move in or out ¹⁄₁₆ inch for every complete turn. A quarter turn will adjust it ¹⁄₆₄ inch, and so on. I keep several stops, as shown in *Adjustable Stop Block*, around my shop and clamp them to fences and jigs as the need arises. If a test piece is off a tiny bit, I stick an Allen wrench in the head of the machine screw and turn it as required to make the adjustment.

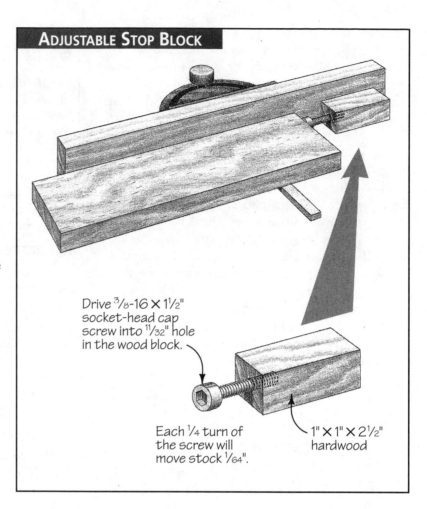

ADJUSTABLE STOP BLOCK

Drive ⅜-16 × 1½" socket-head cap screw into ¹¹⁄₃₂" hole in the wood block.

Each ¼ turn of the screw will move stock ¹⁄₆₄".

1" × 1" × 2½" hardwood

Standard References

"Standard references" is a fancy name for shims and blocks with dimensions that you use frequently. When setting up machines, they are very convenient alternatives to conventional measuring tools like

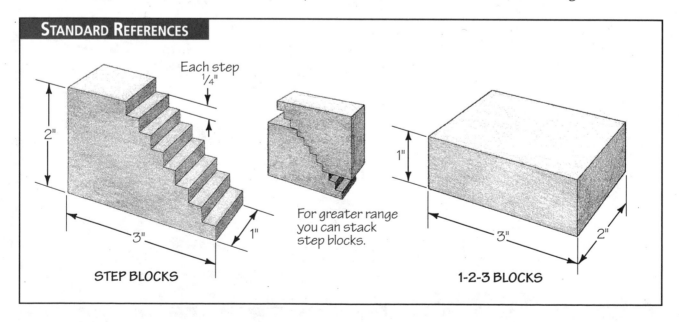

STANDARD REFERENCES

Each step ¼"

2"

3"

1"

STEP BLOCKS

For greater range you can stack step blocks.

1"

3"

2"

1-2-3 BLOCKS

scales and calipers. For example, to adjust a router fence to exactly ½ inch from the cutting edge of the bit, place a ½-inch-thick block up against the cutting edge and set the fence up against the block. You could do it in total darkness and get a more accurate setup than by using the ruler in broad daylight.

Useful standard references include 1-2-3 blocks and step blocks, shown in *Standard References*. The "Combination Mortise and Tenon Jig" chapter on page 240 uses a shim that works the same way. In addition to setting up machines, these blocks are useful for repositioning stock when you need to make several spaced cuts. For example, a step block plus a 1-2-3 block gives four stock positions, each 1 inch apart.

Very often, you need to set up a machine to match the dimensions of existing parts. In these cases don't bother measuring the parts—use the parts themselves as standard references. For example, to adjust a dado head to cut a rabbet for an existing part, set the part alongside the dado head, and adjust the depth of cut so the teeth are flush with the upper surface of the part.

Paired Sticks

A useful alternative to the tape measure is a pair of sticks. Simple as they are, they are very accurate. For example, to size a back panel to fit within rabbets on a cabinet, first clamp two sticks together so their overall length just fits snugly in the rabbets, as shown in *Measuring with Paired Sticks*. You can then adjust your table saw fence using the paired sticks to make the measurement. Carefully done, the setup will be more precise than you could have measured with a tape measure or ruler, and there is no danger of misreading a scale.

Whatever tools or aids you use for setup, don't forget to use an appropriate degree of accuracy—nobody will notice if you're ½ inch off in the length of a flagpole, but you'll hear about it if a table leg is off by that much.

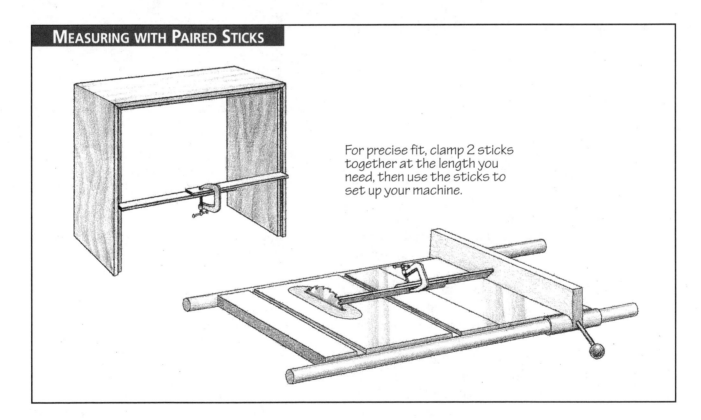

MEASURING WITH PAIRED STICKS

For precise fit, clamp 2 sticks together at the length you need, then use the sticks to set up your machine.

PRACTICAL SHOP GEOMETRY

A compass does more than draw circles; it also copies distances from one part of a layout to another. A large compass like this one is useful for distances too large for a drafting compass but too small to warrant trammels.

A high school friend of mine found algebra so difficult he swore he'd never take another math course. True to his word, he didn't take geometry. But a couple years later in trade school he learned "layout" and loved it. It's a good thing nobody told him that layout is 99 percent pure geometry, because that would have spoiled it for him.

Practical shop geometry, or "layout" if you prefer that term, consists of drawing lines, angles, and curves on either wood or paper. Like the rest of woodworking, simple step-by-step procedures get the job done. The techniques presented here solve problems like accurately laying out dimensions that don't work out to nice round figures on your tape measure, like ⅓ inch. Or drawing an accurate circular arc when the radius is bigger than your shop. Or drawing an accurate 30-degree angle across a 4 × 8-foot sheet of plywood when you only have a 6-inch-long protractor. You'll also find techniques here for drawing useful, common shapes like five-, six-, or eight-sided figures; or curves that meet each other smoothly; or truly elliptical ovals.

One final note before we get down to drawing lines and curves: Some of the later layouts build on techniques from earlier ones without repeating them. For example, instructions might tell you to mark the middle of a line, without repeating the instructions for dividing a line in half. If you come across instructions that seem to skip a lot of steps, look earlier in the chapter for the details.

TOOLS FOR SHOP GEOMETRY

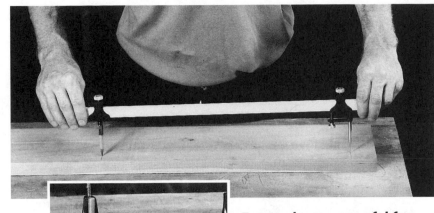

The first step in tackling shop geometry is assembling the right tools. A conventional 1-foot ruler is essential for small-scale layouts, but it's way too small for most shop work. For most work I use a 4-foot stainless steel straightedge that I bought at an art supply store. When that isn't long enough, I use a 6-foot carpenter's level as a straightedge.

Acrylic drafting triangles in large sizes are very handy when drawing layouts with a pencil, but you dare not use them with a marking knife because the knife will cut into the plastic. One way to overcome this shortcoming is to use the drafting triangle to position the line, then butt a steel straightedge or carpenter's square up to the edge, remove the triangle, and scribe with the layout knife against the steel edge.

Perhaps the least familiar tool for many woodworkers is a trammel, also called trammel heads or trammel points. Trammels are large-scale compasses. They clamp to a stick of wood—or beam—of practically any length, allowing you to draw large circles or large-radius arcs and to transfer large dimensions. My personal favorite is the Starrett trammel, shown in the top photo on this page, because it is so well made. You can get perfectly adequate trammels for a lot less money, but many less expensive trammels are really intended for the building trades and have no fine-adjustment mechanism.

Most trammels allow you to substitute a pencil, or at least a piece of drafting lead, for one of the points. Loaded with lead, the trammel makes a more visible but less precise mark than the scribed line of a conventional trammel point.

Suitable beams for trammels vary widely from trammel to trammel. Beams for Starrett trammels must be $\frac{3}{8}$ inch or less in thickness and between $\frac{5}{8}$ and $\frac{3}{4}$ inch wide. The small trammel shown in the inset photo clamps to the edge of any stock not more than $1\frac{1}{8}$ inches thick, so you can use virtually

Trammels are as useful for marking dimensions as they are for drawing arcs and circles. Simply adjust the instrument to the necessary dimension and scribe a short arc to mark the distance. Many trammels allow you to substitute a pencil for one of the two steel scribe points.

any piece of 4/4 (four-quarter) stock as a beam. The biggie shown in the same inset photo is similar in design but has a $2\frac{3}{4}$-inch clamping capacity. On one occasion it allowed me to use a 20-foot-long 2×4 to lay out an arch, but I don't recall ever using it in the shop.

You'll probably want to make a set of beams in various lengths to use in the shop. To make them, rip stock to the required dimensions, plane off the saw marks, and drill a hole in one end of each beam so you can hang them up. I made a set of beams with lengths of 1, 2, 3, 5, 7, and 10 feet.

You'll use trammels for two purposes: transferring dimensions without bothering to measure them, and drawing arcs and circles. The actual practice in both cases is the same. Adjust the trammels to the required distance by parking one point at one end of the required distance and adjusting the other point to the other end. I find that when I'm adjusting a trammel to a measurement, it's usually easier to park the first point at the "1" mark on a scale than to park it at the "0" mark, which is usually the very end of the scale. So to adjust the trammels to 34 inches, I'll park a point at the 1-inch mark and adjust the other to match the 35-inch mark.

To draw an arc or circle, park a steel point at the center and scribe or draw the arc or circle with the second point by pivoting around the first point. To mark a distance, do exactly the same thing, drawing a short arc at the required distance.

Lines, Angles, and Polygons

Most furniture and cabinetwork is straight-line work—squares, rectangles, tapers, and such. Nine times out of ten, the best layout tools for this work are tape measures, squares, and rulers. But the remaining 10 percent of the time you'll be lost without a compass or trammel. These tools are useful in straight-line work for dividing lines and angles, marking lines that are precisely perpendicular to each other, and drawing a variety of geometric shapes.

Dividing a Line or Dimension

Dividing a line in half with a compass or trammel, as shown in *Dividing a Line in Half,* is useful in three situations: First, when the length is a very awkward dimension and the center must be very accurate. Second, when you need to draw a perpendicular line through the halfway point. Third, when dividing a line in half is part of a more involved construction and you already have the compass in hand.

Dividing a line with a compass is even more useful when the goal is to divide the line into some specified number of equal parts. For example, using

arithmetic to divide the 57⅝-inch-wide back of a large office desk into 5 equal panels could give anyone a muscle cramp between the ears. And dividing a 14-foot, 7½-inch stair stringer into 13 equal steps is even worse. But the method shown in *Dividing a Line into Equal Parts* allows you to put the marks right on the money without doing any arithmetic at all.

DIVIDING A LINE IN HALF

First, adjust a compass set to just over ½ the length of the line. Place the compass point at one end of the line and draw an arc, as shown.

Next, with the compass at the same setting, place the point at the other end of the line and draw a second arc, as shown.

Finally, draw a line joining the 2 points where the arcs intersect. This line divides the original line in half. The new line is perpendicular to the original line.

DIVIDING A LINE INTO EQUAL PARTS

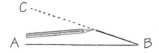

1. Draw a line, BC, at an angle to your original line, AB.

2. Measuring from B, mark off equal segments along BC—as many segments as you want parts in AB.

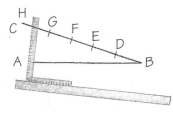

3. Align a leg of a square with point A and the end of the last segment on BC—in this case H. Align a straightedge with the other leg of the square.

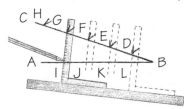

4. Slide the square along the straightedge until it aligns with the next segment on BC—in this case point G—and mark point I. Repeat for each segment on BC.

Measuring Angles

When most of us think of angles, we think of degrees; but we can also measure an angle by the "run" and "rise" of the angle, as shown in *2 Ways to Measure Angles*. This method is especially useful when the object you're working with is large, such as the pitch of a roof. It's also useful when the run and rise are easier to determine than the number of degrees. For example, when laying out a tapered leg, you know how long you want the taper to be, so that gives you the "run." And you know how big you want the leg to be at the foot. Subtract the size of the leg at the foot from the overall size of the stock, and that gives you the amount of stock to remove, which is the "rise."

As a general rule when designing projects, think about how you will actually lay out and cut the angles before deciding whether you want to measure them in degrees or by rise and run. If you'll make the angled cut by tilting the blade on your table saw, design the angle in whole degrees and express it that way; expressing it by rise and run would be a colossal headache when you adjust the saw. On the other hand, it's easier to repeat an oddball angle precisely if you know the rise and run and tilt the stock with a spacer to make the cut. See the instructions for sawing the bevel on a raised panel in Step 3 on page 231 for an excellent example of this.

90-Degree Angles

Perpendicular lines, right angles, square corners—all of which really amount to the same thing—are a special case of angles. Ideally, you have your drawing and woodworking tools and your machines set up so they draw and cut perfectly square corners as a matter of routine. Sometimes, however, when you're designing or laying out a large project, you'll find it most accurate and convenient to construct your right angles with a trammel. A good example is laying out the position of built-in cabinetry in a house with walls that aren't straight or square to each other.

2 WAYS TO MEASURE ANGLES

Use a drafting protractor to design and lay out angles by degrees if you will make the cuts by adjusting a machine to a scale marked in degrees.

But measure angles by rise and run if the layout is large or if your method of cutting is not calibrated in degrees.

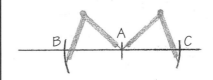

This leg taper has a rise of ³/₄" in a run of 14".

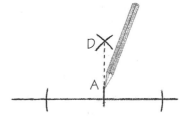

A "9-pitch" roof rises 9" for every foot of run.

DRAWING A PERPENDICULAR LINE THROUGH A POINT ON A GIVEN LINE

First, set a compass to any convenient distance, and with the compass point at the given point (A) on the line, mark points B and C.

Next, increase the compass setting by about 50%; then with the compass point at B and C, draw 2 arcs intersecting at D.

Finally, draw a line connecting D with A.

DRAWING A PERPENDICULAR LINE THROUGH A POINT OUTSIDE A GIVEN LINE

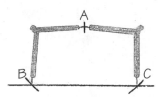

First, set a compass to about 50% more than the distance from the given point (A) to the line. Place the compass point at A and mark points B and C.

Next, from B and C, draw 2 arcs of equal radius intersecting at D.

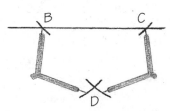

Finally, draw a line connecting points A and D.

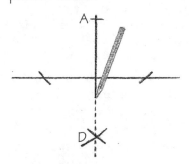

When installing cabinetry, I usually begin by drawing straight, square reference lines right on the floor or on masking tape stuck to the floor. Then I install the cabinetry so it's straight and square, scribing it to the walls and floor. In addition to full-scale floor layouts, both of the methods shown on page 13 and above for drawing a perpendicular line come into use when drawing other geometric shapes, such as the approximate ellipse explained in *Drawing an Approximate Ellipse with a Compass and Ruler* on page 22.

There are a great many times when we want to check that two lines, or parts, are square. The obvious way to do this is to hold a square up to the lines; but on large layouts, or assemblies that are cluttered with clamps and whatnot, it's not always convenient to use a square. Two useful alternatives are given in *Checking the Diagonals to Square an Assembly* and *Checking That Lines Are Perpendicular*.

CHECKING THE DIAGONALS TO SQUARE AN ASSEMBLY

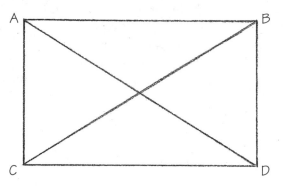

1. Check that AB is the same length as CD.

2. Check that AC is the same length as BD.

3. If checks 1 and 2 are both OK, measure AD and BC. If they are equal, then all 4 corners are square.

CHECKING THAT LINES ARE PERPENDICULAR

To check that 2 lines such as AB and AC are perpendicular to each other:

First put a mark 3 units from A on one line.

Then put a mark 4 units from A on the other line.

If the 2 marks are 5 units apart, then the lines are perpendicular.

The units may be inches or feet or any other handy unit, like three 7" units (21"), four 7" units (28"), and five 7" units (35").

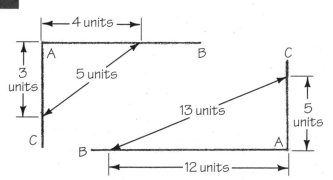

For long, squat constructions, the numbers 5, 12, and 13 also work, as shown here.

Dividing Angles

It would be nice if we could divide an angle into any arbitrary number of equal parts the way we can divide a line. Unfortunately, that isn't possible with geometry as we know it. In fact, geometry teachers sometimes test unwitting students by giving them the impossible problem of dividing an angle into three equal parts. The best we can do is to bisect an angle, as shown in *Dividing an Angle in Half,* and construct certain specific angles, namely those that are a part of the polygons described below. Bisecting an angle is actually quite useful. It allows us to lay out miter joints between parts that come together at an odd angle, as shown in the drawing.

Drawing Polygons

Polygons are interesting as decorative elements. We see them often in chip carving and in Pennsylvania Dutch folk art. As shapes for tabletops, they provide a welcome break from squares and rectangles without requiring the special techniques of curves. A coffee table or end table with a hexagonal or octagonal top can be very elegant indeed.

Strictly speaking, you can draw a polygon with just a pencil and straightedge, but the polygons that are most useful in the shop are the perfectly symmetrical polygons, those with equal sides and angles, known as "regular" polygons. Drawing these requires the compass, or a trammel.

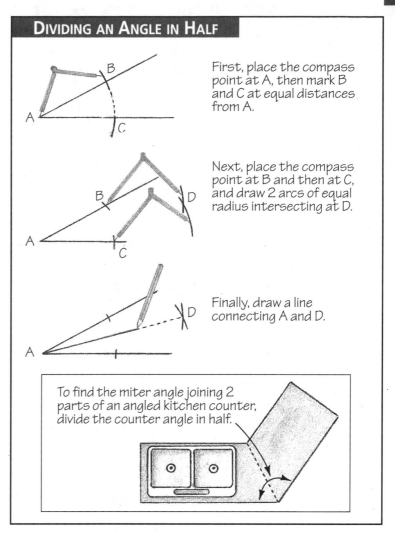

DIVIDING AN ANGLE IN HALF

First, place the compass point at A, then mark B and C at equal distances from A.

Next, place the compass point at B and then at C, and draw 2 arcs of equal radius intersecting at D.

Finally, draw a line connecting A and D.

To find the miter angle joining 2 parts of an angled kitchen counter, divide the counter angle in half.

To draw regular polygons with 3, 5, 6, or 8 sides, see the step-by-step procedures shown in the drawings below. You can double the number of sides of any of these quite easily by dividing the angles in half, but a 10- or 12-sided tabletop is fairly busy-looking unless it's enormous.

DRAWING A TRIANGLE WITH EQUAL SIDES

First draw a line, then set a compass to the length of the line. With the compass point at the ends of the line, draw 2 intersecting arcs, as shown.

NOTE: All 3 angles are 60°

Then draw lines joining the ends of the original line with the intersection of the 2 arcs.

Draw 2 more equal arcs and a line, as shown, to divide one of the angles into two 30° angles.

DRAWING A PENTAGON OR 5-POINTED STAR

1. Draw a circle with diameters AB and CD at right angles. Find the midpoint E of one radius.

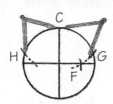

2. With a compass point at E and the compass set to distance EC, mark point F.

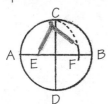

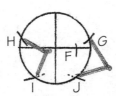

3. With the compass point at C and the compass set to distance CF, mark points G and H.

4. With the compass set to the same distance, CF, and the compass point at H and G, mark points I and J.

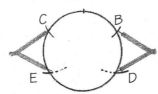

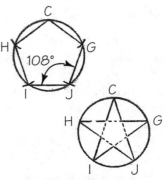

5. Connect the marked points, as shown, to draw a pentagon or a 5-pointed star.

DRAWING A HEXAGON OR 6-POINTED STAR

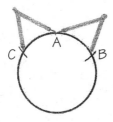

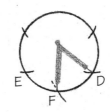

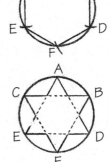

1. Draw a circle and mark a point A on it. With the compass still set to the radius of the circle and the point of the compass at A, mark points B and C.

2. With the compass at the same setting and the point of the compass at B and C, mark points D and E.

3. Move the compass point to D or E and mark point F.

4. Connect the marked points, as shown, to draw a hexagon or a 6-pointed star.

DRAWING AN OCTAGON OR 8-POINTED STAR

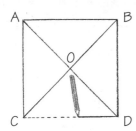

First, draw a square as long and wide as the octagon you require, then draw the diagonals AD and BC intersecting at O.

Next, set a compass to the distance AO, and with the point of the compass at each of the corners, draw arcs as shown.

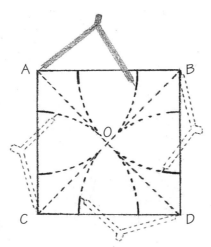

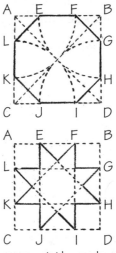

Finally, connect the ends of the arcs, as shown, to draw an octagon or an 8-pointed star.

Circles and Arcs

While most shop work is straight-line work, graceful curves add interest, and often the appearance of lighter weight, to projects. The simplest and most common of these curves are circles and parts of circles, known as arcs. Drawing a circle with compass or trammel is a no-brainer as long as you know where the center is, and as long as the radius of the circle or arc is small enough that the center isn't out in the backyard somewhere. A little geometry is in order when you know where the circle or arc has to go but don't know the radius or center.

Drawing Arcs

A common problem is drawing an arc to cut out the bottom edge of a table apron. Say, for example, you know the length of the cutout and you know how high you want it to be at some point in order to hide structural parts, or at the center, as shown in the inset to

DRAWING AN ARC WITHOUT KNOWING THE CENTER

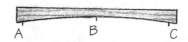

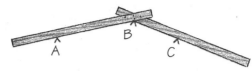

If you know the ends (A and C) of an arc, such as for a table apron, and the height at some point (B), you can draw an arc without knowing the radius.

First, take 2 straight wooden sticks, both longer than the distance from A to C, and align 1 with points A and B, the other with points B and C. Nail them together where they cross.

Next, drive finish nails at A and C.

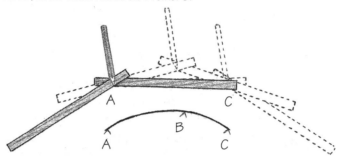

Finally, holding a pencil where the sticks meet, and holding the sticks against the finish nails, slide the sticks along, guiding the pencil, to draw the arc.

Drawing an Arc without Knowing the Center. You can ignore the radius and center and draw the arc as shown in the main part of this drawing. This will work fine if you intend to saw to the line with a

FINDING A CENTER FOR ROUTING AN ARC

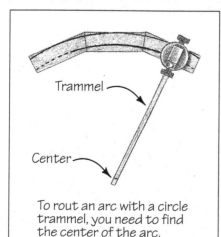

Trammel

Center

To rout an arc with a circle trammel, you need to find the center of the arc.

First, draw lines connecting any 3 points (A, B, and C) on the desired arc.

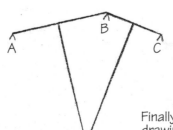

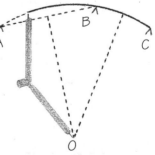

Next, draw lines perpendicular to AB and BC at their midpoints, then extend them to meet at O.

Finally, use O as the center for drawing or routing the arc.

DRAWING VERY LARGE ARCS

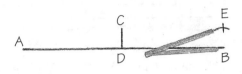
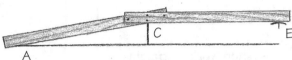

1. If you know the length of an arc, AB, and the height at the center, CD, set a compass to the distance CD and mark point E directly above B.

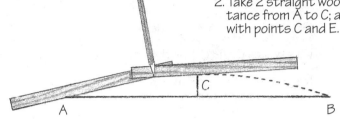

2. Take 2 straight wooden sticks, both longer than the distance from A to C; align one with points A and C, the other with points C and E. Nail them together where they cross.

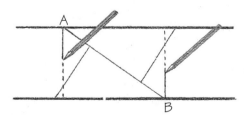

3. Drive finish nails at A, B, and C.

4. Holding a pencil where the sticks meet, and holding the sticks against the finish nails at A and C, slide the sticks along, guiding the pencil, to draw the arc between A and C. Draw the arc between C and B the same way.

JOINING PARALLEL LINES WITH SWEEPING CURVES

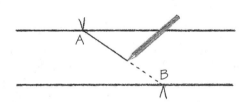

1. Mark points A and B where the sweeping curve will join the parallel lines, then draw a line connecting A and B.

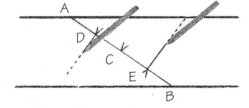

2. Mark the middle of AB at C. Then mark the middle of AC at D and the middle of BC at E. Draw lines perpendicular to AB at D and E.

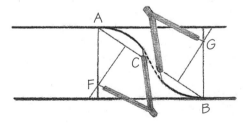

3. From points A and B, draw lines perpendicular to the original parallel lines.

4. Set the compass to the distance FA. Place the compass point at F, and draw the arc AC. Place the compass point at G, and draw arc CB.

band saw and then smooth out the saw marks. If you want to cut the arc precisely with a router and circle-routing jig, as explained in "Routing Arcs and Circles" on page 217, however, you need to find the center and radius, as shown in *Finding a Center for Routing an Arc* on page 17. Notice that both of these methods work even if point B is not at the middle of the arc.

Builders, finish-trim carpenters, and woodworkers who apply their skills to home improvements sometimes face the problem of laying out an arc that is so long, and which has a radius so large, that both of these methods are cumbersome. Say, for example, you're framing or trimming a 12-foot-long arched passage or window that rises 1 foot at the center. To lay it out using the method shown in *Drawing an Arc without Knowing the Center* on page 17, you'd need two "sticks" 13 feet long and a 36-foot-long floor to work on. To use the method shown in *Finding a Center for Routing an Arc* would require a radius of

nearly 19 feet. Layout would require a floor 14 × 20 feet. In a case like this, use the technique shown in *Drawing Very Large Arcs*. With this method you can lay out the arc using "sticks" that are only a little over half the arc length. Drawing the two halves separately, you can lay out the arc on a floor only 4 × 18 feet.

Joining Arcs

Another common problem in the shop is drawing arcs that meet to form sweeping curves that reverse directions, often found in cabinet bases and in feet or table aprons. You can use the old standby method of tracing the curves from the bottoms of paint cans, but this can get to be a very time-consuming trial-and-error procedure. A compass and straightedge make quick work of the task, as shown in *Joining Parallel Lines with Sweeping Curves*. Once you're familiar with the basic procedure, push the envelope, as shown in *Variations on Sweeping Curves*.

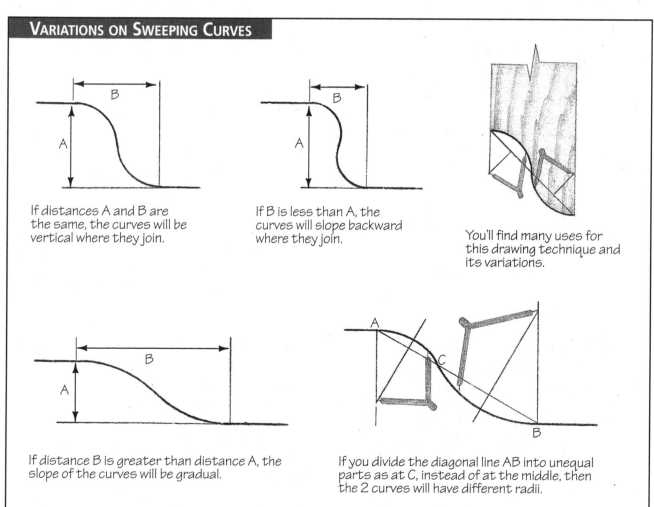

VARIATIONS ON SWEEPING CURVES

If distances A and B are the same, the curves will be vertical where they join.

If B is less than A, the curves will slope backward where they join.

You'll find many uses for this drawing technique and its variations.

If distance B is greater than distance A, the slope of the curves will be gradual.

If you divide the diagonal line AB into unequal parts as at C, instead of at the middle, then the 2 curves will have different radii.

ELLIPSES, A.K.A. OVALS

As useful as the circle is, it is not always the best solution to a design problem demanding curves. Very often a design demands a more elongated shape. The classic elongated shape in architecture is the ellipse, often used in arches and bridges. Some of the finest mansions have elliptical staircases that are even more elegant than grand staircases based on the circle. On the more modest scale typical of home woodworking, the ellipse can be an attractive shape for a dining table or coffee table. A segment of an ellipse often looks better than a circular arc on the bottom edge of a table apron or the top of the glass opening of a glazed cabinet door.

As a practical matter in the woodworking shop, ellipses have an advantage over more free-form shapes—you can cut them with the precision of a mechanically guided tool, as explained in the chapter "Cutting Curves" on page 216. Another advantage of the ellipse over a shape that is almost an ellipse is that many folks with an eye for shape will see the almost-ellipse as almost right, but not quite.

String-and-Pin Ellipses

The simplest method for drawing an ellipse is the string-and-pin method shown in *Drawing an Ellipse with String and Pins*. While not as precise as other methods, it works well enough if your goal is to lay out an ellipse that you'll saw out using a band saw. You will improve its precision by using string that doesn't stretch, by holding the pencil vertically at all times, and by filing a tiny notch near the tip of the pencil so the string won't slip down and off the tip.

DRAWING AN ELLIPSE WITH STRING AND PINS

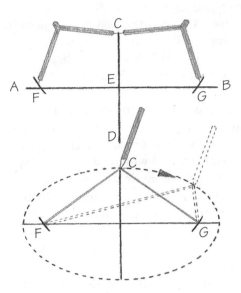

1. Draw 2 lines, AB and CD, that are perpendicular to each other and that cross at their midpoints, E. AB should be the length of the desired ellipse; CD should be the width.

2. Adjust a compass to the distance AE; then with the compass point at C, mark points F and G.

3. Insert pins at F and G, then tie a piece of string into a loop so that when the loop is taut around both of the pins and a pencil point, the pencil point will be at point C.

4. Keeping the string taut, draw the ellipse.

TIP: Notch the pencil to keep the string from slipping off.

Ellipse Trammels

A more precise method for drawing an ellipse is with a device called an ellipse trammel. Years ago you could go out and buy an ellipse trammel from the makers of fine drafting instruments, but no more: Skilled instrument makers are as rare and endangered as good ebony or rosewood, and the demand for ellipse trammels doesn't warrant tooling up for mass production. These instruments worked just like the ellipse trammel for a router shown in the chapters "Cutting Curves" and

"Ellipse (a.k.a. Oval) Trammel" on page 290. If you make a router trammel, you can use it to draw ellipses by fitting a pencil instead of a router to the end of the beam. You can also draw an ellipse using the same principle but without all the work involved in building the trammel. The method is shown in *Drawing an Ellipse with a Makeshift Trammel*.

Approximate Ellipses

Laying out an ellipse on stock with either the string method or the more precise makeshift trammel is fine if you intend to saw to the line and smooth out the saw marks. But if you want to cut the ellipse precisely and minimize the smoothing, there are better alternatives. The router trammel for ellipses just mentioned is a good alternative if you anticipate cutting a lot of ellipses, all within the capacity of a single trammel. For a single, large dining table, or a conference table, or elliptical arches in a building, lay out an approximate ellipse made up of circular arcs and then rout the shape with a simple circle-

routing trammel. You can make the circle trammel in a size to suit the job at hand with little investment of time or materials.

Many geometry books and even some shop manuals show how to approximate an ellipse with arcs of two radii. While these are simple to construct, they aren't close enough to look right. Instead, use the three-radius method shown in *Drawing an Approximate Ellipse with a Compass and Ruler* on page 22. This produces a much closer approximation of a true ellipse—so close that huge stone arches and bridges, all highly visible to the public, have used this approximation for centuries.

There's more to geometry, including parabolas, hyperbolas, cycloids, and other figures with names that sound a little like they belong on alien creatures in a science fiction TV series. But these figures have very little application in practical woodworking. My old classmate George would know nothing of them. George would be quite comfortable, however, going beyond geometric shapes to free-form curves as described in "Free-Form Curves" on page 23.

DRAWING AN ELLIPSE WITH A MAKESHIFT TRAMMEL

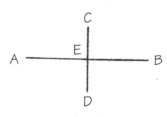

1. Draw 2 lines, AB and CD, perpendicular to each other, crossing at their midpoints, E. AB should be the length of the desired ellipse; CD should be the width.

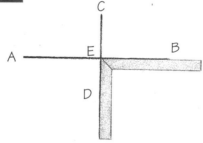

2. Tack or stick straightedges along EB and ED. If your ellipse is small enough, you can stick a framing square to the stock.

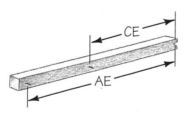

3. Cut a shallow notch in the end of a stick of wood an inch or so longer than AE. Drive fine finish nails through the stick at the positions shown. Clip off the tips of the nails so they protrude slightly less than the thickness of the straightedges.

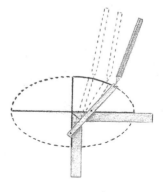

4. Holding a pencil in the notch and the protruding nails against the straightedges, draw ¼ of the ellipse. Reposition the straightedges to draw each of the remaining 3 parts of the ellipse.

DRAWING AN APPROXIMATE ELLIPSE WITH A COMPASS AND RULER

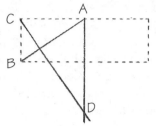

1. Draw a rectangle the length of the ellipse and ½ the width. Find the midpoint, A, of the top of the rectangle, and draw AB. Draw CD perpendicular to AB. Draw AD perpendicular to CA.

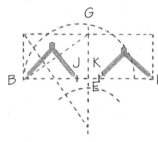

2. Set a compass to the distance AE; with the compass point at E, mark point F.

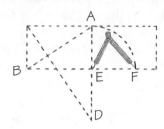

3. Find the midpoint between B and F, and draw a semicircle from B to F.

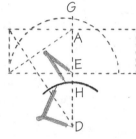

4. Extend EA to G. Set a compass to the distance AG; with the point at E, mark point H. Then set a compass to the distance DH and draw an arc, as shown.

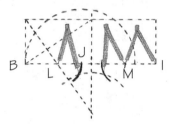

5. Set a compass to the distance EG; with the compass point at B and I, mark points J and K.

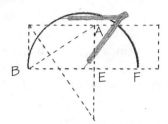

6. Set the compass to the distance BL; with the compass point at I, mark point M. Set the compass to the distance LJ; with the compass point at L and M, draw arcs, as shown.

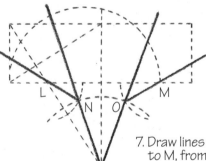

7. Draw lines from N to L, from O to M, from D to N, and from D to O, extending each line a bit beyond the end points.

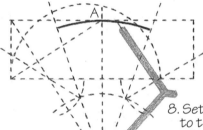

8. Set the compass to the distance DA; with the compass point at D, draw the largest arc of the approximate ellipse, as shown.

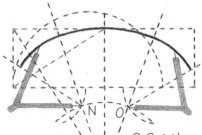

9. Set the compass to the distance from N to the end of the arc you just drew; with the compass point at N and O, draw the intermediate arcs, as shown.

10. Set the compass to the distance from L to the end of the intermediate arc; with the compass point at L and M, draw the last 2 arcs, as shown.

FREE-FORM CURVES

Ellipses and circles won't solve all of your design problems requiring curves. Many projects will look right only with free-form curves. That is when you turn to splines.

A spline is a long, slender piece of wood, plastic, or metal that is springy enough to bend into a smooth and graceful curve. To draw a fair curve, bend a spline into the curve that pleases you, hold it in place with weights or clamps, and draw your line guided by the edge of the spline.

Splines are widely used for designing boats and similar stuff with graceful shapes. Your local dime store won't have them in its stationery department, but you should be able to order them through a drafting supply store. The best width, thickness, and length will depend entirely on how tight and how long your curves must be. The plastic splines that I use most often are about ⅛ inch thick, ½ inch wide, and 3 to 6 feet long. Another set, the same thickness but only ¼ inch wide and made out of a more flexible plastic, also sees frequent use.

The traditional device for holding a spline is a lead weight with an L-shaped hook in the end called a "duck." Judging from the price, I suspect that the commercially available ones are made out of gold instead of lead. Decades ago when I got seriously interested in sailboat design, I cast my own ducks out of lead. But today those 150 pounds of lead ducks are gathering dust in a corner of the shop. I find it more convenient to use sticks of wood with L-screws in the ends, held in place with spring clamps, as shown in *Drawing a Free-Form Curve with a Spline*. They hold more securely than ducks in the woodworking shop.

If you don't want to buy splines, you can make your own out of top-quality, moderately hard, dead-straight-grained wood. Ash is a good choice. Making a set of splines will test your skills as a woodworker. To bend into fair curves, splines must be absolutely uniform in thickness and width. To use them with either ducks or the positioning sticks shown in the drawing, you'll have to cut grooves in the edges. A slotting cutter 1/16 inch wide in a table-mounted router works well for this.

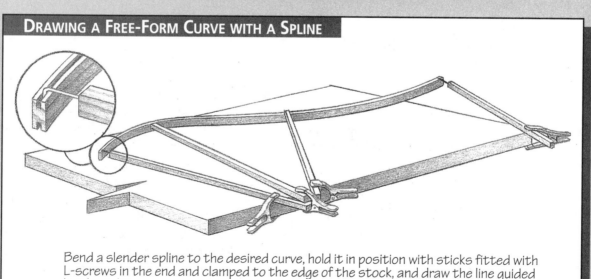

DRAWING A FREE-FORM CURVE WITH A SPLINE

Bend a slender spline to the desired curve, hold it in position with sticks fitted with L-screws in the end and clamped to the edge of the stock, and draw the line guided by the spline.

Sharpening Chisels and Plane Irons

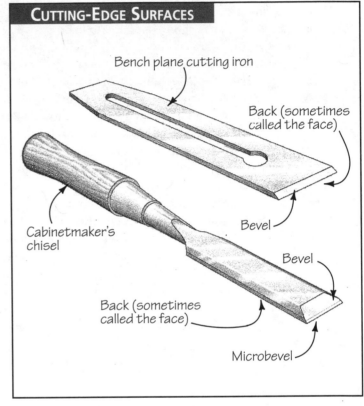

CUTTING-EDGE SURFACES

Bench plane cutting iron

Back (sometimes called the face)

Bevel

Cabinetmaker's chisel

Bevel

Back (sometimes called the face)

Microbevel

A friend was helping us fix supper recently when she found that her knife was dull. She turned over a china bowl that was on the counter and stroked the knife edge on the unglazed rim that formed the foot of the bowl. After just a few strokes, the abrasiveness of the unglazed ceramic restored the cutting edge on her knife. I stood there, amazed, and she laughed at the look on my face. She had been sharpening that way, as taught by her mother, since she was a little girl.

As our friend demonstrated, it doesn't take an expensive sharpening stone or fancy machine to put a sharp edge on a tool. All it takes is an abrasive hard enough to cut steel plus the right rubbing motions. To the casual observer, it's a no-brainer. The trouble is that sharpening is a little like riding a bicycle: Once you know how, it's simple; but until you know how, you're never quite sure what's going wrong.

If you've been frustrated when trying to sharpen tools, take heart. It's a skill that's easy to master once you understand the basic techniques, some background, the tools involved, and the practical limits of sharpening in the home shop. I get a razor-sharp edge on plane irons and chisels, but I don't regularly sharpen my other tools. I send saw blades, jointer and planer knives, shaper and molding head cutters, and router bits out to a professional who has the necessary specialized equipment to do a first-class job.

SHARPENING— AN OVERVIEW

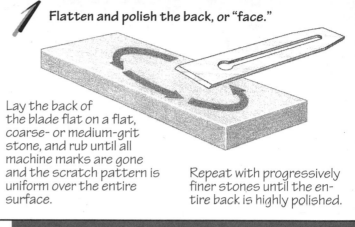

1 Flatten and polish the back, or "face."

Lay the back of the blade flat on a flat, coarse- or medium-grit stone, and rub until all machine marks are gone and the scratch pattern is uniform over the entire surface.

Repeat with progressively finer stones until the entire back is highly polished.

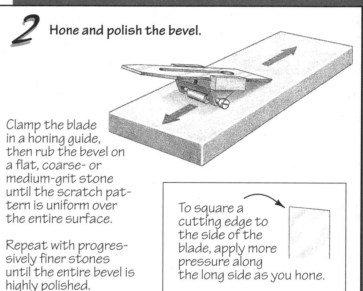

2 Hone and polish the bevel.

Clamp the blade in a honing guide, then rub the bevel on a flat, coarse- or medium-grit stone until the scratch pattern is uniform over the entire surface.

Repeat with progressively finer stones until the entire bevel is highly polished.

To square a cutting edge to the side of the blade, apply more pressure along the long side as you hone.

Many woodworkers struggle along with chisels and planes that are only half as sharp as they'd like them to be. The problem is that the woodworker only *half-sharpens* them. A cutting edge is the intersection of *two* surfaces, the back and the bevel. If you ignore the condition of the back, you'll never get an edge that's more than half sharp. See "What Went Wrong?" on page 34 for some other easily overlooked problems.

Preparing the Back

Flattening and polishing the back is time-consuming, but you only need to do it once, when the tool is new. Just how time-consuming it will be depends on how much of the job the manufacturer did for you. Some new tools are roughly machined and are far from flat. They'll require a lot of effort. Others are smoothly machined and quite flat and need little more than polishing.

To prepare the back side of a cutting tool, lay it flat on a dead-flat, coarse- or medium-grit abrasive and rub it around.

When the surface is entirely free of machine marks and the scratch pattern left by your abrasive covers the entire surface, switch to a finer abrasive. Follow the same process until the scratch pattern on the surface appears entirely uniform again, then switch to a still-finer abrasive. You're done when the finest abrasives have given the surface a mirrorlike gloss like the one shown in the photo on this page.

Be patient—it takes time. I once spent hours on a single plane iron. The important part is the inch or so nearest the cutting edge. Concentrate your efforts in that area by applying the most

The back, or "face," of a cutting edge contributes as much to sharpness as the bevel does. Polish it until it shines like a mirror, especially the area nearest the cutting edge.

SHARPENING A DULL EDGE

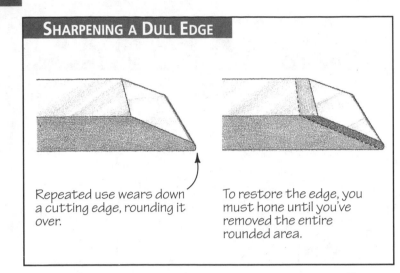

Repeated use wears down a cutting edge, rounding it over.

To restore the edge, you must hone until you've removed the entire rounded area.

pressure there, but don't lift the other end of the tool off the abrasive. If you do, you'll miss the goal of making the surface flat.

Once it's flat and polished, the back will never need further attention, assuming that you don't leave your tools out in the rain.

Sharpening the Bevel

With the back polished, move on to Step 2, honing and polishing the bevel. This is just like flattening and polishing the back, with one exception:

It's hard to keep the bevel flat on the abrasive. With lots of experience you may be able to hold the correct angle by hand; but the better alternative, especially when you're new at it, is to use a honing guide, as discussed below. With the tool in a guide, you can work through the abrasive grits, from coarse to ultra-fine, until the bevel shines like a mirror.

As you hone the bevel, check what's happening after every dozen strokes or so to make sure the abrasive is cutting evenly. If it's cutting more quickly on one side than the other, apply more pressure on the side that is cutting more slowly. If you fail to correct uneven progress, you'll eventually produce a cutting edge that's not square to the side of the tool. The only way to correct an out-of-square cutting edge is by applying heavy pressure on the long side and just enough pressure on the short side to keep it in contact with the abrasive. (See Step 2 on page 25.)

If you use coarse- and medium-grit abrasives aggressively, you may notice that a tiny rolled-over bit of steel, called a "wire edge," has formed on the back of the cutting edge. The temptation to hone it off can be severe, and some woodworkers advise that you do. I strongly advise that you *don't* hone it

GRINDERS

In my opinion the only good use for a bench grinder when sharpening cabinetmaker's chisels and plane irons is driving a buffing wheel for polishing. Grinders save very little time, and if you don't have a lot of skill and experience with them, you'll take the hardness out of the steel by overheating it. (A lot of woodworkers don't realize that heat damages a cutting tool long before the metal turns blue.) Muscle-powered sharpening is fast, is inexpensive, offers much finer control, and requires very little skill if you use an inexpensive honing guide.

If a cutting edge is deeply nicked and you don't want to spend the time to grind the nick out by hand, send it out to a professional sharpening service to have the edge restored. If you

don't want to banish your electric grinder to the garden shed for sharpening shovels, at least replace the grinding wheels with buffing wheels and use it for final polishing, as explained in "Polishing Compounds" on page 35.

A variety of other motorized sharpening devices, such as horizontal wet grinders, have come on the market in recent years. I see them in the catalogs and ask myself two questions:

1. Do I want to spend my limited money, free time, and shop space on sharpening instead of woodworking?

2. Do I have sharpening problems that I haven't solved?

Then I turn the catalog page.

Coarse abrasives leave an edge that does not reflect light.

Medium abrasives replace the coarse scratch pattern with a finer one.

Polishing abrasives remove the fine scratch pattern.

off. I have three reasons for this advice:

First, you don't need to. If you ignore it and carry on honing with finer abrasives until the bevel is polished, you'll find that the wire edge has disappeared.

Second, if you hone off the wire edge with anything but your finest polishing abrasive, you'll scratch the back of the blade. Then you'll have to polish out the scratches.

Third, if you try to remove the wire edge with the back at a shallow angle to the stone instead of flat on the stone, you'll create a secondary bevel on the back. This has all sorts of dire consequences, including a change in the effective bevel angle, which will alter the way the tool cuts. On a chisel it means the tool won't cut where you aim it.

If you think you're finished polishing the bevel and still notice a wire edge on the back, then you aren't finished polishing the bevel.

Resharpening

Sharpening a dull tool is simply a repeat of sharpening the bevel as just described—you only need to recreate the bevel by honing, as shown in *Sharpening a Dull Edge*, and then polish it.

There are two secrets to getting the job done quickly. The first is knowing when to stop. You're done with coarse abrasives when bright light will no longer reflect from the cutting edge, as shown in the first photo above. This indicates you've removed the rounded-over part. You're done with the intermediate grits when the scratch pattern left by the previous grit has been replaced by the scratch pattern of the current grit (middle photo). And, surprise, you're done polishing when the bevel is shiny (right photo).

The second secret to getting the job done quickly is to polish only a microbevel instead of the entire bevel. Microbevels are discussed in "Bevel Angles" on page 28.

These basic steps will sharpen your chisels and plane irons, but a lot of little things can go wrong. I

never managed to get really sharp edges until I understood the whys and wherefores. The understanding helped me discover and correct the mistakes I was making.

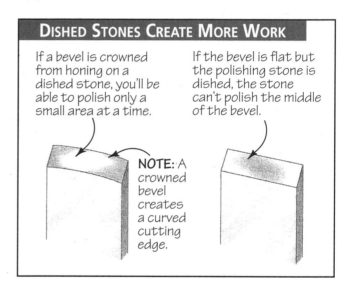

DISHED STONES CREATE MORE WORK

If a bevel is crowned from honing on a dished stone, you'll be able to polish only a small area at a time.

If the bevel is flat but the polishing stone is dished, the stone can't polish the middle of the bevel.

NOTE: A crowned bevel creates a curved cutting edge.

Sharpening Services

Finding a good sharpening service for tools that you don't want to sharpen yourself is not easy: Few of them seem to advertise. By asking around, I've found three types of sharpening businesses:

1. One-man basement or garage operations. Some of these do the best sharpening I've ever seen. Others I wouldn't trust to sharpen a pencil.

2. Services catering to professional shops. These have always done excellent work for me, but some won't touch hand tools.

3. Services that sharpen "wholesale" for hardware stores. I don't use these, because there's no way to explain special requirements to them.

My advice: Always keep your eye open for good sharpening services, but never trust an untested service with your favorite tools.

WHAT MAKES A SHARP EDGE

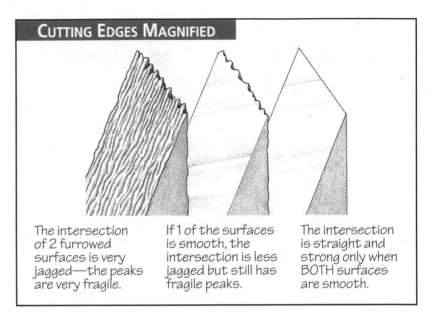

CUTTING EDGES MAGNIFIED

The intersection of 2 furrowed surfaces is very jagged—the peaks are very fragile.

If 1 of the surfaces is smooth, the intersection is less jagged but still has fragile peaks.

The intersection is straight and strong only when BOTH surfaces are smooth.

There are really just two qualities or features of a cutting edge that contribute to the performance of chisels and plane irons. They are the smoothness or polish of the two surfaces that meet at the cutting edge, and the angle at which they meet. Once you have a good understanding of these two characteristics, you'll produce sharper edges with fewer problems, and the problems that remain will be easier to solve.

Polish

The mirrorlike polish of the surfaces is the most striking visible feature of a really sharp tool edge. This fine finish is not just cosmetic. It's the result of making the surfaces smooth at a microscopic level, the level where steel actually severs wood fibers. The smoother the surfaces are, the sharper their inter-section will be, and the easier they will cut.

Polish also has a great deal to do with the durability of an edge. The left part of *Cutting Edges Magnified* is a rather stylized magnification of a cutting edge that has been honed but not polished. The surfaces are furrowed—they appear scratched and gray-looking to the naked eye. In the right part of the drawing, both surfaces have been polished. Edges formed by polished surfaces not only cut more easily, they last much longer because the cutting edge is a single, strong line rather than a series of thin points.

Notice in the middle part of the drawing that polishing just one surface doesn't do much good. This is the kind of edge you'll have if you neglect to polish the back of a new tool.

Bevel Angles

The bevel angle is the angle between the two surfaces that meet at the cutting edge. There is no magic or mystery to bevel angles. A small angle—20 degrees or so—will cut more easily but will also dull and break more easily. A large angle—around 40 degrees—requires more effort to cut but will stand up to more abuse. When I first learned of this simple balance between strength and cutting ease, I experimented with different angles. I wasted a lot of time discovering that woodworkers for the last few centuries were right! Save yourself the wasted time—sharpen your tools to the angles the factory put on them. If you're in doubt, check the bevel angle of your cutting tools against the angles shown in *Recommended Bevel Angles* to make sure they're in the ballpark. If, after considerable experience with these angles, you get an urge to fine-tune your bevel angles, then go ahead, but I'd suggest that you stay within 5 degrees of these recommendations.

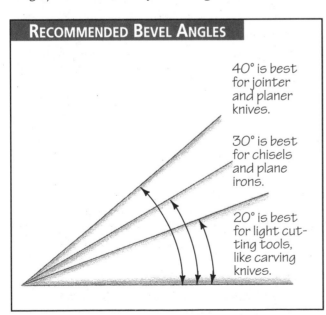

RECOMMENDED BEVEL ANGLES

40° is best for jointer and planer knives.

30° is best for chisels and plane irons.

20° is best for light cutting tools, like carving knives.

SAVING TIME AND EFFORT WITH MICROBEVELS

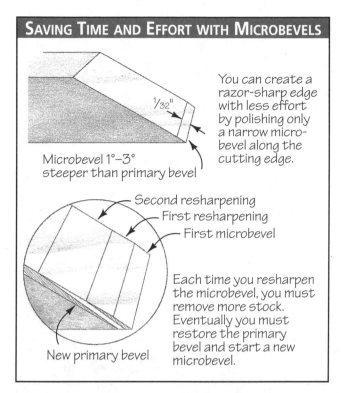

1/32"

You can create a razor-sharp edge with less effort by polishing only a narrow microbevel along the cutting edge.

Microbevel 1°–3° steeper than primary bevel

Second resharpening
First resharpening
First microbevel

Each time you resharpen the microbevel, you must remove more stock. Eventually you must restore the primary bevel and start a new microbevel.

New primary bevel

Microbevel is a ten-dollar word for a simple labor-saving shortcut. Rather than sharpening, honing, and polishing the entire bevel, you just increase the bevel angle slightly so you can hone and polish a narrow strip along the cutting edge as shown in *Saving Time and Effort with Microbevels*. This steeper bevel right at the cutting edge is the microbevel. You can touch up your edge two or three times by rehoning at the microbevel angle; but each time you do, it takes more time because the width of the microbevel increases. Eventually

you'll have to reshape the entire bevel to the original angle and start a new microbevel.

Since the cutting edge is where the work is done and the abuse is absorbed, the angle of the microbevel—not the angle of the original bevel—determines the performance of the tool. The cutting edge shown at the upper right in *Deceptive Bevel Angles* will have the greater strength of a 33-degree bevel but will also require more force to cut than the original 30-degree bevel.

HOW A ROUNDED BACK AFFECTS THE CUT

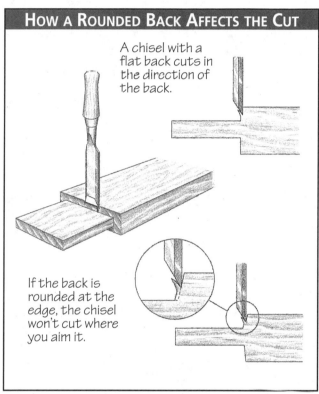

A chisel with a flat back cuts in the direction of the back.

If the back is rounded at the edge, the chisel won't cut where you aim it.

Rounded bevels, both big and small, shown in *Deceptive Bevel Angles*, are also cases of bevels that are not quite what they appear to be. The broadly rounded bevel at the lower left results from using a rocking motion while attempting to sharpen without a honing guide. It takes a lot of rubbing—time and effort—to produce this poor result. It will take even more time and effort to re-flatten it. The most frustrating offender, however, is the tiny roundover at the very edge, shown at the lower right in the drawing. It's frustrating because it's so tiny it may be invisible to the naked eye on a highly polished cutting tool. These tiny roundovers can easily create effective bevel angles of 50 degrees or more, requiring enormous effort to cut.

A roundover on the back of a chisel not only increases the cutting effort, it also makes the chisel

DECEPTIVE BEVEL ANGLES

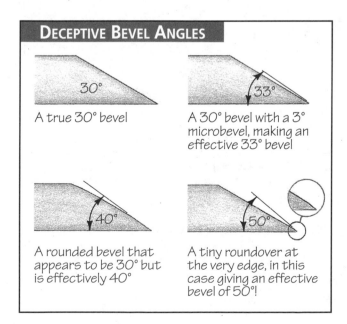

30°

A true 30° bevel

33°

A 30° bevel with a 3° microbevel, making an effective 33° bevel

40°

A rounded bevel that appears to be 30° but is effectively 40°

50°

A tiny roundover at the very edge, in this case giving an effective bevel of 50°!

unpredictable because you never know for sure what direction it will cut, as shown in *How a Rounded Back Affects the Cut* on page 29. "What Went Wrong?" on page 34 describes the most common causes of rounded-over edges.

Crowned Bevels

Broadly rounded bevels and roundovers at the cutting edge are just two examples of surfaces that aren't flat. A bevel can also acquire a crown, as shown in *Dished Stones Create More Work* on page 27. A crown like this usually results from sharpening on a dished coarse- or medium-grit stone. You can prevent the problem by keeping all of your stones flat.

You can flatten stones by rubbing them on silicon carbide wet/dry sandpaper that's backed up with a flat surface such as plate glass. Begin with a grit that is coarser than the sharpening stone. Once the stone is flat, smooth it with a finer grit. This whole process can take some time and wear out several sheets of wet/dry sandpaper if the sharpening stone is fairly hard, like an Arkansas stone. You can also flatten stones with silicon carbide particles on a lapping plate, but your initial investment will be higher because you have to buy the lapping plate. I avoid the whole stone-flattening hassle by sharpening with diamond plates and ceramic abrasives that don't wear away, as explained in "Abrasives" on page 32.

Honing Guides

Some woodworkers belittle honing guides, referring to them as "training wheels." I wonder if they consider a miter gauge a mere crutch for those who can't cut a perfect 45-degree miter by eye, or if they belittle hand planes as crutches for those who can't control chisels. A honing guide, like a miter gauge or plane, is simply a mechanical device for holding something at a specific angle. For plane irons and cabinetmaker's chisels, a honing guide is a valuable aid in sharpening to the correct angle with the least effort.

Honing guides come in a variety of designs, but they all work on the same basic principle: They clamp a roller to the tool. The position of the roller in relation to the cutting edge fixes the angle between the tool and the abrasive, as shown in *Honing Angle Adjustment*. Some guides are designed so the roller rolls on the sharpening stone; others, so the roller is on the workbench in front of the stone. Both designs have advantages. With the roller on

Honing guides may look different, but all of them control the honing angle by clamping a wheel to the cutting tool. The General guide (top) is the most convenient on small stones because the wheel doesn't ride on the stone. The Veritas guide (lower left) uses an eccentrically mounted roller to change the honing angle for a micro-bevel. The Eclipse guide (right) is notable for its secure grip on the tool and for its comfort in the hand.

the stone, you can switch to a finer stone that happens to be thinner, and the honing angle will remain the same. On the other hand, with the roller on the workbench, you can make better use of the entire area of small sharpening stones.

HONING ANGLE ADJUSTMENT

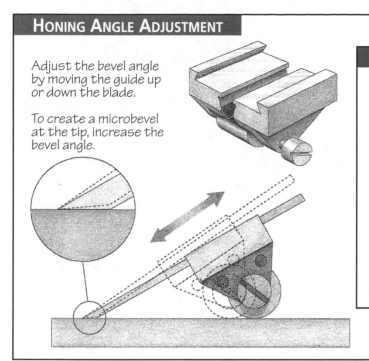

Adjust the bevel angle by moving the guide up or down the blade.

To create a microbevel at the tip, increase the bevel angle.

ADJUSTING A HONING GUIDE

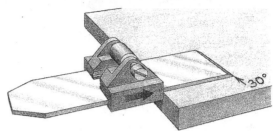

For routine sharpening angles, mark the distance from the cutting edge to the guide on your workbench. To set the guide, hold the tool up to the mark and slide the guide up to the bench edge.

When choosing among the available guides, don't be confused because some of them have a fairly wide roller while others have a narrow one. A wide roller will *not* ensure that the cutting edge remains perpendicular to the side of the tool; only even pressure, and occasional correction when the angle begins to stray, will ensure a square cutting edge.

Of the available choices, I prefer the Eclipse guide, the type shown in the drawings. I find it comfortable to grip, it holds the tool securely, and I can switch stones without readjusting it.

To adjust a guide to the existing bevel angle of a tool, simply hold a straightedge to the bevel and the guide roller, and hold the two up to a light. Move the guide up or down the cutting tool until no light shines between the bevel and the straightedge. This is a lot more accurate than trying to hold the bevel on a flat surface while positioning the honing guide.

For standard angles such as 30 degrees, adjust the guide the first time by trial and error; then mark the distance from the guide to the cutting edge on a convenient surface, such as the edge of your workbench. Next time around, all you'll have to do is hold the edge of the tool at your mark and slide the guide up to the bench edge, as shown in *Adjusting a Honing Guide*.

The best way to grip the tool and guide while sharpening will vary from guide to guide. My usual grip is shown in the photo on this page.

There are three ways to adjust a honing guide from the primary bevel angle to a microbevel angle. The most common method is to move the guide closer to the cutting edge. With the type of guide shown in *Honing Angle Adjustment*, moving the guide about ¼ inch will change the angle about 3 degrees. A method available only with the Veritas guide uses an eccentrically mounted roller that you can turn to change the honing angle a few degrees. The third method, for guides that roll on the workbench instead of the abrasive, is to put a ¹⁄₁₆-inch-thick shim under the roller.

A good honing guide grip lets you use both hands comfortably, lets you apply more pressure on one side of a tool than the other so you can correct out-of-square edges, and works for both plane irons and chisels.

ABRASIVES

Wet/dry sandpaper stuck to plate glass with water is an excellent low-cost sharpening abrasive.

Sharpening abrasives fall into three categories: natural and artificial stones, sandpaper, and polishing compounds. The technique for using each type is similar. Choosing among specific abrasives is a matter of how fast they cut, how flat they stay, how smooth they leave the steel you're sharpening, how much mess they leave behind, and how much they cost. (See the chart "Comparison of Sharpening Abrasives" on the opposite page for the pros and cons of each.)

Most abrasives rely on a lubricant such as oil or water to keep them from clogging with particles of steel and broken-up abrasives. A few, such as ceramics and diamond plates, work without such fluids—you can brush or blow the debris away. Working with wet stones is a bit of a nuisance. If any of the lubricant finds its way onto your stock, it will stain it or interfere with your finish. If your shop is too small for a dedicated sharpening station, consider abrasives that you can use dry—especially for touch-up sharpening.

Coarse abrasives cut fast but leave a rough surface. Fine abrasives cut slowly but leave a smooth surface. You can ask how coarse is coarse and how fine is fine, and a dealer might tell you about grit numbers, but in most cases the answer doesn't help much. The grit numbering system for a Japanese water stone is not the same as for an American oilstone. Furthermore, particles of one mineral don't cut at the same speed or leave the same smoothness as the same-sized particles of a different mineral. So rely on the manufacturer's or dealer's description. I have never found a manufacturer who called a coarse stone fine or vice versa.

My personal preference for sharpening chisels and plane irons is a combination of a diamond plate and a ceramic stone. I use a fine diamond plate with heavy pressure for recreating the bevel, the same plate with light pressure to remove the deep scratches, and an ultra-fine ceramic stone for final polishing of a microbevel. I use them dry, right on my workbench, for touch-up work, and I use them

with slightly soapy water, over the laundry tub, for recreating a bevel.

Arkansas Stones

The only natural sharpening stones still in wide use are Arkansas stones, and their days are numbered—the stone age is ending. The natural deposits of high-quality novaculite, the source of Arkansas stones, are just about exhausted. This makes good Arkansas stones expensive and difficult to get in big sizes. These stones produce very keen edges and wear well, retaining their flatness for a long time. But they cut slowly and are quite a chore to flatten when they do become dished. While you can use them with either water or oil, most woodworkers prefer oil, since it doesn't evaporate as quickly as water. If your grandfather left you a set of these stones, by all means use them and take good care of them. But if you're contemplating buying a complete set, my advice is to keep contemplating.

Oilstones

Artificial stones that are bonded together with resins or sodium silicate work best with oil and are called oilstones. Crystolon and India are trade-names for the most common oilstones sold in the United States. They are economical, are widely available, wear reasonably well, and flatten without too much effort. You can get them in nice big sizes, which makes sharpening a lot easier. Unfortunately, the finest grit available is not fine enough for a good polish. A woodworker who takes his cutting edges seriously will have to switch to a hard Arkansas or ceramic stone or polishing compound for the final edge.

Waterstones

Artificial stones bonded with clay work best with water and are called waterstones. They are reasonably priced and available in big sizes in a range of grits, from fairly coarse to very fine. Their biggest shortcoming is their rapid wear. You'll need to flatten them after just a couple dozen uses. Easy as it is, flattening is a constant chore. It's worth noting that waterstones function both as stones and as loose abrasives. As you begin sharpening, enough of the stone wears away to produce a slurry of abrasive particles. As you continue, both the stone and the slurry abrade the cutting tool. This results in fast cutting that many woodworkers have grown to love. I haven't. I dislike the mess, the need to soak the stones before use, and the need to keep flattening them.

Diamond Plates

Diamonds are too expensive to be bonded together into a stonelike mass, but fusing a single layer of them to a rigid backing brings the cost within reason. The resulting plate (hardly a "stone") is extremely durable, stays flat indefinitely, and works well dry, with oil, or with water. Diamond plates have another advantage that helps to offset their relatively high cost: They cut fast and coarse if you apply heavy pressure, but they produce a much smoother finish if you apply light pressure. Diamonds are the only abrasive hard enough to touch up carbide cutters. I use a small, ultra-fine diamond paddle for this occasional task.

> **NOTE:** A diamond plate may be satisfyingly aggressive yet produce a disappointingly coarse edge when new. Don't despair. Use it to flatten a plane sole or reshape the bevel on a big chisel to break it in. It will then continue to cut quickly if you apply pressure but produce a much smoother surface with light pressure. Don't conclude that it has "worn out." After this initial breaking in, it will work consistently for more years than you'll be around to use it.

Ceramic Stones

Ceramic stones are fused together with tremendous heat and pressure. The result is a stone with many of the features of a diamond plate.

COMPARISON OF SHARPENING ABRASIVES

	RESISTANCE TO WEAR	SHARPENING FLUID REQUIRED	CUTTING SPEED	GRITS AVAILABLE	RELATIVE COST
ARKANSAS STONES	Good	Oil or water	Fair	—	High
OILSTONES	Moderate	Oil	Good	Coarse through medium	Moderate
WATERSTONES	Poor	Water	Excellent	Coarse through ultra-fine	Moderate
DIAMOND PLATES	Excellent, permanent flatness	None, oil, or water	Excellent	Coarse through medium	High
CERAMIC STONES	Excellent	None, oil, or water	Good	Medium through ultra-fine	High
SANDPAPER	Not an issue	None or water	Good	Extremely coarse through ultra-fine	Low
POLISHING COMPOUNDS	Not an issue	None	Moderate	Ultra-fine	Low

$\mathcal{W}$HAT WENT WRONG?

If you sharpen a chisel or plane iron and find that it looks sharp and feels sharp but still doesn't cut well, the time to figure out what went wrong is right away—before you forget some of the little things that you did (or didn't) do. The three most common sharpening mistakes are:

HOW FAR TO HONE

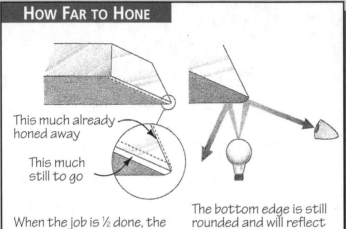

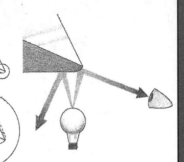

This much already honed away

This much still to go

When the job is ½ done, the edge may look sharp and feel sharp but not cut well.

The bottom edge is still rounded and will reflect light at a different angle than the flat back.

BUFFING ERRORS

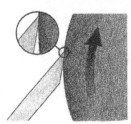

Holding the tool at the wrong angle, applying too much pressure, or using a soft buffing wheel will round-over the cutting edge.

Mistake 1: Insufficient honing.
When you're halfway done restoring a bevel, the edge will feel sharp on your finger but the bottom surface will still be rounded—the effective bevel angle will be way too big. Continue honing until bright light reflects from the back in the same direction right up to the very edge, as shown here.

Mistake 2: Careless buffing.
A buffing wheel can remove an amazing amount of steel in the twinkling of an eye. If the wheel is soft, you press too hard, or you hold the wrong angle, you will round-over the edge, destroying the cutting angle.

Mistake 3: Not stopping when you're done.
Sharpening stones cut steel. That's what they're supposed to do. **DON'T** take one last hand-held stroke at a steeper angle to put the final touch on the edge. That steeper angle will be your effective bevel angle, requiring more effort to cut. The same caution applies to the back: Leave it alone.

Ceramic stones require no fluid to keep from clogging, but you can use oil or water with them if you like. And they stay flat indefinitely. On the down side, they are not available in coarse grits, they are somewhat expensive, they are *very* fragile, and I've heard complaints from a number of woodworkers who said the ceramic stones they purchased weren't flat when new. If you buy one, and I do recommend them, make sure you can return it if it isn't flat.

Sandpaper

Ain't nobody gonna get rich selling sandpaper to potential customers for diamond plates, so the good news about sharpening with wet/dry sandpaper has remained something of a secret. The truth is that this immigrant from the land of auto refinishing is the premier low-budget means to a sharp edge. Wet/dry sandpaper comes in a range of grits from very coarse to super-fine. (Try grits of 200, 600, and 1200 for sharpening, honing, and polishing.) If you really want a super-fine polish, you can now get abrasives on a paperlike backing that are as fine as the finest polishing compounds (up to 12,000-grit).

Procedures for sharpening with wet/dry sandpaper are a bit different from procedures for stones, though just a bit. Start with a flat, waterproof surface at least 10 × 12 inches. Good choices include plate glass, a pastry marble, or even a machinist's surface plate. Douse the surface with water, and lay down a sheet of the paper, abrasive side up, as shown in the photo on page 32.

The water will hold the paper in place. Wet the top of the paper to keep the abrasive from clogging, then use it as you would a conventional stone. If you've been using 2 × 6-inch or even 3 × 8-inch stones, the 9 × 11-inch surface of the abrasive paper will make you feel as if you're standing alone in Yankee Stadium. You sharpen your tools with the same motions you'd use on a stone. When you've finished with a particular grit, peel it off and lay on the next grit.

Polishing Compounds

Sharpening stones, diamond plates, and wet/dry sandpaper all immobilize the abrasive in order to keep it under control. There is another way to go about sharpening: Let the abrasive move around, as long as it stays more or less where needed. (Toothpaste, which has a very mild abrasive in it, works this way.) Polishing compounds consist of very fine abrasives in a waxlike material that

POLISHING WITH COMPOUND

Rub polishing compound on a "stropping board," then polish the cutting edge in the opposite direction from honing.

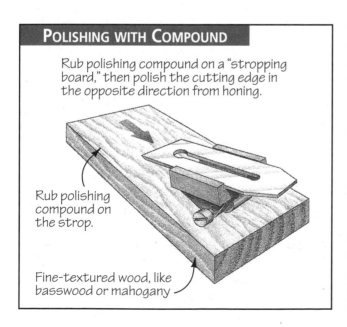

Rub polishing compound on the strop.

Fine-textured wood, like basswood or mahogany

POLISHING WITH A BUFFING WHEEL

For safety and to prevent rounding the edge...

Reverse rotation of the wheel.   OR   Point the tool down instead of up.

sticks to a strop or a buffing wheel. They are effective for putting the final, mirrorlike gloss on an edge. And they can do it at a fraction of the cost of ultra-fine stones.

An inexpensive way to use polishing compounds begins with a *flat* piece of fine-textured quarter-sawn wood, such as basswood or mahogany. Rub compound on the wood, then polish the edge of your cutting tool with the same motion and technique that you would use on a sharpening stone *with one exception:* Go backwards. That is, instead of pushing the tool with the cutting edge leading, push it with the cutting edge trailing, as shown in *Polishing with Compound*. To save yourself time and energy, polish only a microbevel.

A buffing wheel mounted on a grinder is the more common way to use polishing compound. Use only a hard felt buffing wheel to avoid rounding-over the edge. Apply polishing compound to the spinning wheel, then hold the bevel *gently* against the wheel so the wheel is rubbing *toward the cutting edge from the handle side of the bevel,* as shown in *Polishing with a Buffing Wheel.* There are three ways to achieve this direction of rotation:

1. Reverse the direction that the grinder rotates. (Only some grinders allow this.)
2. Point the tool down instead of up.
3. Reverse the guard and work from the back side of the grinder. (Only some grinders allow this.)

Polishing can produce heat quite quickly, so use light pressure, hold the tool to the wheel for only a couple of seconds at a time, and cool the tool in a cup of water when it feels *the least bit warm.* If you let it overheat, the steel will lose its hardness and will no longer hold a sharp edge for any length of time.

CHOOSING THE RIGHT GLUE

A bewildering array of adhesives clutter hardware store shelves. Carefully select two or three, and learn their unique and sometimes peculiar characteristics.

The first glue I ever used on wood was called "Iron Glue." It was thick, brown, smelly stuff. When I read the label, I was duly impressed—it claimed to be stronger than the wood itself. Five years later in high school freshman shop class, I was introduced to hot hide glue. It, too, was thick, brown, smelly stuff, suspiciously similar in odor to Iron Glue. There was no label on the glue pot extolling the virtues of hot hide glue, but I came to respect it and still do. That was four decades ago, and the turned walnut lamp I assembled with that glue is still around, after several winters freezing in a Minnesota garage, 4 years in the humidity of the South Pacific, 16 winters in the dry atmosphere of a wood-heated house in Vermont, and uncounted drops to the floor. I sometimes think that hide glue was made from rhinoceros hide.

I've used more than a few glues since then, and learned some things. One of the most important is that experience with a particular glue is more valuable than a shelf full of different glues. If you know a glue well and you're happy with it, don't buy another on account of anything I say in this chapter *unless* you're sure your current glue won't work for a particular job. If you do need a different glue, choose it carefully—the charts on pages 44, 48, and 51 will help. You want a glue that will not only serve your immediate special need but also add as much versatility as possible to your woodworking in general.

PROPERTIES OF CURED GLUES

The first requirement of a general purpose wood-working glue is that it form a strong and lasting bond. Most of the wood glues mentioned here fulfill the strength requirement when bonding to the sides of wood fibers, as shown in *Grain Orientation and Gluing Strength*. They create bonds that are commonly described as stronger than the wood itself. Hot-melt glue, on the other hand, forms an easily broken bond, which can work to your advantage if you want temporary fastening.

All these glues also meet the "lasting" requirement, meaning they don't deteriorate over time. This assumes, of course, that they are not subjected to the wrong conditions. Many glues must be kept dry. For applications where the parts are constantly wet, such as on a boat, you need a *waterproof* glue like epoxy or resorcinol. And remember that even a patio chair will let you down if you assemble it with glue that is not at least moisture *resistant*.

Glue is considered "stronger than the wood itself" if fibers from one piece remain stuck to the other piece after the joint is broken apart. Even so, when a glue joint fails, it is most likely to break at or near the glue line.

On the other hand, a big advantage of hide glue is that its moisture resistance is so poor that joints can be disassembled for repair by soaking or steaming them. Those who repair antiques, or who

GRAIN ORIENTATION AND GLUING STRENGTH

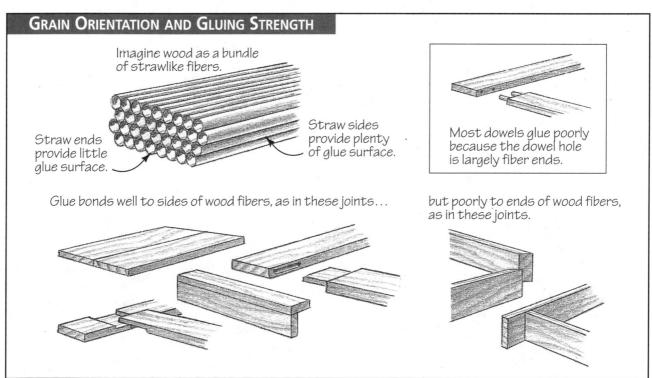

Imagine wood as a bundle of strawlike fibers.

Straw ends provide little glue surface.

Straw sides provide plenty of glue surface.

Most dowels glue poorly because the dowel hole is largely fiber ends.

Glue bonds well to sides of wood fibers, as in these joints...

but poorly to ends of wood fibers, as in these joints.

want their furniture to survive long enough to become antiques, use hide glue exclusively so that any broken parts can be replaced without destroying other parts.

Strength and longevity are not the only physical properties of glue that are of interest to woodworkers. A gap-filling glue can be a lifesaver if you're trying to salvage a joint you've cut too loose. You may even intentionally cut a joint loose and assemble it with a gap-filling glue. (See "Intentional Misfits" on this page.) To qualify as gap-filling, a thick mass of the cured adhesive must be as strong as wood and the mass must not deteriorate over time. Also, the adhesive must cure without significant shrinking. These conditions are not easy to meet. A paste made from yellow glue and sander dust may work as a wood filler in some circumstances, but it doesn't have the strength to stand up as a gap-filling adhesive. The only really good gap-filling adhesives that are readily available and practical in the home shop are the epoxies.

An often-overlooked physical characteristic of some glues is their glacierlike behavior. Even though the ice in a glacier is hard, even brittle, the glacier will flow down the mountain like a slow river because of the enormous stress from all the weight. When a glue tends to flow under stress, we say that it "creeps." The stress can come from an outside source, such as a heavily loaded shelf held up by a glued cleat, or from pressures within the glue joint itself, such as two parts of a joint that expand and contract in different directions when the humidity changes.

Creep is seldom desirable. You may, however, want the corollary to creep: flexibility. When gluing canvas to the back of slats for a tambour, for example, a flexible glue allows the canvas to function as a hinge in spite of being filled with cured glue. Even though creep itself is not desirable, a creepy glue like white glue will still work well *most* of the time. Just remember to use something else if the joint will be under continuous stress, such as in a bent lamination.

*I*NTENTIONAL MISFITS

Some joints are so complex or require such precision that only woodworkers with the mentality of watchmakers ever attempt them. An example is the box-joined tenon construction used in the display stand shown here. The gap-filling strength of epoxy has made many such joints possible for mere mortals who clobber keyboards or wrestle wrenches for a living and work wood on weekends to restore their sanity.

This display stand would be pretty fragile if the tenons from opposite directions didn't join each other; but it would be an impossible nightmare to assemble all eight joints at once if they fit tightly enough for conventional glues. By cutting the box joints a bit loose, chamfering their edges so they find their way together, and assembling them with epoxy, the joint is not difficult at all; and rubber bands are sufficient for clamping the joints.

The point here is not that sloppy workmanship is okay but that your time is better spent getting the visible joint-line tight. Fiddling with hidden details in order to meet the requirements of one adhesive is a waste of energy when another perfectly good adhesive is more tolerant.

The hidden complexity of these joints is practical, thanks to gap-filling adhesives.

WORKING PROPERTIES OF GLUES

Many glues are ready to use when you buy them. Some have to be mixed with water. Still others require that you mix two components in precise proportions. Most glues that you mix have to be used fairly soon after mixing, so if you mix too much it will go to waste. On the other hand, in their unmixed state these glues generally have an unlimited shelf life. And mixing glue is not all that big a chore once you get in the habit of doing it. Some glues, like hide glue and epoxy, offer the opportunity to tailor their working properties to your needs at the time of mixing, an advantage you won't find with ready-to-use glues.

Modern glues like yellow wood glue require no mixing or heating, spread easily and smoothly, bond quickly, and clean up with water.

One of the first characteristics of an adhesive that you will encounter is its cost. Some seem outrageously expensive. When considering adhesives, however, you have to think about the cost of doing a job rather than just the price for a given quantity of the glue. A cyanoacrylate glue may cost 50 to 100 times more than yellow glue, but a dime's worth may give you an instant fix of a mistake, allowing you to work all evening instead of waiting until tomorrow while the yellow glue cures.

Open Time

In many project assembly situations, the most important characteristic of a glue is the amount of time you have between spreading the glue and getting the joint together. This is called the allowable open time, or assembly time, of a glue. It can vary from mere seconds to nearly an hour, depending on the glue and the temperature. If you exceed the allowable open time, you will get weaker joints. I'd like to give you a rule of thumb for determining when open time is nearly over, but there's no rule that applies to all the different kinds of glue. (This is one example of experience with a couple of glues being better than passing acquaintance with many!) Some glues, like white and yellow glues, begin to film over when the open time is past. Others, like the epoxy I use, begin to stiffen but even then will form a strong bond. And contact cement should *not* be closed until the spread glue has completely filmed over and is *no longer* tacky. Most glues have a shorter open time at warmer temperatures. Some have less open time when the humidity is low.

When you face a complex assembly, consider whether you can get it all together within the allowable open time. Check the product label and the charts on pages 44, 48, and 51 for an estimate of the time you have, then plan to stay well within it. If it looks like a tight squeeze, don't push your luck: Glue up subassemblies, and when they're dry, glue the subassemblies together. Equally important, use the available open time efficiently. Have your clamps at hand, make sure you have a cleared area to assemble the parts, and spread the glue without wasting time, as explained in "Applying Glue" on pages 40–41.

Grab

There is a characteristic of glues that I find very important but very difficult to categorize or measure. That is the tendency of the glue to "grab" at some stage during assembly. For example, if you spread yellow glue on two surfaces and then bring them together, they will behave, at first, as though you had spread grease on them. But if you press the

*A*PPLYING GLUE

Getting the right amount of glue exactly where you want it is simple enough, but getting it there quickly so you don't waste the glue's available open time can be a problem with complex assemblies. The best technique depends largely on the kind of joint you're gluing.

For edge joints, I usually use a transfer technique. I clamp one of the pieces in a face vise with the joint edge up and apply a generous bead of glue to the edge. Then I bring the joining edge of the second board together with the first, sliding the edges together—both end to end and side to side—to spread the glue to both surfaces. When I think the glue is well spread, I open the joint and check that both surfaces are fully wetted. If they are, I close the joint again and apply the clamps.

For a single glue line, this technique can actually be too fast. If the wood is quite absorbent, like butternut or basswood, clamping the joint within seconds of spreading the glue can squeeze out so much of the glue that the remainder soaks into the wood, leaving a starved joint. In a case like that, I leave the joint closed for a minute to allow glue to soak into the wood before applying clamping pressure.

If I'm edge-gluing several boards, I still use the vise. After transferring glue between the first two edges, I put the board that was in the vise into the clamping rack, put the second board into the vise with the second joint edge up, and spread the glue for the second glue line, and so on. As each successive board goes into the clamping rack, I close the previous joint to help prevent the glue from filming over. This effectively extends the open time. Then when I've got glue on all the joints, I clamp up the assembly.

I've tried this same technique on the broad surfaces involved in face-gluing and found it didn't work nearly as well—it took too much squishing around of the boards to get both surfaces fully wetted. The technique I prefer for these big areas is to remove the nozzle-cap from the glue bottle and pour out a big puddle. I then spread the glue with a squeegee. I've used squeegees made from plastic laminate, old credit cards, even Masonite; but the best are flexible, almost rubberlike squeegees used by auto body repairmen and available from auto parts stores that cater to this trade.

Rubber rollers, the kind artists use to spread ink, work even better than squeegees and are worth buying if you spread glue over large areas fairly often. Whether you squeegee or roll the glue out, time is your enemy when face-gluing with most glues. It takes time to spread a thin, uniform film over a large area, and just as soon as you get a thin film over part of the area it begins to dry out. On more than a few occasions, I've face-glued with epoxy for the sole reason that spreading out a thin film doesn't shorten the open time. The best tool for spreading the epoxy, I've found, is a thin paint roller made of foam, distributed by the makers of the epoxy.

When spreading glue on joints like dovetails or two surfaces together with hand pressure, after a few seconds they will stick, or grab—further adjustment will require that you first knock them apart. How quickly the surfaces grab depends on the glue. Contact cement grabs instantaneously with no pressure. Epoxy never grabs; it just slowly cures.

The tendency to grab can be extremely useful or a damnable abomination. When edge-gluing boards, it's great to be able to slide the edges into alignment, apply a bit of hand pressure, and have them stay put while you apply clamping pressure. On the other hand, I will never, *never* forget the time a critical mortise-and-tenon joint grabbed during the split second that it took for me to get a better grip on one of the parts. Then in the three or four seconds it took me to slap a bar clamp on the half-assembled joint, the grab developed such strength that it wouldn't budge. I had to saw off the tenon, cut the inserted part of the tenon out of the mortise, and make a new tenon part. (I can hear evangelists for hide glue, which can be softened with steam, saying "I told you so.") Once again, you can avoid the problem by building experience with the working characteristics of just a couple of glues rather than always trying to choose the perfect product for every situation.

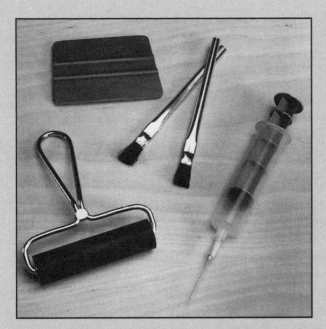

Spread glue with whatever works fast. My favorite off-the-shelf spreaders are (counterclockwise, from top left) squeegees used by auto body repairmen, ink rollers available in craft stores, plastic syringes distributed by the makers of epoxies, and plumbers' flux brushes available from plumbing supply houses.

mortises and tenons, the best spreader is an acid brush—the kind plumbers use for spreading flux. I usually pour the glue into a small yogurt cup lid or coffee can lid, dip the flux brush into it, and paint it onto all of the joint surfaces. It's quick and convenient, and the brush reaches into corners and mortises. When I'm done, I put the brush in a yogurt cup half-full of water. At the end of the day, I clean up all

of the brushes with soapy water, toss out the ones that are beat, and spread the good ones out to dry.

If I'm assembling a whole set of doors or drawers and just need to keep a brush from drying out for a few minutes as I assemble each one, I tape one end of a 3-inch-wide strip of poly film to the bench top. I lay the wet end of the brush on the free end of the plastic strip. Then as I roll the brush handle between two fingers, the plastic rolls up onto the wet end of the brush, keeping it from drying out.

Special glue applicators come on the market from time to time—glue bottles with rollers attached, bottles with special nozzles for spreading glue in biscuit slots, and so on. Every one I tried found its way into the trash after about the third time it clogged up with dried glue. These things may work fine for you if you find yourself diddling with the same difficult application hour after hour, but I suggest that you approach them with caution. They tend to clog quickly for me, and I'm not the sort who puts down a pen without replacing the cap.

In spite of my disenchantment with most special applicators, I do use plastic glue syringes. They really shine at injecting epoxy into complex joints that were intentionally cut loose. I sometimes bore 3/32-inch-diameter injection and air-vent holes so that I can effectively fill all the voids with epoxy resin after assembling the joint dry. Leftover epoxy in the syringe cures solid and then comes out as a plug, clean as a whistle.

Clamping and Curing Times

Glues develop their strength over time. Most glues require that you clamp the joint during the first part of that total time and then handle the joint only gently until the glue has developed full strength. The minimum clamping time varies from glue to glue, as does the time required for full strength. Both times also depend on temperature and should be extended if the temperature of the wood is below 70°F.

A look at the chart on page 44 will show that if you're using yellow glue, you can safely remove the clamps after a half-hour to an hour but you

shouldn't work on the assembly for at least 12 hours. If you're using polyurethane glue, the assembly should stay in clamps for 4 hours and you shouldn't work on it for 24 hours. The difference is substantial but may not matter to you. If you only work evenings, either glue allows you to work tomorrow on an assembly you glue up today (with a bit of fudging). But if you work 8 hours a day in the shop, only the yellow glue allows you to work tomorrow morning on an assembly you glue up at the end of the day today. Similarly, the importance of minimum clamp time depends on how anxious you

REMOVING SQUEEZED-OUT GLUE

Glue squeeze-out is one of the necessary evils of woodworking. You want to see it, because it confirms that you applied enough glue and that the joint is coming together as planned. But you have to clean it off, thoroughly, because a smear of glue under a finish shows up like bird droppings. Here are some techniques worth trying.

• Warm water and a cloth will clean water-soluble glue that hasn't cured too far. If the glue has dried partially, wrap a layer of the rag over an old chisel and coax the glue free, then clean the entire area with a clean piece of the rag. Try to get *all* the glue off, but remember to resand the area after it's thoroughly dry.

• To remove a bead of squeeze-out without spreading it around even further, slide the end of a plastic straw along the joint. With a bit of luck, most of the glue will end up in the straw.

• To remove smeared glue from an inside corner, a hand scraper is often effective. Make sure it's good and sharp so it leaves the wood smooth.

• Use a chisel to dislodge larger clumps of dried glue. Work in the direction of the grain to avoid leaving the wood torn and rough.

• Assemble a joint dry, then apply masking tape to the adjoining surfaces of the wood that will end up coated with squeeze out. After assembling the joint with glue, let the squeeze-out skin over. Then peel away the tape and extra glue.

---

are to reuse the clamps on another assembly. Before you set a clamped assembly aside to cure, consider how you will remove the squeezed-out glue. A few of your options are listed in "Removing Squeezed-Out Glue" above.

Temperature affects more than just clamping and curing time: It may affect whether the glue will form a proper bond at all. The temperature of the air doesn't matter. The temperature of the thin film of glue on the wood does, so you have to watch the temperature of the wood itself. If you work a few hours every evening and don't heat your shop when you're not there, your wood may *never* reach the 70°F minimum temperature for liquid hide glue or resorcinol. When you choose a glue that you intend to stick with (pun intended), consider carefully whether you'll be able to use it during a cold winter.

Pot Life and Shelf Life

Most glues, with the notable exception of liquid hide glue, will keep for a very long time, provided the containers aren't opened and they aren't subjected to extremes of temperature. Once opened, however, some deteriorate more rapidly through exposure to air in the container. Watch for changes in color or consistency, and discard glue that has changed noticeably. Not every change means that the glue is no good, but I am not about

to risk a project for the sake of a half bottle of some stuff that's been gathering dust for six months.

To me, pot life is more important than shelf life. Pot life is the length of time glue is usable after mixing; so it's obviously a concern only with glues like plastic resin and epoxy that require mixing before use. The only advice I can give is to follow the rules the manufacturer lays out. Influences on pot life vary with the product: Hide glue deteriorates because of bacterial action, while the chemical cure of epoxy is extremely temperature-sensitive.

Health Hazards

These days it seems that just about anything you touch may prove to be toxic. Glues are no better or worse. Some glues, like the polyvinyl acetates, seem to be harmless; others, like solvent-based contact cements, definitely contain toxic substances. Skin contact is the danger in some cases. In others, the mischief makers are the fumes or the dust from sanding. Some special-application epoxies are extremely toxic, while those used in boatbuilding seem to be quite safe if you avoid contact with the hardener. Cyanoacrylates are so "safe" they've been tried as surgical adhesives, but of course "safe" only means that we're ignorant of any harm they might cause. Read the product literature, then take the recommended precautions.

GENERAL-PURPOSE WOOD GLUES

In the course of your woodworking lifetime, you'll probably use more general-purpose wood glue than all other types combined. These glues are useful in a broad range of indoor applications, including edge-gluing, case assembly, and solid wood joinery. They are also economical enough for regular use in these applications. A half-dozen glues meet these requirements.

Hide glue is the only adhesive in the world with a 3000-year track record... and still going strong. It's also the only common glue you can "unstick" to make repairs.

Polyvinyl Acetates

Polyvinyl Acetates, or PVAs as they're called in the trade, are the workhorses of wood glues. Included in this group are white "craft" glue, yellow "wood" glue (aliphatic resin), and an improved type of yellow glue (cross-linking PVA) known best by the trade name Titebond II. All form very strong bonds, work well in a wide range of woodworking applications, and are inexpensive. The PVAs bond quickly and cure to thin, translucent glue lines that are nearly invisible to the eye. The minimum application temperature is 50 to 55 degrees—among the lowest of any glues. I've used it at even lower temperatures, breaching what the chemists call the "chalk" temperature. This is the temperature at which a thin layer will turn chalky white instead of filming over as it dries—a clear signal that it's too cold for good bonding.

All PVA glues degrade gradually due to exposure to air, but they have a shelf life of at least a year after opening the bottle and an unknown but very long shelf life in unopened bottles at room temperature.

I've thrown out PVAs that froze and were thick and clumpy after thawing out. A technician at Franklin International (a large PVA manufacturer) has since convinced me that freezing changes the consistency only, not the bonding of the glue.

Clumpy glue, however, is no fun to work with, so avoid storing PVA glue in cold temperatures. The guy at Franklin recommended a simple test for questionable PVA glue: Rub a small amount on a flat surface with your finger. If it spreads evenly, it's still good. If it has deteriorated from exposure to air in the bottle, it will form rubbery globules.

Any one of the three common varieties of PVA will serve you well for most woodworking applications. White glue, the original PVA, is thinner out of the bottle than yellow glue, and dries to a more rubbery consistency. This allows a fair amount of creep, so I wouldn't use white glue for bent laminations. Also, when heated during sanding, white glue clogs the sandpaper. White glue has very little moisture resistance, so it should not be used for projects placed outdoors and should not be exposed to water.

Yellow glue provides notable improvements over basic, white PVA. It's slightly more resistant to moisture, though still not recommended for outdoor use. The cured glue is less flexible than white glue, permitting less creep and making it easier to sand. It works well gluing veneer to a substrate. It's slightly stronger and cures a little faster than white glue. Its only limitation is its fast setup time. If you

GENERAL-PURPOSE GLUES

	PVA		
	WHITE	YELLOW	CROSS-LINKING
PREPARATION REQUIRED	Ready to use	Ready to use	Ready to use
OPEN WORKING TIME	5 minutes	5 minutes	5 minutes
CLAMP TIME/FULL CURE	1 hour/12 hours	30 minutes/12 hours	30 minutes/12 hours
MINIMUM APPLICATION TEMPERATURE	50°F	50°F	55°F
GAP-FILLING ABILITY	Poor	Poor	Poor
MOISTURE RESISTANCE	Poor	Fair	Good
SOLVENT RESISTANCE	Fair	Fair	Fair
CREEP RESISTANCE	Poor	Fair	Fair
OPEN SHELF LIFE	1 year	1 year	1 year
COST	Very inexpensive	Inexpensive	Inexpensive
NOTES	Gums up abrasives	Good general-purpose glue	Moderate moisture resistance

	HOT HIDE GLUE	LIQUID HIDE GLUE	POLYURETHANE
PREPARATION REQUIRED	Mix with water; use hot	Ready to use	Ready to use
OPEN WORKING TIME	1–3 minutes	10 minutes	20–40 minutes
CLAMP TIME/FULL CURE	2 hours/24 hours	2 hours/24 hours	4 hours/24 hours
MINIMUM APPLICATION TEMPERATURE	65°F	70°F	68°F
GAP-FILLING ABILITY	Poor	Poor	Poor
MOISTURE RESISTANCE	Poor	Poor	Excellent
SOLVENT RESISTANCE	Good	Good	Excellent
CREEP RESISTANCE	Good	Good	Excellent
OPEN SHELF LIFE	3-week pot life	1 year	6–12 months
COST	Inexpensive	Moderate	High
NOTES	Good general-purpose glue	Good for occasional repairs of hide-glue joints	New; health hazards not fully tested; foams as it cures

do a lot of complex assembly, you might prefer the longer open time of plastic resin glue (urea-formaldehyde). Yellow glue is my choice for general woodworking.

Cross-linking yellow glues like Titebond II share all the good qualities of the original yellow glue, with one important addition: they pass Type II water resistance tests. This means a glue sample can withstand three cycles of submersion under water for 4 hours followed by 19 hours of oven drying. Cross-linking PVAs are good for outdoor furniture and trim and for indoor work exposed to high moisture levels, such as bathroom vanities and kitchen cabinets. They are not water*proof,* though, and won't stand up to continuous exposure to water. If water resistance is worth a 15 percent increase in cost and a 5° increase in minimum working temperature, this glue is well worth considering for general-purpose use.

Hide Glue

Made from assorted animal proteins (just like cheap hot dogs?) hide glue is the oldest known woodworking glue. It is still holding together furniture entombed in Egypt three thousand years ago. Hot hide glue is made from flakes or pearls that you first soak in water and then heat to 145°F. Electric glue pots just like the one in my high school shop in the mid 1950s are still available, or you can use a baby bottle warmer. The bottle warmer is better suited to the amount of glue you'll need for an evening of woodworking.

Hide glue flakes or pearls will last for years if kept dry. Once mixed with water, however, the glue will spoil just like the cheap hot dog. Some folks reheat leftover glue day after day, claiming that it will keep for up to three weeks. I don't, and I have two questions for those who do. First, how do they know how much water to add to make up for yesterday's evaporation, and second, do they want their glue to be as tender as a hot dog they had reheated to 145°F every day for three weeks?

Hide glue has several unique features. The most widely known is its reversibility. Hide glue joints can be steamed apart, allowing you to remove and repair broken parts. This feature endears it to antique restorers and museum conservators. You can also break down hide glue with papayin, found in juice squeezed out of the skin of the papaya fruit and—much more conveniently—in Adolph's meat

tenderizer. If you take the papayin route, neutralize any residue with peroxide before you apply more hide glue.

A second feature of hide glue that's dear to restorers is that you don't need to remove old hide glue before reassembling the joint with new hide glue. The old and new will combine to form a sturdy bond.

A third handy feature is that hide glue sets in two stages. Recall that when preparing the glue, you add water and heat. When the glue cools, it gels. This is the first stage of the set. Then the water escapes, curing the glue to its full strength. For applications that don't require the full strength of the glue, such as glue blocks holding a drawer bottom, you can rely on the gel stage to "clamp" the parts together while the water escapes. This is called a rubbed joint because of the technique used for making it. Prepare the glue for a quick set, as explained three paragraphs below. Apply the glue and press the parts together, rubbing them back and forth a bit until they grab. The rubbing helps to squeeze out excess glue. Hold the parts together for another few seconds while the glue cools, and you're done—no clamping necessary. Avoid stressing the joint for a day while the second stage of the set develops fully.

You can well imagine a variety of difficult-to-clamp assemblies where this feature of hide glue could be invaluable.

The gelling of hide glue can also be a disadvantage. Thin spreads of the glue will cool and gel quickly. You can minimize the risk of premature gelling by applying the glue to only one surface of a joint and applying it a bit more thickly. The thicker spread will cool and gel more slowly, and the time saved by applying the glue to only one surface will allow you to bring the joint together more quickly.

Few woodworkers are aware that you can change some of the properties of hide glue. For example you can greatly extend the open time by adding up to 30 percent (dry weight) of urea, a readily available garden fertilizer, or by increasing the amount of water mixed with the dry pearls by up to 20 percent. Or you can make your own room-temperature liquid hide glue by adding both urea and water. If you want a glue with more flexibility for making a canvas-backed tambour, substitute glycerine for 10 to 20 percent of the water. This will also increase the working time (and the cure time). If you want the glue to set more quickly, say for rubbing glue blocks into place without having to clamp them, reduce the amount of water in the glue by up to 20 percent.

Hide glue is nontoxic. In fact, a more highly refined version of the same product, gelatin, is used in foods, including marshmallows. (Now you know why roasted marshmallows stick to your kids' faces.) Hide glue cleans up easily with water, and some stains will penetrate it to a degree; so a thin film left on the wood by poor cleanup may not interfere with staining the way a smear of PVA will.

Liquid hide glue is premixed and ready to use right out of the bottle, which is handy if you don't want to mess with a glue pot. However, liquid hide glue has the highest minimum application tempera-

ture (70°F) of any ready-to-use glue. Also, it has a closed shelf life of only about a year, so check the bottle for an expiration date before buying.

Polyurethane Glue

Recent newcomers to the U.S. woodworking market, polyurethane glues are billed as all-purpose woodworking glues—and then some. They are ready-mixed and produce strong, creep-resistant, and waterproof bonds. They have an unusually long open time—one maker claims 40 minutes. Unlike other glues, you can apply them to just one half of a joint and then bring the parts together. This will cut down assembly time and may increase the coverage

WHAT WENT WRONG?

The best mistakes to learn from are the other guy's. Here's a laundry list of mistakes the other guy has made—mistakes that result in weak or failed glue joints.

• *Poor fit.* This is probably the number one cause of failed glue joints. Very few glues provide strength over a gap. If the surfaces don't meet without voids, fix them before gluing. Note that you will also have a poor fit if you cut a joint at 92 degrees but clamp it together at 90 degrees. Always test fit your joinery dry, without glue, to make sure it fits correctly. It's much easier to spot a gap before it's filled with squeezed out glue.

• *End-grain gluing surface.* If either surface of a joint is an end-grain surface, as shown in *Grain Orientation and Gluing Strength* on page 37, expect a weak joint—you're sure to get it.

• *Too much moisture in the wood.* First, glue doesn't stick well to damp wood. Second, damp wood shrinks as it dries, putting additional stress on the joint.

• *Cold temperatures.* The room, the glue, and the wood all have to be at or above the minimum temperature for the glue you're using. If any of the three are too cold, you risk failure. It takes time for wood to adjust in temperature all the way through, so heat your shop well in advance of gluing up a joint.

• *Too little glue.* To get a good joint, both surfaces must be wetted out with a film of adhesive. Further, if the wood soaks up all of the glue before it cures, you won't get an adequate bond.

• *Joint open too long.* The allowable open times for glues are subject to a lot of exceptions. Most glues begin to cure or dry as soon as they're spread, and they may dry quite quickly if temperatures are high, humidity is low, or the glue is spread too thin.

• *Over-hasty clamping.* It takes a few minutes for a wood surface to absorb enough of the glue to form a good bond. Close a joint quickly to prevent it from drying out, but make sure it has a minute or two to soak in before applying full clamp pressure.

• *Too little clamp time.* Just because the boards stay together when you remove the clamps doesn't mean you haven't weakened the joint by removing them too soon. Err on the safe side by exceeding the recommended clamping time.

• *Premature stress.* Working on an assembly with either hand or machine tools (or banging it around or dropping it) will stress a joint and weaken it if the glue has not yet fully cured. Even if the assembly doesn't immediately come apart in your lap, it may fail later.

rate. You can easily scrape dry polyurethane glue from the wood. If you don't get it all off, it takes stain and finish better than most glues. And cutting through dried glue won't dull tools.

Despite all these good qualities, polyurethane glues have a number of shortcomings. Minimum application temperature is a fairly high 68°F. Colder temperatures slow the initial cure time from one hour to as much as four hours. These glues need moisture to catalyze, so you have to moisten the surfaces of old or very dry wood with a damp cloth before applying the glue. And when polyurethane glue dries on your skin, it will stay there for days before it wears away, so if your day job requires that your hands look clean, use gloves when applying it or clean your hands with rubbing alcohol immediately after use. Note, too, that these glues present a health hazard to asthmatics and those who tend to be hypersensitive or highly allergic. Even if you don't have a known problem, use them with lots of ventilation—masks don't help.

One of the peculiar working characteristics of polyurethane glue is that it expands (and foams) as it cures. Many woodworkers interpret this as an indication that it's a good gap filler. It does fill a gap, but it doesn't provide structural strength across the gap. Read the fine print if the label seems to claim otherwise. You may only want cosmetic gap filling; but if you need structural gap filling, polyurethane glue won't provide it. There's also a down side to this foaming and expanding: If a joint is not properly clamped, the expanding glue will push the joint apart.

The cost of polyurethane is either competitive or high, depending on how you classify it. I've included it in the chart on page 44 with general-purpose wood glues because that's how it's being plugged by the makers. Compared to the other general-purpose glues, it's expensive. But since it *is* waterproof, I could just as well have included it with the other waterproof glues. Compared to them it's competitive.

Moisture-Resistant and Waterproof Glues

For projects that may have to stand up to occasional wet or damp conditions, like kitchen and bathroom cabinetry, a general-purpose glue with some moisture resistance is just fine. But when a project will get very wet and get wet quite often, such as outdoor furniture or boats, use a more waterproof glue like those listed below.

Plastic Resin Glue

Also known as urea-formaldehyde glue, plastic resin glue is most common as a powder that you mix with water. The powder has a long shelf life, as long as it's kept in a tightly sealed container. Once mixed, it has a pot life of 4 hours at 70°F, and

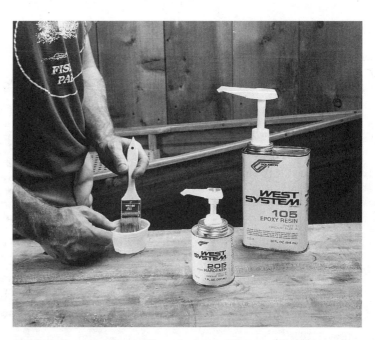

High-tech adhesives like epoxy withstand continuous immersion in water.

1½ hours at 90°. The open time is a generous 20 to 30 minutes, making it a good choice for complex glue-ups. The minimum clamping time is 12 hours,

WATER-RESISTANT GLUES

	PLASTIC RESIN (UREA-FORMALDEHYDE)	RESORCINOL	EPOXY
PREPARATION REQUIRED	Mix powder with water	Mix powder with liquid resin	Mix 2 liquids
OPEN WORKING TIME	20–30 minutes	10–30 minutes	5–60 minutes
CLAMP TIME/FULL CURE	12 hours/24 hours	12 hours/24 hours	No clamp time; full cure varies
MINIMUM APPLICATION TEMPERATURE	70°F	70°F	40–65°F
GAP-FILLING ABILITY	Fair	Good	Excellent
MOISTURE RESISTANCE	Very good	Excellent	Excellent
SOLVENT RESISTANCE	Excellent	Excellent	Excellent
CREEP RESISTANCE	Excellent	Excellent	Excellent
OPEN SHELF LIFE	2–4-hour pot life	2–4-hour pot life	10–60-minute pot life
COST	High	High	High
NOTES	Good water resistance	Excellent waterproof structural strength	Extremely versatile; lacks high heat resistance

which for most of us means overnight. A two-part version, Unibond 800, mixes powder with a liquid resin and has a clamping time of only 4 to 6 hours.

Plastic resin glues are highly moisture-resistant but are not suitable for continuous submersion. They are an excellent choice for outdoor furniture and house trim but not for boats. The minimum application temperature is 70°F—tied for the highest of all the glues. The stuff just won't cure in a cold shop. Plastic resins have good bond strength and creep resistance.

The powders contain toxins, so wear a dust mask when mixing plastic resin glue. In mixed form, the glue irritates the skin, so wear protective gloves. Cured squeeze-out is brittle and hard enough to chip a jointer knife. It sands off easily but the dust is toxic.

Resorcinol

Resorcinol is a two-part adhesive with a resin component and a hardener. It meets the most rigid testing requirements for a waterproof glue.

TECH TIP **SCREWS IN END GRAIN** don't hold very well. But if you drill a pilot hole almost as big as the outside diameter of the screw threads, fill the hole partly with epoxy, and drive in the screw, it will hold extremely well. This is just one of dozens of ways you can use the gap-filling ability of epoxy. Be forewarned, however, that epoxy in a screw hole will hold so well that removing the screw will be a major undertaking.

Once cured, it can withstand continuous salt- or fresh-water immersion, so it's commonly used in boats, laminated structural beams that are exposed to the weather, exterior building projects, and outdoor furniture. It's highly resistant to creep, heat, and solvents and is a fairly good gap filler. On the down side, most resorcinols cure to a deep red or purple color that stands out against almost any wood, so think twice before using it on a fine piece of furniture.

The working properties of resorcinol are similar to those of plastic resin. It has a good long open time and can be cleaned up with water but has a 70°F minimum application temperature. It cures in 12 to 24 hours. The specification sheet from one maker says you need wood with a moisture content between 8 percent and 12 percent for the best bond, and it warns against using the glue on wood drier than 5 percent or wetter than 15 percent moisture content. Resorcinols contain formaldehyde, so use them in a well-ventilated area and avoid breathing dust from the sanded glue.

Epoxy

Superficially, epoxy is similar to resorcinol—you mix two chemicals together, they harden when they react with each other, and they stick to wood. In both cases the new, hard substance is waterproof and resists creeping. Don't be fooled by these similarities. Epoxies are really a huge family of products with enormous variety. As woodworkers, we are primarily interested in epoxy that is formulated specifically for wood. These special formulations offer us physical and working characteristics not found in any other product. In some cases, epoxy's characteristics are the exact opposite of other glues. For example, clamping an epoxy joint during the cure can *weaken* it instead of strengthening it and applying epoxy in a thin coating can offer *longer* open time instead of shorter. You can also change the physical and working characteristics of epoxy with fillers. As explained in the literature available from the manufacturers, you can mix in a wide variety of fillers without seriously changing the strength of the epoxy.

If you add colloidal silica filler to the resin/hardener mix, it behaves a bit like mayonnaise instead of flowing like honey. If you add a lot of colloidal silica, you'll create a very smooth-working, ivory-colored paste.

If you add extremely fine cotton fibers (called microfibers) to the epoxy, the microfibers will give up enough resin to thoroughly wet the surface of the wood but retain enough to prevent the wood from sucking the joint dry. I use epoxy filled with microfibers when assembling mortise-and-tenon joints in outdoor furniture.

Add dust from a belt sander to create a peanut butter–consistency wood filler that will match the color of the wood, provided you finish your project with an oil varnish but no stain.

The pot life, or open working time, and the full cure time of epoxy depend on the hardener and the temperature. A fast hardener used on a hot summer day may give you a pot life of only a couple of minutes. A slow hardener used in a cold shop may allow you to work with mixed epoxy for more than an hour. Even after mixing, and without touching the thermostat, you can adjust the pot life. As epoxy cures, it gives off heat. If you have it in a small cup, this heat will speed up the cure, shortening pot life. If you pour it into a shallow tray so the heat can escape into the air, you will extend the pot life considerably. This is why a thin coating on your wood can offer a longer open time than a thick coating. Adhesives that cure by releasing solvents have a short open time if you spread them thinly.

The good, versatile, woodworking epoxies were originally developed for building wooden boats. Since boatbuilding with epoxy is inevitably a messy operation, the formulators chose the least toxic ingredients. You should avoid skin contact with uncured epoxy, especially the hardener, but a woodworking epoxy is far less hazardous than typical industrial formulations. Once it has fully cured, epoxy does not pose any health problems that anybody is aware of. It may take a month or more for the last vestiges of hardener to react with the resin, however, so avoid breathing dust from sanding operations.

A result of epoxy's gap-filling strength is that you don't need to clamp an epoxied joint. You need to keep the parts immobile while the epoxy cures, and clamps may be the easiest way to immobilize them, but pressure is unnecessary. I've used tape, props, gravity, even braces attached with hot-melt glue to hold parts while epoxy was curing. If you do use clamps, take it easy: Too much pressure will squeeze much of the epoxy out of a joint, weakening it.

Epoxy is completely waterproof, yet it doesn't pass the military's tests for waterproof adhesives. The problem has nothing to do with water: The test requires that the glue joint survive boiling. Epoxies for woodworking begin to soften at about 160°F, so they can't pass the test. Keep this relatively low temperature in mind. I don't usually boil my patio furniture, but I occasionally have to remove a screw that I epoxied in place. A propane torch applied to the screw head will soften the epoxy enough to remove the screw.

SPECIALTY GLUES

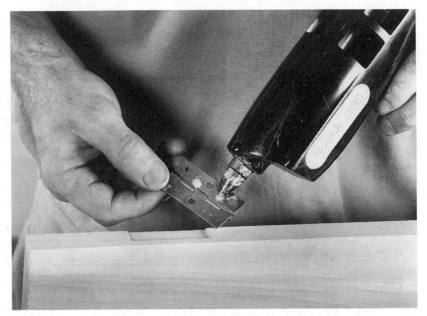

Hot-melt glue, one of many special, limited-purpose adhesives, will hold hardware in place while you drill screw holes.

Once in a while, woodworkers come across a problem demanding an adhesive that is very different from typical woodworking glues. It may be a need for a *weak* glue—one that will break without tearing out a bunch of wood fiber—or a very *quick* stick that will last a long, long time. A few such special-purpose glues have found their way into the woodworking shop. They don't do many jobs; but the ones they do, they do remarkably well.

Cyanoacrylate

Rumor has it that this glue was first developed as a surgical adhesive and was used to close wounds on the battlefields of Vietnam. Name brands like "Super" and "Krazy" are not farfetched.

The first formulas on the market were clear, thin liquids for bonding non-porous surfaces like glass and metal after just seconds of contact. Thicker formulations with better gap-filling capability and slightly longer curing times—10 to 50 seconds—came later. These are the formulas used by woodworkers. Accelerators are available to speed curing time.

Cyanoacrylates are excellent for quick repair of fine cracks or minor defects in wood. Turners fill voids with it, stabilizing fragile-walled vessels. Cyanoacrylates are very resistant to moisture, solvents, and creep, and they're excellent for bonding dissimilar materials like wood to metal.

Cyanoacrylate forms bonds that are brittle, so avoid using it in joints that might be subject to high impact. Price will also limit the use that you make of it: You can buy a gallon of PVA for the price of a shot glass of cyanoacrylate. The glue gives off eye-irritating fumes, and the accelerants can cause headaches and nausea. And keep it off your hands. (Surgical adhesive, remember? You could scratch your ear and then not be able to get your shirt off.)

If you do need to remove it, use acetone or acetone-based nail polish remover.

Hot-Melt Glue

This stuff is like wax—it melts when you heat it up and solidifies when it cools down. To use it, insert a stick of the glue into an electric glue gun; after a few minutes, when the stick reaches about 350°F, apply the melted glue through the tip of the gun. The glue will reharden in about half a minute, depending on the formulation of the glue stick you're using.

Hot-melt glue is economical—pound for pound about the same as hot hide glue. You use only as much as you need, and the sticks never deteriorate. It's completely waterproof, but it can't form structural bonds. I use it to hold parts in position while epoxy cures, to hold hardware in position while I drill screw holes, and to attach the tiny wooden glazing beads that hold glass panes in a cabinet door. A friend of mine uses it to hold turned bowls to a face plate while applying a finish. If you break apart a hot-melt-glued joint, you can remove the residue with a chisel.

Contact Cement

Contact cement is a unique one-part adhesive. You brush, spray, or roll the cement to two surfaces and then, while the parts are separated, allow them to dry for a specified time. When the surfaces are no longer tacky, bring them together. They will grab immediately on contact and allow no adjustment. (If you blow it, you can work the maker's recommended solvent between the parts to dissolve the glue. This will produce an obnoxious but separated mess.) Contact cement is not appropriate for joints that must bear continuous stress.

In the woodworking shop, contact cement is most often used for bonding plastic laminate to core materials like particleboard or plywood. It comes in solvent-based and water-based formulas. Typical applications involve spreading the adhesive over large areas, releasing considerable amounts of solvent. These fumes are hazardous to your health. Provide plenty of ventilation, and wear the

manufacturer's recommended respirator when using the glue. Water-based contact cements tend to cost more, but they're safer to use.

> **TECH TIP** **END-GRAIN SURFACES SUCK UP GLUE,** starving the joint. Don't fight the absorption—fill its thirst. First, apply glue generously. Next, allow the glue to soak in for several minutes. Then scrape off unabsorbed glue and reapply a fresh coat. Finally, bring the joint together and clamp it. This won't make an end-grain joint as strong as a flat-grain joint, but it will add amazing strength to, say, a mitered crown molding.

SPECIAL-PURPOSE GLUES

	CYANOACRYLATE (SUPER GLUE)	HOT-MELT GLUE	CONTACT CEMENT
PREPARATION REQUIRED	Ready to use	Heat in glue gun	Ready to use
OPEN WORKING TIME	2–100 seconds	10–40 seconds	1–2 hours
CLAMP TIME/FULL CURE	N/A	N/A	Momentary pressure plus dry time
MINIMUM APPLICATION TEMPERATURE	40°F	N/A	60°F
GAP-FILLING ABILITY	Not structural	Not structural	Poor
MOISTURE RESISTANCE	Excellent	Excellent	Excellent
SOLVENT RESISTANCE	Excellent	Poor	Poor
CREEP RESISTANCE	Excellent	Poor	Poor
OPEN SHELF LIFE	6 months	Unlimited	6–12 months
COST	Very high	Inexpensive	Moderately high
NOTES	Versatile, durable, instant bonding	Quick for temporary or lightly loaded joints	Well worth learning to use for bonding laminates and veneer

2

PREPARING STOCK

Stock preparation consists of getting wood ready for joinery and final shaping. For the young, patient, and ambitious, that may include watering a tree and watching it grow. But for most of us the process begins with kiln-dried, rough lumber. To make your lumber ready to use, you need to cut it down to manageable length and width, flatten it, plane it to uniform thickness, straighten up the edges, and quite possibly resaw it into thinner pieces or glue it up into wider panels.

Flattening surfaces, known as "jointing," and planing to uniform thickness are the most critical of the preparation operations. All the joinery that will follow depends on flat surfaces and straight, square edges. Start with wood that's twisted, cupped, or bowed, and you're likely to end up with tables that have only three legs on the floor, cabinet doors that close at the top but not the bottom, and drawers that jam tight halfway into their cabinets. But spend some time and effort to flatten and square your rough stock, and these problems will usually disappear, doubling the pleasure of the rest of your woodworking.

CUTTING UP ROUGH LUMBER

A stack of rough lumber is exciting because it marks the beginning of a new project. Cutting it up can be unnerving, though—like scrambling an egg, there's no going back.

A stack of rough lumber can be very intimidating. Many of the boards are likely to be cupped, and those with the most beautiful grain may be twisted and bowed as well. The wide boards in the stack are very appealing but are probably too wide for your jointer. And the long boards will poke out a window or knock a can of stain off the shelf if you try to move them around. To tame the beast, you need to cut stuff down to size, but you also need to keep the rough-cutting to a minimum—lumber is easier and safer to saw *after* it is flat, smooth, and square.

There are three steps to cutting up rough lumber. First, decide how you'd like to use each board, and mark it. These decisions will affect the kind of wood grain in each of the project parts and therefore the appearance of your finished project as a whole. Take your time at this step—it's one of the most important steps in all of woodworking.

Next, crosscut each board just small enough to make the pieces manageable. The best size to crosscut the lumber to will depend on how crowded your shop is and how you intend to surface the stock.

Finally, rip the pieces just narrow enough to fit your jointer. If you intend to hand plane the stock, your best bet will be to leave all the boards full width—hand planing a single wide board flat is much easier than hand planing two or three narrow boards.

PRELIMINARY LAYOUT

Preliminary layout is very different from layout as we normally think of it. Layout usually means carefully marking the size and shape of a part on the lumber so we can cut it to the correct size. The chapter "Measuring, Laying Out, and Setting Up" on page 2 covers this kind of layout. The purposes of preliminary layout are first, to arrange the parts on the available stock so that the grain patterns will form a harmonious whole in the finished project; second, to arrange the parts on the stock to minimize waste; and third, to let you safely cut the lumber into manageable

Preliminary layout requires little precision but a lot of forethought. Examine every board to match it with the best possible use and best grain orientations.

LAYING OUT PARTS ON STOCK

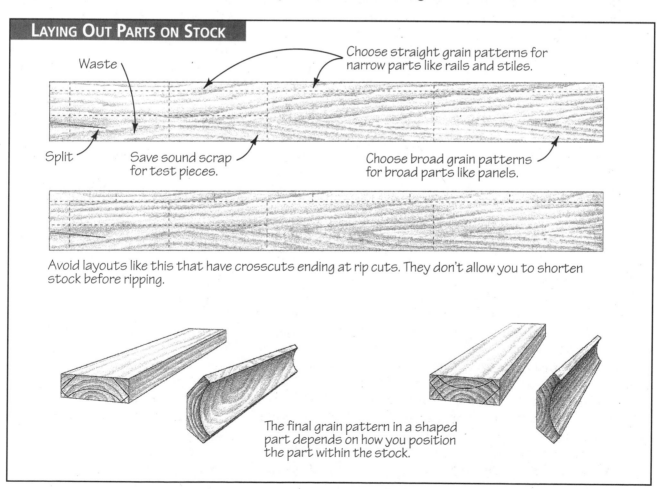

Choose straight grain patterns for narrow parts like rails and stiles.

Waste

Split

Save sound scrap for test pieces.

Choose broad grain patterns for broad parts like panels.

Avoid layouts like this that have crosscuts ending at rip cuts. They don't allow you to shorten stock before ripping.

The final grain pattern in a shaped part depends on how you position the part within the stock.

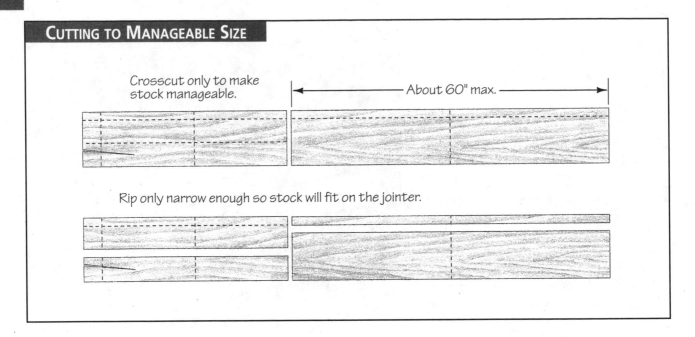

CUTTING TO MANAGEABLE SIZE

Crosscut only to make stock manageable.

About 60" max.

Rip only narrow enough so stock will fit on the jointer.

pieces. Unlike laying out final cuts, the preliminary layout is very rough-and-ready.

My routine for preliminary layout varies little from project to project. My tools are lumber crayons and a tape measure—a wide tape measure because its stiff blade can extend farther before bending. I use crayons in three different colors to help distinguish the purpose of each mark. Here's how I go about it.

First I prepare a place where I can see all of the stock at once. If the shop floor is big enough for all the project lumber, that's the ideal place. If the shop isn't big enough, I move to the garage. For one enormous kitchen cabinet job I did, I spread out on the driveway. For smaller projects I might lean the stock against a wall or lay it on saw horses. When I use a floor, I put down a bunch of 2 × 4s a couple of feet apart. By spreading out the lumber on 2 × 4s, I can go from layout right into crosscutting without having to move the stock first.

Next I examine each board, choose the side with fewer faults, circle the faults with a red lumber crayon, and lay the board on the 2 × 4s with the better side up. Once in a while I'll come across a board with a serious fault on the back side that doesn't show at all on the front, or better, side. I'll mark the location of such faults on the front using a blue crayon. This allows me to allocate that part of the board to a project part that will never be seen on the back, like the bottom of a cabinet. I examine and mark all the lumber this way.

If the project is quite big, I may sort the boards by how I will probably use them. For example, I'll group the boards that I'm most likely to use for door panels and drawer fronts, those I'll most likely use for face frames, door stiles and rails, and so on. This grouping makes the next step easier.

Once the faults are marked, I can decide which parts of the project will come from which parts of the boards. I usually begin by deciding how and where I want to use the most attractive boards. Sometimes that will be the most up-front location in the whole project; but if the boards in question are particularly flamboyant, I may put them where they'll be seen less often, and more appreciated when they are seen.

Most door panels and drawer fronts will come from nicely figured flat-sawn stock. I'll choose plain-looking, straight-grained stock for face frames; door stiles and rails; and other long, narrow parts. Wide boards often contain both kinds of grain, as shown in *Laying Out Parts on Stock* on page 55. I try to avoid laying out the parts so that crosscuts end at a rip cut, as shown in that drawing. It's much easier to crosscut a board all the way and then rip it than to go back and forth between ripping and crosscutting.

I mark each project part about ½ inch over-sized with a black lumber crayon. Most of my marks are freehand—I'll bother with a square only if there's very little wood to waste. If the project is at all complex, I label the parts on the lumber and check them off the cutting list.

CROSSCUTTING

A portable circular saw is the most practical tool for rough-crosscutting. It's sufficiently accurate and quick. Also, it's much easier to move a saw around the lumber than vice versa.

With the lumber all spread out and marked, I crosscut it with either a portable circular saw or a small chain saw. Keep in mind that the purpose here is to make the pieces manageable, not to cut out individual project parts. For me, lumber in the 4- to 6-foot range is manageable. While I crawl around on the lumber making the crosscuts, I adjust the position of boards and 2 × 4s as necessary to avoid sawing the 2 × 4s or the adjoining boards.

A small **electric chain saw** is the handiest tool for rough crosscutting. It's fast, sufficiently accurate, and unlikely to bind up in a cut, and it allows me to rough-crosscut a lot of lumber in very little time. I've used a chain saw for years. But, chain saws are wicked dangerous, and the cost is totally unwarranted unless you have other uses for it or unless you cut up thousands of board feet a year.

A **portable circular saw** is almost as handy as a chain saw, and far more practical since most woodworkers already own one. However, if the circular saw rocks on the uneven surface of warped lumber, the blade will bind. To minimize this danger, adjust the depth of cut to just barely cut through the stock. If it still binds, start the cut over again a half kerf to the left or right. By widening the kerf in this way, you prevent the binding. You can widen the kerf as often as necessary to get through an ornery piece of wood.

Another way you can minimize binding is to cut halfway through the stock from both faces, but this requires readjusting the saw, turning the board over, and laying out a second line on the other side.

If you really need to minimize the amount of waste in order to get specific project parts out of a particular board, your best choice again is the portable circular saw. Lay out the cut with a framing square and then guide the saw with the framing square or a saw protractor.

Some woodworkers use a **radial arm saw** for crosscutting rough lumber. This can work if you shim the stock on the table so that there is no tendency for it to rock and bind up the blade. Binding exaggerates the natural tendency of the radial arm saw to overfeed, which in turn stresses the saw and risks knocking it out of alignment.

I never use my **table saw** to crosscut long or warped rough lumber—it's just too dangerous and difficult. There is no satisfactory and practical way to feed long, warped stock sideways without rocking the wood and binding the blade. And when the blade binds suddenly, as it does when crosscutting, you risk damage to the blade as well as serious kickback.

TECH TIP **WHEN BUYING A PORTABLE CIRCULAR SAW: Keep in mind that bigger blades tend to bind more than smaller ones. My 6¼-inch-diameter portable gives me far less trouble than a friend's whoppin' great 10-inch portable.**

Ripping

The band saw is the safest tool for ripping cupped, bowed, or twisted stock. An outfeed support—or a helper—is essential.

I rip rough lumber only to make it narrow enough to fit on my jointer. I postpone ripping boards into narrow project parts until at least one face of the stock is flat. By jointing before ripping, I eliminate one cause of binding: stock rocking on the saw table.

The three best saws for ripping rough stock are the band saw, the table saw, and the portable circular saw. Rough-ripping by hand disappeared along with apprentices.

If you have a band saw and the shop space for auxiliary infeed and outfeed tables or roller stands, you have the safest setup for rough-ripping. Band saw blades seldom bind and never kick back. Mark the cut with a chalkline if your preliminary layout was freehand, and then rip to the line. A ½-inch, 3 or 4 tooth-per-inch, hook-tooth blade works well. You'll find the band saw a bit slower than the table saw in making the actual cut; but if your stock is at all ornery, the lost time will be more than made up by the lack of binding hassles.

To rip on the table saw, you need one straight edge on the stock so the rip fence can guide the stock in a straight line. The jointer will produce the straight edge for you; and if you set the depth of cut to ⅛ inch or more, it will do it fairly quickly. (See the chapter "Surfacing Rough Lumber" on page 62 for straightening edges on the jointer.) You can also tack a straightedge on the rough lumber, as explained in "Dealing with Waney Edges" on page 60.

Many woodworkers think of the table saw as the ideal ripping saw, and in many ways it is, but the table saw can run into problems when ripping wide stock. Lumber often has internal stresses—one part of a board tending to bend in one direction, while another part is tending to bend in the opposite direction. Ripping such a board may allow the two parts to bend in their opposite directions. If they do, you can have one of two problems, depending on which way the parts bend as you rip the board.

SAWS FOR ROUGH-CUTTING

	CHAIN SAW	PORTABLE CIRCULAR SAW
CROSSCUTTING	Excellent	Excellent
RIPPING	Not recommended	Very good
DANGERS AND LIMITATIONS	Always requires great caution	Limited power, especially ripping
BOTTOM LINE	A good choice for crosscutting if you already own the saw	Best all-around choice, especially if you have a powerful one

AUXILIARY RIP FENCE PREVENTS BINDING

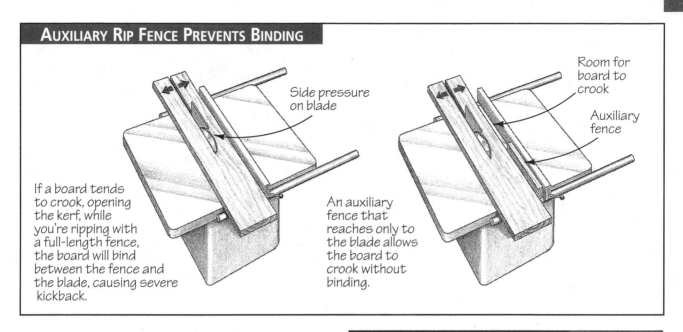

Side pressure on blade

Room for board to crook

Auxiliary fence

If a board tends to crook, opening the kerf, while you're ripping with a full-length fence, the board will bind between the fence and the blade, causing severe kickback.

An auxiliary fence that reaches only to the blade allows the board to crook without binding.

If the stock bends to open the kerf, it will jam between the blade and the fence, as shown in *Auxiliary Rip Fence Prevents Binding*. This can be quite dangerous because the blade will tend to throw the stock back at you. Protect yourself with an auxiliary fence that gives the sawed stock room to bow without pushing against the blade. The auxiliary fence should stop at the leading edge of the blade.

If the stock bends to close the kerf, the splitter on a table saw should prevent the kerf from closing against the blade, but the stock may grip the splitter itself. If it does, turn off the saw and insert a stubby screwdriver or wedge in the kerf beyond the splitter, as shown in *Wedge Prevents Pinching*. Push it in just enough to relieve the squeeze on the splitter.

WEDGE PREVENTS PINCHING

If a board tends to crook, closing the kerf and binding on the blade or splitter, hold the kerf open with a wooden wedge or stubby screwdriver.

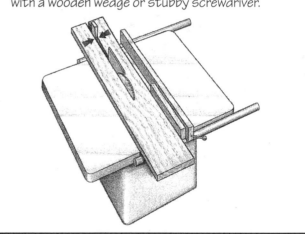

BAND SAW	TABLE SAW	RADIAL ARM SAW
Not usable	Not recommended	Fair
Excellent	Very good	Not recommended
Requires outfeed support	Requires auxiliary rip fence for safety	Prone to overfeed, especially if it binds
The best choice for ripping badly warped lumber	The best choice for ripping lumber with little or no warp	Better than either cutting torches or black powder for crosscutting

DEALING WITH WANEY EDGES

Some of the nicest and most interesting lumber you can buy comes from small sawmills that saw "through and through," meaning that the log is sawed into layers without rotating it between cuts. This produces a mixture of lumber that is flat-sawn, quarter-sawn, and everything in between. The lumber is usually sold with irregular edges, making the first rip cut a challenge. There are two ways to deal with these "waney" edges. The simplest is to clamp a straightedge to the board and rip with a portable circular saw. An alternative is to tack on a wooden straightedge overhanging one of the waney edges. With the straightedge following the table saw fence, you can rip the opposite edge of the stock, removing the wane, as shown in the drawing.

WANEY LUMBER

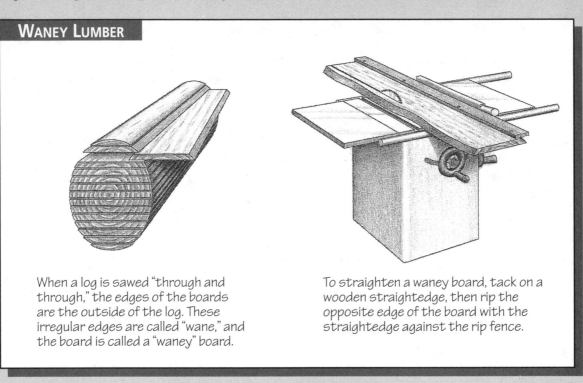

When a log is sawed "through and through," the edges of the boards are the outside of the log. These irregular edges are called "wane," and the board is called a "waney" board.

To straighten a waney board, tack on a wooden straightedge, then rip the opposite edge of the board with the straightedge against the rip fence.

Ripping a cupped board can be a challenge. If you rip with the concave side down, the stock is stable on the saw table during most of the cut but problems arise at the end of the cut: When the two halves come apart, the half between the fence and the blade will jam against the blade. But ripping with the concave side up isn't any better: The same jamming can occur at the end of the cut, plus if the stock rocks on the saw table in the middle of the cut, the blade will bind in the kerf. If the stock is no more than an inch thick and no more than 4 feet long, and the cup is no more than ¼ inch, I will rip it on the table saw with the cup up but holding the stock down alongside the blade with a push stick, as shown in *Avoiding Kickback on Cupped Boards*. For more unruly boards, rip on the band saw or with a portable circular saw.

A portable circular saw is especially handy for rough-ripping big, awkward boards because you can use it without first straightening an edge. Snap a chalkline on the board, and saw freehand or clamp a straightedge to the stock for the saw to follow. The only disadvantages of the portable circular saw are the need to prop up the stock to provide blade clearance underneath and—with many saws—a lack of power.

AVOIDING KICKBACK ON CUPPED BOARDS

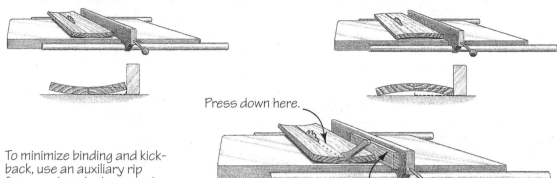

Cupped boards tend to jam between the standard fence and the blade at the end of a cut, whether ripping with the cupped face up or down.

To minimize binding and kickback, use an auxiliary rip fence and apply downward pressure from a push stick alongside the blade.

Press down here.

Auxiliary rip fence

POWER FOR RIPPING

Ripping requires more power than crosscutting but not necessarily more than you have available. If you're unhappy with the ripping performance of your table saw or portable circular saw, check the following suggestions for making the most of the power that you do have.

1. Use a proper rip blade when ripping. Such a blade for a 10-inch saw will have 20 to 30 flat-top teeth, with a hook angle in the neighborhood of 20 degrees. A 7¼-inch blade will have about 18 teeth. A combination blade, with its smaller gullets and lower hook angle, requires more power to make the same cut.

2. Make sure the blade is sharp. If in doubt, send it out. A good sharpening service (one that sharpens saw blades for professional woodworkers in your area) will make most blades perform better than they did brand new. The best indication that a blade needs sharpening is the need for more feed pressure than when the blade was new.

3. If a sharp rip blade slows down significantly when ripping, switch to a thin-kerfed rip blade. These thinner blades remove less wood and therefore require less power.

4. Use a smaller-diameter blade. An 8-inch blade on a 10-inch table saw will have less maximum depth of cut but more than enough for most ripping. The 8-inch blade will cut more slowly, but it will have more torque—less tendency to overload the motor.

5. Make sure the saw motor is getting the electricity it needs. Provide your table saw with its own circuit—20-amp if you run it on 110 volts. Portables are often strangled by extension cords that are too long and don't have adequate capacity. Try ripping with your portable plugged directly into a 20-amp outlet to see if your extension cord is guilty.

Note: Feeding stock slowly in order to give the saw more time to do the work may be self-defeating. Much of the heat generated in sawing is carried away by the sawdust. When you slow down, there's more heat from friction and less sawdust to carry it away. If the blade overheats, warps, and binds in the kerf, you've gained nothing by slowing down.

Surfacing Rough Lumber

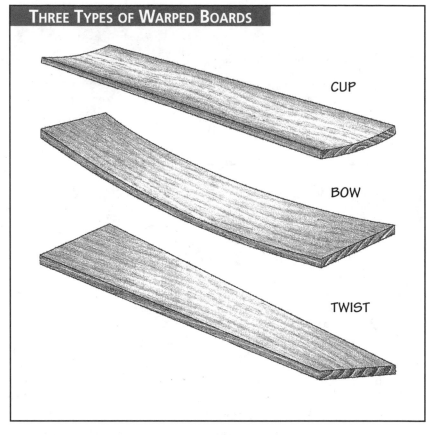

THREE TYPES OF WARPED BOARDS

CUP

BOW

TWIST

Newcomers to woodworking usually think of planing as making wood smooth. Planing does that, but its primary role in stock preparation is taking the cup, bow, and twist out of wood—and making the edges straight and square.

There are several ways to go about flattening rough lumber. The best approach for you will depend on your skills, your budget, your personal preferences, and even on the professional services available in your area. The tools you can use vary from hand planes to heavy machines—even your router in some circumstances. When you plane rough lumber, you have two goals: You want to make the two faces perfectly flat and parallel to each other; then you want to make the edges straight, square to the faces, and parallel. The steps toward these goals begin with removing any warp—cup, bow, or twist—from one face of the stock, then truing the remaining three surfaces using the first face as a reference.

Many woodworkers, especially those with limited space or a tight budget, find it impossible to surface their own rough lumber. If you're among them, you'll be interested in the tips in "Buying Planed Lumber" on page 73. Those tips point out that wise buying involves more than shopping for price.

SIZING UP YOUR STOCK

Some traditional woodworkers use winding sticks to determine whether a board is warped; but I find a long straightedge, such as a carpenter's level or a steel rule, more versatile. Winding sticks reveal only twist, while a straightedge laid on the stock lengthwise, crosswise, and diagonally reveals cup and bow as well as twist.

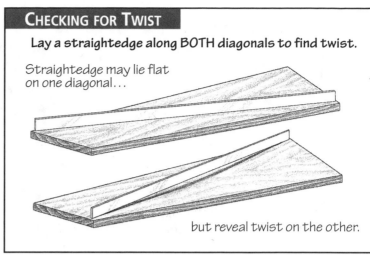

CHECKING FOR TWIST

Lay a straightedge along BOTH diagonals to find twist.

Straightedge may lie flat on one diagonal...

but reveal twist on the other.

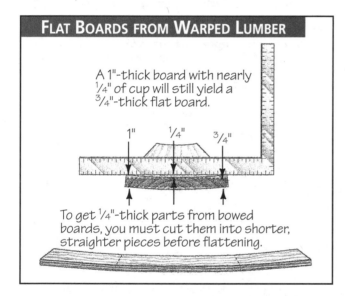

FLAT BOARDS FROM WARPED LUMBER

A 1"-thick board with nearly ¼" of cup will still yield a ¾"-thick flat board.

1"   ¼"   ¾"

To get ¼"-thick parts from bowed boards, you must cut them into shorter, straighter pieces before flattening.

But be thorough when using a straightedge to check your stock. A straightedge laid diagonally on a twisted board may show the board to be apparently flat, as shown in *Checking for Twist* (top), yet when laid on the opposite diagonal reveal twist, as shown at bottom in that drawing. As you notice high spots, mark them with a lumber crayon: It makes a bold mark and doesn't demand repeated sharpening.

You need to know more than just where the high spots are. You also need to know how much thick-ness will be lost to flattening the board. The straightedge reveals this as well. As you check the board with the straightedge in every imaginable position, note the position that leaves the biggest gap between the board and the straightedge. Measure the gap, as shown in *Flat Boards from Warped Lumber*, and add ¹⁄₁₆ to ⅛ inch for smoothing off the rough saw marks. Then subtract this total from the thickness of the board. The answer is the thickest surfaced board you can get. If you plunge right in and start cutting wood before you check, you can wind up with a board that you can't use as planned and may not be able to use for other parts, either.

Cupping is the most common defect in lumber, but bow and twist are more likely to limit how you can use a board. A 1-inch-thick board with almost ¼ inch of cup across its width will still yield ¾-inch-thick parts for your project. But if a long board is bowed and you need ¾-inch-thick pieces from it, you will probably need to cut it into shorter lengths, as shown at the bottom of *Flat Boards from Warped Lumber*.

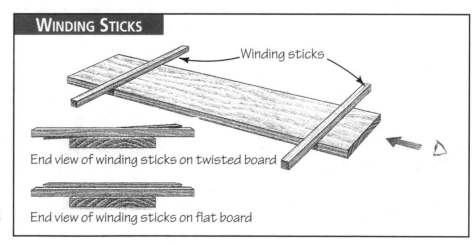

WINDING STICKS

Winding sticks

End view of winding sticks on twisted board

End view of winding sticks on flat board

Machines for Planing

Combination jointer/thicknessers use a single cutter-head and motor. The jointer tables are above the cutterhead, and the thicknesser table and feed rollers are below. With this arrangement the jointing capacity is the same as the thicknessing capacity, typically 1 foot or more, and the single machine takes up far less space than two separate machines would.

It takes two machines to surface rough stock: one to make a surface flat, the other to make the second surface parallel to the first. A jointer planes a surface flat. It's fairly expensive, but it's essential in a shop that uses a lot of lumber. A thickness planer, often called just a planer or just a thicknesser, makes the second surface of a board parallel to the first. Keep in mind that its function is to make a board uniform in thickness—it will make the second surface of a board flat only if the first surface is flat. (But see "Flattening Stock with a Thicknesser" on the opposite page for some exceptions.) The two machines form a complementary pair: Joint a face flat, then plane the opposite face parallel to the first.

Ideally, you should have a jointer as wide as your planer. But few home-shop woodworkers can afford to buy and house a jointer more than 8 inches wide, and few thickness planers are less than 12 inches wide. A solution to the space problem is a combination jointer/thicknesser, as shown in the photo on this page. Unfortunately, there's no good solution to the cost problem.

Both jointers and thickness planers use a rotary cutterhead with two to four knives. The knives travel in an arc and scoop out the surface of the wood. The surface they leave behind is not truly flat—it's scalloped, as shown in *How Mill Marks Happen*.

These scallops, called mill marks or planer marks, may be invisible to the naked eye on unfinished wood. When you apply a finish to your project, however, the changing grain direction in the scallops will stand out and the mill marks will be disgustingly obvious. Never, NEVER consider a machine-planed surface ready for finish. Hand plane, scrape, or sand the surface to remove the mill marks.

When surfacing rough stock with a jointer or planer, you want it to be more than just flat; you also want to minimize grain tear-out so your final smoothing will be as easy as possible. To get the smoothest possible surface, make sure your cutterhead knives are sharp, take a very shallow cut with each pass, and plane "with the grain."

First, try to get the grain direction right. Orient the stock so the visible grain on the edge of the stock goes in the direction shown in *How Mill Marks Happen*. Then check the quality of the cut. The actual wood fibers are not necessarily going in the direction of the visible grain. If the quality of the cut is not as good as you'd like, try feeding the

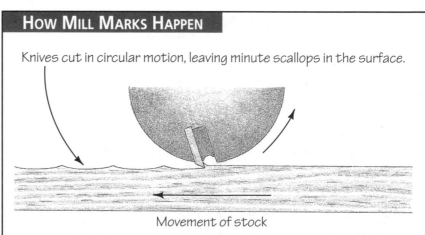

HOW MILL MARKS HAPPEN

Knives cut in circular motion, leaving minute scallops in the surface.

Movement of stock

FLATTENING STOCK WITH A THICKNESSER

To trick a planer into flattening a cupped surface, you need to understand why it doesn't do it in the first place. The reason is primarily the pressure applied by the feed rollers. If a cupped board is fed into a thickness planer, the feed rollers tend to bend the wood flat while the knives are cutting away the surface. When the board leaves the machine, it unbends, and you still have a cupped board. If you can prevent the feed rollers from bending the wood flat, the knives will cut it flat.

Step one in minimizing the bending is minimizing the feed-roller and chip-breaker pressure. Check the manual for your planer, and adjust these pressures to the minimum recommended in the manual.

Step two is supporting the stock close to where the feed rollers apply pressure. Then the strength of the stock can resist the bending pressure. Several ways of supporting the stock are shown below.

You can run into another kind of problem if you thickness-plane rough lumber that hasn't been jointed: The stock jiggles up and down as the rough surface rolls over the planer's table rollers. If you remove or lower the table rollers so that the stock is supported by the table itself, it will jiggle much less. The stock will be harder to feed—you may have to do some pushing and pulling to get it through—but the planed surface will be smoother.

PLANING CUPPED STOCK FLAT

To plane a cupped board, you need to support it close to the center. Otherwise the pressure of the rollers will bend the board flat, then allow the board to spring back after it leaves the planer.

Roller pressure bends the board flat…

because a cupped board is supported only at its edges.

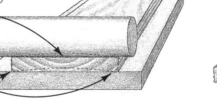

3 WAYS TO MINIMIZE BENDING

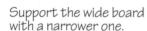

Support the wide board with a narrower one.

Cut a rabbet along the edges of the wide board.

Or flatten part of the board with a hand plane.

stock in the opposite direction. Don't be surprised if reversing the stock improves the quality in some areas of the surface but makes it worse in others. Some wood has "roey" grain—bands of wood with grain running in opposite directions.

Next, experiment with depth of cut. Easily machined wood like straight-grained poplar may allow you to take as much as ⅛ inch in a single pass with no loss of quality. Difficult wood like curly

maple may allow no more than 1/64 inch per pass and then only with barely acceptable quality.

Finally, even if your knives seem razor-sharp, try giving them a touch-up honing with an ultra-fine ceramic stone. You can touch them up right in the machine, unplugged of course. Just make sure you hone at an angle that's no more than a couple of degrees steeper than the primary bevel on the knives.

Using a Jointer

To use a jointer, lay the stock on the infeed table and push it forward into the knives. The stock will push the cutterhead guard out of the way, and the knives in the cutterhead will shave off the bottom layer of wood, as shown in *How a Jointer Works*. With successive passes, great irregularities get shaved down until the entire surface is flat.

When the leading edge of the stock passes onto the outfeed table, press down on it there with your left hand. This will ensure that the remainder of the cut will be in the same plane as the beginning. Feed the stock forward with your right hand, as shown in the photo on page 68.

For the jointer to work properly, the outfeed table must be exactly in line with the cutting arc of the knives. If your jointer is cutting a concave surface, the outfeed table is probably lower than the knives. If the cut surface is convex, the outfeed table is probably higher than the knives.

NOTE: If you notice that your jointer is cutting a slightly convex surface, but the outfeed table is no higher than the knives, the problem may be dull knives. Knives that are not razor-sharp will compress the wood slightly and not remove quite as much as they should. Once the stock is past the knives, the wood will expand back to below the level of the outfeed table. The net effect is the same as the outfeed table being higher than the knives.

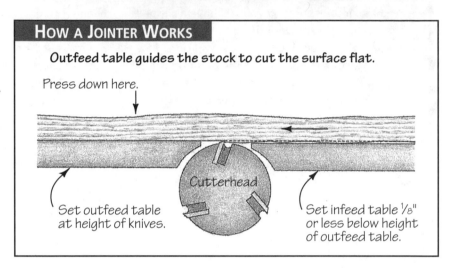

HOW A JOINTER WORKS

Outfeed table guides the stock to cut the surface flat.

Press down here.

Cutterhead

Set outfeed table at height of knives.

Set infeed table ⅛" or less below height of outfeed table.

Using a Thickness Planer

To use a thickness planer, lay the jointed surface of the stock on the infeed side of the planer table. Push the stock forward so that it engages the infeed roller. The roller will press it down tightly against the table and feed it into the knives. The knives will shave off the top layer, down to a thickness equal to the distance between the knives and the table, as shown in *How a Thickness Planer Works*. As the stock passes the cutterhead, it will engage the outfeed roller. This roller will keep the stock pressed down and continue to feed it after the trailing edge has gone past the infeed roller.

In addition to the cutterhead and the feed rollers, a thickness planer may have rollers in the table to reduce friction, a chip breaker that presses down on the stock just ahead of the knives to minimize tearout, and a pressure bar that presses down on the stock just behind the cutterhead. While these added parts improve performance, each in its own way, they may also increase the planer's tendency to "snipe"—to cut the ends of the stock thinner than the rest. "Snipe" on the opposite page explains more about snipe and how you can minimize it.

HOW A THICKNESS PLANER WORKS

Cutterhead shaves off irregularities on the upper surface of the stock. Table height governs the thickness of the planed stock.

Outfeed roller

Infeed roller

Cutterhead

Planer table

$\mathscr{S}$NIPE

Thickness planers often cut the first 3 or 4 inches and the last 3 or 4 inches of a board thinner than the middle of the board. This is known as "snipe." The primary cause of snipe is the table rollers. The front edge of the table and the first table roller support the stock when it first contacts the knives, as shown in the top part of *How Planers Snipe a Board*. When the stock reaches the outfeed roller and the second table roller, the leading edge is pushed down, as shown in the center of the drawing. This changes the position of the board and the depth of cut. At the end of the pass, the trailing edge comes out from under the infeed roller and jumps up, as shown in the bottom part of the drawing. This is snipe at its simplest. The behavior of the board is often further complicated by chip breakers and pressure bars, but the basic problem remains the same: The two table rollers do not uniformly support the stock throughout its passage. You can minimize the problem and sometimes eliminate snipe entirely by removing the table rollers or adjusting them flush with the table. But then feeding the stock becomes more difficult.

Some lightweight portable planers cause snipe because the tables actually flex during operation. When the stock enters the planer, only the infeed roller is applying pressure; but when the stock reaches the outfeed roller, the downward pressure on the table increases significantly. If the table is not absolutely rigid, it will bend slightly downward, decreasing the depth of cut. A change of only a thousandth of an inch or so will be quite noticeable on the stock. There is little you can do to overcome the shortcomings of such a cheaply built machine. Your best bet in this situation is to start with stock that's longer than the finished dimension and cut off the sniped ends after planing.

HOW PLANERS SNIPE A BOARD

As a board enters the machine, the first infeed roller cocks the board up, increasing the depth of cut.

Cutterhead

Outfeed roller

Infeed roller

Table rollers

Then the outfeed roller pushes the leading edge of the board down to its proper position, decreasing the depth of cut.

END OF FIRST SNIPE

Finally, as the board exits the machine, the trailing edge cocks up, again sniping the board.

BEGINNING OF SECOND SNIPE

My Fix for Snipe

I took the table rollers out of my thickness planer years ago and have never put them back. I fitted a ½-inch-thick Baltic Birch plywood auxiliary table over the cast iron. This auxiliary table had cleats on the bottom that fit into the openings where I had removed the table rollers. I covered the top surface with a mixture of epoxy resin and graphite to reduce friction. I find the absence of snipe and the smoother planed surface worth the occasional frustration of having to coax the wood through the machine.

Surfacing with Machines

The steps involved in surfacing stock with machines quickly become a routine: Joint a face, thickness the stock, joint an edge, rip to width. In practice, it's usually most efficient to work with batches of boards rather than individual ones. I'll gather up all the stock that needs surfacing to a particular thickness, joint a face of each piece, then thickness them all, and so forth. Then I'll repeat the routine for all the stock that needs some other thickness.

To create a flat surface with a jointer, hold the stock snugly against the outfeed table just ahead of the cutterhead with your left hand while feeding the stock with your right hand.

If a board you want to joint is twisted, balance the board so both of the "high" corners are more or less the same distance above the infeed table on the first pass. On subsequent passes make sure the leading "low" corner is tight against the infeed table. If it's cupped or bowed, avoid the balancing act by jointing the concave face; leave the convex face for the thicknesser.

Once the stock is flat and uniform in thickness, straighten out the edges. Joint the first edge with the concave side down, as you do when jointing the first face. I've gotten into the habit of moving the fence over so that my edge-jointing uses the middle portion of the jointer knives. It's a minor point, but over the years I've found that face-jointing cupped stock tends to dull the outer thirds of the knives faster than the middle third. By edge-jointing with the middle third, I lessen my usage of the parts that dull the fastest.

The table saw is the ideal machine for cutting the second edge straight and parallel to the first. Check that the blade is perpendicular to the table; then rip the second edge, keeping the jointed edge tight against the table saw fence. A good, modern, carbide-tipped rip blade on a well-tuned table saw with minimal runout will cut an edge so smooth that a single stroke with a hand plane will clean it up. That's as good as the jointer will do, since you'd have to remove the scalloped surface left by the rotary cutterhead of the jointer anyway.

TECH TIP — PLANE STOCK TO FIT YOUR DADOES

rather than cutting dadoes to fit your stock. Make a test dado in a piece of scrap with the router bit or dado cutter that you intend to use. Then use the test dado as a gauge to check the finished thickness of your stock. This will give you a much better fit than trying to thickness the stock to a measurement, and it will save the aggravation of hand planing to fit a routed dado or shimming a dado cutter on the table saw.

STEP-BY-STEP
MACHINE SURFACING

1 Joint one face.

Joint cupped or bowed boards concave-side down.

2 Plane second face parallel to the first.

Shallow cuts produce the smoothest surface.

3 Joint one edge.

Joint crooked boards concave-edge down.

4 Rip to width.

Keep jointed edge tight against the rip fence.

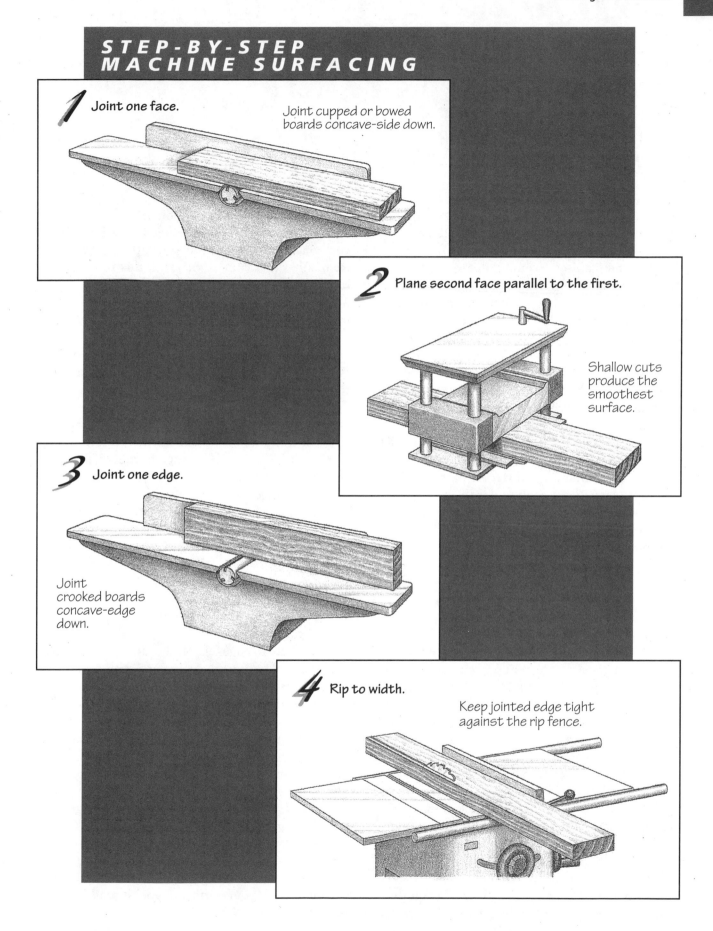

Surfacing with Hand Planes

Engineers can design machines to do just about anything, but that doesn't mean you can afford to buy them or put a roof over them. And machines don't offer the pleasures that many woodworkers find in hand planing. Even if you own and prefer to use machines, you need to know how to flatten a board with hand planes. There are just too many occasions when hand planes are the only practical choice, like when you have a beautiful board that is an inch too wide for your jointer.

Machines and hand planes are not necessarily an either/or choice. With wide boards it often makes sense to flatten one surface with a hand plane, then thickness the board by machine. Then you remove the mill marks with a finely set, razor-sharp hand plane or scraper, as described in the chapter "Smoothing Surfaces" on page 108. In this way, you've used each tool to best advantage and haven't exhausted yourself doing grunt work.

To flatten a board with hand planes, first clamp the board to your workbench, but avoid obstructing the surface you'll be working on. Bench dogs and a tail vise are the best method, but you can also wedge the board, as shown in Step 1 on the opposite page. Shim a bowed or twisted board so that it won't bend or rock while you're working on it.

Mark the high spots where you need to remove the most stock. When hand planing, you have to keep marking and re-marking as you progress because you keep planing off the marks. The lumber crayon is handy for this marking, as long as you still have a lot of stock to remove; but the closer you get to flat, the more frequently you'll want to mark those high areas. A handy way to re-mark them is to rub lipstick on the edge of a 4- or 6-foot carpenter's level, then rub the level over the board. The lipstick will transfer to the wood at the high spots.

The traditional plane for hogging off a lot of waste is a scrub plane, a medium-length, rather narrow plane with a curved cutting edge on the iron. Few woodworkers today invest in this single-purpose tool. They begin with a plane 18 to 24 inches long, called a fore or jointer. Since a plane this length can't dip into the low areas, it helps you concentrate on planing down the high areas. Remember that your objective at this stage is to flatten the board, not to smooth it, so concentrate on removing stock in the high areas that you've marked rather than removing the rough saw marks. As you plane, check the stock frequently with a straightedge and re-mark the high spots. When the board is flat, smooth it as described in the chapter "Smoothing Surfaces."

When one side of the board is flat, you can surface the other side with a thickness planer, or you can continue with hand planes. To carry on by hand, first set a marking gauge to the finished thickness that you want, and scribe the thickness on all four edges of the stock. Some woodworkers then chamfer the edges down to the scribe mark, as shown in Step 3 on the opposite page. This makes it easier to see at a glance how close you are to the final surface. Work the second surface the same way you worked the first surface, planing the high areas and checking regularly with a straightedge. You're done when you reach the scribe mark.

To joint an edge, clamp the stock on edge in a face vise and support the other end with a stick of scrap clamped to a leg of the bench. Use the longest plane you have, preferably 18 inches or more, and make sure the plane is adjusted so the depth of cut is uniform across the width of the plane. When jointing edges with hand planes, you have to check regularly with a square to make sure that the edge is perpendicular to the face. If your plane is properly adjusted and the planed edge is out of square, you're tilting the plane during the cut. If you have trouble, try to remember how many times you fell down while learning to ride a bicycle.

Don't bother ripping the stock to width until you've laid out your parts and you're ready to cut to final size.

STEP-BY-STEP HAND SURFACING

Clamp stock on the bench.

If you don't have a bench with a tail vise and bench dogs, wedge your workpiece between 2 clamped scraps.

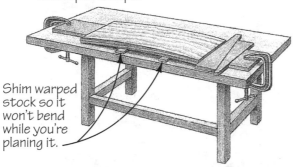

Shim warped stock so it won't bend while you're planing it.

Mark and plane down high areas until the stock is flat.

Plane in this direction...

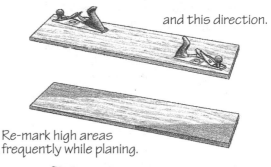

and this direction.

Re-mark high areas frequently while planing.

Planed areas will merge when the board is flat.

Plane second face parallel to the first.

Scribe the finished thickness from the flat surface, and chamfer the edges to the scribe marks.

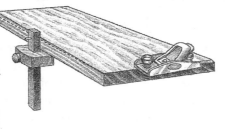

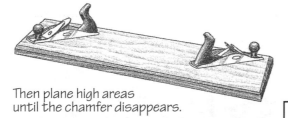

Then plane high areas until the chamfer disappears.

Plane one edge straight and square to the faces, then rip to final width.

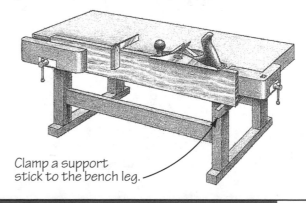

Clamp a support stick to the bench leg.

SURFACING ON THE ROUTER TABLE

Woodworkers occasionally try to figure out a way to surface rough stock with their router. If this idea occurs to you, take two aspirin and get a good night's sleep. Hopefully, by morning, you'll start thinking of hand planes or having the stock surfaced by someone else. Routing surfaces flat is just too cumbersome and laborious.

But there is an exception. A table-mounted router can joint and thickness small pieces of wood such as jewelry box parts. You don't need an elaborate gizmo. Two straight sticks and a bit of double-sided tape will do, as shown in *Surfacing on the Router Table*. Make sure you limit the depth of cut to ¹⁄₁₆ inch or less, and rout both sides before raising the bit for a second pass.

You can also make an edge-jointer out of a router table, as shown in *Making a Router Table Jointer*. The fence will function like the jointer's infeed and outfeed tables. The table will function like the jointer's fence. To mimic the depth-of-cut adjustment of a jointer, attach a strip of plastic laminate to the outfeed side of a router table fence. The drawing provides the details.

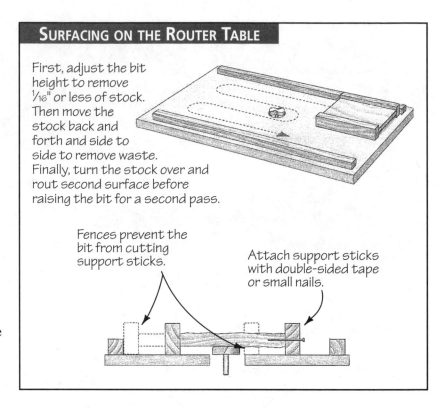

SURFACING ON THE ROUTER TABLE

First, adjust the bit height to remove ¹⁄₁₆" or less of stock. Then move the stock back and forth and side to side to remove waste. Finally, turn the stock over and rout second surface before raising the bit for a second pass.

Fences prevent the bit from cutting support sticks.

Attach support sticks with double-sided tape or small nails.

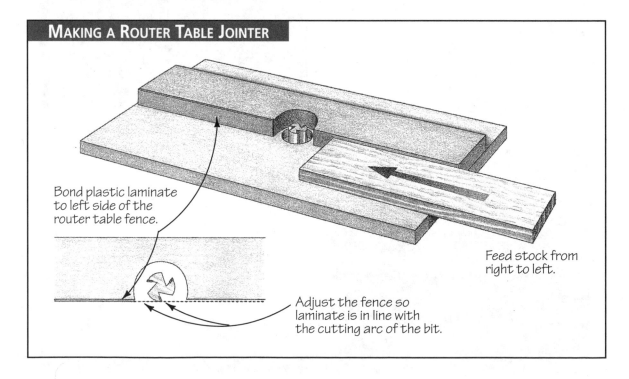

MAKING A ROUTER TABLE JOINTER

Bond plastic laminate to left side of the router table fence.

Feed stock from right to left.

Adjust the fence so laminate is in line with the cutting arc of the bit.

BUYING PLANED LUMBER

A great many woodworkers have neither the money nor the space for a jointer and thicknesser, and have neither the time nor the inclination to hand plane rough lumber. They buy their lumber surfaced. This is a great solution to the problem of surfacing lumber, as long as the stock is truly flat and stays that way. Here's how to make this solution work.

Get a moisture meter. Wood changes shape when its moisture content changes. If you want to buy flat wood and have it stay that way, you have to keep it at the same moisture content. The best place to begin taking control of wood moisture is in your own home—specifically, in your shop and in the rooms where your projects will spend the rest of their lives. Stick a board under your living room sofa for a month. Then measure its moisture content and the moisture content of a board in your shop. If the shop board measures more than a percent or two higher than the sofa board, install a dehumidifier in the shop. (You'll find that the dehumidifier also helps control rust on your tools.) When the sofa board and the shop board measure the same, you're ready to go lumber shopping.

Measure the moisture content of the boards you are considering buying. If they differ from the lumber in your shop by more than two or three percentage points, the new stock will probably change shape after you bring it home. Shop around for lumber closer in moisture content to the lumber in your home.

When you find lumber with an appropriate moisture content, check it with a straightedge to see if it's truly flat. Not all dealers joint lumber before they thickness it. If they don't, you're likely to find cupped, bowed, and twisted boards mixed up with the nice flat ones, so check every board before buying it.

If the dealer will surface the boards after you pick them out, make sure he intends to joint them before thicknessing them. If he expects you to buy them after he surfaces them, whether or not they come out flat, go elsewhere.

Many woodworkers find it far more practical to separate the buying of lumber from the surfacing of lumber. If you can find a cabinet shop with a big jointer and thicknesser, the owner may be willing to surface your stock for a reasonable price. In this case, take your rough lumber home and let it acclimate to your shop. When you're ready to begin work on it, take it out for surfacing and then get it back to the controlled humidity of your shop.

RESAWING

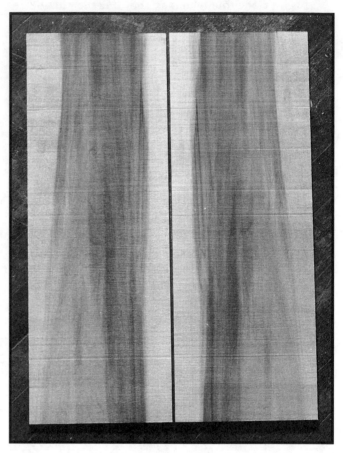

Book-matched boards for a pair of cabinet doors are just one of the many opportunities opened up by resawing.

When I look back at some of the really ugly stuff I made when I first got into woodworking, I realize how important it is to have the right thickness of stock. Trying to make attractive projects with just 1-inch- and 2-inch-thick stock is like trying to find comfortable shoes when your choices of size are "small" and "large."

Resawing, the process of sawing thick boards into thinner ones, gives you all the in-between sizes—thin dividers in a secretary desk, an end-table top that's more than ¾ inch thick but less than 1¾ inches, and even shop-made veneer. Resawing also opens up a whole new realm of matched-grain possibilities like book-matched boards—

two halves of a resawn board opened up like a book.

A typical 14-inch band saw or 10-inch table saw can resaw stock up to 6 inches wide. That capacity has been adequate for most of my projects, but it was too little for some of the best. When a project requires greater resaw capacity than you have, don't give up on the project—check out the alternatives in "Resawing Wide Stock" on page 80.

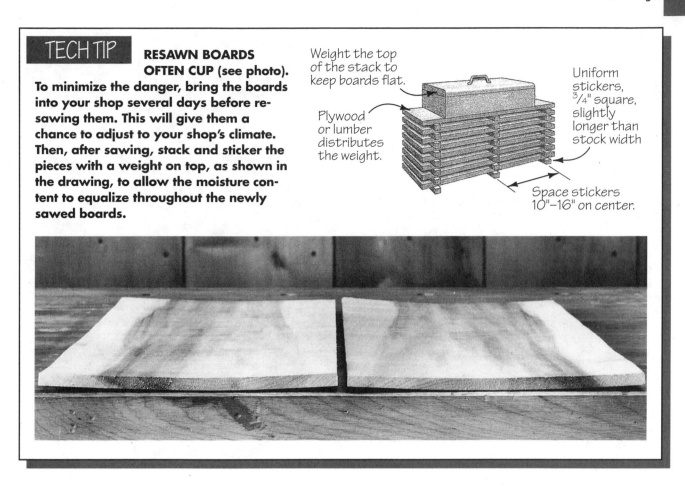

TECH TIP **RESAWN BOARDS OFTEN CUP** (see photo). To minimize the danger, bring the boards into your shop several days before re-sawing them. This will give them a chance to adjust to your shop's climate. Then, after sawing, stack and sticker the pieces with a weight on top, as shown in the drawing, to allow the moisture content to equalize throughout the newly sawed boards.

Weight the top of the stack to keep boards flat.

Uniform stickers, ³/₄" square, slightly longer than stock width

Plywood or lumber distributes the weight.

Space stickers 10"–16" on center.

Stock Preparation

Accurate resawing starts with accurate stock preparation. You need flat and square surfaces as references when you make your cuts; otherwise, you'll end up with pieces that vary in thickness. Begin by flattening one face of your stock. If you're flattening pre-planed stock that has warped, mark this good face so you won't mistake which face is truly flat. If you're sawing a board into more than two pieces, you'll have to flatten the sawed face after each cut to give you a true surface to guide the next cut.

Next, straighten and square an edge in relation to the good face. The easiest way to prepare these two surfaces is with a jointer. For more on that tool as well as some alternate methods of flattening stock, see the chapter "Surfacing Rough Lumber" on page 62.

That's all there is to stock preparation if you intend to resaw on the band saw. If you'll resaw on your table saw, you'll need to rip the second edge straight, parallel to the first edge, and square to the good face.

Once you've established a flat face and square edges, you can lay out your first cut. Allow some extra thickness for cleaning up the saw marks you'll create. Also, keep in mind that your stock is apt to warp slightly after you cut it, as shown in the photo on this page. This can result from the difference in moisture content between the inner and outer parts of the board, or from internal stresses that might have developed as the board was dried. When re-sawing an average 6-inch-wide board, I allow at least ¹/₁₆ inch for cleanup and warpage. For example, if I need ¼-inch finished thickness, I'll lay out the saw cut ⁵/₁₆ to ³/₈ inch from the good face of the stock. Since I "once upon a time" made a mistake, I also place an X on the side of the line where the blade must go.

Don't be greedy and try to resaw too many pieces from a single board. For example, don't try to get four ½-inch boards from a piece of 8/4 (eight-quarter) stock, even if it is on the thick side. Instead, saw the plank into thirds, and you'll have pieces you can plane to a full ½ inch.

RESAWING ON THE TABLE SAW

If I have one or two narrow pieces to saw in half, I turn to the table saw. It cuts quickly, and it's a snap to set up since the fence is right there waiting. But the table saw does have some limitations. Even with a thin-kerfed blade, resawing on the table saw wastes more wood than making the same cut on the band saw. So it's not my tool of choice if I'm trying to squeeze as many pieces out of a board as possible. I also avoid resawing wide boards on the table saw if the resulting boards will be less than ¼ inch thick. Such thin pieces can occasionally buckle or split, and if they do so while they're between the blade and the fence, the results can be unpredictable and dangerous.

Ripping thin pieces from the edge of thick boards, such as for bent laminations, presents a different problem. The pieces can slip down through the slot in the saw's table insert. Pieces that do slip down can cause the blade to bind, which can damage the saw's motor. They can also fly back at you. Prevent problems by making a new plywood table insert with a close-fitting blade slot. Cut the slot by raising the running blade up through the insert while holding it down with a push stick.

Resawing tends to be a power-hungry operation. If your saw bogs down or trips a circuit breaker, see "Power for Ripping" on page 61 for tips on improving its performance. A good, well tuned, contractor-style table saw with a 1½-horsepower motor should make a full-depth cut in most stable woods. If, even with a sharp rip blade, your saw won't take such a big bite, make the cuts in two or three passes each, raising the blade a bit each time.

The actual process of resawing on the table saw is simple, as shown in Steps 1–4 on the opposite page. Use your right hand to feed the stock through the cut at a steady rate while your left hand holds it against the fence just in front of the blade. If your stock is narrow enough to make the full cut in a single pass, use a push stick to feed the tail end past the blade.

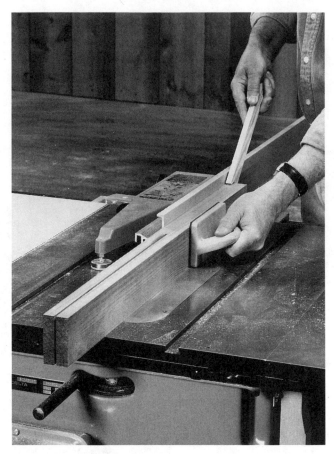

The table saw works well for resawing if the blade is sharp and has deep gullets and if the stock is stable. If the kerf closes and binds the blade, try making the cut in several passes of increasing depth.

Note that resawing on the table saw can be deceptive. Since the blade is buried within the board for much of the cut, it is easy to misjudge exactly where it will appear as it exits. Don't allow your fingers to dangle down along the board's trailing edge, or you may end up with an unpleasant manicure.

One final precaution: You *can't* use most saw guards or splitters when resawing, so you won't have the kickback protection that these devices offer. This is worth considering because resawn boards occasionally warp and pinch the blade during the cut. This can result in a nasty kickback. So stay alert to the way your boards are responding to the saw.

If I'm suspicious about the stability of a board, I'll make my cuts in several passes, starting with the blade an inch or so above the table and raising it two or three cranks per pass. This way, if the kerf does start to close up, the subsequent cuts will open it again.

STEP-BY-STEP RESAWING ON THE TABLE SAW

1 Set blade height to leave a thin strip (about 1/16") down the middle of the board.

This strip keeps the pieces together, giving you better control. Split the pieces apart after sawing.

2 Set the fence for stock thickness + warpage and cleanup allowance.

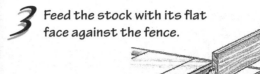

3 Feed the stock with its flat face against the fence.

4 Flip the stock end for end, and saw the second edge with the same flat face against the fence.

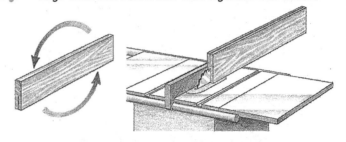

SAWS FOR RESAWING

	TABLE SAW	BAND SAW	HANDSAW
SETUP	Easy	Requires resaw fence; may require adjusting fence for blade lead	Easy
QUALITY OF CUT	Excellent	Good (with a sharp blade)	Acceptable; creates "steps" where table saw and handsaw meet
STRENGTHS	Fast; little cleanup necessary to remove saw marks	Minimal wasted wood; can resaw as thin as 1/16"	Resaws wide stock with minimal investment; good exercise!
LIMITATIONS	Limited to resawing boards 6" wide and narrower; wastes more wood than other methods	6"-wide boards with most band saws; 12" with riser block	Slower than machines (but faster than taking a few boards to someone else for resawing)
SAFETY	Cannot use blade guards	Excellent	Excellent
BOTTOM LINE	Good choice for resawing a few boards that are not more than 6" wide	Best choice for most resawing, especially for thin veneers	Good choice for resawing limited quantities of wide stock

RESAWING ON THE BAND SAW

If I have to resaw more than four or five boards, or if I want to cut a board into very thin slices, I'll take the time to set up my band saw. A band saw's kerf is thinner than even a thin-kerfed circular saw blade, so I'm not losing as much wood to sawdust. Also, the pace is much less intense than that of the table saw.

The typical 14-inch band saw has another advantage over the table saw: You can increase the resaw capacity to 12 inches by adding a 6-inch-tall cast-iron riser block to the column. Many band saw manufacturers make them.

The trade-off with band saws is the coaxing they need in order to saw straight. Unless your saw is well tuned, it may produce resawn boards that are crooked, tapered, or of uneven thickness. Once you get it set up, however, a band saw with a sharp blade can slice ⅛-inch-thick veneers off a board, one after another, with a minimum of fuss.

To resaw effectively on the band saw, you need a good blade and a resaw fence. I use a good ½-inch-wide rake-tooth blade with 3 teeth per inch. The rake-tooth grind is a little more aggressive than a standard-grind. Start with a new blade and use it only for resawing. Cutting curves has a tendency to dull the teeth that are set to one side faster than those that are set to the other. The blade then tends to curve toward the dull side.

Next, you'll need to make a fence to guide your stock through the cut. Some folks have no trouble with a single-point, pivot-style fence, as shown in *Resawing with a Pivot Fence*. It helps keep the stock perpendicular to the table, but you still have to draw a line on your stock and then follow the line. I prefer a fence that runs from the

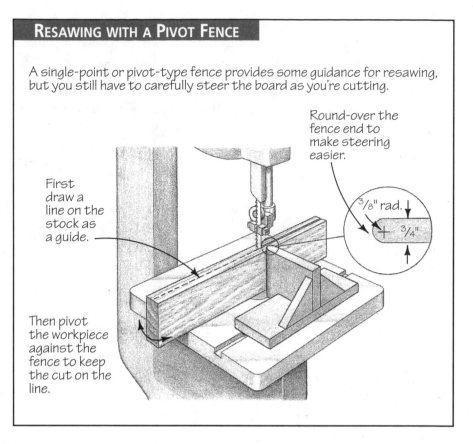

RESAWING WITH A PIVOT FENCE

A single-point or pivot-type fence provides some guidance for resawing, but you still have to carefully steer the board as you're cutting.

First draw a line on the stock as a guide.

Round-over the fence end to make steering easier.

⅜" rad.

¾"

Then pivot the workpiece against the fence to keep the cut on the line.

front of the table to the back of the blade, as shown in Steps 1–4 on the opposite page. This provides plenty of support and frees me from having to steer the board through the cut. Since the fence ends at the blade, the resawn piece can cup or bow as it leaves the blade without pushing against the fence. The fence can be a straight, square 2 × 4 clamped to your saw table, or you can make the more elaborate fence shown in the drawing. Plans for this fence are in the "Resaw Fence for the Band Saw" chapter on page 280.

Tune up your saw, paying particular attention to blade tension and correct adjustment of the blade guides. Then clamp the fence in place, as shown in Step 3 on the opposite page.

Start the cut with one hand applying feed pressure and the other hand holding the board tight to the fence, just in front of the blade. Don't overdo the feed pressure. Think of it as spoon-feeding a baby: You have to keep the groceries coming but you also have to let the kid do the swallowing. You could choke up the band saw blade as easily as you could choke the kid. Keep a push stick handy and use it to feed the board through the final few inches of the cut.

A lot has been written about adjusting the

fence on a band saw to compensate for the blade's tendency to cut to one side or the other, a nasty habit known as "lead." Well tuned and with a good sharp blade on its wheels, my saw doesn't lead. If yours does, even when it's properly tuned, mount the fence at the angle your blade cuts, as shown in Steps 1–4 on page 80. The fence shown clamps to the table at an angle if necessary.

STEP-BY-STEP RESAWING ON THE BAND SAW

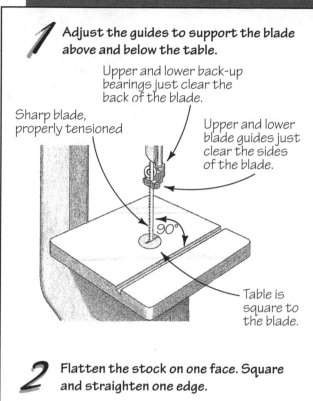

1 Adjust the guides to support the blade above and below the table.

Upper and lower back-up bearings just clear the back of the blade.

Sharp blade, properly tensioned

Upper and lower blade guides just clear the sides of the blade.

90°

Table is square to the blade.

2 Flatten the stock on one face. Square and straighten one edge.

3 Set the fence for required stock thickness plus allowance for cleanup and warpage.

Fence extends from front of the table to back edge of the blade.

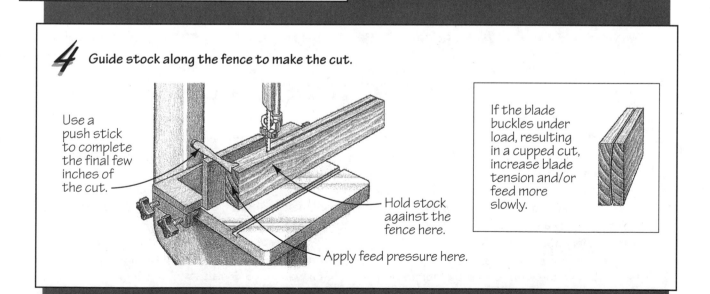

4 Guide stock along the fence to make the cut.

Use a push stick to complete the final few inches of the cut.

Hold stock against the fence here.

Apply feed pressure here.

If the blade buckles under load, resulting in a cupped cut, increase blade tension and/or feed more slowly.

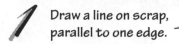

STEP-BY-STEP
COMPENSATING FOR BLADE LEAD

1   Draw a line on scrap, parallel to one edge.

2   Saw to the line. Adjust the angle of the board as necessary to follow the line.

3   Stop sawing when further adjustment of the angle is no longer needed.

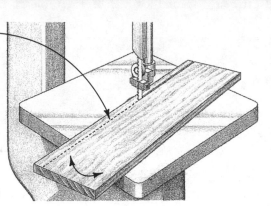

4   Clamp a fence to the saw so it's parallel to the edge of the scrap.

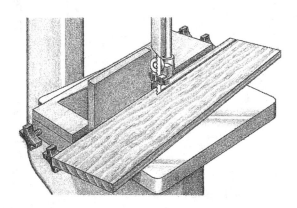

RESAWING WIDE STOCK

Most table saws and band saws can resaw stock 6 inches wide. Band saws with a riser block can resaw stock 12 inches wide. Hand resawing works on very wide stock but gets tedious on large quantities of lumber. If you need to resaw a lot of wide stock, you have three other choices.

1. Have the work done at a cabinet shop with a big band saw. This is a particularly wise choice if you're considering buying such a saw yourself because it lets you see that kind of saw in action.

2. Buy a specialized resaw band saw. Smaller than industrial saws, these have tall throat openings and take blades up to 3 inches wide.

3. Locate a mobile band-saw mill. These portable sawmills are designed for sawing logs but a well tuned rig can saw ¼-inch slices from a plank in practically no time.

RESAWING BY HAND

A third alternative for resawing is to make your own muscle-powered resaw. This isn't as crazy as it might seem. I built one in a few hours, and it works amazingly well. (It's very impressive hanging on the shop wall, too.) The saw is simply a 4-foot length of 1¼-inch-wide, 3-tooth-per-inch band saw blade with a wooden frame to hold it. Complete plans for this saw are in the "Frame Resaw" chapter on page 282.

I make a two-step process out of hand resawing. First, I saw both edges as deeply as I can on the table saw. I see no sense in doing more work by hand than I have to, and the kerfs help keep the hand saw on track as I'm cutting. Then I clamp the board at an angle in a vise and cut it, as shown in Steps 2–3 on this page.

Resawing by hand is surprisingly practical. Full-length strokes make the work go quite fast.

This works, and it works well. I tip my hat to antique tool guru Patrick Leach and the other self-proclaimed Neanderthal woodworkers on the Internet who encouraged me to stop wondering about it and just do it.

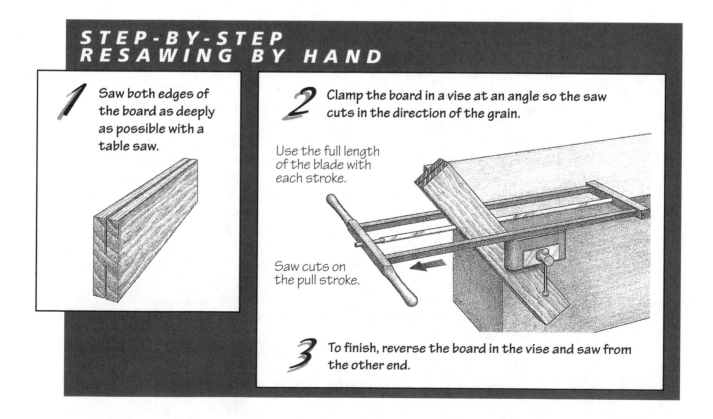

STEP-BY-STEP RESAWING BY HAND

1 Saw both edges of the board as deeply as possible with a table saw.

2 Clamp the board in a vise at an angle so the saw cuts in the direction of the grain.

Use the full length of the blade with each stroke.

Saw cuts on the pull stroke.

3 To finish, reverse the board in the vise and saw from the other end.

GLUING UP WIDE BOARDS

A friend of mine has a magnificent table. The top is 8 feet long, more than 3 feet wide, and nearly 2 inches thick, and it's made from a *single* piece of Spanish walnut. The table is hundreds of years old. At the opposite extreme, a major modern furniture manufacturer I know glues up tabletops out of highly figured, narrow pieces of low-grade lumber; so the top of one of their 1½-foot-wide end tables just might have a dozen pieces glued together. Like it or not, a tabletop that we make for ourselves is more likely to resemble this glued-up tabletop than the antique single-piece tabletop. These days we're lucky to find stock wide enough for narrower parts like door panels.

Fortunately, modern woodworking tools, techniques, and adhesives have made it very practical to create wide boards through edge-gluing. The main five steps in making these joints are:

1. Arranging the boards to create a long-lasting panel

2. Preparing the edges for a good glue joint

3. Maintaining the alignment of the edges with each other

4. Clamping the assembly while the glue dries

5. Cleaning up and resurfacing the assembled panel

Once you've learned the techniques for making these joints strong and durable, you'll find that the greatest challenge is arranging the available boards to create a pleasing composition of wood grain.

ARRANGING BOARDS

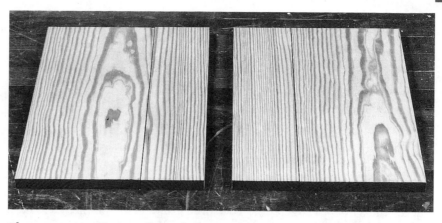

The way you arrange boards for a glue-up can significantly affect the appearance. An unbalanced arrangement of grain (right) leads your eye away from a glued-up panel, while a symmetrical arrangement (left) draws your attention to it.

The appearance of your finished, glued-up panel is at least as important as the tools and techniques that you use in making it. A couple of centuries from now when the antiques auctioneer brings out your masterpiece, the bidders won't praise your choice of glue or your choice between hand planes and machines; they'll praise the masterful arrangement of the figure in your wood.

There's a lot for you to keep in mind when you're deciding how to arrange boards for a glue up. You want to arrange the boards so that:

▶ The assembled grain patterns are pleasing, drawing the viewer's attention rather than leading the eye off in some other direction.

▶ Joints don't creep out of alignment over time, creating little ledges that cast shadows.

▶ Final surfacing of the assembled panel is straightforward and doesn't require planing in two directions at once.

▶ Applying your finish doesn't produce unpleasant changes in appearance caused by varying grain directions.

▶ The panel doesn't cup with seasonal variations in humidity. ●

The solution to one potential problem is often the solution to another as well. For example, arranging for the most pleasing grain patterns often prevents creeping edge joints, and simplified surfacing often also means no surprises after finishing. Both of these examples are further explained below.

Giving advice on arranging boards to please the eye is about as promising as giving advice on choosing a marriage partner. Nevertheless, here goes. First, don't leave the appearance of the grain to chance. You don't need a degree in fine arts to know what you like and what you don't like. Try several different arrangements of the available boards, and note the one you like best. Listen to what others,

even kids, have to say, but don't let them dictate to you. It's your hobby and your project, not theirs.

Second, avoid sharp contrasts in grain along an edge joint. That is, avoid the arrangement shown at the lower left of *Avoiding Steps at Glue Lines* on page 84, where one board has parallel or nearly parallel grain lines, such as in quarter-sawn stock, and the other has perpendicular or nearly perpendicular grain lines, such as in flat-sawn stock.

Third, try to achieve some symmetry in the arrangement. I'm getting onto pretty thin ice here—there can be a lot of exceptions to this rule. The photo on this page shows symmetrical and unsymmetrical arrangements of boards; normally you would choose the symmetrical arrangement shown on the left. But if you are arranging boards to glue up two door panels that will hang side by side in a cabinet, then you might prefer symmetry in the two doors as a pair instead of symmetry in each door viewed individually.

This leads to my fourth and final suggestion, which is to arrange all of the glue-ups for a project at the same time. Lay them out so you can see them all at once, arranged as they will be after assembly in the project. Take your time, and try different arrangements. Once you've glued the boards together it's pretty hard to change your mind.

Dealing with Creep

Appearance is not your sole concern when arranging boards. You also want to avoid joints that creep out of alignment over time. When the humidity changes, wood expands and contracts twice as much tangentially as it does radially, as shown in *Avoiding Steps at Glue Lines*. If you arrange boards so that adjoining ones change thickness at different rates, they will develop steps at the glue lines. The steps may be extremely small, but they'll still be visible as the afternoon sun strikes your waxed tabletop at a low angle. You may also notice very fine steps as you run your hand over the tabletop. Try to arrange your boards as shown in the three right-hand drawings to minimize the possibility of steps. As mentioned earlier, this is a case where aesthetic concerns and structural concerns lead to the same arrangement: The three grain orientations that don't develop steps also look better than the orientation that does develop steps.

> **NOTE:** A glue with high resistance to creep, such as a plastic resin glue, is not a solution to the problem of steps developing at glue lines. The glue may not creep, but the wood itself will distort along the joint, producing rounded "steps" that are still visible.

Minimizing Cupping

Some furniture parts, like drop leaves on a table, have no framework or support to keep them from cupping with seasonal changes in humidity. As you arrange boards for these parts, give some

---

AVOIDING STEPS AT GLUE LINES

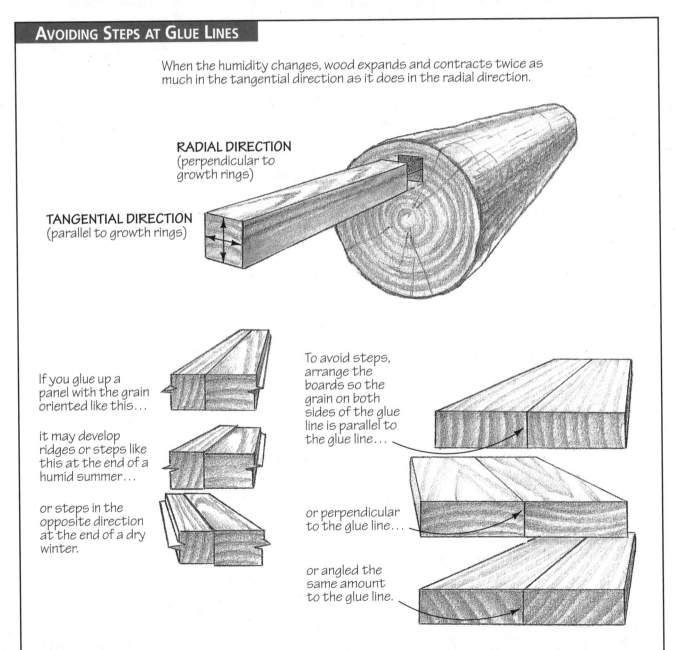

When the humidity changes, wood expands and contracts twice as much in the tangential direction as it does in the radial direction.

RADIAL DIRECTION (perpendicular to growth rings)

TANGENTIAL DIRECTION (parallel to growth rings)

If you glue up a panel with the grain oriented like this...

it may develop ridges or steps like this at the end of a humid summer...

or steps in the opposite direction at the end of a dry winter.

To avoid steps, arrange the boards so the grain on both sides of the glue line is parallel to the glue line...

or perpendicular to the glue line...

or angled the same amount to the glue line.

thought to which way the growth rings in the wood curve. As wood loses moisture, the growth rings tend to straighten out, cupping the board, as shown in *Limiting the Effect of Cupping*. As it picks up moisture during a humid summer, the growth rings tend to return to their original curvature. You can minimize the overall cupping in a glued-up panel by alternating the curvature of the growth rings. Then if the panel gains or loses considerable moisture, it will develop a very slightly wavy surface instead of a broad overall curvature.

You can eliminate cupping entirely by selecting edge-grain boards for the entire panel. This, however, will produce a panel with a significantly different appearance: plain parallel grain lines instead of highly figured grain.

Simplifying Smoothing and Finishing

You still have one more concern as you arrange boards for glue-up: fiber direction within the boards. You are familiar with fiber direction when planing. In one direction a plane slices off a shaving, leaving a smooth surface, but in the opposite direction it tears out the grain. Simplify final surfacing of your glued-up panel by arranging the boards so they all plane in the same direction, not so that some plane best in one direction while adjoining boards plane best in the opposite direction.

Fiber direction also affects the way a panel reflects light after you've applied a clear finish. Two boards that look identical in color and tone when you arrange them for glue-up may appear quite different after you've applied a finish. This is the result of the fibers in the two boards going in opposite directions. The change can ruin an otherwise appealing arrangement, and you can't see it until the project is all done and the finish is applied.

The way to minimize the risk of this kind of surprise is to mark each board with an arrow indicating the direction that it planes best, and to arrange all of the boards with the arrows pointing in the same direction. Once again we have a case where the solution to one problem—this time, planing—also solves another problem, aesthetics.

If it seems that there's a lot to keep in mind when arranging boards for glue-up, you've got the picture. On the other hand, you can ignore all of the above advice on arranging boards and still produce good, functional projects. Think of it as an aspect of woodworking that will allow you to grow and get better even after you've mastered everything else.

LIMITING THE EFFECT OF CUPPING

As wood dries, growth rings straighten; as wood gains moisture, growth rings curve more.

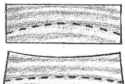 HIGHER MOISTURE
 LOWER MOISTURE

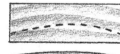 LOWER MOISTURE
 HIGHER MOISTURE

If all the growth rings curve in the same direction, then broad cupping will occur over the width of the board when the moisture content changes.

If the growth rings curve in alternating directions, then moisture changes will cause a less-noticeable wavy surface.

FACE AND EDGE PREPARATION

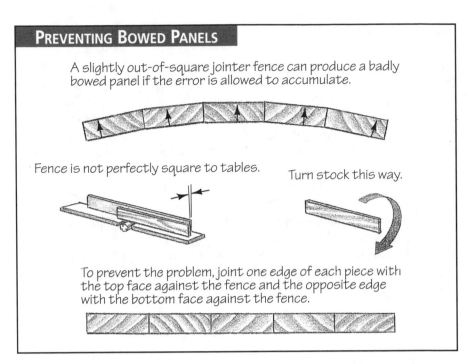

PREVENTING BOWED PANELS

A slightly out-of-square jointer fence can produce a badly bowed panel if the error is allowed to accumulate.

Fence is not perfectly square to tables.

Turn stock this way.

To prevent the problem, joint one edge of each piece with the top face against the fence and the opposite edge with the bottom face against the fence.

When preparing stock for glue-up, you need to decide how much face preparation to do before assembly and how much to do after. You need to flatten the faces before the glue-up so you can reference them when preparing the edges. But you can't plane the boards down to final thickness, because after assembly you'll have to plane off misalignment at the glue joints.

If you have a planer wide enough to plane the glued-up panel, then you will probably find it easiest to do most of the planing on one big piece after the glue-up. On the other hand, if your glue-up will be wider than your planer, it will pay to plane the separate pieces to within 1/16 inch or less of the final thickness and spend a little extra time carefully aligning the edges. Then you can hand plane any remaining misalignment with a minimum amount of work.

Preparing Edges

A good glued-up panel is flat, with invisible glue joints that are as strong as the wood itself. If the edges of the boards are square to the faces, then the panel will be flat. But the panel will also be flat if out-of-square edges compensate for each other, as shown in *Preventing Bowed Panels*.

For the individual joints to be strong and invisible, the two edges must come together without any gaps. That means that neither of the edges can have any hollows or humps, that portions of the edges cannot be out-of-square, and that the edges must be free of saw blade score marks and torn-out grain. The edges must also be free of burn marks, which interfere with the bonding of glue.

A well-tuned jointer is the best machine for creating these joints—if you have one. An excellent alternative is a long, sharp hand plane—if you have the skill, which takes a lot of practice. Basic

instructions for both of these techniques, plus a technique for jointing edges with a router table, are included in the chapter "Surfacing Rough Lumber" on page 62.

However, the most realistic alternative to a jointer for edge preparation is often a combination of good table-saw work and limited hand-plane work. This technique can produce excellent edges for gluing, and it will help you accumulate skill and experience with hand planes as you do so.

There are four steps to this technique. Begin by hand planing one edge of each board straight. Your purpose here is to make an edge that will follow a rip fence in a dead-straight line. An edge that is slightly out-of-square is not a problem. Similarly, short dips or hollows are okay. Humps, on the other hand, must be planed off. Test your work with an accurate straightedge, preferably one at least as thick as your stock, such as a long carpenter's level.

Next, place the hand-planed edge against the rip fence, and rip the opposite edge of the board dead-straight. Keep in mind that your purpose here is edge preparation, not ripping to width; so adjust the fence to remove just a half-kerf, or about 1/16 inch, from the edge of the board. Make sure the fence is parallel to the blade, as explained in "Tuning a Table Saw" on page 98, in the section "Fence Alignment." I use a good combination blade, but try whatever blades you have and use the one that gives you the smoothest surface. When making the trimming cut, make sure you keep the

STEP-BY-STEP
PREPARING EDGES WITH A TABLE SAW
AND HAND PLANE

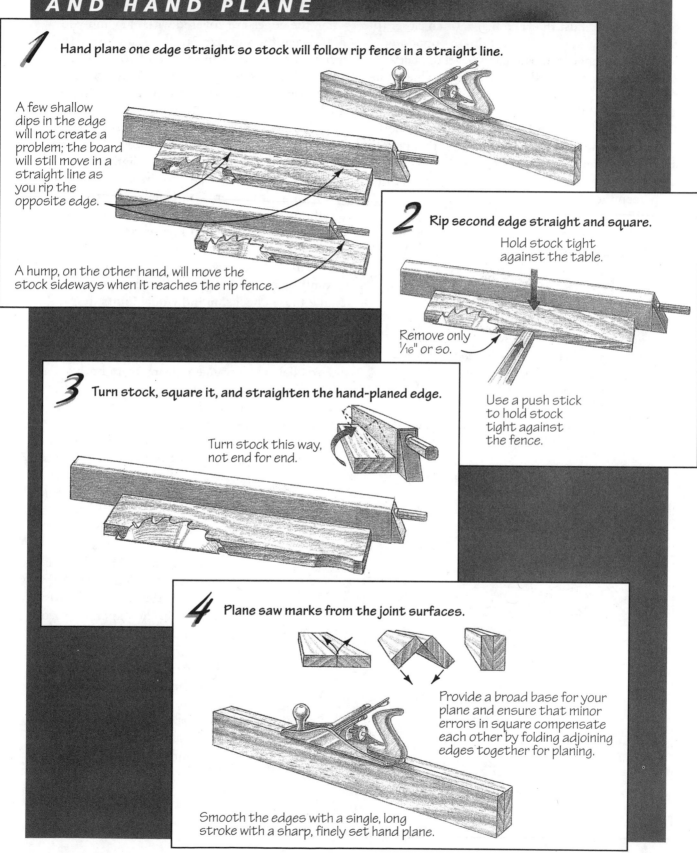

1 Hand plane one edge straight so stock will follow rip fence in a straight line.

A few shallow dips in the edge will not create a problem; the board will still move in a straight line as you rip the opposite edge.

A hump, on the other hand, will move the stock sideways when it reaches the rip fence.

2 Rip second edge straight and square.

Hold stock tight against the table.

Remove only 1/16" or so.

Use a push stick to hold stock tight against the fence.

3 Turn stock, square it, and straighten the hand-planed edge.

Turn stock this way, not end for end.

4 Plane saw marks from the joint surfaces.

Provide a broad base for your plane and ensure that minor errors in square compensate each other by folding adjoining edges together for planing.

Smooth the edges with a single, long stroke with a sharp, finely set hand plane.

bottom face of the stock tightly against the saw table, and the hand-planed edge tightly against the rip fence. Also, keep the stock moving at a uniform rate to prevent burning.

Next, readjust the rip fence 1/16 inch closer to the blade; turn the board; and trim the opposite, hand-planed edge, removing any bevel or short hollows. Prepare all of the boards in the glue-up in this way.

Finally, if the smoothest surface from your best blade leaves saw marks on the edges, smooth them with a single, full-length stroke with a razor-sharp, finely set hand plane. Planing both edges of a joint at once, as shown in Step 4 on page 87, will help keep the plane square to the faces.

> **NOTE:** *A surface must be smooth in order to glue well, but how smooth depends on the species of wood. Relatively soft, easily compressible woods like pine, basswood, butternut, and catalpa glue well even if there are visible saw marks on the edges, provided the saw marks are shallow. Moderate-density woods like cherry and elm require a smoother surface, such as the surface from very good blades on a table saw. I've found that to get the best bond with dense woods like oak and hard maple, the surfaces must be as smooth as possible.*

Checking Edge Joints before Gluing

There are two wrong times to find out that your edges don't meet each other snugly. One is when the edges are covered with glue and you notice that the squeeze-out is not uniform. The other is when a joint in the top of your dining room table fails as you set your Thanksgiving turkey on it. The right time is just before you apply glue to the edges.

To check for unwanted bevel on the edges, stack the boards on edge, as shown in *Checking Flatness before Applying Glue*. No light should pass between the straightedge and the boards. If it does, go back to Step 4 on page 87 or take another pass on the jointer, paying particular attention to the advice in *Preventing Bowed Panels* on page 86.

There are two ways to check for gaps within a joint: by eye and with the tissue-paper test. Make these checks on individual joints, not the entire assembly of several boards. To test visually, clamp the two boards together just tightly enough to keep the clamps from falling off. Lay the boards flat, and arrange lighting from both sides but not from above. Examine the joint closely. Gaps will appear dark because they're in shadow. Check both sides of the joint.

If you have doubts about any part of the joint (and you *should* if you're new to edge-gluing), use the tissue-paper test. Stack two of the boards on edge, with a single thickness of very thin wrapping tissue between the edges in the area that you have doubts about. If the stacked boards don't grip the paper, then you have an unacceptable gap.

There is only one way to fix a gap, and that is to resurface the edges. Once you acquire some hand-plane skill and establish a routine, you'll find that resurfacing is only very rarely necessary.

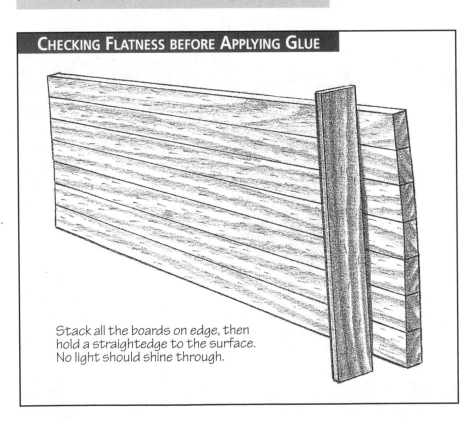

CHECKING FLATNESS BEFORE APPLYING GLUE

Stack all the boards on edge, then hold a straightedge to the surface. No light should shine through.

TECHNIQUES FOR MAINTAINING ALIGNMENT

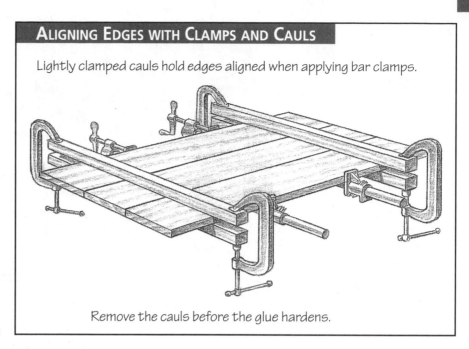

ALIGNING EDGES WITH CLAMPS AND CAULS

Lightly clamped cauls hold edges aligned when applying bar clamps.

Remove the cauls before the glue hardens.

If you have never before glued up several boards, you're in for a surprise. The wet glue makes the edges of the boards so slippery they won't stay aligned. Once a little pressure has been applied by the clamps, the glue will grab; but if you do much gluing up, you'll want a positive method of maintaining alignment. You can make the boards interlock, align the boards with cauls, or add grit to the wet glue.

Interlocking Edges

You might think that shaping edges so they interlock will also make the joint stronger. Well, theoretically it will, but shaped surfaces seldom fit as well as well-prepared butt joints, so they turn out weaker. You rarely need more strength anyway, so shaping the edges to maintain alignment makes sense only if it happens to be the quickest and easiest way to do it.

If you joint the edges with a router table setup as described in "Surfacing on the Router Table" on page 72, you can substitute a glue-joint bit for a straight bit and produce interlocking shaped edges with no added work at all. That makes it about as quick and easy as it gets.

Another way to interlock the edges is by using biscuits. If you have the biscuit joiner handy, it will only take a few seconds to cut slots every foot or two along the joints. When I've used biscuits this way, I haven't bothered to ensure good gluing of the biscuits themselves; I've trusted the strength of the glued butt joint and relied on the biscuits only to aid alignment.

Cauls and Clamps

The most obvious and direct way to keep the edges of boards aligned is to sandwich the boards between straight sticks, or cauls, as shown in *Aligning Edges with Clamps and Cauls.* Simple as this approach is, there are a few details to watch out for.

▶ Don't clamp the cauls too tightly. If you do, they'll grip the boards, and that will prevent the bar clamps from applying adequate pressure to the edge joints when you crank them down.

▶ Make sure the cauls don't get glued to the panel. You can prevent a bond by applying wax or polyethylene tape to the edges of the cauls or by removing the cauls right after you've tightened the bar clamps.

▶ Don't spend so much time arranging and clamping the cauls that you weaken the joint by exceeding the allowable open time of the glue. (See the chapter "Choosing the Right Glue" on page 36 for open times for various glues.) ●

"Shop-Made Bar Clamps" on page 274 shows clamps that are specifically designed to hold edges in alignment and clamp the glue joint at the same time.

True Grit

You can stop boards from slipping around during glue-up by sprinkling a small amount of fine-cracked corn in the wet glue before clamping the boards together. Cracked corn is hard enough to press into the wood and stop the slipping but not hard enough to ruin a cutting tool later on.

Clamps and Clamping

Bar clamps for edge-gluing come in various styles. Steel I-beam clamps (bottom) are the most rigid and durable. Aluminum bar clamps (center) are much lighter than steel but not as rigid. Pipe clamps (top) are more economical if you have a source for used pipe. You can also lengthen them with a pipe coupling.

Clamps for edge-gluing are called bar clamps. The most common variety uses a length of ½-inch or ¾-inch iron pipe for the bar. The style preferred by those on a bigger budget uses a steel I-beam for the bar. A few types use a wooden or aluminum bar.

A good glue joint results from uniform clamping pressure over the entire area of the joint. To get this uniform pressure, use a clamp every 12 to 18 inches—closer if the boards are less than about 3 inches wide.

Align the axis of the clamp screws with the center of the panel, as shown in *Positioning Bar Clamps*. This is quite important. It keeps the clamping pressure on the joints uniform over the width of the joint, not all along one edge. It also keeps the clamp bars out of contact with the squeezed-out glue. Steel bars react with many glues, staining the wood.

Some woodworkers advocate alternating clamps so some are on top of the assembly and some are underneath it. Supposedly this helps keep the whole assembly from buckling when heavy pressure is applied. I don't think it makes a whit of difference,

provided the axis of the clamp screw is properly aligned and the edges of the boards are square to the faces. But I do it anyway because I find it easier to clamp panels in a clamping rack this way. I put half of the required clamps in a rack like the one shown in *Panel-Clamping Rack,* then I add the remaining clamps from above after I've double-checked the edge alignment and tightened the first set of clamps.

Removing Excess Glue

The chapter "Choosing the Right Glue" on page 36 provides a lot of information about glues and gluing, but edge-gluing presents a particular problem not encountered in most gluing operations:

POSITIONING BAR CLAMPS

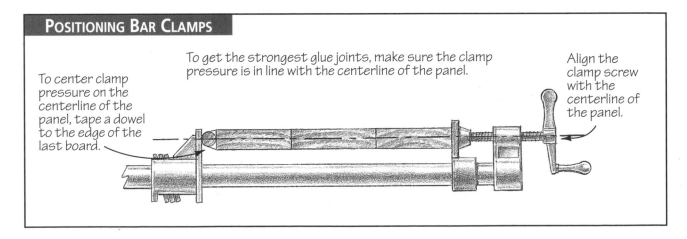

To get the strongest glue joints, make sure the clamp pressure is in line with the centerline of the panel.

To center clamp pressure on the centerline of the panel, tape a dowel to the edge of the last board.

Align the clamp screw with the centerline of the panel.

how to deal with the squeeze-out from so many feet of glue joint. An ideal spread of glue will produce a small but uniform bead of glue squeezed out of the joint when you apply clamping pressure. A real-world spread of glue will produce a nonuniform, often large and runny bead of squeeze-out. You can't simply cut back on the glue to avoid squeeze-out, because you'll inevitably starve the joint in some areas. So you need to figure out how to remove the excess after clamping. Your best options are wiping it up while it's wet, scraping it off after it dries, and sanding it off after it dries.

You can wipe up water-soluble glues immediately after applying clamping pressure. Use clean rags wet with hot water—adding a little detergent doesn't hurt a bit. Don't be afraid of getting the wood too wet: The glue itself is largely water, soaking into your wood. Just don't leave water pooled on the surface. Some woodworkers are afraid that wiping up with hot water will dilute the glue in the joint, weakening it. If your joints fit well, the fear is unfounded—if they don't fit well they'll be weak regardless of the effect of the water. If you have a sink and hot running water in your shop, so that you can frequently rinse out your rag, this technique will probably be the easiest and cleanest way to deal with squeeze-out.

A big paint scraper—the bigger the better—is the fastest way to remove squeeze-out, but the speed comes at a price: The scraper is likely to

> **TECH TIP** — **LEAVE A CLAMPED ASSEMBLY FLAT** instead of standing it on edge while the glue dries. This will prevent the squeeze-out from running across the faces of the boards, which would make it harder to remove.

remove wood as well as glue. Don't take this approach unless your panel is thick enough that you can plane off any tear-out. If you've got the necessary thickness, wait until the glue has fully cured, then clamp the panel on your workbench. Grab the scraper in both hands and pull it briskly along the joint, applying enough downward pressure to keep it from skipping along the top of the beads. With some practice, a single stroke along each joint will remove all of the squeeze-out.

Hardened glue on a panel that doesn't have much extra thickness requires some care. Make sure the glue has *fully* hardened before removing it. White and yellow glues remain soft on the inside of the bead long after they seem quite hard on the outside. Once the glue has fully cured, you can sand off the squeeze-out. White glue, however, will be frustrating: It softens as it warms up, clogging sanding belts and discs. Regardless of the glue type, use a fairly coarse, open-coat abrasive: 60- or 80-grit is appropriate. Switch to a finer abrasive as soon as the bead is gone.

PANEL-CLAMPING RACK

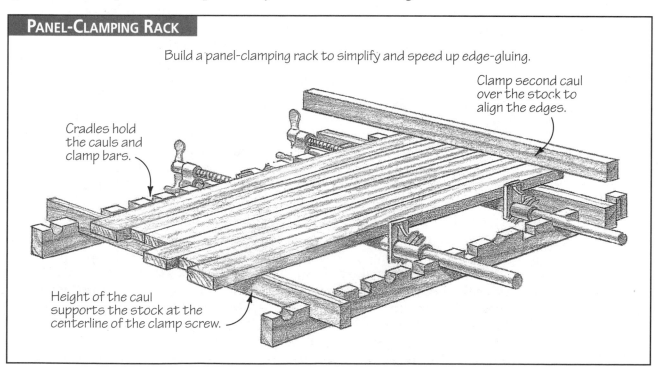

Build a panel-clamping rack to simplify and speed up edge-gluing.

Clamp second caul over the stock to align the edges.

Cradles hold the cauls and clamp bars.

Height of the caul supports the stock at the centerline of the clamp screw.

Saws, Crosscutting, and Ripping

A well-tuned saw, properly used, makes consistent, precise, smooth cuts—piece after piece after piece.

Sawing wood accurately to size is arguably the most basic process in all of woodworking—not necessarily the one requiring the most skill, but the most basic. No matter what you're making, you have to cut every single piece in a project to final length and width. To make these cuts, most woodworkers choose from a short list of powered circular saws, a list that includes the table saw, the radial arm saw, and the chop saw. But since the chop saw is specialized for crosscutting relatively narrow stock, either the radial arm saw or the table saw will be the hub of activity.

Both table saws and radial arm saws have their fervent advocates. Since I wouldn't be able to hide my personal preference even if I tried, I'll put my cards on the table right up front. I owned a radial arm saw...once. I put up with its eccentricities for four years. Then I sold it, bought a table saw, and never looked back.

This chapter focuses primarily on cutting to size with the table saw, though owners of radial arm saws will find much of interest. (If you're still weighing which saw to buy, see "Table Saws, Radial Arm Saws, and Chop Saws" on page 94 for the pros and cons of these saws as I see them.)

Your main concern when cutting work to size is getting the best cut out of your machine. That is a matter of keeping it well adjusted, as explained in "Tuning a Table Saw" on page 98, and choosing the best blade for your needs, as explained in "Circular Saw Blades" on page 106. Once you have a handle on those aspects, you can concentrate on appropriate techniques.

CROSSCUTTING ON THE TABLE SAW

The key to smooth, accurate crosscuts lies in moving the stock sideways smoothly and accurately. Adequate support and a smoothly moving guide are both essential for success.

Owners of radial arm saws are now cordially invited to chuckle smugly as I discuss the problems of crosscutting on the table saw. My first advice goes to those with a frequent need to make accurate cuts on the ends of long stock, like interior trim for a house. The advice is to get a chop saw. My next advice goes to those with an occasional need to make that kind of cut: Get a miter box.

Now with the subject matter whittled down a bit, we can look at the real options that are available for typical woodworking projects. There are three devices that help guide stock sideways over a table saw: the miter gauge, the crosscut sled, and the sliding or rolling table. Since there is some variation in how woodworkers use these terms, I'll define how I use them.

▶ A *miter gauge* consists of a bar that fits a slot in the saw table, and a fence attached to the bar. The fence can be angled for miter cuts. The stock slides on the surface of the table, pushed by the fence.

▶ A *crosscut sled* is just like a miter gauge but with a thin subtable separating the bar from the fence. The stock rests on the subtable, eliminating friction between the stock itself and the saw table. Most sleds are built by the woodworkers themselves.

▶ A *sliding or rolling table* is like a crosscut sled, except that it rides on rollers that follow tracks instead of sliding along on top of the saw table. Sliding tables are standard equipment on a few saws and are manufactured and sold as optional accessories for the typical 10-inch table saws used in small shops. ●

Miter Gauges

Miter gauges are often maligned for being inaccurate and inadequate, but they remain the most convenient and useful of all crosscut guides for small pieces of wood. There are two secrets to maintaining a long and happy relationship with your miter gauge. First, tune and equip it to work accurately; and second, never ask it to work beyond its capacity (as I'll explain below).

The fit between the miter gauge bar and the slot in the table can be quite sloppy without seriously affecting the angle of the cut. For example, even if your miter gauge bar is ¹⁄₆₄ inch narrower than the slot, and the miter gauge is pulled back so far that only half of its length is in the slot, the angle you cut will only be off by a tenth of a degree—not enough to change the fit of parts small enough to crosscut with the miter gauge, like cabinet door rails. But the effect of a poorly fitting miter gauge on the location and smoothness of the cut *is* a concern. If the miter gauge bar moves side to side in the slot, your cut will be inaccurate and rough. You can eliminate the problem by holding the miter gauge against the side of the slot *away* from the blade during the cut, as shown in *Miter Gauge Technique* on page 96. Holding it against either side will solve the problem, of course. But by holding it away from the blade, it's easier to measure from a stop

(continued on page 96)

TABLE SAWS, RADIAL ARM SAWS, AND CHOP SAWS

Choosing a primary saw for a shop can be difficult because the different types are so *very* different. The biggest difference between them, however, is in the type of cut that the basic design is best suited for: An unadorned table saw is best suited for ripping while a radial arm saw is best suited for crosscutting.

Reference Surfaces

The depth of cut of a table saw is a measure of how deep the cut will go into the reference surface, as shown in *Depth-of-Cut Adjustment*. The depth of cut of a radial arm saw is a measure of how *close* the cut will come to the reference surface; how deep the cut goes depends on the thickness of the stock. If the table of a radial arm saw is not parallel to the radial arm, dadoes and rabbets won't be uniform in depth over the length of the cut.

Capacity

The length of stock that a saw can handle is limited by the size of your shop and by obstructions within the shop. *Space Requirements* shows the minimum requirements for typical home-shop saws. As a *practical* matter, however, stock over 8 to 10 feet long becomes very unwieldy when crosscutting on the table saw. The radial arm saw crosscuts stock of any length with equal ease.

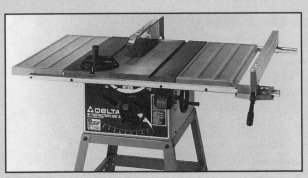

Home-shop wood-workers choose a table saw (above) more often than a radial arm saw (below) as their primary sawing machine because they find it more convenient for precise work. Many later buy a chop saw (left) to complement their table saw.

I've found that radial arm saws have a fairly limited *practical* depth of cut when ripping—they overheat and trip their thermal overload devices much sooner than contractor-style table saws with equivalent nameplate horsepower.

Rigidity and Accuracy

The blade of a radial arm saw is at the end of a long mechanical arm connecting it to the table. Inevitably that long arm will flex. Even if the flex produces no more than a minute vibration, it will affect the smoothness of the cut. The net result is more flexibility in the radial arm saw than in a table saw of equally robust construction. You may not

---

DEPTH-OF-CUT ADJUSTMENT

On the table saw, the height of the blade determines the depth of cut, regardless of the stock thickness.

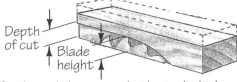

Depth of cut — Blade height

On the radial arm saw, both stock thickness and blade height affect the depth of cut.

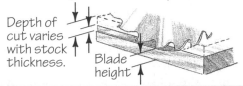

Depth of cut varies with stock thickness. — Blade height

SPACE REQUIREMENTS

Both table and radial arm saws require an 18'-long unobstructed space to rip 4' × 8' sheet stock.

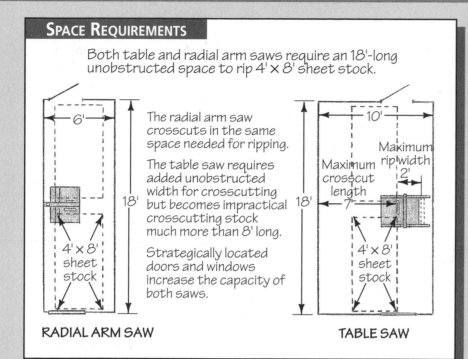

The radial arm saw crosscuts in the same space needed for ripping.

The table saw requires added unobstructed width for crosscutting but becomes impractical crosscutting stock much more than 8' long.

Strategically located doors and windows increase the capacity of both saws.

RADIAL ARM SAW

TABLE SAW

notice the flexibility when crosscutting a small piece of knot-free pine, but you'll notice it trimming the end of a thick oak tabletop 22 inches wide.

Keeping Control

As you feed wood into a table saw blade, the teeth tend to push the stock down against the table and back toward you, as shown in *Forces from Blades*. Pushing the stock back toward you is fine because your muscles are already tensed against thrust in that direction in order to feed the stock.

The cutting forces of the radial arm saw pull the blade into the stock. Since you begin the cut by pulling the saw into the stock yourself, your muscles are ill prepared to resist a saw that tends to pull *itself* into the stock. Crosscutting becomes a delicate balance between keeping the blade engaged and preventing it from jumping toward you. Special blades with shoulders behind the teeth help

to limit this tendency, but they don't eliminate it.

When ripping with a radial arm saw, as shown in the last drawing below, the blade tends to lift the stock off the table. To rip safely, you need to keep the blade guard rotated so the hold-down spring holds the stock against the table. Both saws will kick stock back at you if the stock binds between the blade and the fence.

Chop Saws

Chop saws sacrifice some of the versatility of radial arm saws in favor of reliable precision and smoothness in crosscutting. Their features make chop saws an excellent complement to table saws for crosscutting. Chop saws can't rip and can't crosscut wide stock; but they crosscut stock of any length, they stay aligned, and they produce a cut surface as smooth as you'll get from any other saw.

FORCES FROM BLADES

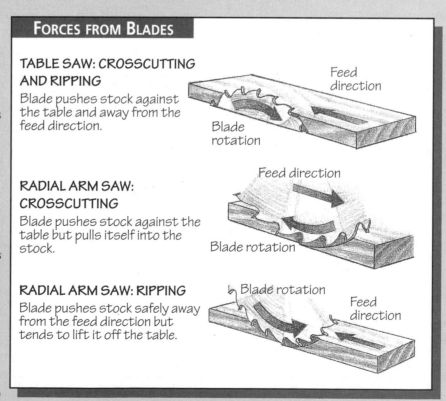

TABLE SAW: CROSSCUTTING AND RIPPING
Blade pushes stock against the table and away from the feed direction.

RADIAL ARM SAW: CROSSCUTTING
Blade pushes stock against the table but pulls itself into the stock.

RADIAL ARM SAW: RIPPING
Blade pushes stock safely away from the feed direction but tends to lift it off the table.

Feed direction

Blade rotation

Feed direction

Blade rotation

Blade rotation

Feed direction

MITER GAUGE TECHNIQUE

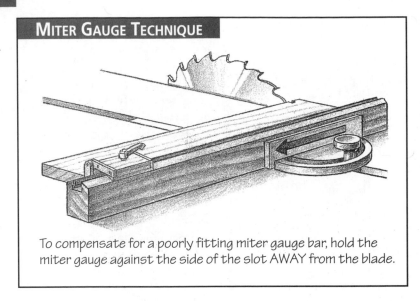

To compensate for a poorly fitting miter gauge bar, hold the miter gauge against the side of the slot AWAY from the blade.

block to the blade; it's easier to hold stock against a stop block; and if your hands should slip during a cut, they won't slip into the blade.

If you're concerned that your miter gauge has way too much slop, measure the gap between the bar and the slot with automotive feeler gauges. If the gap is more than 0.025 inch, get a roll of 20-mil low-friction (high-molecular-weight polyethylene) tape from a woodworking tool dealer, and stick it to the left side of the bar. Some woodworkers fine-tune the fit of their miter gauge bar by raising little dimples on the side of the bar with a machinist's center punch, but I'm not convinced

that the amount of correction this allows is worth the effort.

You can improve the convenience and accuracy of your miter gauge by adding a wooden auxiliary fence to it, but be careful that you don't overdo it. The miter gauge is useful largely because it's so convenient. If you encumber it with too large an auxiliary fence, you'll lose its convenience. I suggest a fence that reaches almost to the blade on the right side, just to the edge of the table on the left side, and is no more than 3 inches high. The auxiliary fence that I use on my miter gauge is identical to the one shown on the sled in Steps 2–4 on page 101. Instructions for making it are found in the "Adjustable Stop Block and Fence" chapter on page 250.

You're bound to be disappointed with your miter gauge if you exceed its capacity. You know you've gone too far if you're having trouble keeping the stock tightly against the fence during the cut. I have two hard-and-fast rules: First, never crosscut stock so long that its midpoint is beyond the end of the fence; and second, never crosscut stock so wide that the fence is not on the table at the start of the cut. If my stock is too long or too wide to abide by these rules, I switch to a crosscut sled.

TECH TIP — SQUARE YOUR MITER GAUGE TO THE BAR, NOT THE SAW BLADE.

SQUARE YOUR MITER GAUGE TO THE BAR, NOT THE SAW BLADE. The bar, not the saw blade, determines the line of travel of your stock. To set the gauge, hold a square up to the bar with the blade of the square along the miter gauge fence, and check for light shining through between the square and the fence. If you adjust the miter gauge fence perpendicular to the side of the saw blade, your adjustment will be off by the amount of your blade runout plus any error in the parallelism of the miter gauge slot. I'm convinced that squaring a miter gauge fence to the saw blade instead of the gauge bar is the most common source of inaccurate crosscuts.

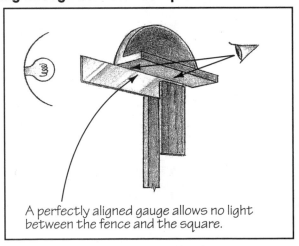

A perfectly aligned gauge allows no light between the fence and the square.

Crosscut Sleds

Crosscut sleds pick up where miter gauges leave off. Bigger and bulkier than miter gauges, they are much less convenient—but they keep bigger and bulkier stock under control.

As you design and build crosscut sleds, keep in mind that these are custom table-saw accessories to meet your individual needs, such as crosscutting long boards, trimming the top and bottom of cabinet doors, mitering moldings, or sawing odd angles accurately. I may want a sled that's specialized for mitering the corners of picture frames, but you may never frame pictures. On the other hand, you might want a sled that's specialized for crosscutting spindles that you've turned on the lathe, a task I never encounter. If my favorite design happens to meet your needs, that's all well and good; but if you can modify it to meet your needs better, then do it.

You'll find that two, or three, or four specialized sleds will be more convenient than one cleverly designed universal sled. If the thing is so big and heavy and complicated that it takes three men and a boy to haul it onto the table saw, then you probably won't use it much.

When designing a sled, plan ahead so you'll be able to make it accurate and so it will stay accurate. To achieve this, I usually fit the bar into a shallow groove in the bottom of the subtable and attach the fence to the top of the subtable, rather than the subtable's edge. This allows me to make tiny adjustments to its position before fastening it down. The "Crosscut Sleds" chapter on page 266, which includes several sled designs and how-to instructions, goes into these details more thoroughly.

There will probably be times when you will want to screw or temporarily glue stops or fences to your sled. If you've made the sled into a work of art, you'll be reluctant to harm it; but if you've made it to be utilitarian, out of the least-expensive materials that will serve the need, then you'll be more willing to make it work hard for you. You can also design your sleds so you can remove labor-intensive parts like fences and stops when the original one gets beat up and use them on a new sled.

Clamping stock *down* on a sled is a bit of a problem. Since few of us can make the subtable out of rigid materials like cast iron or cast steel, we use materials like plywood, particleboard, or plastic laminate–covered hardboard. If we attach a clamping device like a toggle clamp to these somewhat-flexible subtables, or arrange a clamp that presses against them, the sled is likely to flex and lose some of its accuracy. To get around this problem, I always try to arrange the fence so I can clamp to it conveniently, rather than clamping to the subtable, and I frequently apply adhesive-backed fine sandpaper to fence and subtable surfaces so that hand-held stock is less likely to move during a cut.

Sliding Tables

The sliding or rolling table is not a new invention. When the table saw was first adapted for crosscutting, it was fitted with a two-part table with the left part on rollers so that it could move forward and back. When table saws spread from shops to construction sites, manufacturers needed a lighter and less costly crosscutting device. That's when the miter gauge was born.

Sliding tables come in a variety of designs. Some exquisitely built saws crafted in out-of-the-way corners of Europe have the original split table design. Then there are mammoth industrial saws with rolling tables that will carry a stack of full sheets of plywood past a blade as big around as a coffee table. Between these extremes you'll find a handful of good, functional sliding tables of interest to serious amateurs and small-shop professionals.

Sliding tables are the premier setup for crosscutting on the table saw. Their only drawbacks are their cost, the space they take up, and occasionally their sheer weight—trimming a hundred 8-inch-long muntins to length by pushing a massive cast-iron table back and forth deserves a bit of rethinking.

If you're shopping for a sliding table, keep in mind that the usefulness of a feature depends on the kind of woodworking you do—you won't have

The sliding table on this saw is an optional accessory, offering precise crosscutting of stock up to 48 inches wide.

(continued on page 100)

Tuning a Table Saw

Smooth saw cuts are the result of sharp, high-quality saw blades and well-aligned saws. "Circular Saw Blades" on page 106 explains the characteristics of carbide-tipped saw blades and will help you choose appropriate ones. Tuning and maintaining your saw is the other half of the battle. Not all saws are created equal, of course, and some are capable of finer work than others. Many woodworkers would be surprised, however, at how well even a cheap saw will perform if given a bit of tender, loving care.

The teeth on a circular saw blade pass through the wood twice: once when cutting the kerf, and then back through the kerf when coming around to have another go at the wood. Ideally, these returning teeth hit the existing kerf without scoring either side of it. But that would happen only with a perfectly aligned saw. The more accurately you align your saw, the closer you'll come to the goal and the smoother your cuts will be.

Runout

Check the runout first. Ideally the blade rotates in a plane that is perfectly perpendicular to the shaft. Runout, a measure of how far off it is, causes a blade to cut a kerf that is rough, and wider than the teeth themselves.

Runout results from imperfections in both the saw and the blade. A very good saw with a very good blade may have as little as 0.002 or 0.003 inch of runout. As much as 0.010 inch is tolerated by some woodworkers.

Since imperfections in both blades and saws contribute to the runout, the two can either add up or tend to cancel each other. Try loosening the nut and rotate the blade a quarter-turn on the arbor. If that changes the amount of runout, experiment to find the position that gives you the least runout. Then mark the blade and the flange on the saw so you can remount the blade in the same position every time.

CIRCULAR SAW BLADE RUNOUT

Ideally, the blades are perpendicular to the saw arbor.

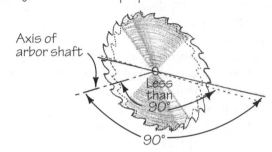

Axis of arbor shaft

Less than 90°

90°

In reality, they are never perfectly perpendicular.

MEASURING RUNOUT

IF YOU OWN A DIAL INDICATOR:

Set it up to find the nearest and farthest positions of the rim of the blade. This difference is the runout.

TO CHECK RUNOUT WITHOUT A DIAL INDICATOR:

1. Rotate the blade by hand while holding a block of hardwood up to the blade.
2. Find that part of the blade closest to the block side.
3. With the block just barely touching the blade, clamp the block to the saw table.
4. Rotate the blade 180° and measure the gap between the block and the blade by inserting pieces of paper in the gap.

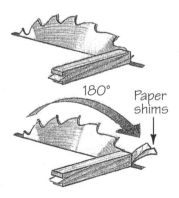

180°

Paper shims

A gap that takes only 1 thickness of paper is good, 2 is OK, 3 or more is bad.

Miter Slot Alignment

The miter gauge slot determines the line of travel of stock during crosscutting. If the slot is perfectly parallel to the plane of the blade, then the teeth rising at the back will hit the kerf exactly. If it isn't parallel, the amount that it's off is known as the "heel." As shown below, you can check for heel without any fancy measuring tools. (By marking a tooth and making both measurements from that tooth, the measurements will be independent of runout.) If the miter slot is not parallel to the blade, you need to readjust the table or trunnions. See your saw manual for specifics.

CHECKING CROSSCUT HEEL

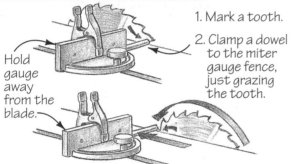

Hold gauge away from the blade.

1. Mark a tooth.

2. Clamp a dowel to the miter gauge fence, just grazing the tooth.

3. Rotate the blade and move the gauge forward.

If the dowel just grazes the tooth, your slot is perfectly parallel to your blade.

If the dowel bumps the tooth, readjust the dowel to just graze the tooth; measure the gap at the first position.

If the dowel misses the tooth by more than 1 or 2 thicknesses of paper, readjust the table or trunnions to eliminate the gap.

Fence Alignment

If a rip fence is not parallel to the blade, the result is the same as crosscut heel: Teeth rising at the back of the blade score the sides of the kerf. To check your saw, begin by checking that the fence locks to the front rail before locking to the back rail. If it doesn't, get out your saw manual and adjust it.

Next, check that it locks parallel to the blade. I prefer a direct test as described below. Check twice: once when moving the fence to the right before locking and again when moving to the left.

If both checks come out the same, you have a fence that locks up in a reliable position. Get out your manual and adjust the fence to lock parallel to the blade, which is indicated by both surfaces being equally smooth and free of crosshatching and burns.

If the two checks give you different messages, start saving up for a good aftermarket fence. In the meantime, try adjusting the fence so that it locks parallel when moved in one direction, and then always move it in that direction just before locking it.

Some woodworkers adjust the fence so it angles away from the blade in order to provide room for stock that bows during the cut. Don't do it. When ripping solid lumber, allow for bowing stock by using a short rip fence, as shown in *Auxiliary Rip Fence Prevents Binding* on page 59.

CHECKING FENCE ALIGNMENT

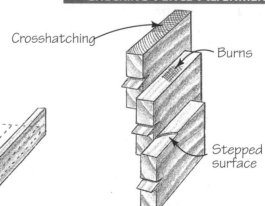

Crosshatching

Burns

Stepped surface

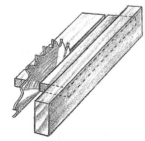

1. Rip a scrap of stable, fine-textured hardwood, like cherry, stopping and turning off the saw in the position shown.

2. Remove the 2 pieces and fold them open so you can examine the cut edges.

3. If the left board shows any of these faults, the fence angles away from the blade. If the right board shows them, the fence angles toward the blade.

4. See the saw manual to realign the fence.

much use for 52-inch crosscutting capacity if you never use plywood or particleboard. Here are some of the features to consider.

◗ *A rigid table with built-in stock clamps:* Since neither miter gauges nor crosscut sleds are well suited for clamping stock in place for the cut, make sure your rolling table overcomes this deficiency.

◗ *A long, rugged crosscut fence that locks securely at commonly used angles:* The fence should stay put and make it easy to position long, thick hardwood.

◗ *Quick and easy removal of the crosscut fence:* Unless you're shopping for a saw just for crosscutting, remember that fences and clamps have to get out of the way every time you need to rip.

◗ *A miter gauge slot in the fixed table:* A rolling table that's ideal for handling big materials is a pain in the shoulders when crosscutting small parts. A miter gauge will save you from muscling the iron works back and forth when you need to cut up a bunch of 2-inch glue blocks.

◗ *Extension wings to support long boards and full sheets of plywood:* Few of us measure our shop size by the acre. A good rolling table supports big stock but also breaks down into less space when you need the room for other tasks.

◗ *Long travel for crosscutting full sheets of plywood:* For those who work with 4 × 8-foot sheet stock, a 50- or 52-inch travel may be the single most important feature of a rolling table.

◗ *Shielded tracks, rails, or bearings:* This is an easily overlooked feature. If sawdust can find its way to the bearings or tracks, the table will rumble along like a Tonka truck on a gravel road, and the saw cut will look like you used a dull chain saw. ●

Repeat Cuts

More often than not, a project calls for several parts cut to the same length. These might be legs or drawer parts or any of dozens of project parts—all to the same length. Whether cutting them with a chop saw, with a radial arm saw, or on the table saw, you'll get more accurate results in less time if you align the stock against a stop block.

These can be as simple as scraps of wood clamped to a fence; but once you form the habit of using them, you'll want a more convenient arrangement. A good stop block has the following features.

◗ It clamps and unclamps from a fence with no more than a half turn of a knob or lever.

◗ When clamped it stays put and doesn't pivot in a tee slot, moving a fraction of an inch.

◗ It flips out of the way while you trim one end of a board, then flips back for cutting the other end.

◗ When positioned for use, it doesn't wiggle at all—the hinges allow no play or backlash.

◗ It allows you to adjust the stop position in tiny increments.

◗ It works on a wide variety of machines and jigs so you don't need several of them. ●

The usefulness of stop blocks has not escaped the attention of tool manufacturers, who make a variety of stops that clamp to fences. I have yet to see one that scored very well on my grocery list of requirements, however. I suggest that you make the stop block shown in the photo on page 250, which was born of frustration with the commercial ones.

Stock Support for Crosscutting

Adequate support for stock during a crosscut is essential for both your safety and the quality of the cut. If a board tends to tip off the saw table during *or after* the cut, you have to occupy both your brain and your muscles to keep it on the table. You have more important things to do—like minding where your fingers are. The quality of the cut is affected because stock held on the table by pressure from your hands tends to move jerkily through the cut.

Woodworkers, myself included, have cobbled together a variety of supports of questionable value. Most of these are too rickety or a nuisance to set up, the stock doesn't move along them smoothly, or they aren't long enough. If you've been down this road, I'm sure you can add to the list of problems.

Only recently I contrived a solution that works better than anything else I've ever used. It's shown in the photo on page 93. Plans and instructions for making it are in the "Crosscut Support" chapter on page 298. The support is rigid because it's well braced and attaches to the saw. It's convenient because it swings up for use and down, out of the way, when it's not needed. It's also convenient because it sports a hinged rail that flips up to support stock on a crosscut sled, or down to support plywood sheets. Low-friction (high-molecular-weight polyethylene) tape on the support surfaces will help the stock slide smoothly and easily.

STEP-BY-STEP CROSSCUTTING

1 Adjust the blade height.

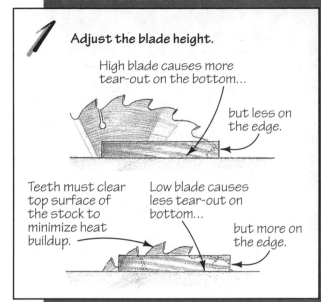

High blade causes more tear-out on the bottom...

but less on the edge.

Teeth must clear top surface of the stock to minimize heat buildup.

Low blade causes less tear-out on bottom...

but more on the edge.

2 Adjust a stop block to the required distance.

If precise length is critical, cut and measure a test piece before cutting the workpiece.

Measure from the tooth, NOT from the blade plate.

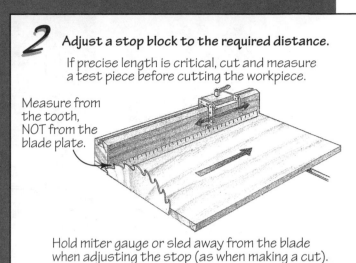

Hold miter gauge or sled away from the blade when adjusting the stop (as when making a cut).

3 With the stop block up out of the way, trim one end of the stock square and smooth.

With left hand, hold the stock back against the fence and down against the table.

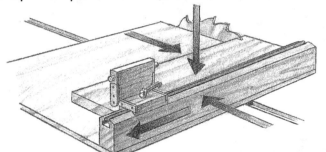

Feed stock without pausing. Moderately slow feed gives a smoother cut but may burn wood like maple or cherry.

Feed with right hand; hold gauge or sled away from the blade.

4 Reverse the stock end for end, flip the stop block down, hold the stock against the stop block, and trim to length.

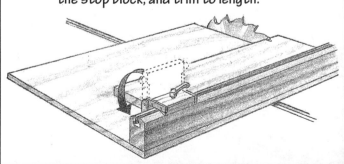

TECH TIP

TO MINIMIZE EFFECTS OF A MISALIGNED MITER GAUGE SLOT, withdraw narrower stock before it reaches the rear teeth of the blade.

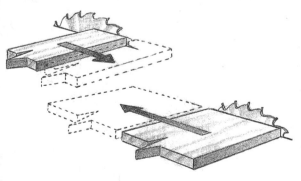

If stock is already alongside the teeth at rear when the cut is complete, continue until the entire piece clears the blade.

CROSSCUTTING BY HAND

Most woodworkers can handle their crosscutting needs with two handsaws: a backsaw, also called a tenon saw, with a blade 12 to 14 inches long and about 15 teeth per inch; and either a dovetail saw or a gent's saw with a blade 8 to 10 inches long and about 18 teeth per inch. The smaller saw should have only very slight set to the teeth (0.015 to 0.020 inch) so it will leave a very smooth surface. Use it for crosscutting stock no more than 1 square inch in cross section, and for hand-cutting dovetails, as explained in "Cutting Dovetails by Hand" on page 192. Use the backsaw for other joinery and for crosscutting stock up to 4 square inches in cross section. A saw of this type will usually have the teeth set 0.030 to 0.050 inch.

A backsaw in a handy and convenient size will crosscut stock as large as ¾ inch thick × 6 inches wide, but it does better on smaller stock.

The handiest way to crosscut stock is with a bench hook, as shown in *Bench Hook/Shooting Board*. Hook the bench hook over the near edge of

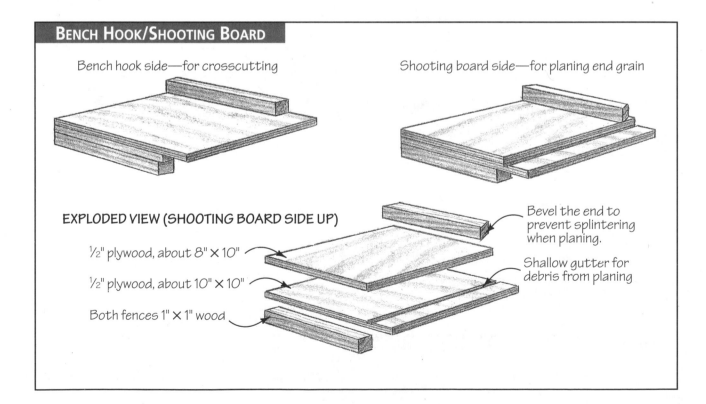

BENCH HOOK/SHOOTING BOARD

Bench hook side—for crosscutting

Shooting board side—for planing end grain

EXPLODED VIEW (SHOOTING BOARD SIDE UP)

½" plywood, about 8" × 10"

½" plywood, about 10" × 10"

Both fences 1" × 1" wood

Bevel the end to prevent splintering when planing.

Shallow gutter for debris from planing

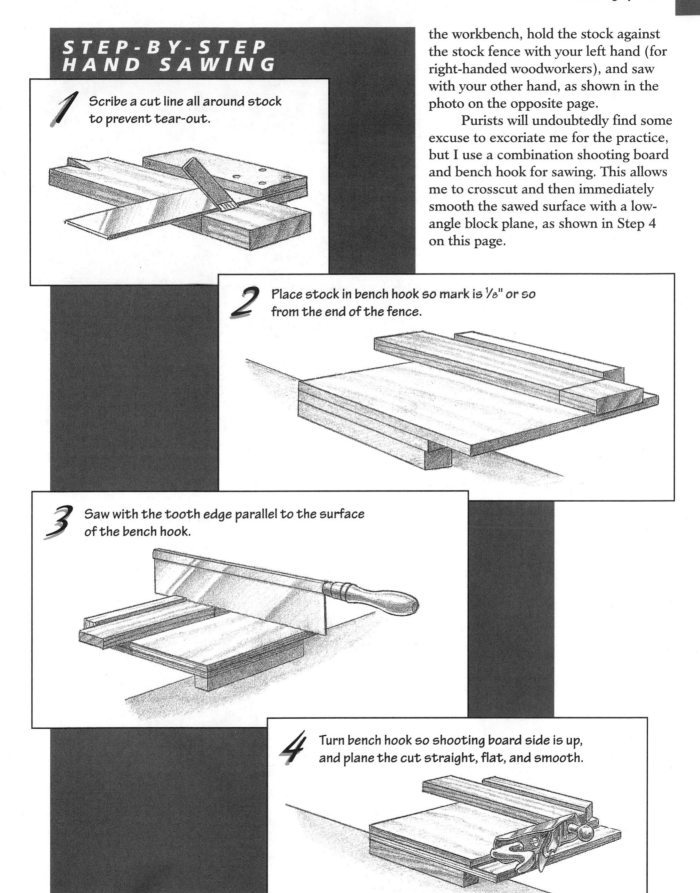

STEP-BY-STEP HAND SAWING

1 Scribe a cut line all around stock to prevent tear-out.

2 Place stock in bench hook so mark is ⅛" or so from the end of the fence.

3 Saw with the tooth edge parallel to the surface of the bench hook.

4 Turn bench hook so shooting board side is up, and plane the cut straight, flat, and smooth.

the workbench, hold the stock against the stock fence with your left hand (for right-handed woodworkers), and saw with your other hand, as shown in the photo on the opposite page.

Purists will undoubtedly find some excuse to excoriate me for the practice, but I use a combination shooting board and bench hook for sawing. This allows me to crosscut and then immediately smooth the sawed surface with a low-angle block plane, as shown in Step 4 on this page.

Ripping and Sawing Plywood on the Table Saw

The table saw is beyond doubt the most efficient and practical saw for ripping in small to medium-sized shops. It's simple, accurate, easy to use, and reasonably safe, and it produces a smooth cut. There are four secrets to accurate and safe cuts. First, when ripping solid lumber, use a half-fence, as shown in *Auxiliary Rip Fence Prevents Binding* on page 59, so stock that bows after the cut won't jam between the blade and fence. Second, make sure the fence is parallel to the blade, as explained in "Tuning a Table Saw" on page 98. Third, use push sticks, as shown in *Push Sticks*, to keep your fingers away from the blade. And fourth, provide outfeed support—and if that's another person, train the person to support the stock in a straight line, as shown in the photo and accompanying drawing on this page.

If you walk backwards normally when tailing a board, your body will sway from side to side, making it difficult to avoid moving the board from side to side.

Instead, place your feet in a straight line, angling your toes out to help keep your balance.

Sawing Sheet Stock

We normally think of ripping as sawing with the grain and crosscutting as sawing more or less across the grain. But plywood as well as other

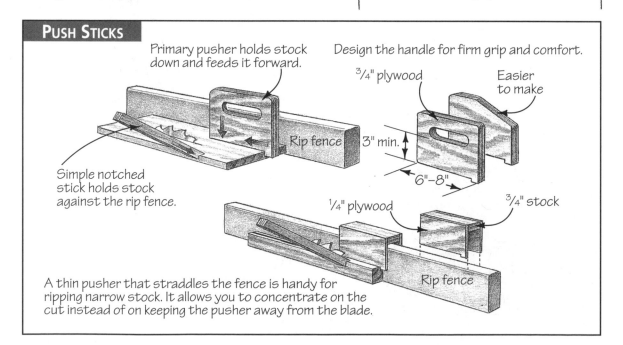

PUSH STICKS

Primary pusher holds stock down and feeds it forward.

Design the handle for firm grip and comfort.

³/₄" plywood

Easier to make

Rip fence

3" min.

6"–8"

Simple notched stick holds stock against the rip fence.

¼" plywood

³/₄" stock

Rip fence

A thin pusher that straddles the fence is handy for ripping narrow stock. It allows you to concentrate on the cut instead of on keeping the pusher away from the blade.

manufactured sheet stock has grain going in both directions, or all directions. It differs from solid lumber in the way we use it as well. We usually use solid lumber in pieces that are much longer with the grain than they are wide across the grain. But a more typical use of plywood is in pieces with length and width more nearly the same, such as the back of a cabinet or bottom of a drawer.

When sawing sheet stock, use a combination or crosscut blade, not a rip blade. If you cut a lot of sheet stock, talk to your blade dealer about an appropriate special-purpose blade. Then ignore the grain direction of the surface veneer. Use the rip fence whenever you're sawing parallel to the longer dimension of the stock, and a crosscut guide when sawing parallel to the shorter dimension. When guiding the stock with the fence, use the full-length rip fence, not the half-fence recommended for ripping solid lumber. The longer fence makes it easier to control wide plywood parts, and there is no need to allow room for distortion as there is with solid lumber. Finally, provide both "crosscut" support and outfeed support when breaking down full sheets.

*S*TOP SPLINTERING

Materials with a thin surface layer—like melamine-faced particleboard and some hardwood plywood, especially oak—tend to splinter and tear out badly on the bottom surface. Saws designed especially for these materials use a separate scoring cutter ahead of the regular blade to minimize this tear-out. With care, you can achieve the same result with an ordinary table saw.

Adjust the fence to the necessary width of cut, and make sure it's solidly locked at both ends. Adjust the depth of cut to $\frac{1}{32}$ to $\frac{1}{16}$ inch.

Now score the stock by feeding it backwards over the saw, from the outfeed side toward the infeed side, as shown below. Only a few blade guards will allow this—you'll have to remove others, as you do for dado cuts. Hold the stock firmly down against the table so the shallow scoring cut doesn't miss spots, and hold it firmly against the fence so the score is exactly where you want it. Be aware that this is a "climb" cut, tending to feed itself. At this shallow a cut, pieces a couple of square feet or more in area won't be thrown by the blade, but you may notice a difference in the amount of push needed to feed the stock. I don't suggest the technique for pieces less than 1 square foot in area. Finally, raise the blade so the teeth clear the top of the stock, and saw it in the normal direction, from infeed side to outfeed side. This cut must coincide with the scoring cut exactly.

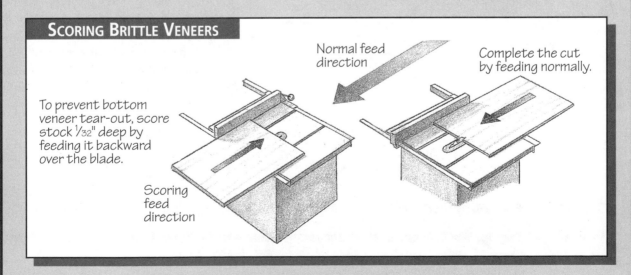

SCORING BRITTLE VENEERS

Normal feed direction

Complete the cut by feeding normally.

To prevent bottom veneer tear-out, score stock $\frac{1}{32}$" deep by feeding it backward over the blade.

Scoring feed direction

CIRCULAR SAW BLADES

Today's carbide-toothed saw blades are a vast improvement over the all-steel blades of a few decades ago. Much of the improvement is due to the carefully designed angles on the two sides, the front face, and the top. If you understand how these angles affect sawing, you will be better able to choose the right blade for specific applications.

The **top bevel angle** is the most visible facet of a tooth. A tooth with an angled or beveled top does a cleaner job of crosscutting wood fibers than one with no angle. Blades with alternate-top bevels, known as ATB blades, cut both sides of a kerf cleanly. Top bevels of up to 15 degrees are good for general crosscutting. Angles as high as 40 degrees are found on some special-purpose blades.

On the minus side, ATB blades leave a small ridge running down the center of the kerf, a nuisance when you're cutting rabbets or tenon shoulders. If the ridge is a problem for you, try a blade with the top of every fourth or fifth tooth ground flat instead of beveled. This "raker" tooth cleans out the ridge left by the beveled teeth. (ATB blades with a raker are sometimes designated "ATBR blades.")

The **relief angle** of a tooth allows the stock to feed forward so the next tooth can take a bite. You can safely assume that the manufacturer has provided an appropriate relief angle.

The **hook angle** of a tooth affects two aspects of a saw blade's performance: its aggressiveness and its tendency to produce splinters when exiting the kerf. Hook angles can vary from +20 degrees to –7 degrees. High hook angles feed aggressively but tend to splinter the wood. Low or negative hook angles require more feed pressure but splinter less. Rip blades can use higher hook angles to good advantage. Crosscut blades seldom benefit from more than 10 or 15 degrees of hook.

Chop saws and radial arm saws crosscut best with blades that have minimal hook angles. Negative hook angles are best for man-made materials like Corian, plastic laminates, chipboard, and plywood.

Gullet size is directly related to the *number of teeth* on a blade. Bigger gullets leave room for fewer teeth. You need big gullets when ripping because the waste tends to be stringy and clogs small gullets. Smaller gullets, and hence more teeth, are possible on crosscut blades because the waste consists of very short fibers. This works out well in practice because you need more teeth to get a smooth crosscut than to get a smooth rip.

The tradeoff between number of teeth and gullet size is a problem

BLADE AND TOOTH PARTS

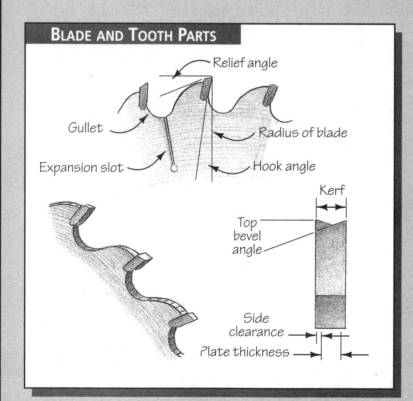

Relief angle

Gullet

Radius of blade

Expansion slot

Hook angle

Kerf

Top bevel angle

Side clearance

Plate thickness

when designing a combination blade for both ripping and crosscutting. The usual solution is one flat-top ripping tooth with a large gullet followed by four closely spaced ATB teeth for crosscutting. This compromise neither rips as well as a good rip blade nor crosscuts as well as a good crosscut blade—but it does both reasonably well and saves a lot of blade switching.

The plate has the unenviable job of keeping all of the teeth moving along the straight and narrow even while the blade is heating up from friction, and doing it without buckling or warping. **Expansion slots** in the outer edge of the plate accommodate the expansion of the plate due to heat. The plate is also pre-tensioned to help maintain flatness over a broad range of temperatures. Unfortunately, you have to depend on the reputation of the manufacturer to get a good plate. The only way to detect a bad one is by buying it and finding out it cuts roughly and overheats quickly. As a rule of thumb, don't expect to find a high-quality plate on a cheap blade.

Side clearance between the plate and the teeth allows the plate to turn in the slot cut by the teeth without building up excessive heat from friction. Blades with minimal side clearance usually cut smoother than blades with more side clearance, but they're more likely to bind, overheat, and warp. Some manufacturers coat their plates with Teflon to minimize friction.

When referring to a saw blade, **kerf** is the width of the teeth. The term is also used for the slot that the blade cuts. The width of the slot is the width of the teeth (blade kerf) plus the total runout of the blade and the saw. (See "Tuning a Table Saw" on page 98.) You need more power to cut a wide kerf than to cut a thin one, but a robust and stable plate and adequate side clearance limit how thin a kerf can be. Advances in metallurgy and blade technology have made thin kerf blades more practical today than they were 10 or 15

years ago, but to use one you still need a more finely tuned saw than when using standard blades. Blade stabilizers or stiffeners (see below) are even more desirable on thin-kerfed blades than on standard ones.

Blade Recommendations

No one blade does all jobs perfectly. The best blade for the job depends on the material you're cutting, on whether the job is a rip or a crosscut, on whether you're primarily concerned with speed or smoothness of cut, and on the thickness of the material. I've always taken the advice of my sharpening service. The owner consistently recommends good blades at good prices. So my first recommendation is that you find out who sharpens blades for professional shops in your area, and bring that person your sharpening and blade business.

That said, my own suggestions for the woodworker who saws mostly solid wood in the range of ¾ to 1½ inches thick and occasionally saws plywood and other man-made wood products are the following three blades:

1. A 40- or 50-tooth ATBR combination blade for general use

2. A 26- or 28-tooth rip blade for extended ripping sessions, all deep ripping, and sawing tenon cheeks

3. A 60- to 70-tooth crosscut blade to use only for joinery where a particularly smooth cut is needed

Next, I strongly recommend that you buy and use blade stabilizers or stiffeners. In fact, I suggest that you get both 4- and 6-inch-diameter stiffeners and use the largest that will allow you the depth of cut you require at the moment. These accessories dampen vibrations in the overburdened saw plate, giving you a smoother and quieter cut.

SMOOTHING SURFACES

Abrasives, planes, and scrapers are all effective for smoothing surfaces. The best choice depends on the species of wood, the individual board, and even the grain direction in a specific area within the board.

When you work with wood for the pure pleasure of it, the technique that you use is obviously very important—some woodworkers get more pleasure from a hand-planing workout than from shepherding a sander, while others like nothing better than climbing aboard a locomotive-sized belt sander. But the final product is equally important, because we all get a second pleasure from pride in an especially attractive and well-made project. When choosing a technique for smoothing wood, you may have to compromise one or the other of those pleasures because the technique that produces the best results depends largely on the species of wood.

There are three basic techniques for smoothing wood: hand planing, scraping, and sanding. All three, properly done, produce very good results, but the results differ in subtle ways. Often a hand plane will produce a smoother, glossier surface than a scraper or sandpaper, even if you sand with extremely fine grits. The softer woods, like pine and basswood, for example, seldom show any benefit from sanding with abrasives finer than 220-grit, and a scraper just pulls out tiny fibers. A well-tuned, razor-sharp plane, on the other hand, will give a shine to these woods that sandpaper can't achieve.

Other species respond very well to abrasives. Years ago I picked up a couple hundred board feet of a tropical hardwood sold to me as "bloodwood." It was hard, heavy, and close-grained. I found it very difficult to plane or scrape this wood, but I could polish it with sandpaper that was finer than I had ever used before, and the results improved with each finer grit.

That surprised me because I had never before used a wood that showed visible benefits from sanding with abrasives finer than 440-grit. After polishing this stuff with 1200-grit paper, it had the best sheen that I had ever seen on unfinished wood.

Scraping works best on the moderate-density woods, like cherry, walnut, mahogany, and maple. The scraper doesn't tear out ultra-fine fibers the way that even the sharpest, most finely tuned hand plane does, and it doesn't leave the microscopically fuzzy finish that abrasives leave on many species.

If you really take your woodworking seriously and you work with a variety of woods, you'll want to learn all three methods for smoothing and choose the best one for the species you're working. But you should know three things ahead of time: First, sanding is the most versatile way to smooth wood. You can get very good—if not the very best—surfaces with any species of wood by sanding. Second, planing and scraping by hand require skill that you can get only with practice—considerably more skill and practice than you need to achieve fine surfaces using sandpaper. Third, the differences in appearance produced by these three methods are subtle. Your neighbor

probably won't notice any difference at all. If you spend the time it takes to get good at hand planing and scraping, do it for your own satisfaction and pleasure.

TECH TIP

FLAWS SHOW UP much more clearly under a coat of finish than they do on bare wood. Scratches, dings, and dents that are visible only with very close scrutiny on the unfinished wood are often quite distracting after the piece has been stained or varnished—when it's too late to do anything about them. Prevent this kind of disappointment by examining the surface very carefully under strong side lighting.

NOTE: *Don't confuse smoothing with flattening. When you smooth a surface, you remove very little stock and don't change its shape significantly. When you surface rough stock, you intentionally remove as much stock as necessary to give it the shape you want—usually flat and square. Planing machines like jointers and thicknessers do a good job of removing stock to produce a flat board but do not produce acceptably smooth final surfaces—they leave mill marks, as shown in* How Mill Marks Happen *on page 64. Even hand planes differ for smoothing and flattening: long planes—tuned and adjusted for relatively coarse cuts—are best for flattening, while short ones—tuned and adjusted for very fine cuts—are best for smoothing. Your skills will grow more quickly if you keep these two operations, flattening and smoothing, separate in your mind.*

SANDING

Belt sanders (upper right) are wood hogs, but sanding frames (upper left) give them some manners. Orbital sanders are strictly for smoothing, not leveling. The conventional type (lower right) is slow and safe, while the random-orbit type (lower left) gets the job done faster.

At first glance sanding seems to require little skill, but doing a good job requires attention to details. For example, when sanding, you have to look quite hard to gauge the results of your efforts. You can't rely on how smooth the wood feels to tell you how it will look. Since you usually can't feel mill marks from a jointer or planer, you certainly won't be able to feel when they're sanded away.

It's faster and easier to acquire skill at sanding than skill at hand planing or scraping, but it still takes some learning. The following general rules will help you avoid some of the more common problems.

▶ Sand parts before assembly. Inside corners, such as where a table apron meets a leg, are extremely difficult to sand after assembly.

▶ Vacuum or thoroughly brush off the dust each time you switch sandpaper grits. The dust includes particles of abrasive from the previous (coarser) grit as well as wood dust. If you don't remove those coarser abrasive particles, they will continue to scratch the surface as you push them around.

▶ If you brush instead of vacuum between grits, then wipe the wood with a cloth dampened in mineral spirits. This gets the dust out of the scratches, so you can see any you've missed.

▶ If you intend to apply a stain or finish that contains water, then you should wet the wood after final sanding, allow it to dry, and resand lightly with the finest grit you used previously. Some woodworkers use a wet rag for this process, which is called "raising the grain." I prefer a mist from a household plant mister.

▶ Never move on to a finer grit until you've removed all of the faults in the surface. Either the finer grit won't remove the faults you left, or it will take much more time and effort to remove them.

▶ If you discover that you overlooked a fault and moved on to a finer grit, go back and remove the fault with a coarser grit, then rework your way up to the finer grit. ●

Sanding: The Right Sequence

There's no real mystery to the sanding sequence: The first grit levels the surface and removes mill marks, glue, scratches, and dents. The second grit removes the scratch marks left by the first, and so on, until the surface is sufficiently smooth for finishing. The grit to start with depends on the density of the wood and the depth of the flaws you need to remove.

Your goal is to start with a grit that will remove the flaws in the wood with the minimum amount of time and effort. If you start with too coarse a grit, you'll remove the flaws in a flash, but then you will have to sand out the scratch pattern of the coarser abrasive. If you start with too fine a grit, it will take

ABRASIVE MATERIALS

Tiny granules of natural stone like flint or garnet were once the only raw material for making sandpaper. Today, most sanding belts, discs, and sheets use man-made abrasives like aluminum oxide or silicon carbide. They're hard, sharp, and long-wearing—a combination that none of the natural abrasives can match.

The abrasive grit is glued to a paper or cloth backing material. The weight of the material determines how durable and how flexible the abrasive sheet or belt is. Paper backings are labeled "A" through "F," with A being the lightest and F the heaviest. Cloth backings are labeled "J," "X," "Y," "T," and "M," with J being the lightest and most flexible and M the heaviest. Belts for portable belt sanders are always "X"-weight cloth. When buying cut sheets for hand sanding or for use on orbital sanders that clamp the abrasive material in place, you'll have little choice—finer grits will be available only on lighter paper, and coarser grits will be available only on heavier paper.

Coated abrasives (sandpaper) are further classified as "open-coat" or "closed-coat." Open-coat abrasives have open spaces between the individual pieces of grit on the backing. Closed-coat abrasives are completely covered with grit. As a general rule, use closed-coat abrasives because they work faster. If you find that they clog up excessively with some particular species of wood, then switch to open-coat abrasives. An alternative solution to the problem of excessive clogging is stearate paper, which is treated to release the particles without clogging. You'll recognize it by its white or gray appearance.

too long to remove the flaws. Since hard wood abrades away more slowly than soft wood, it will pay to start with a somewhat coarser grit here than you would use on a soft wood with equally deep flaws. Keep in mind that a coarse abrasive cuts just as fast making a mistake as it does removing the stock you want removed. So whether your sanding device is your bare hands or a 6-inch-wide stationary belt sander, don't use an abrasive coarser than 100-grit until you have experience with grits that are a step finer. Given these rules, some guidelines for when to use various grit abrasives are listed below.

CHOOSING AN ABRASIVE GRIT

ABRASIVE GRIT	APPROPRIATE TASK	EXAMPLE
24–50	Heavy stock removal (but not for soft wood)	Leveling a board in a hardwood glue-up if it's proud of its neighbors
60–80	Light stock removal	Sanding out a moderately deep scratch or dent or unusually deep mill marks
100–150	Initial smoothing	Leveling mill marks from a well-adjusted planer
180–240	Finer smoothing	Removing the scratch marks of coarser grits and those from factory sanding of plywood
280 and up	Polishing	Putting a sheen on very hard, close-grained wood

As you can see, the first grit to use depends entirely on the task at hand and can range from the extremely coarse grits below 50 to as high as 150.

The sequence of grits to follow after the first depends partly on whether you're sanding by hand or by machine. When sanding by machine, I generally make each new grit 50 percent finer than the previous one. So if I start with 80-grit, I'll progress to 120, then 180, then 280. When sanding by hand, which is slower, I space the grits a bit closer—say 80, 100, 120, 150. The task for each of these grits is to remove the scratch marks left by the previous grit.

Whether you're sanding by machine or hand, the end of the sequence—the finest grit—depends on the species of wood, the finish you'll apply, and the look you want to achieve. If you intend to apply a film finish like shellac or polyurethane then the feel of the wood is not relevant—all you will feel is the film finish. For looks, there's no point in using a grit that leaves a scratch pattern much finer than you're able to see. On coarser-grained woods like butternut, grits higher than 120 are a waste of time—you won't see any improvement after applying a finish. The harder the wood the more it pays to use finer grits.

Another consideration is whether you intend to stain the wood. Stain will darken a coarsely sanded surface more than a finely sanded one. The concern is uniformity: Make sure you sand all the parts with the same grit so they all stain the same.

If you intend to apply an oil finish, then the feel of the wood is important because the finish won't disguise the texture. Your best guide is your fingers. If you can't feel any difference between 180-grit and 220-grit on the wood, then it's a waste of time and effort to go beyond 180.

Finally, I have to concede an exception to the above guidelines. Some woods are so dense and so close-grained that you can polish them to a gloss that will still be evident after applying an oil finish. Ebony is such a wood. Keep polishing these treasures until finer grits show no improvement.

Belt Sanders

Belt sanders are aggressive stock removers. They're ideal for leveling the joints of glued-up panels if you don't have a planer. They can also do a lot of damage if you allow them to tip. Learning to control them is a matter of practice, but it's important that you form good habits while gaining the practice. Keep the following in mind:

▶ Keep the cord over your shoulder so you won't have to worry about running over it with the sander—you have better things to occupy your mind. If you wear shirts with epaulets, button them down over the cord to keep it from slipping off your shoulder.

▶ Never move the machine in the direction it's pointed; instead, move it at a slight angle. The slight sideways movement will minimize the risk of sanding a groove with the edge of the belt, but it will increase the tendency to tip, so be careful.

▶ Never, NEVER move the sander so that its center of gravity is off the stock.

▶ Ignore advice to start the machine before putting it down on the stock—this is sure to gouge the wood. Instead, lift slightly to take most of the weight off the belt but not enough to raise the machine, then start the machine running and allow the weight back onto the belt as you begin to move the machine forward.

▶ To avoid creating shallow areas, never concentrate your sanding in an area smaller than 3 times the length of the pad × 3 times the width of the pad. (And never sand stock narrower than the pad.) ●

Consider equipping your belt sander with a sanding frame, as shown in the photo on page 110. These attachments virtually eliminate the danger of tipping the sander. Properly adjusted, they prevent sanding a hollow if you sand too long in a small area. On the other hand, they have two disadvantages that can work together to cause a lot of damage. First, they prevent the sander from working up close to corners and walls. Second, they prevent you from gaining experience controlling the machine by yourself. If you use the frame routinely and then remove it to sand near an obstruction, you risk a big, unhappy surprise as the machine tips and gouges your work.

Orbital Sanders

There are two types of orbital sanders: conventional pad sanders, which move the abrasive in a circular motion, and random-orbit sanders, which combine the circular motion with rotation of the entire disc. Random-orbit sanders work faster, an advantage for the careful worker but a danger for the careless, because they can do more damage in less time. Both types create a scratch pattern so tiny and shallow that you usually can't see it.

The conventional orbital sander has a rectangular pad that takes a quarter, third, or half sheet of sandpaper. The random-orbit type has a 4½-, 5-, or 6-inch-diameter circular pad that takes precut abrasive discs. The pads on both types are either foam rubber or felt. The soft surface pushes the abrasive down into shallow hollows in the surface. This is good for smoothing out the scratch marks of a belt sander but not so good for leveling mill marks.

Generally speaking, orbital sanders are easier to learn to use than belt sanders, and conventional orbital sanders are easier to learn than random-orbit sanders. A few things to keep in mind:

▶ Don't try to remove large amounts of stock with an orbital sander. Use a belt sander or plane.

▶ Keep the surface of the stock free of dust so the abrasive can reach the stock. I prefer sanders that I can handle with one hand so that I can keep a brush in my left hand while sanding with my right.

▶ Let the weight of the tool do the work. Bearing down heavily usually just slows the orbiting motion.

▶ Start and stop a conventional orbital sander off the stock, but start a random-orbit sander as you would a belt sander—down on the stock but relieved of most of its weight.

▶ Experiment to find the most efficient combination of tools and techniques. I find that if I finish sand close-grained wood like cherry or maple with an orbital sander, I must progress all the way to 220-grit. But if I use the orbital sander with grits up to 120 and then follow with hand sanding in the direction of the grain with 150-grit, I get the same results with less time and effort. ●

DUST

Sanding dust is so fine, it hangs in the air and drifts with the air for hours before settling out. By then it can be anyplace—in your lungs, in the ducts of your forced-air heating system, and in every nook and cranny of your shop, with special preference for places where you can't sweep. For many woodworkers it's a health hazard, causing either respiratory problems or skin problems. There is no one good way to lick it—the best solution to the problem is to use every weapon at your disposal. A few suggestions for your arsenal:

• Wear a dust mask.
• Use sanders with dust bags or vacuum attachments.
• Install window fans to exhaust dusty air.
• Install commercially available shop air filters with blowers.
• Install a high-volume, low-pressure dust collector and use it to suck up the air where you're sanding. (Shop vacs are low-volume, high-pressure. They can't suck up enough air to catch the dust before it's all over the room.)
• Sand outdoors.

SANDING SHAPES

Sanding curves and shaped edges can be a challenge. You want to sand them smooth, but you don't want to ruin the crisp lines of your work by rounding-over the edges any more than is necessary to remove their sharpness. Here's what I do. For convex shapes like a bull-nose or quarter round, I shape the paper around the work with my hand. For concave shapes I either wrap sandpaper around dowels or cardboard tubes or I make a sanding block that matches the profile. *Sanding a Cove* shows how I make a sanding block to clean up cove molding that I make on the table saw.

Sanding sharp inside corners is a problem. I try to cut them in the first place with tools that require a minimum of sanding, such as razor-sharp router bits, then I sand them only as needed with A-weight sandpaper wrapped tightly around a hardwood block that has sharp edges.

Convex curved edges that are square to the face of the stock are fairly easy to sand with a stationary disc sander, as shown in the left photo on this page. You can get similar results from table-saw disc sanders. These look like toothless saw blades, and you can mount conventional sanding discs on their sides. Sanding large-diameter concave edges is more of a problem. I usually stick self-adhesive sandpaper to a flexible batten for sanding these sweeping curves.

SANDING A COVE

First, stick 80-grit sandpaper into the cove.

Then sand a foam block to the shape of the cove.

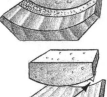

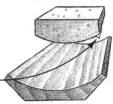

Finally, stick sandpaper to the foam and smooth the cove.

Self-stick sandpaper

The table on a stationary sanding machine helps you keep the edge square to the face of the stock.

Portable belt sanders with accessory feet work like miniature stationary belt sanders, perfect for freehand smoothing of small parts.

Hand Planing

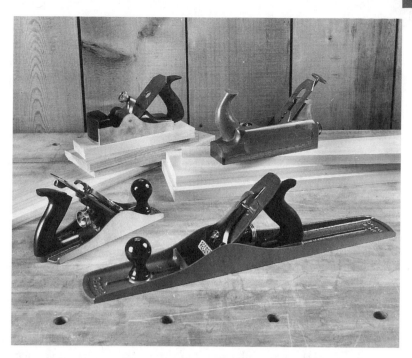

The most common plane design today is the Bailey (front left and right). The longer models like the #7 "jointer" smooth wood just as well as the shorter #4 "smooth" plane, but they're more fatiguing. More expensive planes of either wood (back right) or metal (back left) may be easier to adjust or fine-tune and may be more comfortable to use.

Sharp, well-adjusted hand planes smooth the traditional furniture woods admirably well. They're quiet, reasonably priced, and efficient. And they're delightful gems of ingenuity. The 9- to 10-inch-long plane referred to as a #4 is usually the best choice for smoothing, but shorter or longer planes of equal quality and adjustability will produce equally smooth surfaces. Longer planes like #5 and #6 are more fatiguing to use, but they're more versatile because they do a better job straightening and flattening than the #4. If you work mostly on smaller projects like boxes and small chests, you may prefer the shorter #3 or #2.

The less expensive models of hand planes have a place in woodworking, but that place is in rougher work, not in smoothing. If a plane does not have an adjustable frog or other means of narrowing the gap between the cutting iron and the opening in the sole, don't expect top-notch quality in the rest of the plane. The most common plane design is the "Bailey," shown in the photo on this page, but there are variations on the Bailey and other plane designs that are often very high quality and quite expensive. Wooden-bodied smoothing planes with modern adjustment mechanisms are lighter in weight and less fatiguing than metal planes for big smoothing jobs.

There are a few basics to good planing that you will need to consider. First, all planes have to be carefully tuned and adjusted, as described in "Tuning a Plane" on page 118. While you're at it, consider tuning and adjusting your workbench. You can't do a good job of smoothing stock with a hand plane if you're in an awkward position; so adjust your bench to a comfortable height. I'm 5 feet, 10 inches tall, and I like a bench 36 inches high.

Next, you need to keep the stock from running away from you as you plane. A pair of bench stops near the left edge of the bench (if you're

right-handed) works well. If you don't have stops, you can clamp a cleat to the bench top; but keep the clamps out of the way so the plane won't bang into them. You simply butt the stock against either the stops or the cleat. You can only plane toward the stops, of course; so if the grain of the wood demands that you plane in both directions, as explained below, you have to reverse the board. But unless you're perfectly ambidextrous, you'll want to do that anyway. Bench dogs and a tail vise also work fine and hold the stock regardless of the direction you're planing; but if you're smoothing a lot of pieces, a simple stop is quicker.

As a general rule, aim the plane straight down the board and plane in the same direction. Skewing the plane reduces the effective angle of the cutting iron and increases the tendency of fibers to tear out. Skewing also reduces the force required to push the plane. You may find some boards that plane more cleanly with a skew cut, but they're the exception. Most often pushing the plane straight, even though it's harder, will give you the smoothest surface.

With almost every board, you'll find that it planes more easily and smoothly in one direction than the other. This direction is called "with the grain." I have been hearing and reading all my life that you can tell which direction is "with the grain" by examining the edge of the board, with some exceptions. I find that the exceptions account for about 50 percent of the total. My method for figuring out the grain direction has an equally good track record—I make a blind guess. Then after discovering by experiment which direction is "with the grain," I plane in that direction.

Unfortunately, with some boards, both directions are "against the grain." These boards fall into two groups. The first group includes boards that plane best in one direction at one end of the board and in the opposite direction at the other end, and also boards that plane best in one direction along one edge and in the opposite direction along the other edge. Plane any boards in this group by giving in to their preference, planing in both directions as demanded by the particular parts of the board.

The other group contains certain species of tropical wood that are blessed with what is called "roey" grain. Mahogany is the best-known example. Roey grain in a board means that alternate narrow bands running the length of the board plane best in opposite directions. If you plane in one direction, half of the bands come out smooth and the other half tend to tear out. If you switch directions, the previously torn-out bands come out smooth and the previously smooth bands tear out. If you have a very, very fine plane and get really good at using it, you'll be able to plane roey boards smooth. The rest of us will use scrapers.

Unless the grain demands otherwise, plane the full length of the stock with each stroke. On long boards this will mean walking the plane down the length. If the plane is so hard to push that you can't walk it, you may have it set too deep, or it may be dull, or you may need a narrower plane. (I'm a li'l guy. I prefer 2-inch-wide planes over the 2⅜-inch versions and sometimes wish I had a 1¾-inch #3.) Overlap each stroke with the previous one by the minimum amount you can get away with without too many missed spots. When you're new to hand planing, that may mean a 50 percent overlap. That's okay—just keep pushing the envelope. Always try to set the plane for the thinnest possible shaving, as shown in the photo on this page. If the first series of passes covering the entire surface hasn't smoothed the board sufficiently, take another series of passes over the entire surface.

You won't smooth boards with hand planes for very long before you run into boards with localized areas of erratic grain. If your plane is set for the finest cut possible and this local area still tears out, finish smoothing the rest of the board, then tackle the squirrelly area with a scraper.

Press down evenly on the plane throughout the stroke. This takes a bit of practice, especially at the beginning and end of each stroke. You want to develop a continuous and fluid motion, but to get there it helps to break it down into three segments, as shown in *Using a Hand Plane*. With a little practice you'll blend the three segments into a smooth, unbroken sweep of the plane.

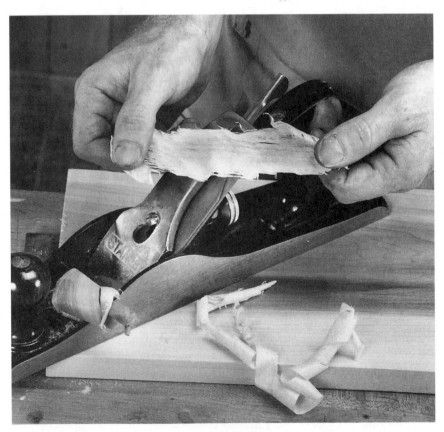

Razor-sharp cutting irons and finely tuned planes produce paper-thin shavings and the smoothest surfaces.

USING A HAND PLANE

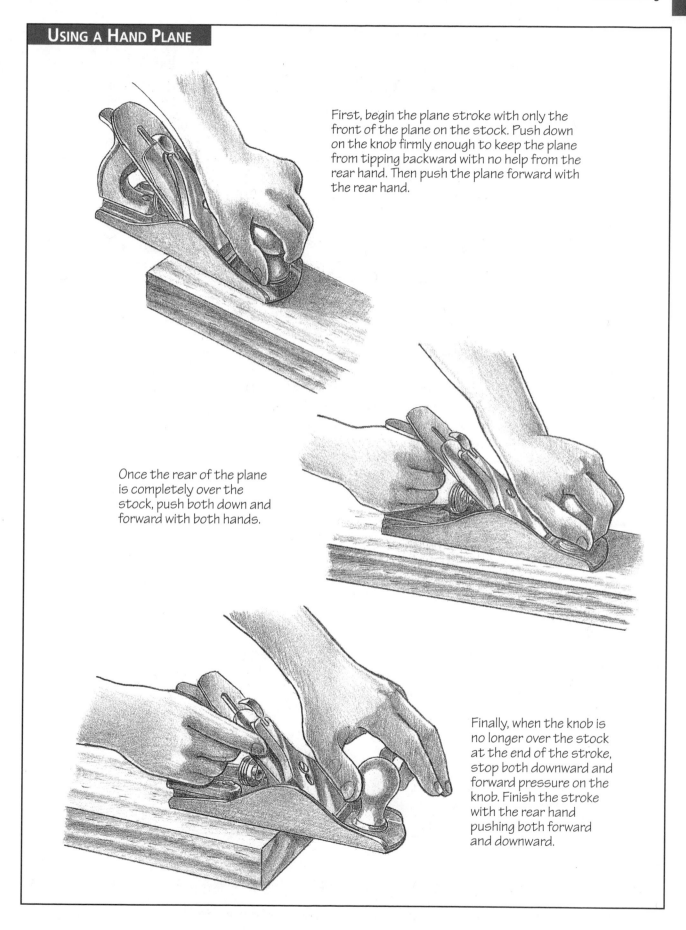

First, begin the plane stroke with only the front of the plane on the stock. Push down on the knob firmly enough to keep the plane from tipping backward with no help from the rear hand. Then push the plane forward with the rear hand.

Once the rear of the plane is completely over the stock, push both down and forward with both hands.

Finally, when the knob is no longer over the stock at the end of the stroke, stop both downward and forward pressure on the knob. Finish the stroke with the rear hand pushing both forward and downward.

TUNING A PLANE

Hand planes symbolize the craft of woodworking more than any other tool. Yet many of them sit on shelves, gathering dust produced by belt sanders. Plane owners become frustrated because their planes tear wood, dig in, and fail to produce a smooth surface. And these woodworkers don't realize that they only need to tune and sharpen the plane to overcome the problems.

If you want to get the best performance from your plane, the first thing to check is the flatness of the plane's sole. Adjust the depth of cut so the cutting iron doesn't project below the sole at all, then hold an accurate straightedge to the sole the same way you would check the flatness of lumber. (See "Sizing Up Your Stock" on page 63.)

If it's out-of-flat enough that you can get more than one thickness of paper between the straightedge and the sole, flatten the sole with abrasives the same way you would flatten a sharpening stone, as explained in "Crowned Bevels" on page 30. The entire sole doesn't need to be dead-flat, but the

four outside edges and the front edge of the mouth need to be coplanar. (Sorry about the five-dollar word, but I can't say the edges need to be in the same plane, can I?)

Adjusting a plane so that it works well is neither difficult nor time-consuming. Start by disassembling the plane, as shown below, then sharpen the cutting iron, as explained in the chapter "Sharpening Chisels and Plane Irons" on page 24. You may want to round the corners of the blade, as shown in *Rounding Corners*, so that the edges of each pass of the plane will blend into the surface of the stock.

The cap iron bends the shaving sharply, as shown in *Preventing Tear-Out*, taking the strength out of the shaving so it won't pry fibers out of the workpiece. But the cap iron must fit dead-flat against the cutting iron; otherwise, shavings will jam up in the gap. If you can jam a piece of paper between the cap iron and the cutting iron, hone the cap iron so that its leading edge contacts the blade,

---

EXPLODED VIEW OF A PLANE

DISASSEMBLY

First, lift the lever cap cam and remove the lever cap.

Then loosen the screw holding the cutter iron to the cap iron.

Finally, turn the cap iron 90° to the cutter iron, and slide the cap iron along the cutter iron so the screw head disengages from the cutter iron.

FROG ADJUSTMENT

First, loosen both frog screws ¼ turn.

Then turn the frog adjusting screw clockwise to close the mouth, or counterclockwise to open.

Finally, tighten both frog screws.

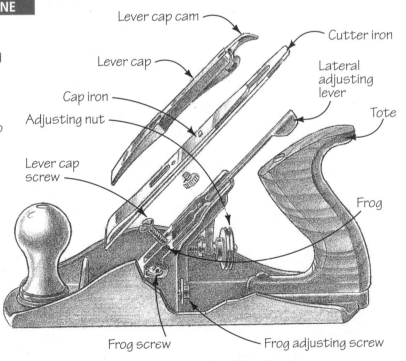

Lever cap cam

Cutter iron

Lever cap

Lateral adjusting lever

Cap iron

Adjusting nut

Tote

Lever cap screw

Frog

Frog screw

Frog adjusting screw

as shown in the drawing. The front edges of the cutting iron and cap iron must be parallel, so make sure both are square to their edges. Then set the distance between the cutting edge and the cap iron to 1/64 inch or less.

NOTE: *Here and elsewhere the distances given for tuning a plane are suggestions for where to start experimenting. Don't measure them; eyeball them.*

PREVENTING TEAR-OUT

Cap iron breaks shavings, so fibers aren't pried out.

Front of the mouth opening holds fibers down, so they tear out less.

Cap iron

Cutting iron

Thinner shavings bend more easily and tear out less.

The position of the frog determines the gap between the cutting iron and the mouth. Adjusting it is a matter of trial and error. The goal is to get the smallest gap that won't clog with shavings. The catch is that you have to adjust the frog with the plane irons removed, and then you can't see the size of the gap. The first time around, adjust the frog by trial and error to create a gap between the cutting iron and the front edge of the mouth roughly 1/64 inch wide.

With the cap iron and the frog at these trial settings, move the lateral adjusting lever so the cutting edge is parallel to the sole. Then turn the adjusting nut so the iron projects 1/100 inch or less below the sole. Quite frankly, this will be a wild guess unless you have pretty phenomenal eyesight. I focus on the "or less" and then try cutting, gradually increasing the setting until the plane starts to cut.

Different species of wood behave differently, so fine-tune the plane on the wood you use most frequently. Here are the guidelines to follow when fine-tuning:

• Always strive for the shallowest cut that will give you a fairly continuous shaving. This will produce the smoothest surface.

• After decreasing the depth of cut, take up slack in the mechanism by turning the nut in the opposite direction until you feel some resistance.

• If the plane doesn't cut, try planing a wide variety of places on the stock. A finely set plane will only cut the high spots of a board that isn't perfectly flat.

• If the mouth of the plane clogs with shavings, try reducing the depth of cut before readjusting the frog to create a larger gap at the mouth.

• If fibers jam in the corners of the mouth, round the corners of the cutting iron.

• If fibers tear out, set the cap iron closer to the edge of the cutting iron and reduce the depth of cut.

• If fibers still tear out and you can neither set the cap iron closer nor reduce the depth of cut, then adjust the frog to close the gap at the mouth further.

ROUNDING CORNERS

To minimize plane marks on stock, round corners of a cutting iron on a medium-grit sharpening stone, then polish its edge.

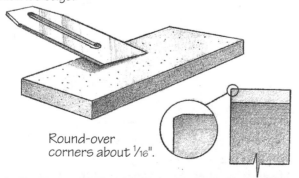

Round-over corners about 1/16".

SCRAPING

Rectangular hand scrapers (right) smooth flat surfaces. Curved scrapers (left) allow you to smooth coves and other moldings. Cabinet scrapers (top) are easier on your fingers on big jobs.

Scrapers have an aura of mystery about them. Many woodworkers don't even consider using them, assuming that only Black Forest elves have the necessary magic to make them work. This is unfortunate because mere mortals can use scrapers with fine results, producing very smooth surfaces quite quickly.

Some of the mystery that surrounds scrapers results from the cutting edge, the burr, being so tiny that you can't see it—you can only feel it. But that ultra-tiny cutting edge is the reason the scraper can smooth wild, squirrelly, contorted grain without tearing it out. The shavings from a scraper are so thin that you can scrape veneered work with little risk of scraping through to the underlying material.

There are two types of scrapers: hand scrapers and cabinet scrapers. Hand scrapers are just flat pieces of steel used freehand. Cabinet scrapers have a metal body, like a spokeshave or plane, and they hold a scraper blade at a nearly vertical angle.

Hand scrapers, shown in the photo on this page, have several advantages and several disadvantages. On the plus side, they're quite inexpensive, costing only a few dollars apiece, and you can use them right up to an obstruction, which allows you to smooth surfaces that meet at an inside corner. On the other side of the ledger, hand scrapers can be very fatiguing to the fingers because you have to flex the scraper to use it properly. Next, they can get so hot that they'll burn your fingers if you use them aggressively on a large surface. Finally, they require practice to use well.

Cabinet scrapers, on the other hand, are ideal for smoothing large surfaces. I use the old rosewood-handled cabinet scraper shown in the photo on page 108. It smoothed the tops of grand pianos for many years before I bought it. Cabinet scrapers don't permit the fine control that's possible with a hand scraper, but you can use them for hours and still have functioning fingers.

Hand Scrapers

The first secret of success with scrapers is the preparation of the tool, just as it is with hand planes. The hand plane requires careful sharpening of the cutting iron and positioning of the cap iron; the scraper requires careful turning of the burr. Having prepared a hand scraper as described in "Sharpening a Hand Scraper" on page 122, hold it in both hands with a sharp edge resting on the stock. Next, if you're scraping a flat surface with a rectangular scraper, bow the scraper slightly away from you. Then tilt it forward a few degrees, and push, as shown in the right photo on the opposite page. "Slightly" and "a few" are not very exact

SCRAPER BURR

A scraper works like an extremely finely set plane. The main part of the scraper breaks the shavings just like the cap iron on a plane, while the burr on the scraper cuts the wood just like the cutting iron on a plane.

Scraper blade

Burr

Shown highly magnified

You can also cut on the pull stroke by spreading your thumbs, bringing your fingers closer together, flexing and tilting toward you, and pulling, as shown in the left photo on this page. Some woodworkers prefer this method, but the consensus seems to be that pushing is easier. I find pushing *much* easier, but only pulling allows you to get right up to an inside corner.

You can hand scrape as big a surface as your thumbs will tolerate, but most woodworkers use hand scrapers primarily on localized areas, such as:

◗ Patches of difficult grain in surfaces being hand planed
◗ Areas around joints where glue was smeared
◗ Inside corners
◗ Where rails meet stiles, and similar flush joints
◗ Small projects, like jewelry boxes ●

descriptions. I use these fuzzy terms because how much you flex the blade and how far you tilt it depend on the actual angle of the burr, which you can't see; the hardness of your stock; and how deeply you want to cut. To increase the depth of cut, flex or tilt more. It's best to start a stroke with too little flex and tilt and then increase both until you get the cut you want—that avoids getting stopped abruptly by too deep a cut. End the stroke by decreasing both the flex and the tilt until the scraper stops cutting entirely.

NOTE: *Flexing a scraper prevents the corners from digging in or leaving a visible edge to the cut. When using a curved hand scraper, skip the flexing part of the procedure. There are no corners to dig in, and you can tilt to get the depth of cut you want.*

A hand scraper works just as well whether you pull it (left) or push it (right). Experiment to see which way your fingers work best.

Sharpening a Hand Scraper

Burnishing a burr on the edge of a scraper has as much mystery about it as scraping itself does; but here, too, a little explanation and a little practice should clear the mist. If you rub a hard oak dowel along the edge of a soft pine board, you'll distort and crush the sharp corner of the pine board. A burnisher is made out of harder steel than a scraper. By rubbing the burnisher along the edge of the scraper, you'll distort and mold the edge of the scraper. The burr will be too tiny to see; you have to rely on getting the technique right in order to get the burr right, and then try it out to "see" if you got it right.

Putting an edge on a scraper is a three-step process. First remove the old worn-out burr. Then shape the edge into a good starting point for burnishing. Finally, massage the steel into a useful cutting edge. The procedure is similar for hand scrapers and cabinet scrapers, but a few details do differ. See *Sharpening a Cabinet Scraper* on page 125 for the differences.

To remove the old burr, clamp it in a vise and file the edge with a mill or a flat smooth-cut file. Hold the file lengthwise to the edge to keep the edge straight, and use a simple wooden jig, as shown in Step 1, to keep the edge square to the face of the scraper.

You want the edge of the scraper to be as smooth as possible. But smoothing it can be a bit tricky because any rounding-over of the edge will seriously hurt your final burr. Just polishing the edge lengthwise on a sharpening stone will quickly wear a groove in the stone, and a groove is guaranteed to round-over the edges. Many woodworkers file with a bastard-cut file. They polish the edge by holding the scraper perpendicular to a fine sharpening stone and then rubbing sideways. I use a smooth-cut file, as mentioned above, and skip the polishing.

Filing and polishing may create some unwanted burr on the face of the scraper. Remove it by honing the face of the scraper *flat* on a fine sharpening stone. The scraper should now have a perfectly flat edge with crisp 90-degree corners—absolutely no secondary or microbevels or rounding-over. This is the starting point you want for massaging a burr onto the edge.

To produce the burr, hold the scraper flat on the edge of your bench with the edge of the scraper overhanging very slightly. Spread a thin film of oil on the scraper, and rub the length of the edge *hard* 20 or 30 times with the burnisher. Keep the burnisher very nearly flat on the face of the scraper, as shown in Step 3—raised no more than a couple of degrees to concentrate the force near the edge. The purpose of this operation is to consolidate the steel along the scraper edge and to begin creating a burr.

To turn the burr, hold the scraper vertically in the vise and apply oil to the edge. Burnish the edge by rubbing lengthwise *hard* 20 or 30 times. Start with the burnisher horizontal, flat on the square edge. Gradually tilt the burnisher so that by the end of your 20 or 30 strokes it is tilted about 15 degrees. When you're done, you should be able to feel a distinct, sharp burr on the face of the scraper.

Sharpen all four long edges (both faces along both sides) of rectangular scrapers. With curved scrapers, sharpen only the part with the curve you need. You can re-form the burr three or four times before filing and honing the edges again. An evening or two of experience will teach you far more than any book ever could.

STEP-BY-STEP
SHARPENING A HAND SCRAPER

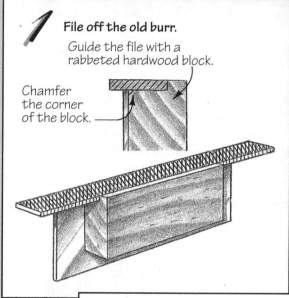

1 File off the old burr.

Guide the file with a rabbeted hardwood block.

Chamfer the corner of the block.

2 Hone the faces.

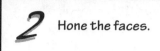

Edges (highly magnified) should be flat, smooth, and at right angles.

Fine sharpening stone

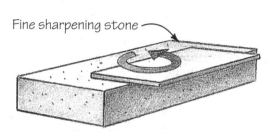

3 Burnish the faces, raising a burr.

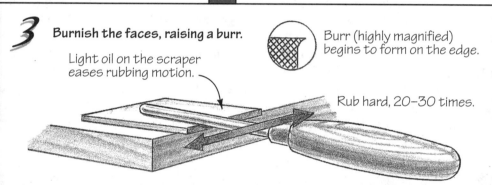

Light oil on the scraper eases rubbing motion.

Burr (highly magnified) begins to form on the edge.

Rub hard, 20–30 times.

4 Burnish the edge, turning the burr, creating a cutting edge.

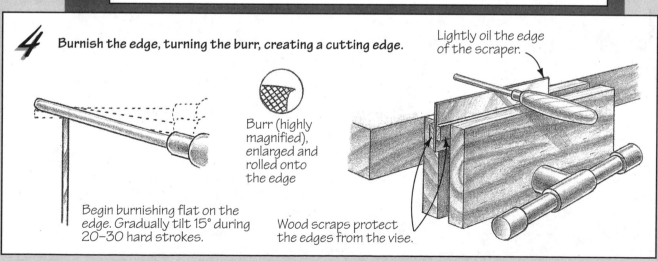

Lightly oil the edge of the scraper.

Burr (highly magnified), enlarged and rolled onto the edge

Begin burnishing flat on the edge. Gradually tilt 15° during 20–30 hard strokes.

Wood scraps protect the edges from the vise.

Cabinet Scrapers

If you think of a plane as a fancy gizmo to help guide and control a chisel, which is really all it is, then a cabinet scraper is no more or less than a fancy gizmo to help guide and control a hand scraper and to keep your fingers cool. The smaller type shown in the photo on page 120 holds the scraper and allows you to flex it with a thumbscrew but doesn't allow you to change the tilt of the blade. The bigger kind shown in the photo on page 108 allows you to adjust the tilt with a pair of knurled nuts but doesn't allow you to flex the blade. With both types, you make fine adjustments to the depth of cut by adjusting the flex or tilt as provided for.

To set up a cabinet scraper to cut, place it on a flat surface, like a piece of plate glass, and gently insert the blade so it touches the glass; that is, with zero protrusion below the sole of the scraper. Clamp the blade in the holder, then create some depth of cut by flexing the blade with the thumbscrew or tilting it with the pair of knurled nuts, depending on your type of cabinet scraper. With the tilting-blade type, start with the blade vertical and tilt forward to create cutting depth. Now start testing the cut and adjusting the depth to suit your needs.

This is the safe way to start because it guarantees that you can adjust the depth back to zero. Once you have experience, however, you may find situations when this method of setting the blade doesn't allow as much depth of cut as you want. In that case, start with more blade by placing one or two thicknesses of paper under the front of the scraper as a shim when you first install the blade.

Now practice and experiment. With the flexing-type scraper, experiment with slightly different burnishing angles when you sharpen. With the tilting-type scraper, experiment with slightly different initial blade installation angles so that the angle after creating some depth of cut is farther forward. Find out what works best for you with different hardnesses of wood, with straight and mellow grain, with gnarley grain, with whatever you customarily work with.

When tackling sizable surfaces, which is where cabinet scrapers do their best work, scrape the surface systematically so you don't miss some areas or over-scrape other areas. Work "with the grain" unless a little on-the-spot experimentation proves that some other angle works better in some localized area. And keep in mind that you're doing it for your own satisfaction. If you're having a hard time, put the scraper aside and try another day, because eventually all the little variables will fall into place, right there in your own hands.

COMPARISON OF SMOOTHING TECHNIQUES

	TOOLS NEEDED	EXPERIENCE NEEDED	VERSATILITY	BEST APPLICATION
SANDING	Belt and orbital sanders	Minimal	Works well with any wood	Polishing extremely hard woods; smoothing areas that tear out easily
HAND PLANING	Bench plane with adjustable mouth	Moderate	Best with soft to moderately hard woods	Smoothing wood with fairly consistent grain
SCRAPING	Hand scraper; optional cabinet scraper	Moderate	Limited to moderately hard woods	Smoothing difficult grain

SHARPENING A CABINET SCRAPER

Cabinet scrapers are a bit different from hand scrapers because the edge is beveled 45 degrees. But sharpening them is essentially the same—only a few details differ from the steps shown in *Step-by-Step Sharpening a Hand Scraper* on page 123.

Begin by filing the bevel with a file guide, as shown below. Polish the edge on a fine sharp-ening stone if you can do so without creating any secondary bevels or rounding-over; otherwise skip the polishing. An edge free of secondary bevels is more important than a polished edge.

Hone the face flat on a fine stone to remove any undesired burr from the filing. Then burnish the face as described for hand scrapers, but keep the burnisher *dead-flat* on the blade. Your sole objective here is to consolidate the steel—you are not producing a burr that you will then turn.

Finally, clamp the blade vertically in a vise with the bevel toward you and apply a bit of oil. Burnish the edge as you would a hand scraper, beginning with the burnisher flat on the edge—in this case at 45 degrees. Tilt the burnisher gradually as you burnish, stopping about 15 degrees *before* you reach horizontal, as shown in the drawing. If your cabinet scraper is the type that flexes the blade but doesn't allow you to adjust the angle, you will probably want to experiment with variations from the 15-degree burr suggested here, but 15 degrees is a good starting point.

45° FILE GUIDE

File the cabinet scraper blade using a 45° hardwood block as a guide.

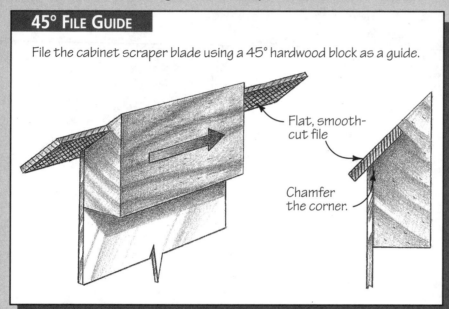

Flat, smooth-cut file

Chamfer the corner.

BURNISHING A CABINET SCRAPER

Begin with a burnisher flat on the blade's 45° bevel. Gradually tilt the handle upward 30° during 20–30 hard strokes, ending at 15° below horizontal on the last stroke.

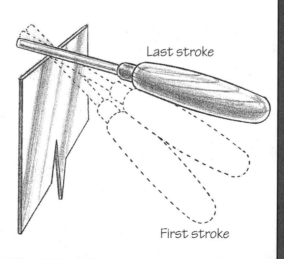

Last stroke

First stroke

Burr (highly magnified) on cabinet scraper

3

CUTTING
JOINTS

Joinery, the art and craft of making things by joining pieces of wood, is at the very heart of woodworking. In fact, many woodworkers think of woodworking and joinery as the same thing. While joinery isn't *all* there is to woodworking, it's certainly an enormous part.

The importance and usefulness of some particular joint doesn't depend on its complexity, however. Simple dadoes and rabbets are as essential to bookshelves and wall cabinets as the more complex mortise-and-tenon joint is to tables and chairs. In many cases you can choose between a fairly simple joint and a more involved, more robust one. For example, you can join

drawer parts with a simple, routed, interlocking drawer joint or with tough, traditional dovetails. Pick and choose to meet the requirements of your project and to match or even slightly exceed your skills and tools.

As you explore new joinery, keep in mind that it can be more than just structure—it can also be a part of design, a part of the aesthetics of the things you make. When you put a project together with visible, strong, hand-crafted joints that were first used thousands of years ago, your project will convey a comfortable feeling of security in a world where way too much is way too transient.

RABBETS, DADOES, AND GROOVES

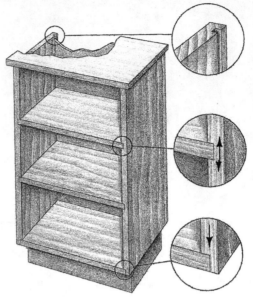

Groove: a trough with square sides and flat bottom cut in the direction of the grain. Used to join drawer bottoms and cabinet backs.

Dado: a groove cut across the grain. Used to join shelves to cabinet sides.

Rabbet: a groove with 2 sides cut along an edge. Often used to join corners.

Dadoes and grooves provide mechanical strength in 2 directions, useful for holding parts captive or preventing cupping.

Rabbets provide mechanical strength in 1 direction to help carry loads.

Rabbets, dadoes, and grooves are the bread and butter of cabinet joinery. Though they lack the decorative potential of joints like dovetails or wedged tenons, they're easy to cut with the table saw or router and they provide structural strength where other joints are inappropriate.

The mechanical strength of these joints is their major contribution; they seldom improve the gluing strength. For example, consider the dado joint commonly used where shelves join the side of a cabinet, as shown in *Strengths and Uses of Rabbets, Dadoes, and Grooves.* The dado provides excellent support to hold up the weight of the shelf and everything loaded on it. The dado also effectively prevents the shelf from cupping. However, the dado does nothing to prevent the shelf from pulling out. Only glue in the joint or mechanical fasteners provide that strength, and the glue strength is limited since all of the gluing surfaces involve end grain.

The rabbet joint shares the strengths and weaknesses of the dado joint, with a couple of exceptions. Properly oriented, it provides the weight-bearing mechanical strength of the dado but does little to prevent cupping. On the other hand, rabbet joints that are parallel to the grain, often used instead of grooves for joining cabinet backs, may glue quite well.

Grooves are most commonly used to hold a part captive while allowing it to expand and contract with changes in humidity. Typical applications include holding drawer bottoms, cabinet backs, and raised panels. Glue is not used at all in these situations.

Using Dado Cutters

A table saw equipped with a dado head has several advantages when cutting dadoes, rabbets, and grooves. It has the power to make most cuts in a single pass and at higher feed rates than routers. Setup is quick and familiar because the procedures are mostly identical to crosscutting and ripping. And with 20 to 40 teeth per blade, plus chippers, dado cutters run cooler and stay sharp longer than router bits. There are also disadvantages, of course. A good dado cutter for a table saw will carry a three-digit price tag; and if you don't get a good one, you have to expect a lot of tear-out along the edges of dadoes. (See "Circular-Saw Dado Cutters" on page 130.) Also, dado cutters are not very prac-

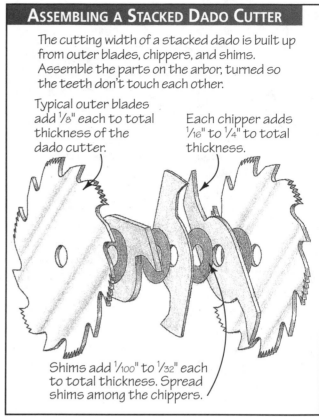

ASSEMBLING A STACKED DADO CUTTER

The cutting width of a stacked dado is built up from outer blades, chippers, and shims. Assemble the parts on the arbor, turned so the teeth don't touch each other.

Typical outer blades add ⅛" each to total thickness of the dado cutter.

Each chipper adds ¹⁄₁₆" to ¼" to total thickness.

Shims add ¹⁄₁₀₀" to ¹⁄₃₂" each to total thickness. Spread shims among the chippers.

The typical dado cutter consists of two outer blades very much like saw blades, separated by a stack of chippers. Using it is very much like ripping or crosscutting on the table saw.

tical for stopped dadoes because the stopped end is inevitably a lengthy curved ramp.

Think of sawed dadoes, rabbets, and grooves as very wide kerfs that only go partway through the stock. The critical steps in making them are adjusting the width of the dado cutter, adjusting the depth of cut, and—in some cases—adjusting the rip fence.

When using a dado cutter, you'll need to replace your saw's throat plate with one specifically made for dado cutters. Saw makers supply such inserts; but if you make your own, you can make it a "zero-clearance" insert by cutting the blade slot with the dado cutter. This will help reduce tear-out along the edges of your dadoes. I usually make a dozen insert blanks at a time and then cut slots in them as needed.

To cut rabbets with a dado cutter on the table saw, you'll need to make an auxiliary fence, as shown in *Making a Rabbeting Fence* on page 132. The fence covers part of the dado cutter, allowing you to expose just the width that you need. By making the cutout big enough for the fully raised dado cutter, you will allow room for chips and dust to move about and find their way down through the table insert. A 1-inch-thick fence reduces the chances that you'll inadvertently bump the cutter with the steel fence.

(continued on page 132)

CIRCULAR-SAW DADO CUTTERS

When choosing a dado cutter, you have two quite different types to choose from: wobble cutters and stacked sets. The final choice between them boils down to price versus clean cuts. Most wobble dado cutters have a single blade or cutter mounted between tapered plates, as shown in the bottom right photo on this page. The tapered plates tilt the blade so it's not perpendicular to the saw arbor. Turning the plates adjusts the amount of tilt and therefore the width of the swath that the spinning blade will cut. This approach makes wobble dado cutters comparatively economical and easy to adjust; but the geometry results in a dado with a rounded or sloped bottom, as shown at the top in the photo below, which makes a good glue bond virtually impossible. Wobble dado cutters also produce more tear-out at the surface of the stock than stacked sets do.

A stacked dado set, as shown in the top right photo, consists of a pair of matched blades that cut the edges of the dado plus chippers that

Stacked dado cutters create a wide kerf by sandwiching chippers between a pair of saw blades.

Wobble dado cutters hold a single blade at an angle to the saw arbor. The spinning, wobbly blade cuts a wide swath.

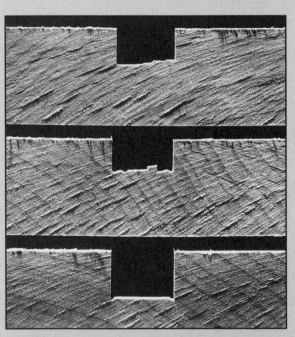

Wobble dado cutters leave a curved or sloped bottom (top). Some stacked dado cutters leave a rough or ridged bottom (center). Only a quality stacked dado cutter leaves a smooth, flat bottom (bottom).

remove the stock between the edges. The blades are typically ⅛ inch thick and have anywhere from 18 to 48 teeth. The chippers may have 2 to 6 teeth each and vary in thickness. Most dado sets include one ¼-inch chipper, two ⅛-inch chippers, and one 1/16-inch chipper. Various combinations of blades and chippers allow the set to cut dadoes from ¼ inch to 13/16 inch wide in 1/16-inch increments. This type of dado cutter, if well made with accurately ground teeth, cuts a dado with a flat, clean bottom and crisp edges with minimal tear-out. Fine adjustment of dado width by adding shims between the chippers can be tedious but is easy to reproduce if you note which chippers and shims are necessary to produce a specific, exact width. A good set of this type may seem expensive, but consider what you're buying: two high-quality carbide-tipped saw blades that match each other exactly, plus the chippers that space them apart. If the set only costs double what you'd pay for a comparable-quality saw blade, you're getting a bargain.

Cutting dadoes to match the thickness of plywood panels is a problem with many stacked dado sets because plywood is usually 1/32 inch thinner than its stated thickness. To produce accurate fits for plywood, some dado cutter makers include a 3/32-inch chipper in the set. This allows adjustments in 1/32-inch increments. A more versatile alternative is a set of brass or plastic shims. These begin at 0.010 inch and go up to 0.031 inch, which is the same as 1/32 inch. These sets of shims are fairly new on the market—we used to shim dado cutters with paper, playing cards, matchbook covers, and all sorts of other garbage. Don't even think of going back to those days of frustration—if the shim sets were made of gold, their convenience would still be worth their price.

You might expect outside blades with more teeth to cut more smoothly. I don't know why, but in actual practice the blades that produce the

---

Dado Cleanup Bits

Use a dado cleanup bit in your router to clean up rough-bottomed dadoes and rabbets like those produced with a wobble dado. These bits have a ball bearing that rides against the sides of the dado or rabbet while the end of the bit cleans up the bottom. Note that they work only in dadoes and rabbets that are at least 3/16 inch deep.

---

best cuts have about 24 teeth. The most difficult task for a dado cutter is cutting across the grain on oak plywood—it tends to splinter and tear out horribly. The blades that do best in this difficult situation have negative hook angles of 5 to 10 degrees. (See "Circular Saw Blades" on page 106.)

Stacked sets clearly cut cleaner dadoes than wobble cutters, but consider your needs before deciding which is better for you. If you want a dado cutter primarily for cutting grooves for drawer bottoms, a good wobble dado will do the job for less money. It will leave acceptably smooth edges cutting with the grain, and since drawer bottoms are not normally glued in place, the rounded bottom won't matter.

Eliminate Shims

If you thickness your own stock, you can forget about shimming a stacked dado. Just make sample dadoes in plywood cut with your dado cutter but no shims. Then mark, right on the sample, the size and number of chippers used to cut each dado. When preparing stock for parts that will be housed by dadoes, thickness the stock to fit a sample dado. When you're ready to cut the dadoes, simply assemble the chippers marked on the sample.

ADJUSTING THE TABLE SAW FOR A DADO OR GROOVE

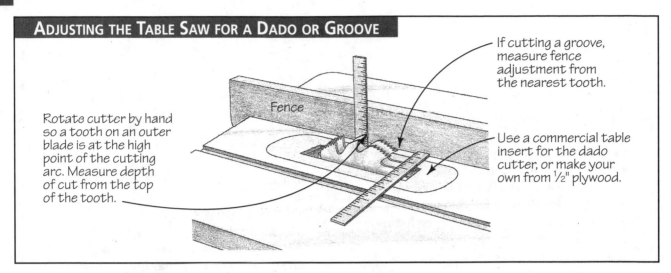

If cutting a groove, measure fence adjustment from the nearest tooth.

Rotate cutter by hand so a tooth on an outer blade is at the high point of the cutting arc. Measure depth of cut from the top of the tooth.

Fence

Use a commercial table insert for the dado cutter, or make your own from ½" plywood.

MAKING A RABBETING FENCE

First, trace a fully raised dado cutter onto the side of a 1"-thick auxiliary fence.

Next, saw out an arc slightly larger than the tracing of the cutter.

Finally, install the fence, and adjust to cover the unneeded part of the dado cutter.

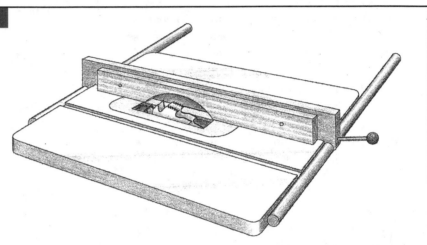

The biggest single problem that you're likely to encounter when using a dado cutter on the table saw is cutting dadoes across long stock, like the sides of a tall bookcase. The problem, moving a long board sideways smoothly, is identical to the problem of crosscutting on the table saw, as discussed thoroughly in "Crosscutting on the Table Saw" on page 93. Cutting the dadoes on a radial arm saw might seem like an attractive alternative, but be forewarned that this is one of the most problematic cuts you can make on a radial arm saw. The radial arm saw's tendencies to overfeed, flex under load, and produce an inconsistent depth of cut are aggravated when the saw is equipped with a dado cutter instead of a standard saw blade. (These three tendencies are discussed in "Table Saws, Radial Arm Saws, and Chop Saws" on page 94.)

The tendency to overfeed is a danger because the saw moves unexpectedly. The overfeeding, in turn, causes more flexing and forces the table out of adjustment, changing the depth of cut. If you do try

fitting a dado cutter to a radial arm saw, use only a stack-type cutter that has cut-limiting shoulders following each tooth. While some woodworkers insist, correctly, that the climb-cut rotation of the radial arm saw gives a cut with minimal tear-out, I'd rather save my fingers by using a router.

> **TECH TIP**   **EVENLY SPACED DADOES** are ideal for locating and holding dividers in storage cabinets for audiocassettes or compact discs, but these cabinets require a lot of dadoes. To cut multiple evenly spaced dadoes, adapt the techniques for cutting box joints described in the chapter "Corner Joints" on page 172 and make a jig similar to the "Box Joint Jig" on page 277. If you think of the box joint as a series of parallel dadoes cut into the end of a board, adapting the procedures to cutting a series of parallel dadoes into the face of the board will be easy.

ROUTING RABBETS, DADOES, AND GROOVES

Routing rabbets, dadoes, and grooves has several advantages over using dado cutters. A significant one for many woodworkers is the much lower price tag for clean, splinter-free cuts: You can buy ten clean-cutting router bits for the cost of a top-of-the-line dado cutter. A second big advantage is the router's versatility. Use it hand-held on project parts too big to handle on a stationary machine, or mount it in a router table for small parts or large numbers of medium-sized parts. If your project requires stopped dadoes, rabbets, or grooves, you'll find it much easier to square up the end of a routed cut than a cut made on the table saw. You can even design your projects to eliminate the need to square up the ends of routed dadoes. For example, if you design shelves with rounded-over front edges, they will fit into routed dadoes without any squaring up at all, as shown in *Routed Dado*.

But these advantages come at a price: Router bits don't stay sharp as long as a table-saw dado cutter, they won't cut deeply in a single pass, and they usually require far more time to set up.

Hand-Held Cuts

When routing across long stock or near the middle of wide stock, it's far easier to move the router across the work than to move the work over a saw table or router table. To do that, however, you have to clamp a fence or straightedge to the stock to guide the router. That guiding edge has to be positioned accurately, usually either perpendicular or parallel to an edge of the stock.

Upon reaching that point in a project, a neophyte usually lays out the two sides of the dado or groove, then measures the distance between the edge of the router base and the edge of the bit, and finally lays out the position of the necessary straightedge guide. After a few mistakes from arithmetic or measuring errors, the neophyte will probably figure out the better way shown in *Positioning a Straightedge*. The gauge blocks are a good example of a useful standard reference, as described in "Standard References" on page 8.

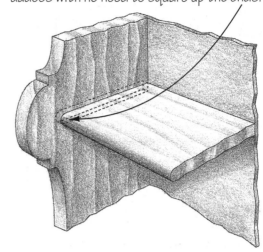

ROUTED DADO

Shelves with rounded front edges fit routed dadoes with no need to square up the ends.

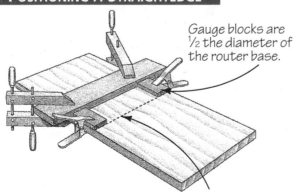

POSITIONING A STRAIGHTEDGE

Gauge blocks are ½ the diameter of the router base.

1. Lay out the centerline of the dado.
2. Clamp gauge blocks alongside the layout line.

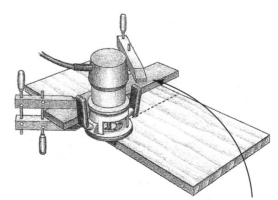

3. Clamp a straightedge alongside the gauge blocks.
4. Remove gauge blocks and rout the dado.

If you rout a lot of dadoes (or if you enjoy making jigs and fixtures as much as you do competing with Ethan Allen for display space in the living room), you'll be interested in two aids that simplify positioning a straightedge. One is a router T-square, and the other is a flip fence.

The router T-square is an industrial-strength version of the traditional drafting T-square, as shown in *Router T-Square*. It allows you to lay out the centerline of the cut on just one edge of the stock instead of two, and to align the straightedge perpendicular to the stock edge without the need to line up two marks at once. When using this jig, clamp *both* ends of the T-square to the stock before routing the dado—otherwise it's sure to move during the cut.

The router guide shown in *Flip Fence* is handy for longer dadoes and in situations where dadoes or grooves are not perpendicular to the stock edge. It is really no more than a straightedge with a long, built-in gauge block. The hinged leaf, like a gauge block, is exactly half the width of your router base. By aligning the hinged leaf with the centerline of the dado, the edge of the fixed leaf is in the right position to guide the router. The fixed leaf is twice as wide so that the clamps that hold it won't interfere with the hinged leaf when you flip it over.

If you need to rout a dado slightly wider than the bit diameter, just put a shim between the guiding straightedge and the router and take a second pass. The shim can be as thin as a piece of masking tape on the edge of the router base or as thick as a strip of wood laid alongside the straightedge.

When routing rabbets and grooves near the edge of the stock, the best guide is an edge guide like

ROUTER T-SQUARE

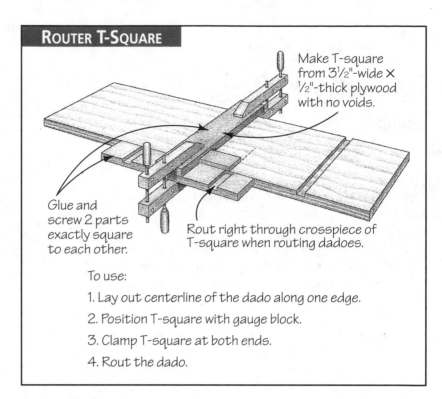

Make T-square from 3½"-wide × ½"-thick plywood with no voids.

Glue and screw 2 parts exactly square to each other.

Rout right through crosspiece of T-square when routing dadoes.

To use:

1. Lay out centerline of the dado along one edge.

2. Position T-square with gauge block.

3. Clamp T-square at both ends.

4. Rout the dado.

FLIP FENCE

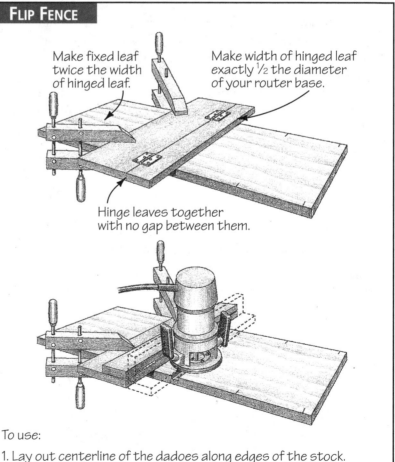

Make fixed leaf twice the width of hinged leaf.

Make width of hinged leaf exactly ½ the diameter of your router base.

Hinge leaves together with no gap between them.

To use:

1. Lay out centerline of the dadoes along edges of the stock.

2. Align hinged leaf with layout marks and clamp fixed leaf to stock.

3. Swing hinged leaf over and rout the dado.

the ones that come with routers. The edge guide eliminates all the marking and clamping associated with the straightedge, replacing it with a fairly simple adjustment of the edge guide. How simple that adjustment is depends on how well the guide was designed and manufactured, of course. Not all edge guides are created equal, and some are quite a nuisance to adjust.

All of the edge guides that I've used—good, bad, and indifferent—benefited from a longer, shop-made, wooden auxiliary fence. A fence 18 inches long helps you control the router at the beginning and end of the cut when only half of the fence is in contact with the stock.

If you have a good router with a poor edge guide, make a replacement edge guide, as shown in *Shop-Made Edge Guide*. The drawing is intentionally vague about the length of the guide. A great big long guide is a cumbersome nuisance but allows you to rout a groove farther from the edge. If you don't cut grooves far from the edge, or if you have a good dado cutter for your table saw for cutting them, keep the edge guide conveniently small. Even if the router is your only means of cutting grooves, I suggest that you keep the length of the edge guide down to 18 inches or so, with a fence 18 inches long. This will allow you to rout grooves a foot or more from the edge of the stock; and if you need one farther away than that, you'll get better control over the router by clamping a straightedge to the stock.

When using an edge guide, always feed the router counterclockwise around the stock—in this direction the cutting action of the bit tends to pull the edge guide tightly against the edge of the stock instead of pushing it away.

Bearing-guided router bits, as shown in the photo on this page, are a popular alternative to the edge guide for routing rabbets. These bits cut a rabbet with a specific width, determined by the diameter of the cutter and the diameter of the bearing. Some have interchangeable bearings, allowing a single cutter to rout rabbets of several widths.

I might as well concede that I don't like bearing-guided bits. Perhaps the cheapskate in me resists plunking out green money for a bit that does only one job, but I do have other objections:

▶ Those teeny-weeny bearings follow any ding or bump in the edge of the stock, reproducing the imperfection in the rabbet.

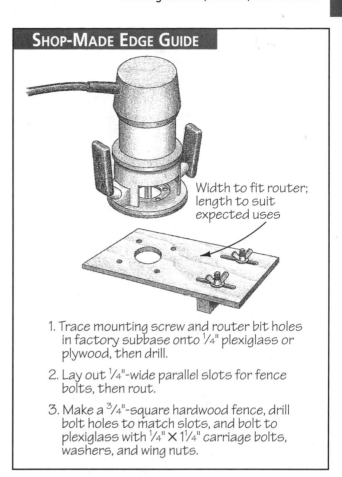

SHOP-MADE EDGE GUIDE

Width to fit router; length to suit expected uses

1. Trace mounting screw and router bit holes in factory subbase onto 1/4" plexiglass or plywood, then drill.

2. Lay out 1/4"-wide parallel slots for fence bolts, then rout.

3. Make a 3/4"-square hardwood fence, drill bolt holes to match slots, and bolt to plexiglass with 1/4" × 1 1/4" carriage bolts, washers, and wing nuts.

A rabbeting bit with interchangeable bearings can cut rabbets of several widths. The bearing follows the edge of the workpiece—including any irregularities in the edge.

▶ Those teeny-weeny bearings ride up and over stray wood chips instead of pushing them out of the way like an edge guide.

▶ Those teeny-weeny bearings burn out, freeze up, spin with the bit, and burn the edge of the stock. ●

But in spite of my dislike of them, bearing-guided bits are great for rabbeting curved edges.

Router Table Cuts

Hand-held router cuts require that you immobilize the stock, usually by clamping it to a workbench. Then if the cut requires a straightedge, you have to lay out the center-line of the cut and clamp a straightedge on each and every piece of stock. If the parts that you're working on are modest in size, you can save yourself a lot of this hassle by mounting the router in a router table instead of hand-holding it. This gives you the economy and clean cutting characteristics of the router with the convenience usually associated with table-saw work. To use this technique, choose a bit the width of the cut you want to make, set the bit height, set the fence, and make as many cuts as you need without any further adjustments.

TECH TIP   **ROUT TWO SIDES IN HALF THE TIME:** When dadoing the sides of casework, like bookshelves, rout both sides at the same time. Put the two sides together, front edge to front edge, and align the ends. Then lay out the dadoes, clamp on a straightedge, and rout as though the sides were one piece. This saves you half of the layout and clamping time, and it also eliminates tear-out on the front edges because the two pieces will support each other. If the dadoes must be blind, stopping before they reach the front edge, then routing the two sides together will provide a place to clamp a stop block so you won't overshoot the end of the dadoes. If you're working in sheet materials, like plywood, you can carry this technique a step further: Rout the dadoes into a double-width piece of stock and then cut it in half to make the two sides.

ROUTER TABLE DADOES

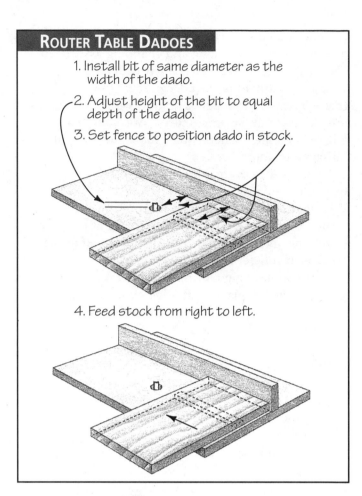

1. Install bit of same diameter as the width of the dado.
2. Adjust height of the bit to equal depth of the dado.
3. Set fence to position dado in stock.
4. Feed stock from right to left.

BLIND DADOES

For blind dadoes, clamp a stop block to the router table fence.

This distance = length of dado.

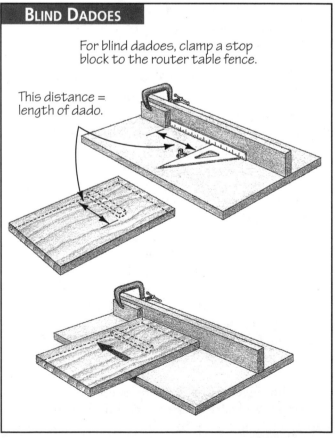

VARIATIONS ON THE DADO JOINT

Lap joints, whether crossing, forming an angle, or forming a tee, are made by cutting wide dadoes (or rabbets) across the two pieces that will join. The challenge in cutting lap joints is getting the depth of cut just right. If the depth of cut is not exactly half the thickness of the stock, the joint will miss being flush by twice the amount of error. The best way to check the depth of cut is to make test cuts into *both* faces of a piece of scrap exactly the thickness of the project parts, as shown in *Depth-of-Cut Test for Half-Laps* on page 138.

A combination rabbet-and-dado joint is another variation on the basic joint. At a corner where you might normally use just a

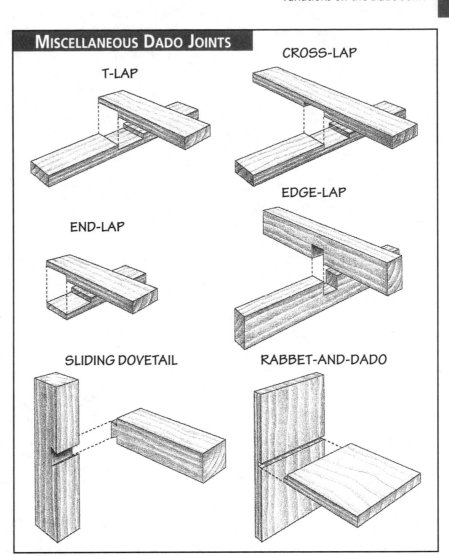

MISCELLANEOUS DADO JOINTS

T-LAP

CROSS-LAP

END-LAP

EDGE-LAP

SLIDING DOVETAIL

RABBET-AND-DADO

DADO, RABBET, AND GROOVE CUTTERS

	STACKED DADO CUTTERS	WOBBLE DADO CUTTERS	ROUTER
DADOES IN LONG STOCK	Impractical	Impractical	Very practical
DADOES IN SHORT STOCK	Ideal	Rough cuts	Best in router table
GROOVES AND RABBETS	Ideal	Quite good	Quite good
COST	$100 and up	$50 +/–	$10 and up per bit
QUALITY OF CUT	Poor to very good; varies with quality of cutter	Very poor to good; varies with quality of cutter— "good" only for grooves	Very good
EFFICIENCY FOR MULTIPLE CUTS	Very efficient	Very efficient if further cleanup not required	Poor when hand-held; efficient in router table

DEPTH-OF-CUT TEST FOR HALF-LAPS

Rout a test piece from both sides.

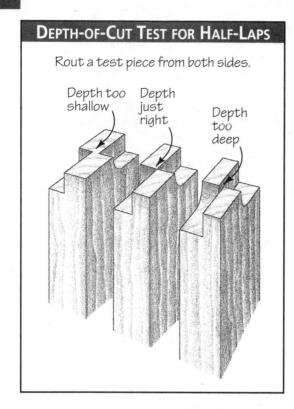

Depth too shallow

Depth just right

Depth too deep

COMBINATION RABBET-AND-DADO JOINTS

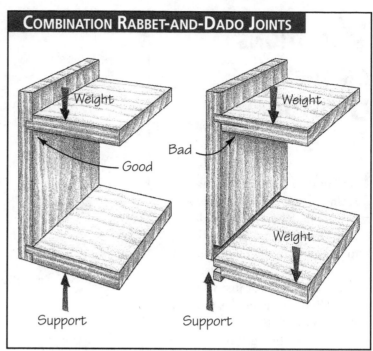

Weight

Weight

Good

Bad

Weight

Support

Support

rabbet, the combination helps align the parts during assembly. But don't expect the combination to give you increased joint strength in this situation, because the outer edge of the dado piece is prone to splitting off. You might also use the combination to join the end of a shelf to a cabinet side. If you rout dadoes, you may find it easier to rabbet the end of a shelf so it fits a given dado than to widen the dado to fit a shelf of unusual thickness. Note that the shelf will carry more weight if the rabbet is in the top surface than if it's in the bottom surface, as shown in *Combination Rabbet-and-Dado Joints.* Whether using the combination to replace a simple rabbet or a simple dado, cut the dado first, and then rabbet the second piece to fit.

The sliding dovetail joint is sometimes found where you would normally expect to see a simple dado joint, such as joining a drawer rail to an end table's leg. It provides mechanical strength where the simple dado joint is weakest, resisting with-drawal. In the case of the drawer rail, this is impor-tant because sliding the end table along the floor tends to pull the rail out of the leg.

To make the joint, begin by laying out the "dado" half of the joint on the leg. Since the dove-tail "dado" is wider at the bottom than at the top, you can't rout it in multiple passes of increasing depth. You *can,* however, rough it out with a straight bit and then enlarge it into the proper

TECH TIP   **SAWING RABBETS: If you're getting by with an inexpensive dado cutter that produces less than perfect cuts, you may find that you get better rabbets by making two cuts with a regular saw blade. Two passes with a saw blade—one with the stock flat on the table and the other with the stock on edge, as shown here—will take less time than cleaning up the ragged rabbets made with inexpensive dado cutters.**

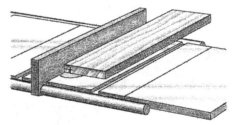

Make first cut with stock flat on the table; rabbet against the fence.

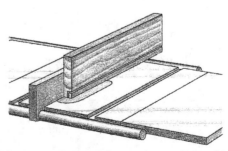

Make second cut with stock on edge; rabbet away from the fence so waste can fall free.

STEP-BY-STEP
CUTTING A SLIDING DOVETAIL

1 Lay out and cut dovetail "dado" as you would any other dado, but use a dovetail bit with cutting diameter equal to the thickness of joining piece.

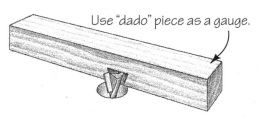

2 Chuck a bit in a table-mounted router, and adjust the height to exact depth of "dado."

Use "dado" piece as a gauge.

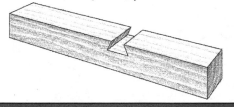

3 Adjust the fence so most of the bit is housed, exposing only about 1/16" for the first test.

Router table fence

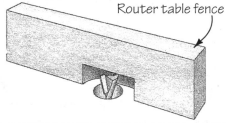

4 Cut both sides of the "tail" in a test piece the same thickness as the project part. Use a square push block to guide the stock.

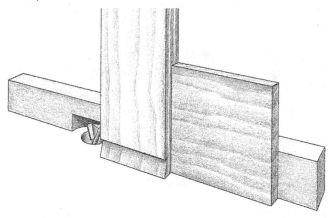

5 Adjust the fence and retest until the fit in "dado" is just snug. Then cut the project parts.

dovetail shape with the dovetail bit. Unless you have an unusually powerful router, I suggest that you follow this two-step procedure. Other than this use of two bits for two passes, rout the "dado" as you would any other, as explained above.

The "tail" is best cut on the router table. Adjusting the router table fence to cut a snug-fitting "tail" is pure trial and error—mostly error if you don't adjust the fence in small increments. Keep in mind that any adjustment to the fence changes the dimension of the tail by twice the amount because you're cutting both sides. Like other dovetails, arrange your work schedule so you can assemble the joints before changes in humidity can change the fit.

TECH TIP   **AVOID LONG SLIDING DOVETAILS. Before you go designing a library full of bookshelves using long sliding dovetails to join the shelves to the uprights, you should know that cutting a sliding dovetail that fits well requires very careful workmanship. Assembling a well-fitted sliding dovetail a foot long can be challenging because the further the joint comes together the more friction there is to prevent the joint from coming together any more. And trying to assemble the foot-long well-fitted joint when it's covered with a tacky glue will turn a grown man into a whimpering, forlorn child.**

EDGE JOINTS

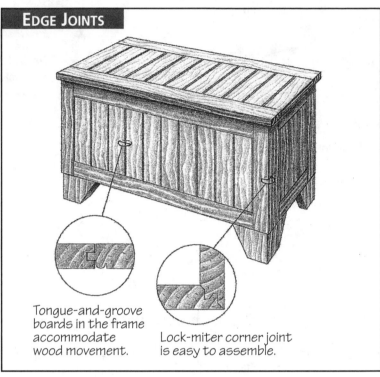

Tongue-and-groove boards in the frame accommodate wood movement.

Lock-miter corner joint is easy to assemble.

Trees are tall and slender, so boards are long and narrow. Assembling them to make short, wide furniture and cabinetry requires edge joints, like those shown in *Edge Joints*. Glued edge joints, like the corner joint shown, are very strong because the long grain found in both surfaces of the joint glues well and because dimensional changes caused by changes in humidity seldom stress the joints unduly. Joints that interlock but are not glued, like the tongue-and-groove joint shown, allow the wood to move with changes in humidity, without affecting the overall width of the assembly. Edge joints are not sophisticated joinery like mortises and tenons, or dovetails, or raised panels, but they're an essential part of even the most sophisticated projects.

There are three common types of edge joints:

1. Flat, butted and glued joints make wide boards out of narrow ones. They have a chapter of their own, "Gluing Up Wide Boards" on page 82.

2. Flat, interlocking edge joints, like the tongue-and-groove and shiplap, join narrow boards without glue when you're covering wide areas such as cabinet backs.

3. Corner edge joints, including butt joints and miter joints, form the vertical corners of cabinets and columns.

Working on the long edges of narrow stock to make these joints is most convenient on the table saw, router table, or jointer. A hand-held router is awkward with stock less than 6 or 8 inches wide, because there's no place to clamp a straightedge. If you prefer hand tools, use a plow plane to cut grooves and a bench rabbet plane, a combination plane, or a multiplane to cut tongues and rabbets.

FLAT EDGE JOINTS

Interlocking edge joints create broad, flush surfaces—like the backs on furniture, paneled walls, wainscoting, and floors—out of fairly narrow pieces of wood. Since each joint can accommodate the little bit of movement expected of a narrow board, there will be no significant change in the overall width of the assembly when the humidity changes. Also, a bead or chamfer along the edge can disguise the movement.

The interlocking edges of tongue-and-groove joints keep the surfaces flush and prevent gaps when the wood shrinks. The shiplap joint's overlapping edges prevent visible gaps but don't keep the surfaces flush. This difference makes the tongue-and-groove joint clearly superior; but the shiplap joint is adequate if the wood is stable and the design allows you to fasten the parts at frequent intervals, as you can when attaching a back to every single shelf of a bookcase or hutch. The advantage of the shiplap joint is that you can cut it with limited tools. A table saw and dado cutter will do the job, or even just a rip blade, or a router and just one straight bit, or a bench rabbet plane.

Tongue-and-Groove Joints

Tongue-and-groove joints are usually proportioned so that the thickness of the tongue is about one-third the thickness of the stock. This makes the tongue and the two sides of the groove all about the same strength. If you're making wall paneling or wainscoting using stock of ¾-inch finished thickness, this suggests tongues about ¼ inch thick and grooves to match. For the back of the top half of a hutch, however, ¾-inch-thick stock is pretty heavy

FLAT EDGE JOINTS

TONGUE-AND-GROOVE JOINTS

Simple tongue-and-groove joint

V-groove

Bead the tongue edge, not the groove edge.

Bead

Tongue ⅓ of stock's thickness is typical.

From back, nail here.

From front, nail here.

Rabbets are ½ of stock thickness.

SHIPLAP JOINTS

Bead only the rabbeted edge of the face.

From front, nail here.

From back, nail here.

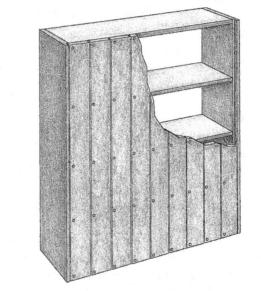

Nail tongue-and-groove boards every 18" to 36". Nail shiplap boards every 8" to 12".

construction—my preference here is for stock about ½ inch thick. For these furniture backs, I make the tongues ³⁄₁₆ inch thick.

The length of the tongues (and depth of the grooves) is less important than the thickness. If the boards are less than 3 inches wide, and therefore unlikely to expand and contract very much, I make the tongues as long as they are thick and the

TECH TIP **EASE TONGUE ASSEMBLY:**
If you don't use router or
shaper cutters that round the leading
edges of the tongues, ease the edges with
a sanding block. This minimizes the risk of
a splinter from a broken edge lodging in
the bottom of a groove, preventing the
tongue from seating properly.

grooves to match. If the boards are wider, I may make the tongues as long as half the stock thickness. For ¾-inch-thick stock, this means tongue length (groove depth) in the range of ¼ to ⅜ inch. For the ½-inch-thick stock I use for furniture, the range will be from 3/16 to ¼ inch.

There are several ways to make a tongue-and-groove joint. The most versatile, but by no means the fastest, is to make the groove half of the joint with a dado cutter in the table saw, as explained in "Using Dado Cutters" on page 129, and then make a matching tongue by cutting a pair of rabbets, also with a dado cutter, as explained in that same section. If your stock is unusually thin, or unusually thick, this technique may be your only choice because special tongue-and-groove cutters for the router or molding head are available in only a few sizes.

By far the fastest way to cut tongues and grooves is with a shaper, but the shaper's kid brother, the router table, also does a respectable job. With either setup, you can use the special tongue-and-groove cutters mentioned above. These cutters have subtle nuances in their shape, including a very slight taper to the tongues and grooves and very lightly rounded edges. The tapers make it easier to fit the pieces together, and the rounding prevents splinters from breaking off the edges and preventing the joint from coming together tightly. Unfortunately, these cutters are available in only one size, suitable for ¾-inch-thick stock.

To cut tongues and grooves for thinner stock on the router table, use an arbor and slotting cutters. These two- or three-wing cutters are available in a wide range of sizes in increments of 1/32 inch. You can stack two of them on an arbor with spacers between to cut tongues in a single pass. This is virtually identical to the standard shaper technique of stacking cutters on the shaft.

The poor man's tongue-and-groove cutter, remembered with some nostalgia but little fondness by those of us old enough to antedate the router, is a molding head cutter on a table saw. I don't mean to disparage the molding head—it's a grossly under-appreciated accessory for the table saw—but using it to cut tongues and grooves requires feeding all of the stock on edge. While this is certainly practical, and no more difficult than cutting a groove in an edge with a dado cutter, it requires more attention to keep the stock tight against the fence than to keep it flat on a table as in router table work.

Hand tool enthusiasts can cut the joint with just plow and rabbet planes, but combination planes and multiplanes come with special tonguing cutters that make cutting tongues a one-step instead of two-step operation. These cutters lack the tapered and rounded refinements of specialized shaper cutters, or router bits, or molding head cutters; but they do come in two sizes, 3/16- and ¼-inch-wide. The narrow one is ideal for ½-inch stock on furniture.

Chamfering and Beading Edge Joints

The bead or V-groove commonly seen on the face of a tongue-and-groove joint is camouflage. It's there to disguise an opening that varies in width due to the seasonal expansion and shrinkage of the boards. Choosing between the bead and the double chamfer that makes up the V-groove is a practical as well as aesthetic consideration. If you're cutting the tongues and grooves with a shaper or router table, you can buy cutters that make the chamfers in the same operation. These cutters are possible because you can cut a chamfer from the edge of the stock, just as you cut a tongue or groove. This is an obvious money saver in a commercial shop, and it may appeal to the home-shop woodworker undertaking a big project like a kitchen full of cabinets or wainscoting for several rooms. Since you can cut a bead only from the face of the stock, it's impossible to make a cutter that cuts both a bead and the two sides of a tongue. Cutting a bead has to be a separate operation.

If you choose not to use these special cutters, however, the bead has a practical advantage. The V-groove requires two separate chamfers, one on the tongue edge and one on the groove edge, while the bead requires only a single pass along the tongue edge.

From an aesthetic point of view, I suppose the V-groove fits better with designs that are primarily composed of flat surfaces and may use chamfers on other corners. From my prejudiced point of view, however, choosing between the bead and the

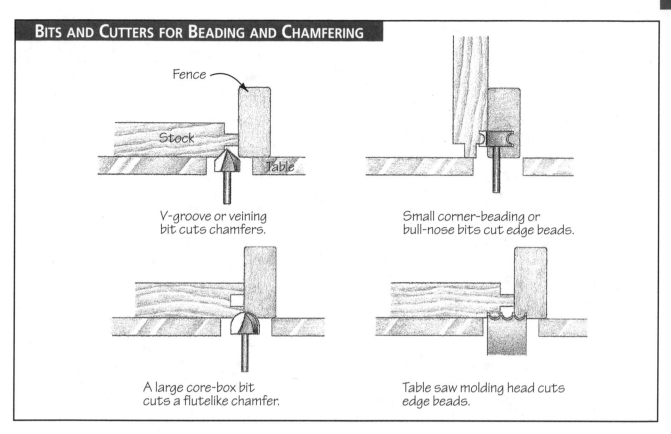

BITS AND CUTTERS FOR BEADING AND CHAMFERING

Fence

Stock

Table

V-groove or veining
bit cuts chamfers.

Small corner-beading or
bull-nose bits cut edge beads.

A large core-box bit
cuts a flutelike chamfer.

Table saw molding head cuts
edge beads.

V-groove is a simple matter of the bead being attractive and the V-groove being ugly.

Use a V-groove bit or large veining bit for chamfering because the tongue will get in the way of a regular chamfering bit. Use a corner-beading router bit, a molding-head beading cutter for your table saw, or a half-round concave shaper cutter to cut beads. I prefer the molding head because the stock runs through flat on the saw table.

Assembling Tongue-and-Groove Stock

Plan for the expansion and shrinkage of the wood when assembling tongue-and-groove joints. If you own a moisture meter and you're a compulsive tester, then you probably know how dry wood gets in your part of the country during the driest season of the year and how high the moisture content gets during the most humid time of the year. You can then measure the moisture content of your project stock and know whether it's likely to expand, shrink, or do a little of each after going into service. The rest of us will have to make a sophisticated guess. If it's near the end of the driest time of year, say late January in northern climes, assume the stock will only expand. If it's near the end of the most humid time of year, say late August, assume the stock will only shrink.

If the stock will only shrink in service, assemble the joints tight. If the stock will only expand, leave a gap at each joint of about the thickness of a dime (0.05 inch). If you think the stock may do a little of both, expanding and shrinking, then leave a gap of about $1/32$ inch—that's the thickness of the wire in a #1 paper clip. These are all

TECH TIP   SAVE STOCK WITH SPLINES:
You can save a modest amount of expensive wood by cutting a groove in both edges of your stock and inserting a spline to join the two parts. This joint makes more efficient use of your wood, since none of it is hidden as a tongue. You can use plywood or even Masonite for splines. Keep in mind, however, that for camouflage you'll be limited to either a V-groove or a very tiny bead, since a larger bead will weaken the face side of the groove too much.

TONGUE-AND-GROOVE PANELS

You can frame tongue-and-groove stock the same way you would frame a raised panel, as explained in the chapter "Frame-and-Panel Construction" on page 226. The result is a door or cabinet side with the overall dimensional stability that characterizes framed panels but with a somewhat more homey, less sophisticated appearance, appropriate in many kitchens and family rooms.

The frame is exactly the same as a frame for a raised panel. The assembled tongue-and-groove boards must have tongues on all four sides. This means that all the boards must have tongues on both ends, one must have a tongue on both sides, and the rest must have a tongue on one side and a groove on the other side. The tricky part is calculating the overall width of each piece so the width of all the flat faces is the same.

First, decide on the length and width of the opening in the frame and the number of tongue-and-groove boards you want to use. Next, decide how much total allowance to make for expansion and contraction; ¼ inch is reasonable for most cab-inet doors. Subtract this allowance from the width of the frame opening, and call the result the "assembled face width." Then measure the width of a bead plus a quirk and call it the "bead width."

Notice that if you have five boards, you will have six beads because one board must have two tongues and therefore two beads. Multiply the "bead width" by the number of beads, and subtract this amount from the "assembled face width." This gives you the combined width of all the flat faces. Divide this combined width by the number of boards to get the width of each flat face. The overall width of the board with two tongues must be the flat face width plus twice the "bead width" plus twice the tongue width. The overall width of the boards with a tongue and a groove must be the flat face width plus one "bead width" plus one tongue width.

The length of the tongue-and-groove boards will be the length of the frame opening plus two tongues—no allowance is necessary for expansion because this is the direction of the grain.

ANATOMY OF FRAMED BOARDS

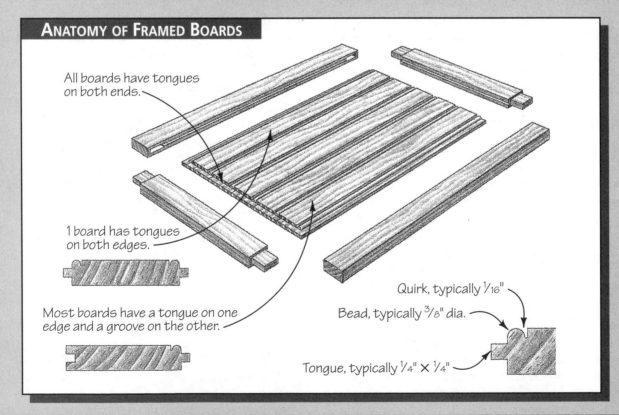

All boards have tongues on both ends.

1 board has tongues on both edges.

Most boards have a tongue on one edge and a groove on the other.

Quirk, typically ¹⁄₁₆"

Bead, typically ³⁄₈" dia.

Tongue, typically ¼" × ¼"

guesstimates, of course, and they assume that your boards are only 3 or 4 inches wide. If your stock is wider, increase the gaps proportionally.

When assembling an interlocking joint, nail the stock along one edge only, allowing the other edge to move. If you're nailing from the front surface, such as nailing up wainscoting, place the nails in the corner between the tongue and the adjacent shoulder, as shown in *Flat Edge Joints* on page 141. Then set them below the surface with a nail set. When nailing from the back side, such as installing the back on a hutch, you can face nail along either edge but be careful that you don't nail into the groove.

Shiplap Joint

The shiplap joint (which is *not* a boat builder's joint) is an easy-to-make substitute for the tongue-and-groove joint. It's easy to make because the joint consists of two simple rabbets that you cut with the same machine setup, usually a table saw and dado cutter. You can also rout the joint, preferably on the router table, but it will take longer than the dado cutter because you'll have to feed the stock more slowly and may have to make several passes.

When preparing stock for shiplapping, make sure all of the boards are exactly the same thickness so they'll come out flush when installed. (Since the easy way to cut the rabbets references both surfaces, *neither* side will be flush if the stock varies.) Adjust the dado cutter height to half the stock thickness and check the setup, as shown in *Depth-of-Cut Test for Half-Laps* on page 138. Chamfer or bead the showing face and allow room for expansion, as explained in "Tongue-and-Groove Joints" on page 141. Be sure to drive the fasteners on the overlapping side of the joint, as shown in *Flat Edge Joints* on page 141, and keep them back from the edge so they don't catch the underlying piece.

CORNER EDGE JOINTS

CORNER EDGE JOINTS

Butt-joined random boards often produce distracting appearances.

Careful selection of boards for butt-joining avoids the distraction.

A rabbet-and-chamfer joint can disguise the edge surface, but this takes more time to make.

Miter joints avoid the edge surface but require more time and care to cut and assemble.

The vertical corners of cabinets and furniture present a problem in combining strength, ease of assembly, and clean, good-looking appearances. Since both pieces coming together present long grain, the joint will glue well if adequately clamped. But the easiest arrangement to clamp, the simple butt joint, will look good only if the grain of the stock is very carefully selected, as shown in *Corner Edge Joints*. In some cases a rabbet joint chamfered on the outside works well, but to clamp it effectively and easily it's best to cut the chamfer after the joint is assembled. That can be quite awkward, as explained below. In the greatest number of cases, the miter joint *looks* best; but clamping a simple, noninterlocking miter joint so it lines up properly is horrendously difficult. To make assembly easier, you can make a splined miter or lock-miter joint; but this increases the time spent cutting the parts. Biscuits will also make clamping up a miter joint easier. Choosing among the alternatives requires that you balance appearance, time spent selecting stock, time spent cutting the joint, and ease of assembly.

Butted Corner Joints

The easiest corner joint to cut is a simple butted corner joint. All you need is well-prepared stock with straight, flat, smooth surfaces. The parts require no further preparation, and they will glue up into a very strong assembly. The joint's shortcomings are its appearance and the difficulty of keeping it aligned during assembly.

The appearance of the joint suffers when the grain of the exposed edge of the overlapping piece contrasts with the grain on the face of the adjoining piece, as shown in *Corner Edge Joints* on page 145. However, by carefully selecting stock with growth rings that intersect the face at roughly 45 degrees, you can usually create a joint with very little contrast—in some cases the joint will be virtually invisible. These will not be pieces with strikingly beautiful grain patterns, but their more staid appearance is usually more appropriate at a corner anyway. The cost to you of this fix is the time it takes to select the stock and to check how it will appear.

Keeping a butted corner joint aligned during assembly is not an insurmountable problem. The best solution depends on your temperament and the depth of your pockets. If you're careful, unflappable, easy-going, and working wood for pleasure rather than for your livelihood, then the solution is simply a matter of taking the time to realign the parts after you've applied clamping pressure and they've inevitably squished out of place. If you prefer direct, preventive intervention, treat yourself to a biscuit joiner and use a biscuit every 8 inches to maintain alignment. Some woodworkers go to the bother of cutting grooves for a full-length spline within the joint. This, to me, is serious overkill for a butted joint: It uses up a significant amount of good gluing surface to solve a problem that has easier solutions.

Rabbeted Corner Joints

One occasionally useful corner joint combines a rabbet with a chamfer. If the available stock requires that you use fairly flat grain on the two parts of the joint, use a chamfer, as shown in *Corner Edge Joints* on page 145, to separate the two flat-grain faces with a narrow, angled strip of edge grain. This can be quite attractive, provided it's appropriate for the rest of the design.

The rabbet helps you keep the parts aligned during assembly because you can clamp the joint in

A biscuit joiner is the handiest tool for preventing a butted corner joint from squishing out of alignment.

both directions. Since the chamfer is at an angle to both faces, it won't look inappropriate even though its grain pattern is different. Naturally, resolving these two problems presents a third: You will get the most even clamping pressure on the joint if you cut the chamfer *after* assembly, particularly with wide chamfers, but then the stock will be much less convenient to handle. If the project is big, you'll have to chamfer with portable tools or hand tools.

> **NOTE:** *Stopped chamfers usually look much better than full-length chamfers, but you can't rout a stopped chamfer—the radius of the ramp at the end of the chamfer would differ at the two edges of the chamfer, as shown in* Rabbet-and-Chamfer Corner Joints.

Cut the rabbet, as explained in the chapter "Rabbets, Dadoes, and Grooves" on page 128. Keep in mind that the depth of the rabbet determines the width of the chamfer, as you can see from *Rabbet-and-Chamfer Corner Joints*. The sole function of the rabbet is to aid alignment during assembly: If you want a wide chamfer, you can make the rabbet as shallow as ⅛ inch.

RABBET-AND-CHAMFER CORNER JOINTS

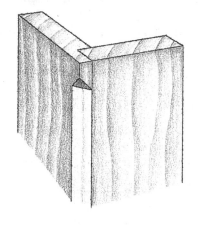

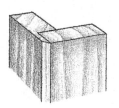

Deep rabbets require narrow chamfers. You can clamp this combination after chamfering.

Stopped chamfers usually look better than unstopped chamfers; but a stopped, routed chamfer needs hand finishing.

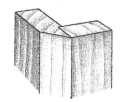

Shallow rabbets require wide chamfers. You must chamfer this combination after assembly.

Mitered Corner Joints

A miter joint presents only two wood surfaces to view, avoiding the visible edge that creates aesthetic problems with butt joints. It also has more gluing surface than butt joints: 1.4 times the gluing surface, to be exact. But its advantages end there. To cut and assemble a mitered corner, you have to choose between very difficult assembly and more-involved shaping of the joint.

Assembling a **simple mitered edge joint** with no alignment aids is enormously difficult because the only way to apply clamps applies pressure at 45 degrees to the joint, inevitably sliding it out of alignment. In fact, you risk exceeding the allowable open time of the glue as you fiddle around with the clamps and try to tame the slipping and sliding halves of the joint. If you're stubborn, patient, and determined to prove me wrong, then try it. Otherwise, plan on using a spline, biscuits, or interlocking shapes to keep the joint aligned as you apply clamping pressure.

A **splined miter joint** begins with accurate 45-degree bevels on the stock. Don't trust the scales on your saw when you set this critical angle. Use a drafting triangle to check the tilt of the blade. Adjust the tilt with the blade as high as it will go,

then lock the tilt. Double-check the adjustment by making test cuts in two pieces of scrap. If they form a square corner when you bring their bevels together, your setup is right.

If your saw blade tilts to the right, don't attempt to rip the bevels with the fence to the right of the blade; this will trap the stock, risking kickback. Protect yourself by setting up the fence to the left of the blade.

There is no practical way to adjust the rip fence by direct measurement from the tilted blade. Instead, lay out the bevel cut on the end of the stock, align the layout with the blade, and bring the fence alongside the stock. I find it easier to perform this ritual with the stock on the outfeed side of the blade, as shown in Step 2 in *Step-by-Step Sawing an Edge Miter* on page 148, but suit yourself.

After cutting the bevels on all of the stock, lay out the spline groove on the end of a piece. Keep it fairly close to the inside of the joint—1/8 to 3/16 inch is appropriate for 3/4-inch-thick stock—in order to avoid weakening the tip of the bevel. Then install a dado cutter on the saw and adjust the fence. Once again, set up the fence so the blade tilts away from it to avoid trapping the stock. This will require

STEP-BY-STEP
SAWING AN EDGE MITER

1 Adjust blade tilt to 45° with the aid of a drafting triangle.

2 Lay out a cut on the end of the stock, align with the blade, then lock the fence along the stock edge. (Tilt of blade makes direct measurement impractical.)

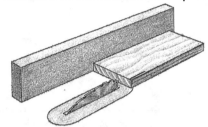

3 Hold stock tightly against the table while making the cut.

Blade tilts away from the fence.

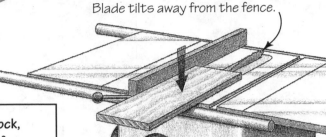

NOTE: Some saws tilt left, allowing miter cutting in the more familiar ripping position to the left of the fence.

STEP-BY-STEP
SAWING SPLINE GROOVES IN MITERS

1 Lay out a groove on the end of the mitered stock.

Poor: Groove weakens stock here.

Good: Strength is preserved here.

¼" × ¼" groove is typical for ¾" stock.

2 Install dado cutter, typically with 2 outer blades of cutter only for ¾" stock.

4 Cut the groove.

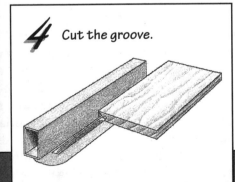

3 Align layout with the dado cutter, then lock the fence along mitered edge of the stock.

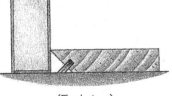

(End view)

STEP-BY-STEP
ASSEMBLING SPLINED MITERS

1 Prepare splines to fit snugly in grooves; test fit of the joint without glue.

2 Stick cauls to edges of the stock with hot-melt glue or double-sided tape.

3 Apply glue to all mating surfaces and assemble.

4 Clamp lightly in both directions, then increase pressure evenly on all clamps.

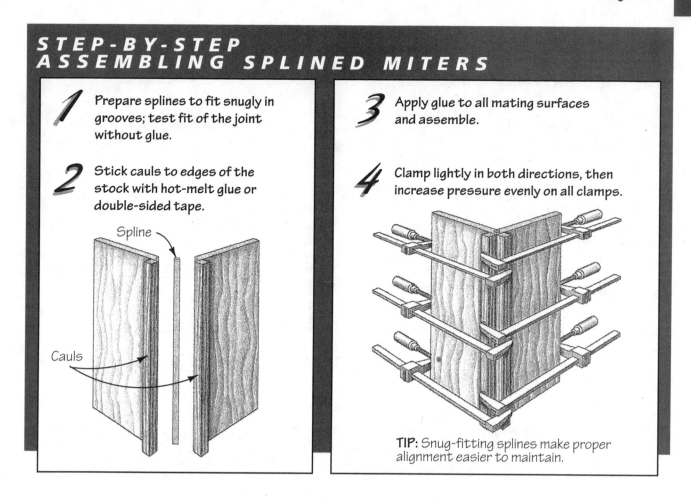

Spline

Cauls

TIP: Snug-fitting splines make proper alignment easier to maintain.

feeding the stock with the sharp edge of the bevel against the fence, so be careful that you don't bang up the edge as you cut the groove.

Plane a board to a thickness equal to twice the groove depth (or just a hair less), and then rip splines from its edge. They should fit snugly in your grooves—the better they fit, the better they will keep the parts aligned as you bring clamping pressure to bear during assembly.

Biscuits in a miter joint function like a spline: They prevent the beveled edges from slipping sideways as you apply clamping pressure. How well they function depends on how snugly the biscuits fit and how closely you space them. Since you don't make the biscuits yourself, you have no control over their fit; but you can improve the job they do by spacing them closely, say every 3 or 4 inches. If you're making just a few miter joints, you'll find the biscuit joiner faster than setting up a dado cutter for splines.

A lock-miter joint begins to show real advantages over the alternatives when the number of joints that you have to make climbs above a half-dozen or a dozen. The advantages include single-pass cutting of both halves of the joint, a single setup of one router bit or shaper cutter for both halves, self-alignment at assembly time, and clamping in only one direction. All of these benefits come from interlocking tongues and grooves, as shown in *Edge Joints* on page 140. If this sounds a bit too good to be true, let me hasten to add that setting up the cutter is time-consuming and you need substantial power to run the bit or cutter. The available bits are designed for 3/4-inch-thick stock; don't try to push them more than 1/8 inch over or under that size.

Setting up a lock-miter router bit or shaper cutter is a teaser because the part of the bit from which you really ought to measure is so difficult to measure from—that is the midpoint of the edge shared by the tongue and the groove, as shown in the first drawing in Step 1 on page 150. You want to set the cutter so that this midpoint is above the table by half the thickness of the stock or slightly less. Setting the fence is a bit easier because you can ignore the midpoint and measure from the

COMPARISON OF CORNER JOINTS

	BUTT JOINT	BUTT JOINT WITH BISCUITS
APPEARANCE	Requires careful stock selection for acceptable appearance	Requires careful stock selection for acceptable appearance
EASE OF CONSTRUCTION	No prep needed beyond straight, square edges	Quick and easy to make, but requires biscuit joiner
EASE OF ALIGNMENT DURING CLAMPING	Tricky; parts tend to slip; requires clamps in only 1 direction	Excellent if biscuits fit snugly; requires clamps in only 1 direction
BEST APPLICATION	For 1 or 2 joints when appearance is not critical	Use it if you have the machine.

STEP-BY-STEP CUTTING LOCK-MITER JOINTS

1. Adjust the setup.

First, adjust the bit height.

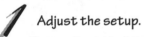

½ stock thickness

Next, adjust fence so this distance = this distance.

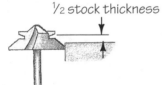

Then lower the bit and move the fence closer no more than 1/32" to produce a tiny flat on the tip.

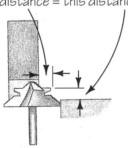

2. Cut one half of joint against fence.

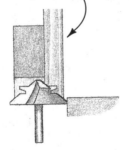

3. Cut second half flat on the table.

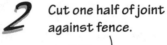
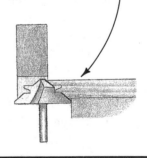

4. Glue 2 halves of the joint together. They require clamping in only 1 direction.

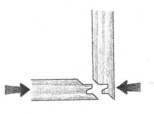

5. Chamfer the corner or plane the faces to remove inverted corner at the tip.

Rabbet-and-Chamfer Joint	Splined Miter	Miter with Biscuits	Lock-Miter
Requires some care in selecting stock	Requires no care beyond choosing face grain	Requires no care beyond choosing face grain	Requires no care beyond choosing face grain
Requires rabbeting 1 part of joint	Requires 2 saw setups, 4 passes per joint, plus making spline	Requires beveling edges, then use of biscuit joiner	Requires tedious setup, then 1 pass per piece
Excellent but requires clamps in 2 directions	Good if spline fits well; requires clamps in 2 directions	Satisfactory if biscuits fit well; requires clamps in 2 directions	Excellent; requires clamps in only 1 direction
For multiple joints when appearance is not critical	For when appearance is important but your tools are limited	If you have the machine, use it instead of a spline.	Best for large numbers of joints

corner shown in the second drawing in Step 1. When you have these adjustments set, make a test cut with the stock flat on the table. Your test will reveal one of three scenarios:

1. If your adjustments were perfect, the setup will produce a sharp edge at the tip of the miter that will just graze the outfeed side of the fence.
2. If the two equal distances of Step 1 are slightly too great, the sharp edge of the miter won't touch the outfeed fence.
3. If the two distances are on the low side, the edge of the miter will be blunt.

Most woodworkers strive for scenario #1. That's fine as long as you get it *exactly* right and then treat the parts with great delicacy to avoid damaging the sharp edge. Scenario #2 has nothing to recommend it, producing an irregular cut similar to snipe on a thickness planer. I tweak the

setup to produce scenario #3, striving for a blunt "flat" that's no more than 1/32 inch wide, preferably less. This gives me a margin of safety in avoiding snipe and produces "sharp" edges that are more resistant to damage. After assembling the joint, I either chamfer the corner just enough to remove the inverted corner that the two flats produce, or scrape or plane the faces of the two parts to eliminate the inverted corner.

Tweaking the setup is time-consuming because you can't readjust *just* the height or *just* the fence; every time you change one, you have to change the other an equal amount. But once you've got it on the money, locked firmly in place, and test pieces fed along both the table and the fence produce identical results, you can feed square-edged stock through it all day long, producing perfect miters that self-align during assembly and require clamping in only one direction.

Mortise-and-Tenon Joints

MORTISE-AND-TENON TERMS

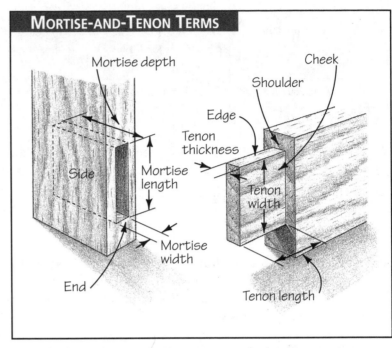

Mortise depth

Cheek

Shoulder

Edge

Tenon thickness

Side

Mortise length

Tenon width

Mortise width

End

Tenon length

Well-made mortise-and-tenon joints are the musclemen of woodworking. They have excellent mechanical strength, very good glue strength, and high resistance to racking, the most severe stress on most joints. They're my first choice for joining table legs to table aprons, door stiles to door rails, chair rungs to chair legs, and face frame corners. But the mortise-and-tenon will stand up to heavy use only if it's well made. The tenon must have square shoulders and broad cheeks and must fit into the mortise snugly.

The right fit is essential to getting the best glue strength from a mortise-and-tenon joint. Most glues require clamping pressure for a good bond, but you can't clamp the sides of a mortise to the cheeks of a tenon. If you make the joint tight enough to apply gluing pressure, most of the glue will be scraped off when you the push the two parts together. And since most common woodworking glues have fairly high tack, a tight-fitting joint is liable to get stuck before it's fully assembled. Tight enough for a really good bond is too tight for assembly, and loose enough to assemble easily is too loose for a good glue bond.

The best solution to this dilemma is usually compromise: cut the joint so that it takes firm hand pressure to assemble it, but not so tight that clamps or mallet blows are necessary. If that seems like a pretty fine distinction, requiring precise cutting of the parts, it is. As you go through this chapter, weighing the pros and cons of the various ways to cut mortises and tenons, keep this need for precision in mind.

Compromise isn't the only way to deal with the dilemma. You can cut a tight joint, ignoring the fact that most of the glue will be scraped off, and then pin or wedge the tenon in the mortise to maximize the mechanical strength, as explained in "Mechanical Refinements" on page 166.

Another alternative is to build a slightly loose-fitting joint and glue it with a gap-filling adhesive like an epoxy. (See "Intentional Misfits" on page 38.) This maximizes the glue strength of the joint. Woodworking epoxies have excellent strength, have very low tack, require no clamping for a good bond, and don't shrink as they cure. Even if you don't routinely glue mortise-and-tenon joints with an epoxy, keep it in mind as a no-compromise way to salvage a joint that you cut too loose.

Strong and Easy Mortise-and-Tenon Joints

Two variations on the traditional mortise-and-tenon joint combine strength and ease in cutting. One is the open mortise-and-tenon joint, also known as a bridle joint. The other is the separate-tenon joint.

The bridle joint is favored by woodworkers who are more comfortable cutting tenons than mortises. It lacks the mechanical strength of the traditional mortise-and-tenon joint, but it glues exceptionally well; the open mortise flexes enough to allow good clamping pressure. Cutting the open mortise is just like cutting the cheeks of a tenon on the table saw. If your saw has adequate power, you can cut the mortise in a single pass with a sharp dado head or grooving cutter.

The separate-tenon joint is favored by woodworkers who are comfortable and efficient at routing mortises. It is my favorite by a wide margin. It uses two mortises instead of one, and a separate tenon piece that is easy to mass-produce.

NOTE: *This joint has a variety of names. Some call it a "loose" tenon, but that term has been more appropriately used for mortise-and-tenon joints that can be disassembled. Others call it a "floating" tenon for reasons that escape me. The term "false" tenon has been used and makes a little bit of sense, but I prefer to call it a separate-tenon joint because the tenon is a separate piece of wood.*

To make the joint, rout both of the mortises, then saw out tenon stock on the table saw and round the edges on the router table. Make the tenon stock in long pieces, and cut tenons to length as needed. This joint can save a lot of expensive cabinet wood in a big project because parts that would otherwise have to include a tenon can now be shorter. Cut the tenons themselves from a less expensive wood.

If this joint strikes you as being a hybrid descended from both mortise-and-tenon joints and dowel joints, then you've got the idea. Like any good hybrid, it combines the best features of both parents and none of their bad features. The separate-tenon joint has the simplicity and ease of the dowel joint combined with the superior glue strength of the mortise-and-tenon joint.

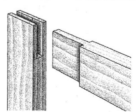

The open mortise-and-tenon or "bridle" joint provides excellent glue strength in an easy-to-make table saw joint.

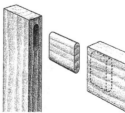

The separate-tenon joint provides totally concealed joinery, good strength, and easy construction for those comfortable with routing mortises.

The width of a mortise, by tradition, is no more than one-third the thickness of the stock. When all mortises were chopped out with chisels, this "rule" ensured that the surrounding stock was strong enough to resist splitting. A well-fitted and glued mortise-and-tenon joint will be stronger, however, if the tenon is one-half the thickness of the stock. With today's machining techniques, you can rout or drill a wide mortise with far less risk of splitting. I routinely rout ⅜-inch-wide mortises in ¾-inch stock and ¼-inch-wide mortises in ½-inch stock. Well-fitted and glued, these joints are quite robust.

A final point before we get into specific techniques: Always cut mortises first, then cut the tenons to fit. The reason is simple: The easiest way to make precise mortises is to make them exactly the width of the tool, whether it's a router bit, a drill bit, or a chisel. Then, once you've established the width of the mortise, you can fine-tune the thickness of the tenon to match it. And if you prefer to cut the parts too tight and then trim them to the right fit, you'll find it easier to shave a tenon to fit a mortise than to shave a mortise to fit a tenon. I've grouped the techniques that follow in this same order: mortises first, then tenons.

ROUTING MORTISES

With all due respect and encouragement to those who prefer nineteenth-century hand-tool methods, the modern router cuts a more precise mortise, in less time, with less effort,

MORTISE-ROUTING SETUP

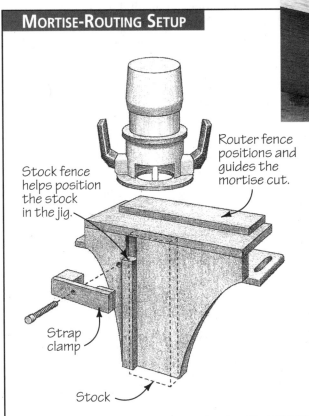

Stock fence helps position the stock in the jig.

Router fence positions and guides the mortise cut.

Strap clamp

Stock

The best bits for plunge-routing mortises are spiral upcut bits. They plunge extremely well, shear the wood efficiently when fed sideways, and clear the waste from even a deep mortise. Machinist's end-mills are identical to woodworker's spiral upcut bits and are often available from machinist's supply firms in a wide range of sizes.

and with less practice. Routing is also less stressful to the stock. You can rout a mortise with thin sides and close to the end of the workpiece, where other techniques might split the stock. The only price you pay for this list of advantages is having to deal with round-ended mortises. A hand-held plunge router is the most versatile tool for routing mortises, but a conventional router in a table has advantages in some situations, as described in "Mortising on a Router Table" on page 156.

STEP-BY-STEP
PLUNGE-ROUTER MORTISING

1 **Lay out centerline and ends of the mortise.**

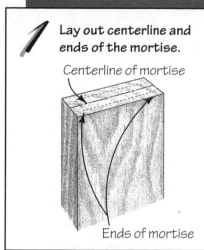

Centerline of mortise

Ends of mortise

2 **Clamp stock to the mortising jig.**

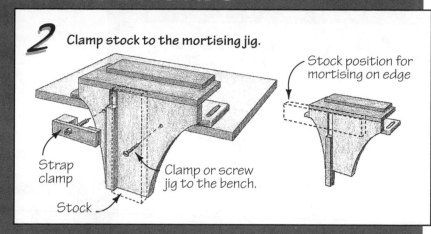

Stock position for mortising on edge

Strap clamp

Clamp or screw jig to the bench.

Stock

3 **Adjust router fence to center the router bit on the layout.**

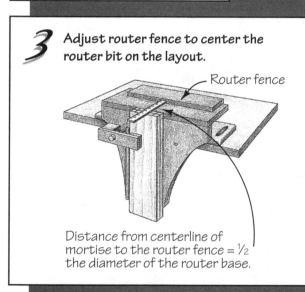

Router fence

Distance from centerline of mortise to the router fence = $\frac{1}{2}$ the diameter of the router base.

4 **Limit length of the mortise with stop blocks.**

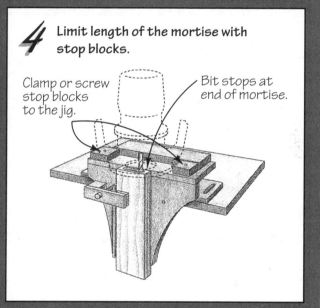

Clamp or screw stop blocks to the jig.

Bit stops at end of mortise.

5 **Rout mortise in several passes.**

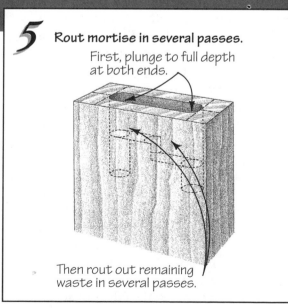

First, plunge to full depth at both ends.

Then rout out remaining waste in several passes.

Plunge-Routing

All you need to plunge-rout mortises, besides a plunge router and a suitable bit, as shown in the photo on the opposite page, is a jig to hold the workpiece and guide the router. Such a jig can be stone simple or quite elaborate. An example of a fairly simple variety is shown in *Mortise-Routing Setup*. Instructions for building the jig are in the "Combination Mortise and Tenon Jig" chapter on page 240. This same jig doubles as a table saw tenoning jig, as explained in "Cutting Tenons with a Tenoning Jig" on page 161. The steps involved in plunge-routing a mortise are shown above using this particular jig but are essentially the same for most shop-built jigs.

STEP-BY-STEP ROUTER-TABLE MORTISING

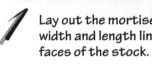

1 Lay out the mortise, then extend width and length lines to adjoining faces of the stock.

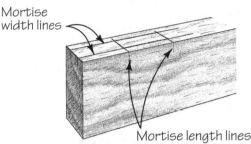

Mortise width lines

Mortise length lines

2 Draw 4 bit-location extension lines on router table.

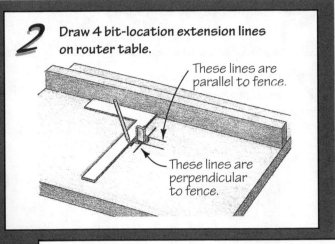

These lines are parallel to fence.

These lines are perpendicular to fence.

3 Adjust router fence to position the stock for the mortise cut.

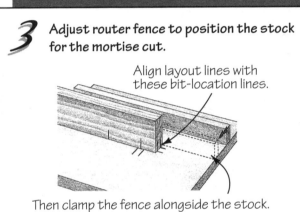

Align layout lines with these bit-location lines.

Then clamp the fence alongside the stock.

4 Limit travel of the stock with stop blocks.

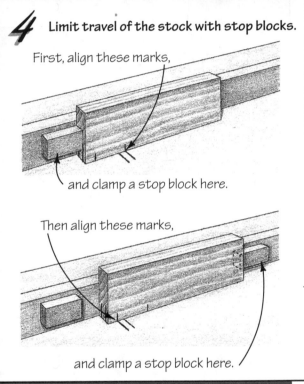

First, align these marks,

and clamp a stop block here.

Then align these marks,

and clamp a stop block here.

5 Raise the bit and cut the mortise.

Hold the stock firmly and lower it onto running bit; then feed back and forth to cut the mortise.

Finally, lift off the stock the same way you lowered it.

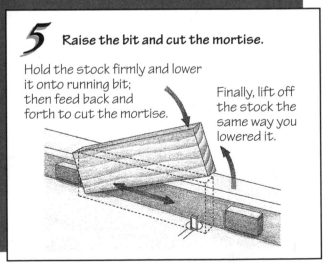

Mortising on a Router Table

Mortises cut on a router table have the same precise and consistent width and smooth sides as plunge-routed mortises. In addition, if you are cutting a series of identical mortises in identical parts, the router table procedure may be more convenient—you don't have to align and clamp each part in a jig. On the other hand, adjusting the depth of cut on a table-mounted router is usually a nuisance, making it much *less* convenient if the depth of your mortises requires routing in several passes.

The router table is *not* appropriate for mortising into the end of stock unless you're prepared to build and use an additional jig to hold the stock on end. And it's not convenient for routing the edge of stock that is longer than the router table fence, because there is no place to install stop blocks. I use a router table only when I have a lot of shallow identical mortises to cut in the edges of small parts.

Cutting Mortises by Hand

While machines are usually the most accurate and efficient tools for cutting mortises, there are times when hand tools are better for a particular job. Mortises that must enter the stock at an angle and mortises that must taper are just two cases suited to hand tools.

While some woodworkers chop out mortises with only a chisel and mallet, I prefer drilling out the bulk of the waste first. In addition to being easier, boring out most of the waste reduces the chance you'll split the stock when chopping and prying with a chisel. A third advantage is that boring out the mortise allows you to clean up with ordinary bevel-edged cabinetmaker's chisels, which aren't stiff enough for the pounding and prying involved in chopping out mortises that haven't been bored.

The steps that follow assume that the mortise is rectangular, and square to the surface. I would normally rout such mortises, but the complex mortises that *demand* hand cutting are so varied that specific instructions for cutting them would fill a book of their own. The basic procedures remain the same, however. Modify and

STEP-BY-STEP CUTTING MORTISES BY HAND

1 Lay out the mortise width with a mortise gauge and the length with a layout knife and square.

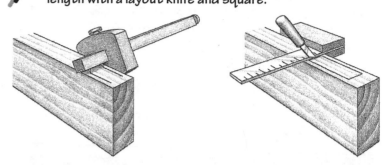

2 Drill out waste with a bit the same diameter as the width of the mortise.

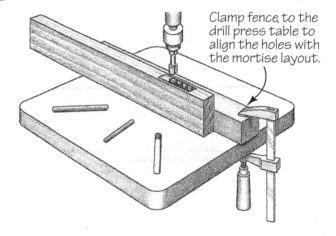

Clamp fence to the drill press table to align the holes with the mortise layout.

3 Clean up the mortise sides.

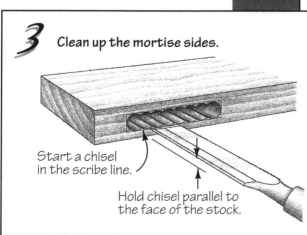

Start a chisel in the scribe line.

Hold chisel parallel to the face of the stock.

4 Square the ends of the mortise.

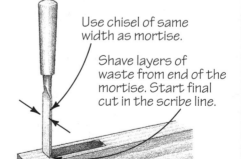

Use chisel of same width as mortise.

Shave layers of waste from end of the mortise. Start final cut in the scribe line.

SQUARE PEG, ROUND HOLE

Many woodworkers cut their mortises with a plunge router and their tenons on the table saw. The result is square tenon edges and round mortise ends. The proverbial square peg doesn't fit the round hole. What do you do?

• Don't even ask which is better, round or square. Chose your technique to produce consistent results with smooth sides: That's more im-

portant than any difference in strength between round and square ends.

• If you think square ends will look better, square the ends of the mortises with a chisel, as shown in Step 4 on page 157.

• If the mortises will be hidden, or if you prefer round ends, then round the edges of the tenons with a chisel or rasp. You'll find that a lot easier than squaring the ends of a mortise.

adapt these steps to suit the demands of the job.

Begin by scribing the mortises on the stock. This will go much faster if you scribe all the identical mortises at the same time, then cut them. If you intend to bore the mortises with a bit that has a long pilot, scribe the centerline of the mortises as well as its sides, and align the pilot with the centerline to bore out the waste. You still need a scribe mark along the side to help in lining up the chisel that will clean up the rest of the waste.

The best bits for boring out a mortise, in order of preference, are Forstner bits, brad-point bits, and spade bits. Twist drills will wander if you try to overlap the holes. Both the boring and the cleanup will be much easier if you use a bit the same size as the width of the mortises. If you can't adapt the mortise size to a bit that you have, you'll need to stagger the drilled holes, positioning half of them along one side of the mortise and the other half along the other side.

HOLLOW-CHISEL MORTISING

Cutting a mortise by running an auger inside a hollow, square chisel is a technique that has been around for a spell. My dad had one of these attachments for his 11-inch Delta drill press in the 1950s. Virtually identical attachments are still being made, and now there are dedicated mortising machines as well.

The principle is a clever combination of drilling and chiseling that take place simultane-

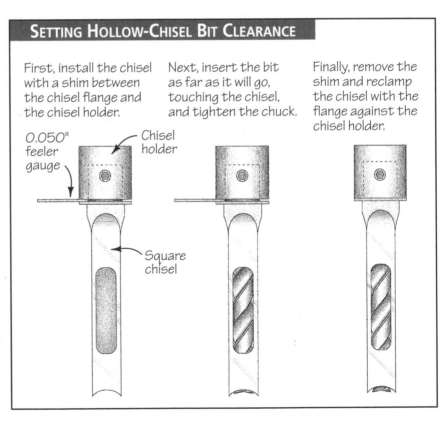

SETTING HOLLOW-CHISEL BIT CLEARANCE

First, install the chisel with a shim between the chisel flange and the chisel holder.

Next, insert the bit as far as it will go, touching the chisel, and tighten the chuck.

Finally, remove the shim and reclamp the chisel with the flange against the chisel holder.

0.050" feeler gauge

Chisel holder

Square chisel

STEP-BY-STEP
HOLLOW-CHISEL MORTISING

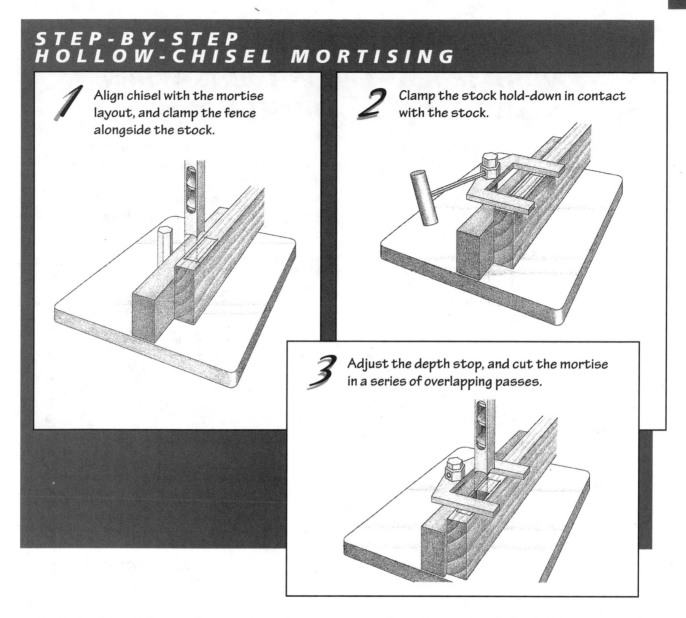

1 Align chisel with the mortise layout, and clamp the fence alongside the stock.

2 Clamp the stock hold-down in contact with the stock.

3 Adjust the depth stop, and cut the mortise in a series of overlapping passes.

ously. Both sides of the mortise are trimmed at once. The auger cuts up and lifts out the bulk of the waste. The hollow square chisel trims the sides of the mortise and feeds its shavings to the auger to be lifted out.

Hollow-chisel mortisers require careful setup. If you don't have proper clearance between the bit and the chisel, or if either the bit or the chisel slips, you could easily ruin both of these expensive tools. The clearance should be between $1/32$ inch and $1/16$ inch. Rather than trying to measure the clearance directly, I take an indirect approach, as shown in *Setting Hollow-Chisel Bit Clearance.*

I find I need a very sharp chisel and a lot of force to cut a moderately hard wood like cherry. You'll have to carefully hand hone the chisel's cutting edges to maintain sharpness, and you'll need

more than a beer can–weight drill press to stand up to the forces. If you try to reduce the needed force by cutting less than half of a full chisel bite with each pass, the chisel will tend to slip over into the existing mortise. One advantage of the dedicated mortisers is that they are specifically designed to withstand heavy stresses.

A word or two about the quality of cut. The business end of these bits is a trifle larger in diameter than the dimension of the matching chisel. Consequently, the sides of the mortise are slightly scalloped, which doesn't do a thing for the quality of the glue bond. Also, the sides of the mortises are less smooth than routed mortises. While the mortises are not flawless, and the tools require some baby-sitting, a glance at the steps above will show how quick and convenient hollow-chisel mortising can be.

MORTISE-AND-TENON JOINTS WHEN THERE ISN'T ENOUGH ROOM

One of the most common applications for the mortise-and-tenon joint is joining table aprons to legs. It's an application that always presents the same problem: not enough room. Two aprons must solidly join the top of the leg on adjoining faces. If the leg is slender enough to avoid looking clunky, then the mortises run into each other. The traditional compromise is shown in *Mitered Tenons* and has served for centuries. Furniture styles have evolved to meet the required dimensions at the top of the legs while minimizing their apparent size. But if you want a table of exceptional durability, or you want to design tables with more delicate legs, there is an alternative: Join the opposing tenons to each other.

A box joint between the tenon of one apron and the tenon of another adds a whole new dimension to the strength of a table. Not only does the box joint add more glue area than the mitered-tenon treatment, it also adds mechanical strength to resist splitting the leg. When joining opposing tenons, I use separate tenons, as shown in *Box-Joined Separate Tenons*. The joint may appear to be a nightmare to cut and fit properly, but the approach that I take makes it surprisingly easy.

After routing the mortises, I saw tenon stock to just over twice the required tenon length and cut loose-fitting box joints in both ends. Then I saw the double-length pieces into two tenons of the proper length. To assemble the joint, I brush epoxy in the mortise and on the tenon surfaces, leaving a small puddle of epoxy where the leg mortises intersect. When I insert the tenons, bringing the box joint together, the small puddle of epoxy fills the gaps in the loose-fitting box joint. I fit the aprons to the tenons last and then band clamp the whole assembly of four legs and four aprons while the epoxy cures.

The first time I tried this technique, I made a prototype joining two ½-inch-thick maple aprons 1 foot long to a maple leg that was only ⅞ × ⅞ inch in cross section. I asked my muscular teenage son if he could break the assembly apart. We were both quite surprised when he couldn't.

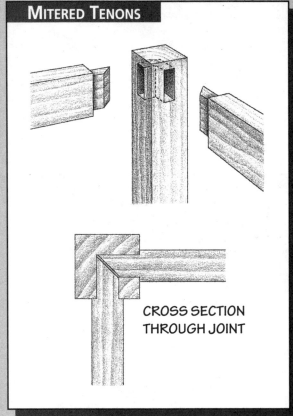

MITERED TENONS

CROSS SECTION
THROUGH JOINT

BOX-JOINED SEPARATE TENONS

Mortises intersect.

Tenons join at intersection of mortises.

MORTISING TECHNIQUES

	PLUNGE ROUTER	ROUTER TABLE	HAND TOOLS	HOLLOW CHISEL
TOOLS REQUIRED	Plunge router Spiral bit Mortising jig	Router Spiral bit Router table	Chisels Drill press	Drill press and mortising attachment OR dedicated mortiser
SETUP DIFFICULTY	Moderate	Moderate	Minimal	Moderate
QUALITY OF CUT	Excellent	Excellent	Fair to very good	Acceptable
STRENGTHS	Clean, precise, easy	Very fast once set up	No machine setup; cuts any size or shape	Fastest way to cut mortises with square ends
LIMITATIONS	2½" depth	2½" depth; can't mortise edges of long stock; can't mortise ends of stock	None	3" depth; no very hard woods
SPEED	Quick	Very quick	Slow	Very quick
SHAPE OF MORTISE	Round ends	Round ends	Square ends	Square ends
BOTTOM LINE	The fastest and cleanest technique for general mortising	Excellent for making large numbers of identical mortises in identical short pieces	Best choice for making unusually large or complex mortises	Good technique for general use but requires more setup than plunge routing

CUTTING TENONS WITH A TENONING JIG

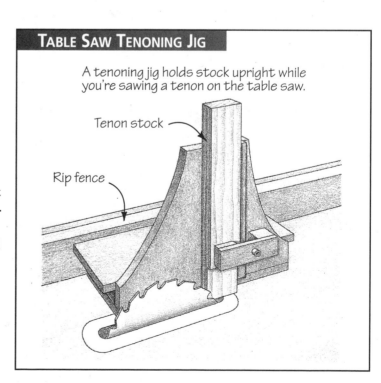

TABLE SAW TENONING JIG

A tenoning jig holds stock upright while you're sawing a tenon on the table saw.

Tenon stock

Rip fence

For centuries, perhaps millennia, the difficult half of a mortise-and-tenon joint was the mortise; a woodworker had to chop it out with a chisel. The tenon was the easy part; all he had to do was saw off the waste. Now the tables are turned. You can rout a mortise with a single setup, but cutting a tenon still requires the same eight distinct saw cuts: two cheeks, two edges, and four shoulders.

If you anticipate cutting many tenons, it will be worth your while to make a jig to hold

STEP-BY-STEP
CUTTING TENONS WITH A TENONING JIG

1 **Lay out tenon on scrap stock.**

Extend tenon thickness and width lines to adjoining faces.

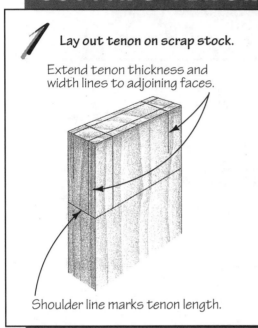

Shoulder line marks tenon length.

2 **Adjust table saw blade height.**

Set blade 1/32" shy of shoulder layout.

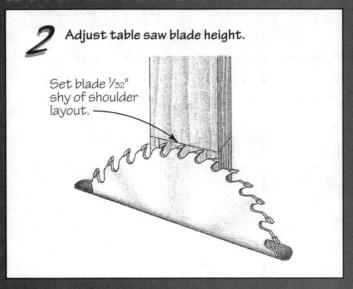

3 **Adjust rip fence and cut the cheek farthest from the fence.**

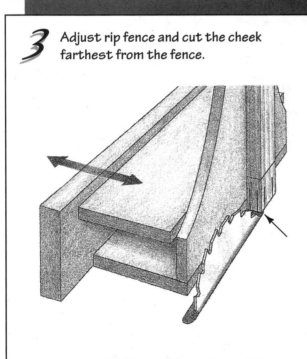

4 **Fit spacer between jig and fence, then cut second cheek.**

Blocks key the spacer to the jig.

Thickness of spacer = thickness of tenon + saw kerf.

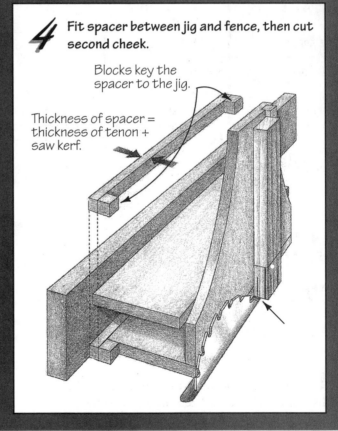

stock vertically on the table saw. I use the same jig that I use for routing mortises, turned upside down, as shown in *Table Saw Tenoning Jig* on page 161. Instructions for building it are in the "Combination Mortise and Tenon Jig" chapter on page 240. Commercial tenoning jigs are also available.

When using the jig, I cut one of the tenon cheeks with the base of the jig against the rip fence. Then I move the jig over with a spacer to make the other cheek cut. The technique is quick, and since I never move the fence, each tenon ends up precisely the same. The first time you cut

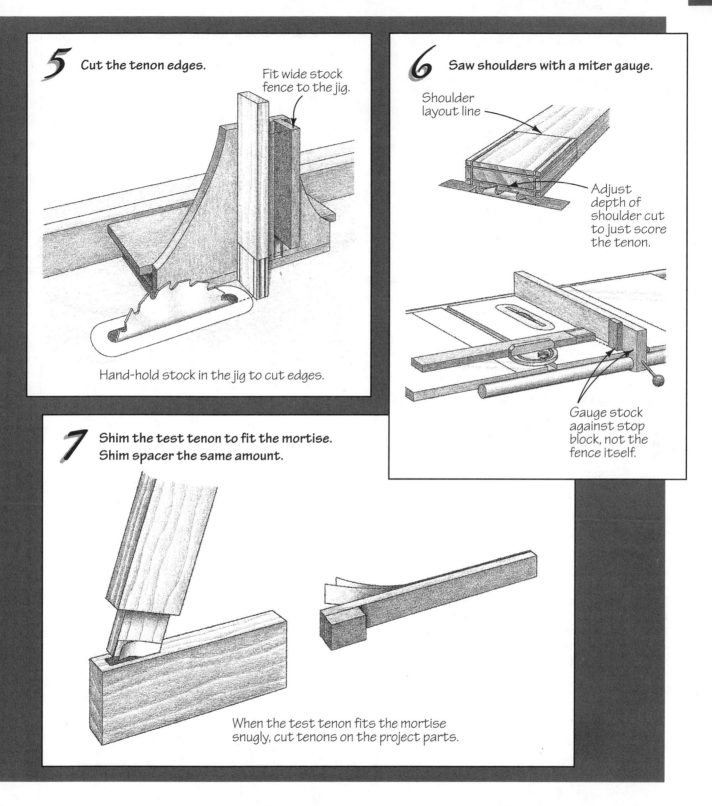

5 Cut the tenon edges.

Fit wide stock fence to the jig.

Hand-hold stock in the jig to cut edges.

6 Saw shoulders with a miter gauge.

Shoulder layout line

Adjust depth of shoulder cut to just score the tenon.

Gauge stock against stop block, not the fence itself.

7 Shim the test tenon to fit the mortise. Shim spacer the same amount.

When the test tenon fits the mortise snugly, cut tenons on the project parts.

a tenon of a particular thickness with a particular saw blade, you'll have to carefully tune a spacer so it equals the thickness of the tenon plus the width of the saw kerf. From then on you'll be able to use the same spacer for all tenons of that thickness, whether they're long or short, wide or narrow, centered or offset. Once you have two or three well-tuned spacers for tenons of different thicknesses, you'll be set for life, at least if you are my age.

Always use a rip blade when cutting tenon cheeks and edges. It will feed faster than a combination blade, remaining cooler. The 2- or 3-inch depth of a tenon cheek cut is enough to overheat and even warp a combination blade. My favorite rip blade is a 24-tooth, 10-inch, thin-kerfed blade.

Set up and adjust the table saw, and test the setup by cutting a tenon on scrap stock. Start by making a spacer that is slightly thinner than the

Note: *Many woodworkers set up their tenoning jig and table saw to cut one of the cheeks, then reverse the stock in the jig to cut the second cheek. I dislike this procedure for three reasons. First, it makes it twice as hard to get a good fit, because any minor error in the setup for the first cheek cut is doubled when you reverse the stock for the second cut. Good techniques should increase accuracy, not lessen it. Second, if your stock isn't consistent in thickness, your tenons will end up thicker or thinner than you want. Finally, this single-setup procedure tempts you to center tenons even in situations where they ought to be offset, such as in many table apron-to-leg joints.*

TECH TIP

CUT BOTH CHEEKS AT ONCE: If you cut many tenons, you can save a lot of time by cutting both cheeks of your tenons at once. Buy a pair of well-matched rip blades and a set of blade spacers and shims (available from Delta dealers; part #34-171). Space the blades a distance equal to the tenon thickness plus the side clearance of the blades.

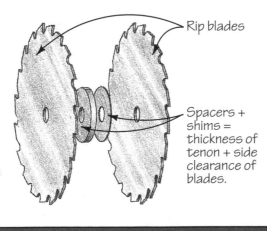

Rip blades

Spacers + shims = thickness of tenon + side clearance of blades.

CLEAN, TIGHT SHOULDER LINES

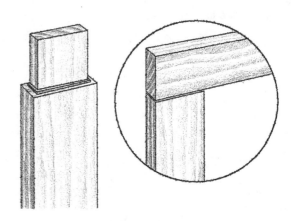

If neither the shoulder cut nor the cheek cut cleans out the corner, a tiny ridge will prevent the tenon shoulder from seating against the mortise piece.

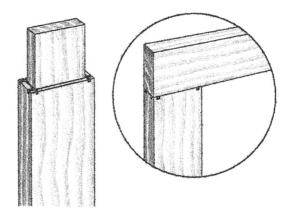

If the cheek cuts clean out the corner but extend into the shoulder, the overcut will show on the assembled joint.

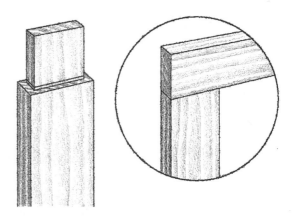

If the shoulder cut cleans out the corner and scores the tenon, the overcut won't show when the joint is assembled.

combined thickness of the tenon and a saw kerf. Then cut a test tenon and shim it with tape to fit the mortise. Shim the spacer with the same amount of tape. This technique saves a lot of testing and retesting.

Cut the tenon shoulders last. They are the only visible part of a mortise-and-tenon joint, so they need to be precise and free of chips or tear-out. But cutting them is a very straightforward operation. Keep the following in mind, and you'll be home free.

◗ Make sure your miter gauge fence is dead-square to the bar.

◗ Use the best crosscut blade you can afford, and make sure it's sharp.

◗ Set the depth of cut to just barely score the tenon, as shown in *Clean, Tight Shoulder Lines*. ●

Cutting Tenons with a Dado Cutter

If you seldom cut tenons, it's probably not worth the effort to build a jig. Instead, cut the shoulders with a crosscut blade and use a dado cutter to waste away the cheeks, as shown in *Quick-and-Dirty Tenons*. In a pinch, you can even waste away the cheeks with multiple cuts with a standard saw blade.

The only drawback to this dado head technique is the need to shave the tenons to final thickness with a chisel or small rabbet plane. There are two reasons for the final shaving. First, the dado head cuts rarely produce the precise tenon thickness you need for a good joint. Second, many dado heads leave a rather coarse cut. Wobble dadoes will leave a particularly messy tenon. Still, for a few tenons, the hand fitting takes less time than building a tenoning jig.

The procedures for cutting tenons with this technique are pretty straightforward. Begin by laying out the tenons on the stock and on several test pieces. Make sure the test pieces are exactly the same thickness and width as your project stock. Then cut the shoulders, as described in Step 6 on page 163.

Next, mount a dado cutter on your table saw and adjust the depth of cut to just shy of your

> ## Quick-and-Dirty Tenons
>
> First, saw shoulders with a crosscut blade.
>
> Next, waste away cheeks with a dado cutter.
>
> Finally, smooth the cheeks and shave them to fit the mortise with a rabbet plane or chisel.

tenon cheek layout line. Hold a test piece firmly in the miter gauge, and waste away both cheeks in a series of cuts.

Test the fit of the tenon in a mortise, and adjust the depth of cut to produce a tenon that is several plane shavings too thick. The rougher the surface, the more you should leave for the hand plane. Remember that the thickness of the tenon will change by twice the amount that you adjust the depth of cut.

When your test pieces meet your approval, cut the tenons on all your workpieces. Then cut the edges the same way you cut the cheeks, readjusting the blade height as necessary.

Chisel or plane each tenon to fit its specific mortise.

MECHANICAL REFINEMENTS

Pins and wedges will hold mortise-and-tenon joints together so securely that glue is quite unnecessary. They're still used in situations where glue is inappropriate: situations like post-and-beam house construction and knockdown furniture. In addition to the mechanical strength that pins and wedges contribute, they can provide a nice decorative touch and can hold the joint together while the glue dries, freeing up clamps.

Wedges are practical only when the mortise goes all the way through the stock, as shown in *Wedged Tenons,* allowing you to insert the wedges after the tenon is fully inserted in the mortise. They are most effective when the mortise is tapered and the wedges spread the end of the tenon into a dovetail shape. When making this joint, cut the small end of the mortise to fit the tenon snugly. This way the mortise will prevent the wedge from splitting the tenon stock when you drive the wedges home.

Pinned mortise-and-tenon joints are locked by pins that pass through both the mortise piece and the tenon, as shown in *Pinned Tenons.* When making this joint, position the pins at the middle of the tenon length rather than the middle of the

width of the mortise piece. This position strikes a balance between the pin splitting out the end of the tenon and the pin splitting off the side of the mortise piece if the joint receives hard racking stress. Timber framers and antiquarian woodworkers sometimes bore the pin holes in the tenon offset slightly from the pin holes in the mortise

Fox-Wedged Tenons

It's *possible* to wedge a blind tenon; this is called a "fox-wedged tenon." Saw kerfs in the tenon, start wedges in the kerfs, and drive the tenon piece into the mortise. As the tenon enters the mortise, the bottom of the mortise will drive the wedges into the kerfs. As long as you get everything perfect the first time, you'll have a strong joint. But if the assembled joint is a trifle loose, or too tight to fully assemble, you'll have a disaster; there is no way to disassemble the joint to make adjustments.

WEDGED TENONS

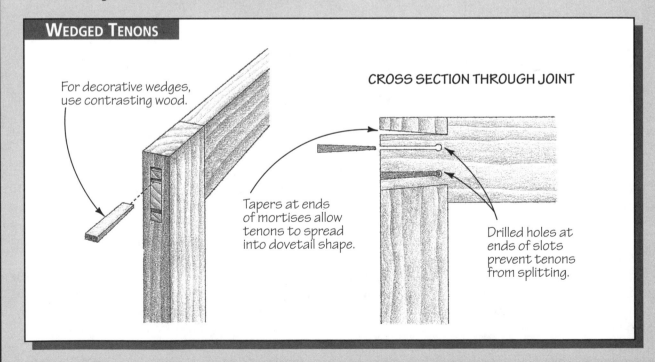

For decorative wedges, use contrasting wood.

Tapers at ends of mortises allow tenons to spread into dovetail shape.

CROSS SECTION THROUGH JOINT

Drilled holes at ends of slots prevent tenons from splitting.

piece. The pin then draws the joint tightly together as it is driven in. While quite practical for the timber framer, this technique of "draw-boring" is a bit out of place if you're adding a pin mostly for decoration and relying on glue primarily to hold the joint together.

A tusk joint, as shown in *Tenon with a Tusk Wedge*, is a second way of pinning a mortise-and-tenon. Here, the tenon passes entirely through the mortise stock and beyond, and a pin or "tusk" locks it where it protrudes. In addition to its fine old-timey flavor, the joint is very functional if the furniture needs to be disassembled from time to time. It's common on trestle tables, beds, and looms. If you use this joint, please do it right, with the tusk vertical. With seasonal swelling and shrinking of the wood and racking of the joint during heavy use, a well-designed tusk with a bit of side clearance will drop farther into its mortise, tightening the joint. A horizontal tusk (yeeech) will just wiggle looser. When making this joint, be sure to angle the second mortise—the one through the tenon—to match the angle on the tusk. Also, be sure to give the tusk enough side clearance that you can drop it into the mortise before giving it a final tap.

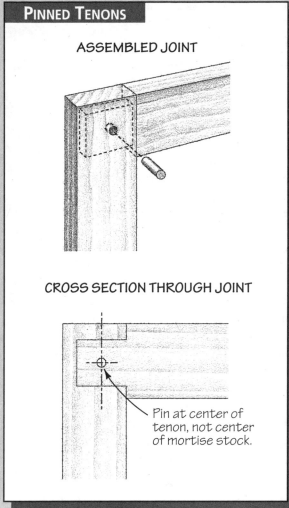

PINNED TENONS

ASSEMBLED JOINT

CROSS SECTION THROUGH JOINT

Pin at center of tenon, not center of mortise stock.

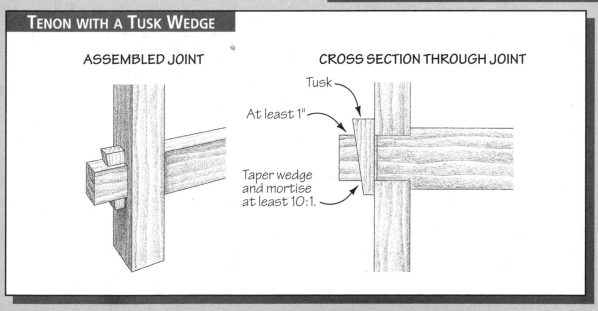

TENON WITH A TUSK WEDGE

ASSEMBLED JOINT

CROSS SECTION THROUGH JOINT

Tusk

At least 1"

Taper wedge and mortise at least 10:1.

CUTTING TENONS WITH A HANDSAW

Some tenons are very difficult to set up for machine cutting. Examples include tenons that are not in line with the stock and tenons with shoulders that are not perpendicular to the faces of the stock, as shown in *Tenons Best Cut with a Handsaw.* When you see tenons this complex on your plans, get out your backsaw.

Cutting an accurate tenon with hand tools is not as difficult as many woodworkers fear. The secrets to success are accurate layout and correct sawing technique. See "Gauges" on page 6 for layout suggestions. If the layout is confusing, do it first with light pencil lines to make sure you're getting it right, then scribe it. Scribing not only gives you a more precise line to follow, it also helps prevent splintering where the saw exits the stock.

Your body will stray into a natural position while you saw. Place your body so the cut will follow the line when your body is in that natural position.

"Handsaw Technique" on page 170 gives some valuable tips on accurate sawing with a handsaw, especially a backsaw.

To saw out a tenon, begin by cutting the cheeks, stopping just short of the shoulder lines. Remember that you can plane down a thick tenon but you can't fatten up a thin one; so if you are going to miss the line, miss it on the waste side rather than the tenon side. Saw down the edges in the same way.

Saw the shoulders with the aid of a bench hook, which you can make yourself, as explained in *Bench Hook/Shooting Board* on page 102. Trimming the end grain on a shoulder is more difficult than trimming a cheek, so make the shoulder cuts as precise as you can.

Fit each tenon to its mortise with a small rabbet plane or chisel. The traditional tool for trimming the shoulders is also the small rabbet plane. In fact, it is often called a shoulder rabbet plane.

TENONS BEST CUT WITH A HANDSAW

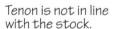

Tenon shoulders are not perpendicular to face of the stock.

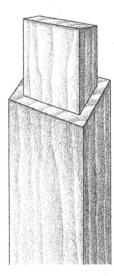

Tenon is not in line with the stock.

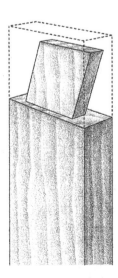

STEP-BY-STEP CUTTING TENONS WITH A HANDSAW

1 Scribe the tenon layout on the stock.

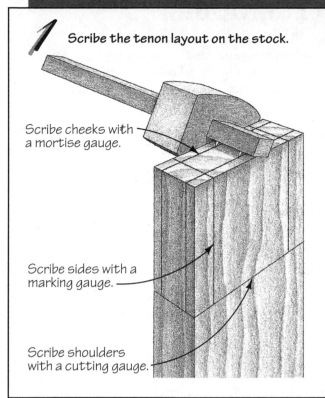

Scribe cheeks with a mortise gauge.

Scribe sides with a marking gauge.

Scribe shoulders with a cutting gauge.

2 Saw cheeks and edges with a backsaw.

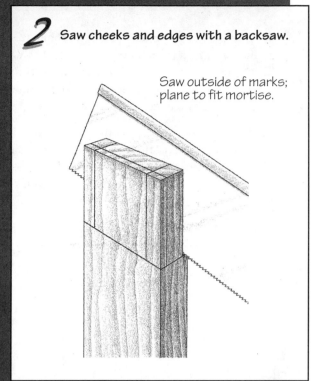

Saw outside of marks; plane to fit mortise.

3 Saw shoulders with the aid of a bench hook.

Align saw blade in the groove.

Scribe shoulder line deeply.

Cut into vee with a knife or chisel.

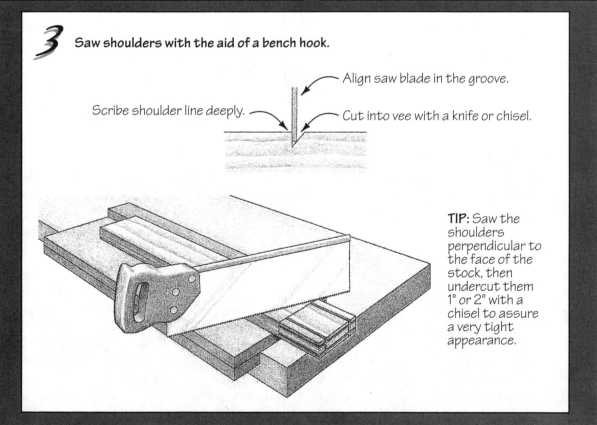

TIP: Saw the shoulders perpendicular to the face of the stock, then undercut them 1° or 2° with a chisel to assure a very tight appearance.

HANDSAW TECHNIQUE

After 30 years of woodworking, I thought I had a pretty good handle on the basics. Then a builder taught me how to use a handsaw. His advice was good, and not at all obvious. Some of his suggestions are included here.

1. Assuming that you are right-handed, arrange yourself and the stock so the waste side of the cut line is on the right. This way the saw blade will be to the right of the line and you'll be able to see what you're doing.

2. When clamping stock in a vise, position it so the cut line is vertical, as shown here,

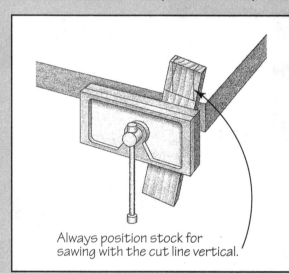

Always position stock for sawing with the cut line vertical.

even if that means that the stock is tilted. It's much easier to saw to a plumb line on cocked stock than to saw to an angled line on plumb stock.

3. Position your stock in the vise so you will be sawing at or slightly below elbow height.

4. Clear away anything within view that is tilted, such as boards leaning against the wall at the back of your workbench. They will distract you and trick your eye.

5. Several lines define a cut: at least one on a face and at least one on an edge. If your kerf is progressing down more than one at a time, it is likely to stray from one of them as you concen-

trate on following another. So always extend the cut down just one line at a time, as shown here.

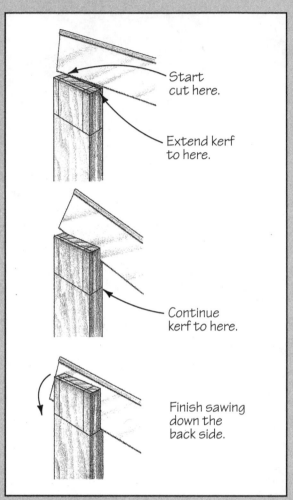

Start cut here.

Extend kerf to here.

Continue kerf to here.

Finish sawing down the back side.

If comfortable and relaxed sawing causes the kerf to extend down the line in back while you're concentrating on the near line, raise the stock higher in the vise. Lower the stock in the vise to extend the kerf down the back side.

6. As you saw, your body will tend to fall into its most comfortable and relaxed sawing position. It will do so regardless of whether that position puts the cut where you want it. Don't try to fight this tendency—use it. If your cut begins to stray from the line, move your feet and therefore your whole body so that the most natural body position puts the cut where you want it.

TENONING TECHNIQUES

	JIG AND SPACER	TWIN BLADES	ROUTER TABLE/ DADO HEAD	HAND TOOLS
TOOLS REQUIRED	Table saw; Rip blade; Tenoning jig with spacer	Table saw; 2 identical rip blades; Blade spacers; Tenoning jig	Table saw and router table OR Dado head on table saw; Rabbet plane	Backsaw; Bench hook; Rabbet plane; Chisel
SETUP DIFFICULTY	First time: complex Thereafter: minimal	First time: complex Thereafter: minimal	Minimal	None
QUALITY OF CUT	Excellent	Excellent	Poor to very good	Fair to very good
STRENGTHS	Ease, consistency, accuracy	Ease, consistency, accuracy	Ease, minimal equipment	Versatility
LIMITATIONS	Tenon length limited to table saw's depth of cut. Good only for straight tenons with square shoulders.	Tenon length limited to table saw's depth of cut. Tenon thickness limited by table saw arbor length. Good only for straight tenons with square shoulders.	Good only for straight tenons with square shoulders	None
SPEED	Quick	Quick	Moderate to quick	Slow to moderate
BOTTOM LINE	Best combination of quality, speed, and economy in most shops	Best when cutting large numbers of tenons	Best for infrequent tenoning	Best when tenons or shoulders are angled

CORNER JOINTS

Dovetail-shaped splines, which create the illusion of a dovetail joint, are just one of many ways to reinforce a corner. If you make the splines out of a contrasting wood, they'll add interest as well as strength.

Making things out of wood without joining the ends of boards is pretty limited. Even the simplest box, bookshelf, table, or chair demands joining pieces of wood end to end, usually at a corner. Unfortunately, it's impossible to join wood end to end strongly without reshaping the ends of the boards so that you're really joining the wood long grain to long grain. All of the better corner joints, like dovetails, box joints, and splines, are examples of this reshaping.

The range of corner joints reflects the broad range of applications for them. If you're making a drawer to hold silverware, and your teenage son will yank it open and slam it shut every time he needs another bowl of Wheaties, then strength and durability are your main concerns. On the other hand, you can expect a music box for your mother to receive gentle treatment. And if your corner joints are on the 150 bluebird houses for your wife's garden club flea market, you probably want joints that you can make quickly and efficiently.

Strength in a corner joint comes from two potential sources: the mechanical interlocking of the pieces and the glue used to hold them together. Joints like a simple end miter that have no long-grain gluing surfaces and don't interlock require reinforcement in the form of splines, or mechanical fasteners like nails.

The dovetail is among the best corner joints, strong and good-looking. There are so many good ways to make a dovetail joint, however, that I've given it an entire chapter, beginning on page 184. This chapter covers the other useful corner joints.

Making Rabbet-and-Dado Joints

Dado joints and rabbet joints are among the simplest joints to cut. They are also fairly easy to assemble since they're self-aligning. Unfortunately, they are not very well suited for boxes and drawers. As shown in *Rabbet-and-Dado Joints in Drawers,* the mechanical strength of a rabbet joint is of little use on a drawer. Likewise, a dado is weak if it's too close to the end of the stock. Neither joint glues well, because of the end grain involved in the joint surfaces. This isn't to say that rabbets and dadoes aren't useful—there are many occasions when nails are quite appropriate—but I don't suggest them when strength and durability are important.

The lock joint is a variation on the simple rabbet-and-dado. Used for attaching drawer fronts to sides, it's stronger than a plain rabbet joint because it provides some mechanical resistance to pulling the front off the drawer. The joint is easy to cut with a simple table saw setup, as shown in *Sawing a Lock Joint.*

RABBET-AND-DADO JOINTS IN DRAWERS

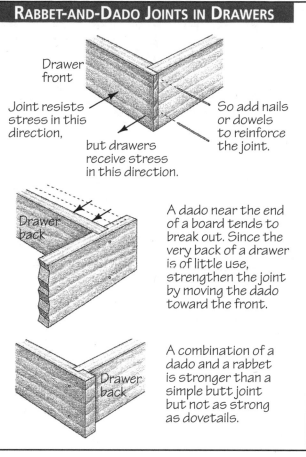

Drawer front

Joint resists stress in this direction,

but drawers receive stress in this direction.

So add nails or dowels to reinforce the joint.

Drawer back

A dado near the end of a board tends to break out. Since the very back of a drawer is of little use, strengthen the joint by moving the dado toward the front.

Drawer back

A combination of a dado and a rabbet is stronger than a simple butt joint but not as strong as dovetails.

You'll find the setup is easiest when the stock thickness is readily divided into thirds, like ¾ inch. But once you understand how the various cuts relate to each other, you can modify the setup to

SAWING A LOCK JOINT

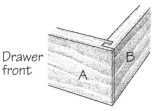

Drawer front

First, set blade height to stock thickness. Cut piece A on end.

Adjust dado cutter width to ⅓ stock thickness.

Adjust fence to center dado cutter in stock. Use same position for all 3 cuts.

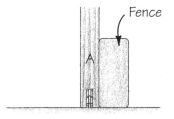

Fence

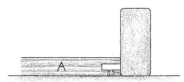

Next, set blade height to ⅓ stock thickness and cut piece A flat on the table.

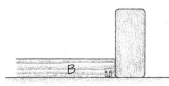

Finally, cut piece B with the same setup as the previous step.

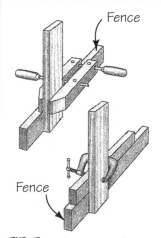

Fence

Fence

TIP: To cut narrow pieces on end, clamp on a straightedge or hand screw to ride on top of the fence.

work with pieces of any thickness. Make test cuts in scrap before you saw your project parts.

You can make a nearly identical joint on a router table, using a drawer lock bit, made just for this joint. It cuts the joint in two passes instead of three. Once set up, as shown in *Routing a Lock Joint*, the bit height remains the same for both cuts. If you need to make a lot of drawers and they don't need to be bomb-proof, routed lock joints are worth considering.

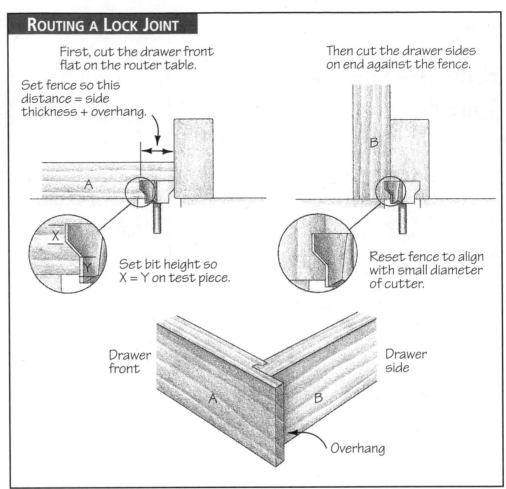

ROUTING A LOCK JOINT

First, cut the drawer front flat on the router table.

Set fence so this distance = side thickness + overhang.

Set bit height so X = Y on test piece.

Then cut the drawer sides on end against the fence.

Reset fence to align with small diameter of cutter.

Drawer front

Drawer side

Overhang

Making Box Joints

It's hard to beat the box joint for strength. Like the lock joint, you can cut the box joint on the table saw or with a table-mounted router. Both machines require that you use a simple shop-made jig. Complete plans for the jig are in the "Box Joint Jig" chapter on page 277.

The box joint's one major limitation is its appearance. The checkerboard effect of the inter-locking pins can be distracting if they're allowed to show in a clean, simple design. Of course, if the joinery is hidden, the looks are of little consequence.

Cutting box joints is straightforward. Whether you use the table saw or a table-mounted router, the procedure and the jig used are the same. Making the

THE BOX JOINT

The interlocking fingers of the box joint provide plenty of long-grain to long-grain glue surface as well as excellent mechanical strength.

Thin fingers are more work but are stronger.

joint requires a series of identical cuts, each one exactly the width of the pins that remain between the cuts, and each cut gauged from the previous one. This works well, provided your setup is accurate. But any error in the setup will increase with each successive cut. An error of 1/128 inch might not seem like much, but after 16 cuts the total error will be ⅛ inch. Getting it right is a matter of patience and test cuts.

Box joints are quite easy to glue together because they are self-aligning and easily clamped. In fact, a well-cut box joint doesn't need to be clamped at all, unless it's to get the joint to seat properly.

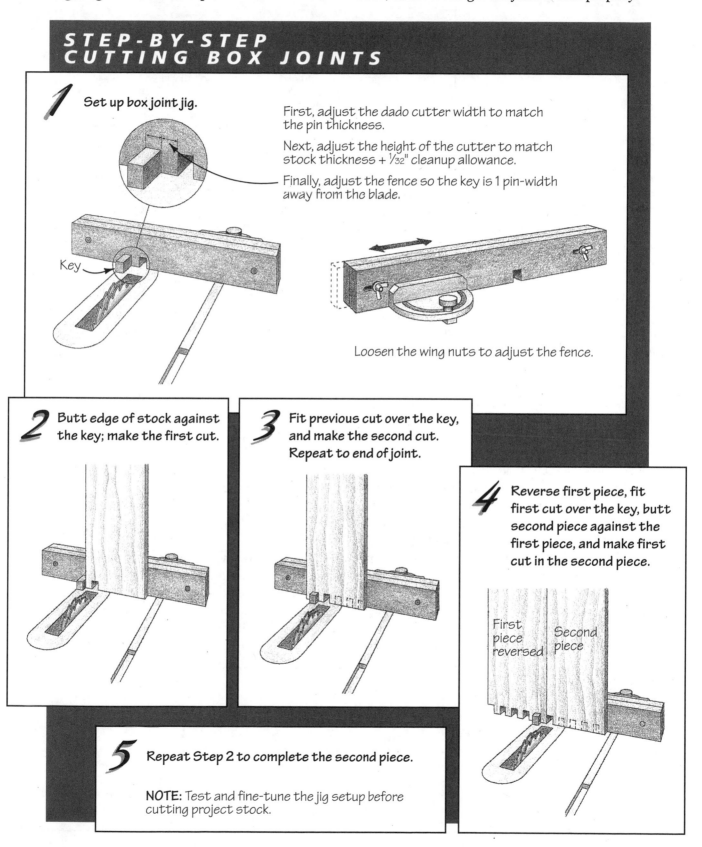

STEP-BY-STEP CUTTING BOX JOINTS

1 Set up box joint jig.

First, adjust the dado cutter width to match the pin thickness.

Next, adjust the height of the cutter to match stock thickness + 1/32" cleanup allowance.

Finally, adjust the fence so the key is 1 pin-width away from the blade.

Key

Loosen the wing nuts to adjust the fence.

2 Butt edge of stock against the key; make the first cut.

3 Fit previous cut over the key, and make the second cut. Repeat to end of joint.

4 Reverse first piece, fit first cut over the key, butt second piece against the first piece, and make first cut in the second piece.

First piece reversed   Second piece

5 Repeat Step 2 to complete the second piece.

NOTE: Test and fine-tune the jig setup before cutting project stock.

Making Mitered Joints

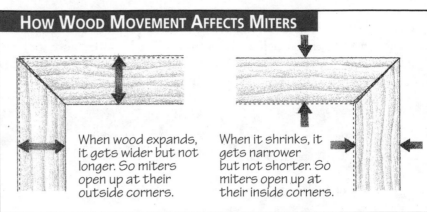

HOW WOOD MOVEMENT AFFECTS MITERS

When wood expands, it gets wider but not longer. So miters open up at their outside corners.

When it shrinks, it gets narrower but not shorter. So miters open up at their inside corners.

Those who've never made a miter joint may think it's a no-brainer—a job for an apprentice once he's proven he can sweep the floor adequately. But the clean, simple appearance of the miter joint belies the difficulty involved in making it. Cutting and assembling a strong, tight miter joint is tough, and it can be nearly impossible in some situations.

By itself, the miter joint is pretty weak. The two pieces don't interlock; and the glue surfaces, though angled, are essentially end grain. In many applications a miter joint is held together primarily by the piece of furniture behind it—a mitered crown molding on a china hutch, for example, is held together by the hutch. If you're using the miter joint for the corners of a jewelry box, you need to add reinforcement to the joint. Splines, either visible or hidden, or box-joined tenons will provide strength.

Another problem with miter joints is that few stay tight over their lifetime, unless it's a short lifetime. As shown in *How Wood Movement Affects Miters,* the seasonal expansion and contraction of wood open up even the best-fitting miter joints. This is more pronounced on wider stock joined to form a flat frame, like a picture frame, but I've seen it happen on box sides that were less than ¾ inch thick. Minimize the problem by using stable stock like cherry, and for a box use flat-sawn pieces because they expand and contract in thickness less than quarter-sawn stock.

If these two concerns lead you to think you're

playing against a stacked deck, you're right. But in spite of its shortcomings, the miter joint is tremendously useful. It allows moldings and grain patterns to continue around corners without interruption, as shown in the photo on page 181.

The sequence of operations for making mitered joints depends on the kind of reinforcement that you intend to use. If you're planning on visible reinforcement, like exposed splines, mock dovetails, or angled dowels, then you will assemble the actual miter joint before tackling any of the reinforcement joinery. If the reinforcement will be hidden, however, all of the joint cutting must be complete before the miter comes together. Keep this in mind because the material that follows can't be organized both ways. I've chosen to present "Cutting Bevels for Miter Joints" and then "Assembling Miters" in this section, followed by "Visible Miter Reinforcement" and finally "Hidden-Miter Reinforcement."

Cutting Bevels for Miter Joints

There is really just one good way to cut the bevels for an end miter: Tilt the blade on your saw to the correct angle and crosscut the pieces, as shown in the photos on the opposite page. The correct angle is half the angle between the two parts of the joint, as shown in *Figuring Miter Joint Angles,*

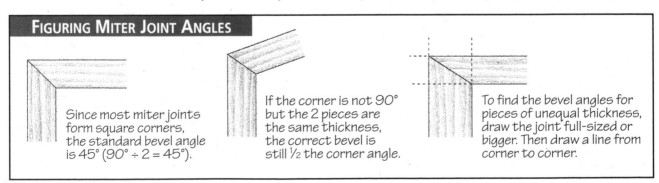

FIGURING MITER JOINT ANGLES

Since most miter joints form square corners, the standard bevel angle is 45° (90° ÷ 2 = 45°).

If the corner is not 90° but the 2 pieces are the same thickness, the correct bevel is still ½ the corner angle.

To find the bevel angles for pieces of unequal thickness, draw the joint full-sized or bigger. Then draw a line from corner to corner.

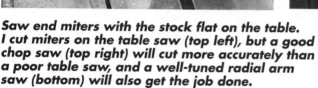

Saw end miters with the stock flat on the table. I cut miters on the table saw (top left), but a good chop saw (top right) will cut more accurately than a poor table saw, and a well-tuned radial arm saw (bottom) will also get the job done.

unless the pieces are not of equal thickness. In that case you'll have to be a little more creative, as shown. Once you have the angle on paper, use a T-bevel to transfer it to the saw.

For the finest cuts, use a sharp, carbide-tipped, precision cutoff blade (a 10-inch blade should have at least 60 teeth). I have a crosscut blade that I keep specifically for joinery cuts—I remove it as soon as I'm done sawing so that I'm not tempted to use it for general shop work.

Note: The blades that come with most chop saws are better suited to carpentry than to furniture work. If you intend to use your chop saw for joinery, invest in the same kind of high-quality blade you'd buy for precision work on the table saw.

Assembling Miters

Gluing beveled surfaces together is like trying to walk up an ice-covered sidewalk—if you take the direct approach, you'll slide all over the place. The best way to glue up a miter is to apply pressure perpendicular to the glue-covered surfaces by attaching clamping blocks, as shown in the left photo and inset drawing on page 178. Attaching the clamping blocks with either double-sided tape or hot-melt glue is fast, but neither is as secure as a paper glue joint.

To make a paper glue joint, spread wood glue

on both pieces you want to join, in this case the clamping blocks and the box sides. Clamp them together with a piece of kraft paper in between (brown paper grocery bags work well), then allow the glue to cure overnight. When you're ready to remove the clamping blocks, a sharp whack with a mallet will split the paper, separating the pieces instantly. This approach combines the ease of removal that tape and hot-melt glue offer with the durability of real wood glue. Just don't knock your miter joint apart when you knock the blocks off.

A popular alternative to angled clamping blocks uses band clamps, as shown in the right photo and inset drawing on page 178. The angled clamping blocks exert more clamping pressure and allow you to concentrate on keeping just one joint at a time properly aligned, but the band clamps make it easier to ensure that opposite sides of the box will clamp up parallel to each other.

Clamping with band clamps but leaving out the blocks has two problems: Squeezed-out glue bonds the bands to the project, and the bands exert very uneven pressure on the glue line. I have, on occasion, done it anyway. I glued the joints with epoxy resin because it doesn't require even pressure, and I wrapped a strip of polyethylene around the assembly before clamping to protect the bands from the epoxy. All indications to date are that only my heirs will be able to properly evaluate the life expectancy of the joints.

After you assemble your miters, leave the

> ## TECH TIP
> **GLUING MITERED GRAIN:** To increase the strength of a white- or yellow-glued miter joint, precoat the beveled surfaces with glue. Allow the glue to soak in, then carefully wipe or scrape away any excess. Apply fresh glue, and clamp the joint together as usual. Precoating the bevels fills the end grain, preventing the wood from wicking glue away from the joint after the pieces are clamped.

clamps on for a good 12 hours before removing them, to give the glue ample time to cure. Then, after you remove the clamps, handle the assembly gently until you've had a chance to reinforce the joints.

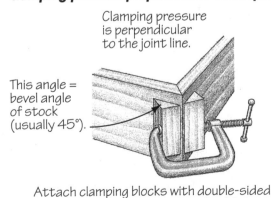

The best way to clamp a miter joint uses angled glue blocks temporarily stuck to the beveled pieces. The blocks let you apply clamping pressure perpendicular to the joint.

Clamping pressure is perpendicular to the joint line.

This angle = bevel angle of stock (usually 45°).

Attach clamping blocks with double-sided tape, hot-melt glue, or paper glue joint.

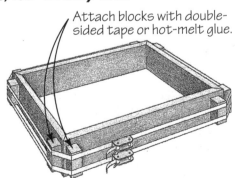

Two inexpensive band clamps will clamp four miter joints at once, but that means you have to keep four miter joints aligned all at once, too—no easy task.

Attach blocks with double-sided tape or hot-melt glue.

Keep checking alignment of all 4 corners as tension is applied to band clamps.

VISIBLE MITER REINFORCEMENT

Reinforcing a miter consists of adding wooden keys or mechanical fasteners that span the joint, providing some interlock between the adjoining pieces. You can make these keys as unobtrusive or as flashy as you like, depending on how much you want to emphasize their role in your design.

For light-duty applications you can reinforce a miter with finish nails. Drive them in from both sides of the joint, as shown in *Nailing a Miter*. Set the heads, dab on a little filler, and they'll practically disappear.

For a stronger, all-wood joint, add wooden splines. These fit in slots cut through the corner of the miter, as shown in the photo on this page. The possible shapes are limited only by your imagination and the available router bits.

Spline Reinforcement

A plain spline is the easiest type of wooden reinforcement to use. Cut the grooves for the splines with the aid of an adapted tenoning jig, as shown on page 180.

Splines do a good job of reinforcing a miter joint because their long-grain surfaces glue well to the long-grain surfaces of the spline slots. By using a wood with a contrasting color, the splines can become decorative details as well.

The thickness of the splines is determined by the width of the saw kerf. Most of the time I use a regular saw blade, so the splines I use are 1/8 inch thick. For thicker splines, use a dado cutter to saw the slots. The spacing of the splines affects both the strength of the joint and the appearance. Lots of splines may look busy, but each glue surface adds to the strength of the joint. You can also gussy up the appearance by angling the splines (tilting the saw blade); but this weakens the reinforcement—the glue surfaces begin to involve end grain, and the box sides along the slots may split off.

Mock Dovetails

The photo on page 172 shows a "mock dovetail" joint. It's simply a decorative variation on the splined miter, made with a dovetail bit instead of a saw blade. For strength, this joint is indeed a mockery of true dovetails; but the strength of true dovetails is not always needed. If you like the look of the dovetail shape, mock dovetails give it to you on two surfaces instead of only one.

NAILING A MITER

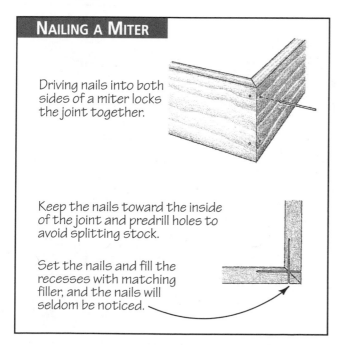

Driving nails into both sides of a miter locks the joint together.

Keep the nails toward the inside of the joint and predrill holes to avoid splitting stock.

Set the nails and fill the recesses with matching filler, and the nails will seldom be noticed.

REINFORCING MITERS WITH SPLINES

1. Set blade height $1/16$" below the inside corner of the joint.

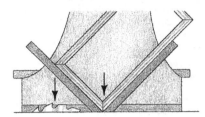

2. Clamp the box to your jig, and saw a slot through the corner.

3. Move fence or use spacers to reposition the jig for subsequent grooves.

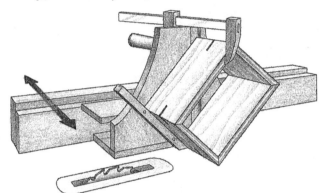

ADAPTING A TENONING JIG

First, remove the tenoning fence and the clamp.

Then screw new $3/4$" square fences to the jig.

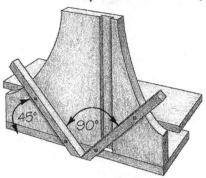

Complete plans for this jig are in the "Combination Mortise and Tenon Jig" chapter on page 240.

4. Saw splines to fit the grooves snugly.

5. Glue splines in the grooves.

6. When dry, use a chisel to trim them flush.

CUTTING MOCK DOVETAILS

Adjust the bit to just miss the inside corner of the joint.

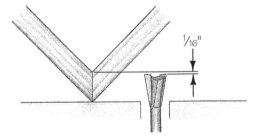

$1/16$"

Use the modified tenoning jig with your router table and a dovetail bit to create the slots for a mock dovetail joint.

To make the joint, chuck a dovetail bit in your table-mounted router and adjust the depth of cut as you would a saw blade for conventional splines. Use the same modified tenoning jig to hold your workpiece, and guide it along the router table fence to make the cut, as shown in the photo on the opposite page.

To make the dovetail splines, plane a 2- to 3-inch-wide board so its thickness is just slightly greater than the widest part of the dovetail slots. Rout the dovetail shape, as shown in *Making Dovetail Splines,* then rip the splines from the board. Saw them to length and glue them in the slots. When the glue dries, use a chisel to trim them flush.

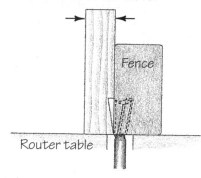
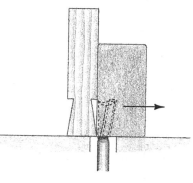

MAKING DOVETAIL SPLINES

Stock is 1/32" thicker than the width of the slots.

Fence

Router table

First, raise the bit about 1/16" higher than the setting used to rout the spline slots. Adjust fence so the bit will just cut to the corner of the stock. Cut the first face of the stock.

Next, make an identical cut on second face of the stock; then test the fit of the spline in the slot. Move the fence away from the bit in tiny increments to deepen the cut, and repeat the second cut until the spline fits just snugly.

Finally, rip the spline from the stock.

HIDDEN-MITER REINFORCEMENT

When I choose a miter joint over a dovetail or box joint, it's usually because I don't want the joinery to show. The splines and variations on splines shown previously won't do in these cases, but the hidden-spline miter and miters with box-joined tenons do quite well. Of the two, the hidden-spline miter is weaker but much easier to make.

Hidden-Spline Miter

You can hide spline reinforcement within an end-grain joint just as you can with a long-grain joint, as described in the "Splined Miter Joint" paragraphs on page 147. The joints are so similar that there is no

Miter joints with no visible reinforcement allow the grain of the wood to wrap right around the corner of the box (bottom). Notice how the box joint gives a mechanical appearance to the box (top).

point in repeating all the details. Instead, I'll simply describe how the end-grain version differs.

One obvious difference is that you'll cut the spline groove with the aid of the miter gauge instead of guiding the stock along the rip fence. Don't dispense with the rip fence entirely, however. Set it up as shown in *Hidden Splines*, and use it to position the stock in the miter gauge.

The biggest difference between these two splined miters is that the end-grain cousin requires splines with grain perpendicular to the joint line, as shown in *Hidden Splines*.

Once you have cut the grooves, prepare spline stock so its thickness just fits the grooves snugly. I usually resaw 4/4 (four-quarter) stock slightly over-sized on the table saw and then hand plane it to fit. Crosscut individual splines just a trifle shorter than the combined depth of the two grooves. They will be pretty flimsy until you get them glued in place. I find it easiest to cut the splines from a fairly narrow board and to use as many as I need to make up the length of the joint.

Box-Joined Tenons

You can have the strength of a box joint concealed within a miter joint, providing great strength, and a very clean appearance. While this combination of features is appealing the joint is *not* quick and easy to make.

As shown in *Hidden Box Joints*, making this joint involves several other techniques, including routing mortises, as explained in "Plunge-Routing"

on page 155; cutting bevels, as explained in "Cutting Bevels for Miter Joints" on page 176; making separate tenons, as explained in "Strong and Easy Mortise-and-Tenon Joints" on page 153; and making box joints, as explained in "Making Box Joints" on page 174. There are no special techniques just for this joint. The only real tricks to making the joint, beyond getting up the courage to try, are:

◆ Design the joint to use several tenon assemblies of modest width rather than one long one. This makes it easier to cut the box joints. I always use tenons 2 inches wide and leave less than 2 inches between mortises. *Hidden Box Joints* shows a typical relationship between mortise length and mortise spacing.

◆ Make the tenons fairly thick in relation to the stock you're joining in order to maximize the strength of the box joint. If I'm joining ¾-inch stock, I make the tenons ½ inch thick. If I'm joining ½-inch stock, I make the tenons ¼ to 5⁄16 inch thick. I've even joined 3⁄8-inch-thick stock with tenons ¼ inch thick, leaving only 1⁄16-inch-thick sides on the mortises.

◆ Design the box joint so the two tenons are identical, having a pin on one end only. This makes cutting the box joints much easier because the two halves are identical.

◆ Draw a cross section of the joint 2 or 3 times the actual size so you can easily see the relationship between the actual tenon length and the mortise depth before cutting the bevels. Plan so the mortises are 1⁄32 inch deeper than the tenons will actually go.

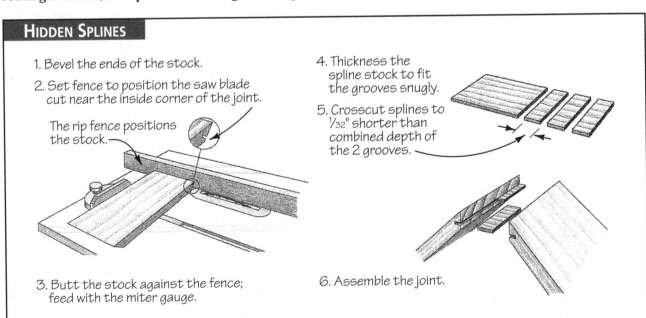

HIDDEN SPLINES

1. Bevel the ends of the stock.

2. Set fence to position the saw blade cut near the inside corner of the joint.

The rip fence positions the stock.

3. Butt the stock against the fence; feed with the miter gauge.

4. Thickness the spline stock to fit the grooves snugly.

5. Crosscut splines to 1⁄32" shorter than combined depth of the 2 grooves.

6. Assemble the joint.

HIDDEN BOX JOINTS

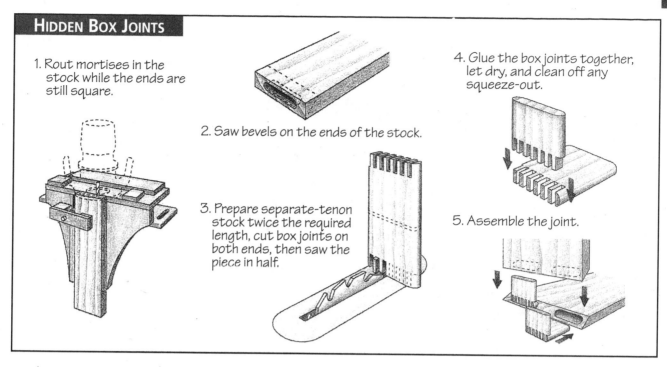

1. Rout mortises in the stock while the ends are still square.

2. Saw bevels on the ends of the stock.

3. Prepare separate-tenon stock twice the required length, cut box joints on both ends, then saw the piece in half.

4. Glue the box joints together, let dry, and clean off any squeeze-out.

5. Assemble the joint.

▶ Cut the tenon stock into pieces that are twice the tenon length plus a saw kerf, cut box joints in both ends, then saw the pieces in half.

▶ Rout the mortises before beveling the ends of the stock. This makes it much easier to rout the mortises and to measure the mortise depth.

▶ Glue the tenon pairs together at exactly 90 degrees, let the glue dry, and clean up any squeeze-out before assembling the miter joint. Gluing the tenons together ahead of time makes it much easier to assemble the miter joint. ●

When is this joint worth the effort? When you enjoy intricate work. When you need a very strong miter joint without visible reinforcement. When you need lots of identical miter joints, like a dozen music boxes. When you just want to prove to yourself that you can.

CORNER JOINTS

	STRENGTHS	WEAKNESSES	USES
RABBETS AND DADOES	Easy to cut Self-aligning	Not very strong Not very attractive	Simple boxes Light-duty drawers
LOCK JOINTS	Easy to cut Very easy to assemble	Not very strong but better than rabbets	Light-duty drawers
BOX JOINTS	Very strong	Mechanical appearance	Boxes; Cases
VISIBLY REINFORCED MITERS	Decorative; Good strength	Fussy to make	Boxes; Cases
HIDDEN-SPLINE MITERS	Clean appearance; Moderate strength	Time-consuming to make	Boxes; Cases
HIDDEN BOX JOINT MITERS	Clean appearance; Very strong	Very time-consuming to make	Strong boxes; Cases

DOVETAILS

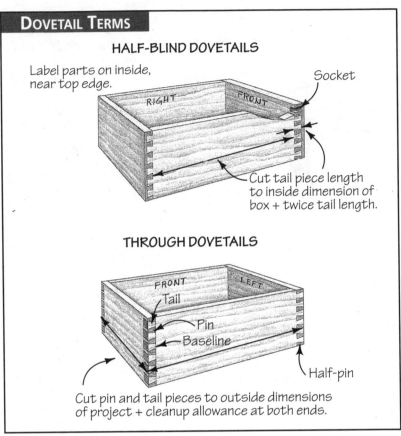

DOVETAIL TERMS

HALF-BLIND DOVETAILS

Label parts on inside, near top edge.

RIGHT FRONT

Socket

Cut tail piece length to inside dimension of box + twice tail length.

THROUGH DOVETAILS

FRONT LEFT

Tail

Pin

Baseline

Half-pin

Cut pin and tail pieces to outside dimensions of project + cleanup allowance at both ends.

In the minds of many, whether woodworkers or not, dovetails are the touchstone of craftsmanship—anything assembled with dovetail joints is seen as finely crafted. It's not a bad criterion. Joining the ends of boards is difficult because the joint area is small and the end grain of the boards glues poorly. Dovetails overcome these difficulties by providing excellent mechanical strength and by creating lots of side-grain surface, which glues well. The joint requires good craftsmanship because each of the large number of surfaces making up the joint must be in exactly the right place and position. When done well, the joint not only provides good strength and long life, it *looks* both strong and handsome. The reputation of dovetails as a touchstone of craftsmanship is indeed well warranted.

Less justifiable, however, is the notion that there is only one right way to make dovetails. The arrangement of the pins and tails gives the joint its strength and appearance; how you cut the joint should be a matter of personal preference and practicality. After all, once the joint is assembled, the technique you used to make it is history.

There are many techniques and jigs to choose from. You can rout strong, utilitarian, half-blind dovetails with an inexpensive and simple jig. You can chop the most elegant and delicate dovetails in virtually any shape, size, or angle with a saw, chisel, and mallet. You can cut parts of the joint with the table saw, band saw, or scroll saw, and then finish with hand techniques. And you can rout decorative through dovetails with a choice of jigs that allow varying amounts of adjustment. Few operations in woodworking offer as many alternatives.

ROUTING HALF-BLIND DOVETAILS

If there were a grand prize for the most clever and elegant jig in all of woodworking, it would have to go to the jig for routing half-blind dovetails. This device guides a router to cut both the pins and the tails at the same time, beveling tails and sockets on three sides, as shown in *Half-Blind Dovetail Jigs*, instead of only two as in traditional hand-cut dovetails. The jig makes it possible to cut both pins and tails at the same time by making the two the same exact size and by offsetting the pin and tail boards in the jig.

HALF-BLIND DOVETAIL JIGS

Tails are angled on 3 sides.

The jig holds the boards inside out for routing tails and sockets at the same time. Fold the tail piece 180° for assembly.

Adjusting the bit shallower makes the fit looser.

Same

Shallow bit cuts narrower tail and wider socket.

Same

Conversely, adjusting the bit deeper makes the fit tighter.

NOTE: *Pins and tails can be confusing. In traditional terminology a "tail" is the part of the joint with the shape of a dove's tail on the face of the stock. A "pin" shows that dovetail shape on the end of the stock. That is how I use the terms in this book. The terms pin and tail are reversed by the makers of some half-blind jigs, however. This makes their instruction manuals a real challenge to follow.*

THROUGH AND HALF-BLIND DOVETAILS

Dovetails that show the ends of both the pins and the tails on the two outside corners of the joint are known as *through* dovetails. They are found in utilitarian traditional woodwork, like blanket chests and candle and Bible boxes, and in contemporary designs that expose joinery as a part of their aesthetic.

More sophisticated traditional woodwork shows no end grain on the outside surfaces. In these designs, drawer corners are joined so the drawer front covers the ends of the tails in a joint known as a half-blind dovetail.

Your choice between through dovetails and half-blind dovetails affects the method of construction. If you prefer hand tools, through dovetails are much easier to cut than half-blind dovetails. But if you prefer the router, half-blinds are considerably quicker to cut. Also, the jig for half-blind dovetails is less expensive than the one for through dovetails.

You pay two prices for the simple efficiency of half-blind jigs. First, the dovetails have a very repetitive, mechanical look to them. This is seldom a real problem since the whole idea behind half-blind dovetails is to hide the joinery. If they're hidden, a repetitive, mechanical appearance hardly matters.

The second price you pay is limited flexibility. If a routed half-blind dovetail joint ends with a part of a socket, the corresponding tail will be quite fragile. To avoid this, the drawer or box must have a height that is a multiple of the dovetail spacing. In some applications you might not have that design flexibility.

In spite of these limitations, the basic half-blind dovetail jig is the most useful jig for large numbers of woodworkers. It's ideal for building strong drawers for everything from delicate end tables to chests of drawers to kitchen cabinets to tool storage lockers. It also happens to cost the least, provided you get one of the versions that isn't designed for high-production shops.

When you first get one of these jigs, make some test joints and save the ones that fit right. Then when you tackle a project, you'll know just how long the tails must be for the joint to fit well. You need to know the exact tail length in order to cut your tail pieces to the correct length, as shown in *Dovetail Terms* on page 184.

One aspect of these jigs that may not seem intuitive is the adjustment of the fit of the joint. If a test joint is too loose, make the depth of cut *deeper;* if the test joint is too tight, make the depth of cut *shallower.* The adjustment is very sensitive—a change of the router's depth of cut of 1/128 inch will produce a noticeable change in the fit of the joint.

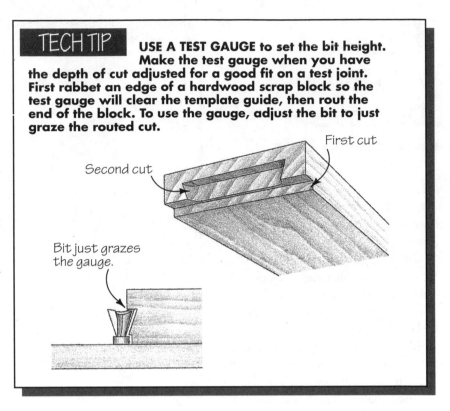

TECH TIP USE A TEST GAUGE to set the bit height. Make the test gauge when you have the depth of cut adjusted for a good fit on a test joint. First rabbet an edge of a hardwood scrap block so the test gauge will clear the template guide, then rout the end of the block. To use the gauge, adjust the bit to just graze the routed cut.

First cut

Second cut

Bit just grazes the gauge.

TECH TIP TO GET THE STRONGEST JOINT, assemble it the same day you cut it. If you leave the pieces to assemble another day, small changes in humidity and moisture content will affect the various pieces in different ways, causing slight changes in the fit. So make sure you don't cut more joints than you'll be able to assemble in the same work session.

You'll also find that the best adjustment for joining two pieces of pine or basswood is not the best adjustment for joining two pieces of hard maple.

Cut all of your parts to length and width before you start cutting the actual joints. Then arrange the parts the way you want them to go together and then *label* them. To place a piece in the jig properly, you'll need to know and be able to double-check the top edge, the inside surface, and where the piece goes in the final assembly. I make a habit of penciling the part name on the inside near the top edge.

To cut the joint, clamp the pin and tail pieces in the jig with the inside surface facing out, with the top edges against the jig's stops. The pin piece goes on the top of the jig, and the tail piece goes on the front, overlapping the end of the pin piece and flush, as shown in Step 3 on the opposite page. Fit the template to the jig as described in the jig manufacturer's instructions, and adjust the bit based on prior tests. Begin routing with a scoring cut along the baseline to prevent tear-out. This should be a climb cut made from right to left along the tail piece. When you reach the left edge of the stock, begin routing out between the tails, creating both the tails and their sockets. Keep the template guide in contact with the template, and work your way from the left edge of the stock to the right edge.

STEP-BY-STEP
ROUTING HALF-BLIND DOVETAILS

1 Install the template guide and bit.

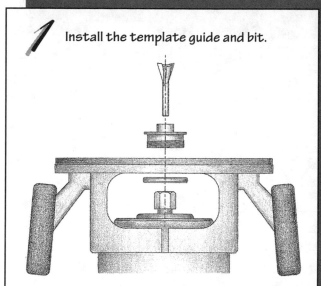

2 Adjust the depth of cut based on prior test joints.

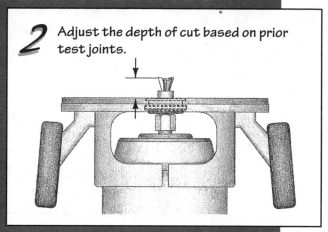

3 Clamp the pin and tail pieces in the jig and install the template.

Pin piece

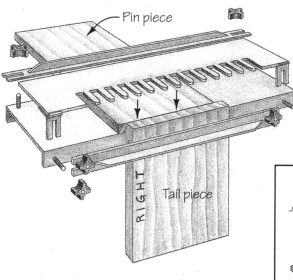

RIGHT

Tail piece

4 Score shoulders on the tail piece, routing right to left.

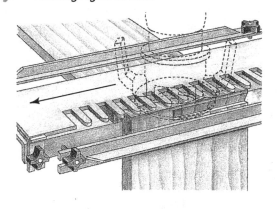

5 Rout the joint from left to right.

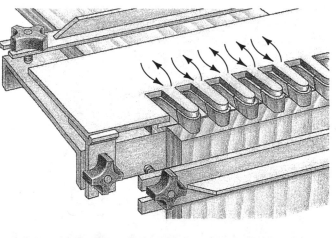

ROUTING THROUGH DOVETAILS

The simple, one-bit approach to routing dovetails that works so well for half-blind dovetails won't work for through dovetails. To rout a through dovetail joint with a conventional appearance, you have to use a dovetail bit for the tails and a straight bit for the pins, as shown in *Through Dovetail Jigs*. You also have to rout both the pin and tail pieces with the stock in the upright position, instead of routing tails upright and pins horizontal as with a half-blind jig. Like half-blind jigs, however, through dovetail jigs require forethought at the design stage in order to have the joint end with the conventional half-pin.

Different jig makers take different approaches to routing through dovetails, as explained in "Choices among Jigs" on page 190, but the actual steps in using the various jigs are quite similar. Specific nitty-gritty details for how to go about each of the steps vary from jig to jig, but the manuals that

Routing through dovetails requires that you use a straight bit for the pins shown here and a dovetail bit for the tails.

come with them are good at those details. The steps shown on the opposite page outline the overall procedure. If you're in the market for one of these jigs, the steps will give you a good idea of what you're getting into. If you own one, they'll help you understand

---

THROUGH DOVETAIL JIGS

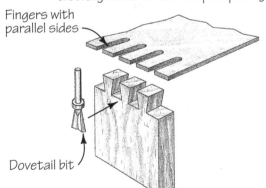

The tail template guides the router in a straight line to cut the pin openings.

Fingers with parallel sides

Dovetail bit

The pin template guides the router at 2 separate angles to cut the tail openings.

Fingers with angled sides

Straight bit

Some jigs use a bit with a bearing on the shank to follow the template.

Others use a template guide that's mounted on the router baseplate.

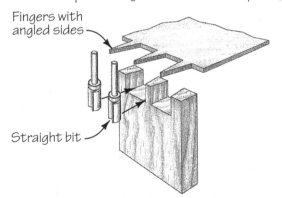

Adjust the pin template to change the fit of the joint. Farther forward makes the pins larger and the fit tighter. Farther back makes the pins smaller and the fit looser.

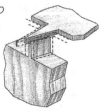

STEP-BY-STEP
ROUTING THROUGH DOVETAILS

1 Clamp the tail piece in a vise or jig, depending on the jig design.

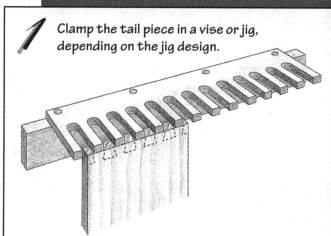

2 Set the tail template (if adjustable) to the required spacing of the pin openings, and clamp in place.

3 Install dovetail bit, and adjust the depth of cut to thickness of stock + thickness of template + allowance for trimming tail ends after assembly.

Template guide or bearing

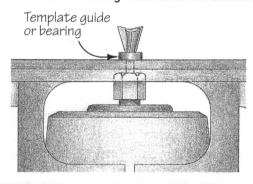

4 Rout the tails.

NOTE: Template shown permits adjustment of tail width. Other jigs work similarly.

5 Clamp the pin piece in the jig, and clamp the pin template in place.

6 Install a straight bit, and adjust the depth of cut to thickness of tail stock + thickness of template + allowance for trimming tail ends after assembly.

7 Rout the pins.

NOTE: Template shown is fully adjustable type. Other jigs work similarly.

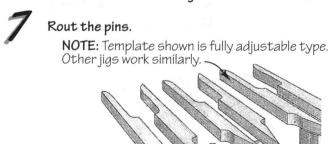

Rout tail openings in sequence shown.

CHOICES AMONG JIGS

Through dovetail jigs are a fairly recent development, dating back only to the late 1970s. Today there are three types of jigs for guiding a router to cut this classic joint. Despite differences in appearance, all three are identical in principle: All use templates to guide the router, and all use a dovetail bit to cut tails and a straight bit to cut pins. They differ in the amount of adjustment you can make to the jig in order to arrange the pins and tails to your liking.

The first of these jigs to come on the market is deceptively simple. It consists of a nonadjustable template for routing tails and a matching template for routing pins, as shown in *Nonadjustable Dovetail Jigs,* and that's all. There is no clamping hardware to limit the width of the stock you can join, which means you have to provide your own means of clamping the template to the stock. You make all of the adjustments for the fit of the joint when you attach hardwood backing blocks to the templates, which makes it harder to fine-tune the adjustment for harder or softer wood. The templates are extremely simple to use—as long as you are happy with the spacing machined into them. To change the spacing, you have to reposition the templates on the stock for each tail and then align the pin template to a scribed line for each pin.

Adjustable jigs are complex in comparison to the nonadjustable variety but not impossibly so once you get used to them. They consist of templates for guiding the router plus clamps for

NONADJUSTABLE DOVETAIL JIGS

The simplest through dovetail jigs consist of 2 aluminum templates, 1 for tails and 1 for pins.

Tail template has parallel sides.

Pin template has angled sides.

securing the stock plus adjustments for spacing the pins and tails and for fine-tuning the fit. Their templates are really assemblies of template sections. You can position these sections pretty much as you like along a mounting bar. In order to ensure that the pins and tails match each other, the angled template surfaces for routing the pins are on the same piece of metal as the straight template surfaces for routing the tails—you can't move one without

what's going on and will provide a "refresher course" if you've been away from the jig for a while. With any of these jigs, be sure to make both the pins and the tails a bit longer than the thickness of the board they

join so that they will stick out a trifle when the joint is assembled. Then after the glue is dry, plane or sand them flush. It's a lot easier to sand the pins and tails flush with the boards they join than to sand the

moving the other to match. To bring the appropriate set of surfaces into use, you reposition the whole template assembly.

There are two kinds of jig with adjustable section templates. On one kind, a section of the template incorporates both a fixed width slot to guide the router when cutting the pin opening and an arrowlike portion to guide the router when cutting the matching pin. This kind of jig, shown in *Adjustable-Tail Jigs,* allows you to adjust the location of the pin openings (and therefore the tail size) but not the size of the pin openings (or the size of the pins themselves).

The other kind of adjustable jig further divides up the template so you can adjust the pin size as well as the pin location, as shown in *Fully Adjustable Jigs.* At first blush this would seem to give you twice as much versatility. But keep two things in mind: First, most woodworkers strive for delicate pins; and second, you can't rout pin openings any smaller than the bit that's cutting them. The added versatility of this type of jig simply gives you the freedom to make indelicate pins.

ADJUSTABLE-TAIL JIGS

This type of jig uses a template assembly. Each section includes a straight portion for routing tails and an angled portion for routing pins. You can adjust the sections to vary pin spacing.

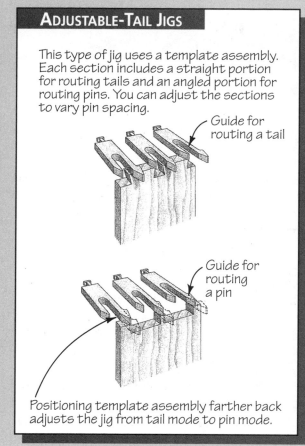

Guide for routing a tail

Guide for routing a pin

Positioning template assembly farther back adjusts the jig from tail mode to pin mode.

FULLY ADJUSTABLE JIGS

Each movable section in this type of jig includes 1 side of a tail-routing template and 1 side of a pin-routing template. You can adjust pin and tail size and position.

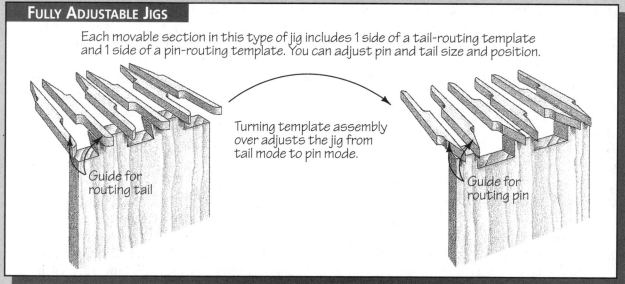

Turning template assembly over adjusts the jig from tail mode to pin mode.

Guide for routing tail

Guide for routing pin

whole surface of the adjoining boards flush with a pin or tail that happens to come out a bit shallow. You can get by with $\frac{1}{32}$ inch extra, but I usually allow $\frac{1}{16}$ inch.

One last word about routed through dovetails. Don't try to fool a knowledgeable woodworker into thinking that you cut them with mallet and chisel—he'll recognize the angles and the pin size.

CUTTING DOVETAILS BY HAND

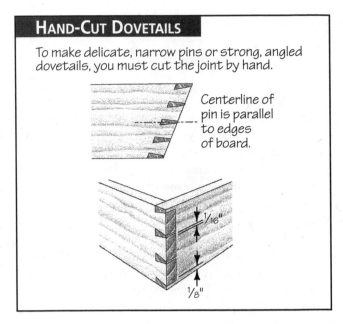

Hand-cut dovetails have some very significant advantages over routed dovetails—and some significant disadvantages. On the plus side, they offer unrivaled flexibility. When cutting by hand, you can make the most delicate of pins—joints with pin openings that taper down to little more than the kerf of the dovetail saw, as shown in *Hand-Cut Dovetails*. Or you can join boards at angles and angle the pins and tails accordingly so that they look right, as shown in the drawing. And you can do them at 10 o'clock at night without waking up the whole household with a whining router.

On the minus side, it takes considerably more skill and practice to produce good-fitting hand-cut dovetails than it does to rout them. Hand cutting is also slower than routing, particularly if you have more than a couple of identical joints to cut. Highly experienced woodworkers may be able to chop out a dovetail joint with hand tools in less time than it takes a neophyte to set up a jig, but I'll stand by my claim that routing is faster in any fair comparison. Whether faster is better is a separate question, of course. If you work wood because it's fun, then faster means the fun is over sooner.

To cut dovetails by hand, do a good job of it, and enjoy the process, you need the right tools. These include:

◗ A dovetail saw or gent's saw about 8 to 10 inches long with about 18 or 20 finely set teeth per inch
◗ Bench chisels in a variety of widths, from quite narrow to a full inch wide
◗ A mallet with a flat face to drive the chisels
◗ A cutting gauge or, second best, a marking gauge
◗ A good try square or combination square
◗ Either a sliding bevel or dovetail markers
◗ Either a scratch awl, a marking knife, a well-sharpened carpenter's pencil, or a *sharp* conventional pencil with hard lead
◗ Clamps ●

Unfortunately, only the expert has the experience to get good results with marginal tools. The inexperienced beginner needs to concentrate on positioning and aiming the tools, not on compensating for tools that don't cut where they're aimed.

The tried and proven procedures for cutting dovetails by hand consist of laying out one-half of the joint, sawing the sides, chopping out the waste with a chisel, tracing the first half of the joint onto the other half, and sawing and chopping the second half of the joint.

There are no really persuasive reasons for cutting the tails first or the pins first unless the pins are especially delicate. In that case tracing deep and narrow pin openings from the tail piece onto the pin piece can be difficult, so it may be wiser to cut the pins first. If the pin openings are roomy, however, you may find it easier to trace from the tail piece onto the pin piece. It won't take you many practice joints to get a feel for the sequence that you find most comfortable.

Layout of the first half of the joint is a combination of noncritical, even freehand, lines and highly critical lines. When laying out the baselines, make both the pins and tails a trifle longer than the thickness of the stock they will join. This will make them protrude by that trifle after assembly. You can then sand or plane them flush for a neat appearance. (If you try to make them the exact thickness of the adjoining piece, there is a risk that they'll wind up a trifle short. Then your only remedy is to plane down the entire surface of the adjoining piece.) The position of the baseline can make allowance for as much or little of this cleanup as

STEP-BY-STEP LAYING OUT DOVETAILS

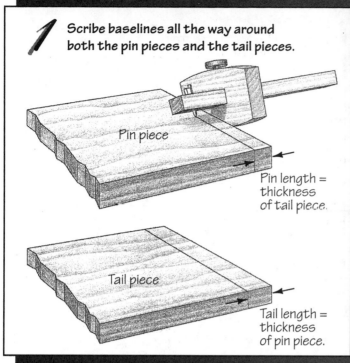

1 Scribe baselines all the way around both the pin pieces and the tail pieces.

Pin piece

Pin length = thickness of tail piece.

Tail piece

Tail length = thickness of pin piece.

2 Lay out the ends of the tails on the end of the tail piece. Scribe a line square across the end of the board.

3 Adjust sliding bevel to the dovetail angle, then scribe the sides of the tails from the layout on the end to the baseline on both sides of the tail piece.

8°–14° (typ.)

Mark pin openings on both sides and on the end.

you like, so it's a bit arbitrary; but the baseline *must* be straight and parallel to the end of the board.

The angle that you choose for the sides of the tails is up to you, but you should be aware of the conventions. Traditional dovetail angles range from about 7 degrees to 14 degrees. You'll often see this expressed as "rise and run," as explained in *2 Ways to Measure Angles* on page 13. A 7-degree dovetail has a rise of 1 in a run of about 8. A 14-degree dovetail rises about 1 in 4. As a general rule, low angles are used with harder woods and higher angles with softer woods. While the position and angle of the pin openings is up to you, the ends of the tails on the end grain of the board *must* be truly square to the face of the stock, and the lines marking the sides of the tails *must* meet the end-grain layout precisely. Any of the four marking tools listed with the tools on the opposite page will work well for this layout.

When sawing to the lines, it's amazingly easy to saw on the wrong side of the line, even after a lot of experience. So don't skip the step of clearly marking the waste areas, then keep the saw on the waste side of the line. It's a lot easier to remove a shaving with a chisel if you err on the waste side than to grow some of the tree back if you err on the "save" side.

The chisel work is the part that worries the

inexperienced the most. There are two keys to superior results. First, make sure your chisels are as sharp as you can get them and make sure there's no rounding or tiny bevel on the back side. Review the chapter on sharpening on page 24 if in doubt.

Second, use a guide block, as shown in Step 2 on page 194. Make it about 2 × 2 inches in cross section, with sides that are perfectly square to each other. Three or 4 inches longer than the width of the pin and tail pieces is a convenient length; so if you cut dovetails in a wide range of stock widths, you'll want guide blocks of several lengths. A strong, stable hardwood like maple is best for the guide block.

When positioning the chisel for the vertical cuts, make sure the cutting edge is right up against the guide block, but tilt the chisel *very* slightly away from the top surface of the guide block—a $\frac{1}{32}$- to $\frac{1}{16}$-inch gap between the chisel and the block at the top is fine. This slight angle creates a bit of hollow, allowing the joint to fit tightly along the baseline. Since the hollow is on

STEP-BY-STEP CUTTING DOVETAILS BY HAND

1 Clamp tail board vertically in a vise, with tails at elbow height, and saw the sides of the tails.

Keep saw kerf on the waste side of the line.

2 Chop out pin openings.

Align guide with the baseline.

Chop down 1/16" or less, then chip out the waste.

Remove 1/2 the waste from 1 side, then turn stock to finish.

Hardwood guide block

If pin opening on the end is too narrow for the chisel, chop out the waste from the face of the stock.

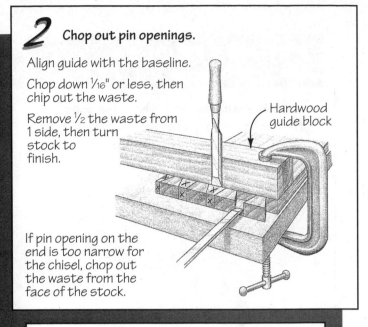

3 Clamp pin piece vertically in a vise, then scribe the pin ends from the tails.

Make sure baseline of tails aligns with the edge of the pin board.

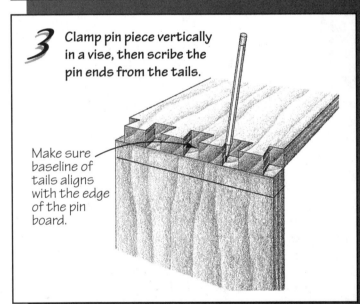

4 Scribe down from the ends of the pins to the pin baseline.

Mark waste areas.

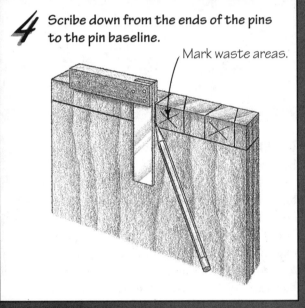

5 Saw pin sides on the waste side of the layout.

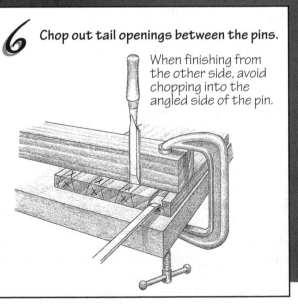

6 Chop out tail openings between the pins.

When finishing from the other side, avoid chopping into the angled side of the pin.

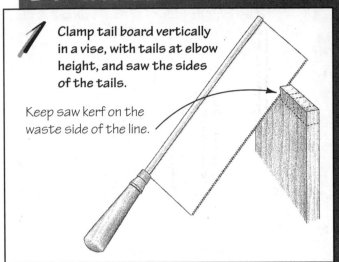

an end-grain surface, where glue won't bond well anyway, strength in the joint is not sacrificed.

When you're cutting very narrow pin openings in the tail piece, you won't be able to chip out the waste from the end grain—the opening will be too small for even your narrowest chisel. The way to deal with this problem is to chop in from the face of the stock at an angle. It's one more skill to acquire; and rather than attempting it when you're new to hand cutting dovetails, I suggest that you design your first few joints with wider pins. That way you can get the other skills down pat before tackling this added complication.

Having cut the first part of the joint, check it to make sure the sides are flat; and if the first part is the tail piece, check also that the sides are square to the face. Then trace the first part onto the second part. If you did the tails first, you'll trace them onto the end grain of the pin piece. If you did the pins first, you'll trace them onto the face of the tail piece. In both cases make sure the baseline of the tails is accurately aligned with the edge of the pin piece. When tracing, you may find that the most convenient marking tool is a scratch awl or standard pencil with hard lead. Being long and slender, they reach into corners more easily than marking knives or carpenter's pencils.

Sawing and chopping out the second half of the joint is just like sawing and chopping out the first half. If this second half is the pins, start from the inside face of the pin board. From the inside, the tail openings that you're chopping flair out. Then after turning the board over to finish from the outside face, angle the chisel so you won't chop into the pin itself.

The final step is trying the fit of the joint and paring back any surfaces that don't fit. A word of caution here: A pin or a tail that won't fit into its opening may be too fat on the left or too fat on the right, and it does make a difference. If you pare the wrong side, it will fit okay but all the rest of the parts will be off. To avoid this problem, align the edges of the two boards and then see which surfaces aren't fitting. You can make the joint fit by making the pin or tail smaller or by making the opening bigger, but make sure you pare the correct side. Your goal is a fit that requires firm hand pressure or light taps with a mallet. A fit that requires too much persuasion to come together is sure to split one piece or the other.

COMPARISON OF DOVETAILING TECHNIQUES

	ROUTING HALF-BLIND DOVETAILS	ROUTING THROUGH DOVETAILS	CUTTING DOVETAILS BY HAND	MARRYING MACHINES TO HAND-TOOL TECHNIQUES
TOOLS NEEDED	Router and jig with 2-digit price tag	Router and jig with 3-digit price tag	Standard general-purpose hand tools	Standard general-purpose hand tools and machines
EXPERIENCE NEEDED	Minimal general woodworking experience	Minimal general woodworking experience	Considerable hand-tool experience	Moderate general woodworking experience
SPACING VERSATILITY	2 or 3 sizes; fixed uniform spacing	Varies with jig	Unlimited	Unlimited
SUITABLE FOR HALF-BLIND DOVETAILS	Yes	No	Yes, but difficult	Sawing tails only
SUITABLE FOR THROUGH DOVETAILS	No	Yes	Yes	Yes
BEST APPLICATIONS	Joining drawers	Large numbers of exposed, robust-looking joints	Limited numbers of very elegant or angled joints	Large numbers of hand-cut look-alikes

Marrying Machines to Hand-Tool Techniques

General-purpose shop machinery like the table saw can't cut a complete dovetail joint, but it can speed up parts of the job. A dado head, for example, can cut dovetail pins.

Woodworkers, being a clever lot, have come up with various ways of using standard shop machinery to speed up the cutting of large numbers of dovetails without sacrificing all of the flexibility of hand-cut joints. The most versatile of these techniques are cutting pins with a dado head on the table saw, sawing the sides of tails with either a band saw or scroll saw, and drilling out some of the waste in the pin openings with a drill press. If you combine all three of these techniques, very little hand work remains. Or you can use just one or two of the machine techniques and do more of the work by hand. Keep in mind that the basic sequence of steps is still the sequence of hand cutting, and some hand work is still required; the machines simply aid one or more of the steps.

It's worth noting that these machine techniques preserve most of the flexibility of hand-cut dovetails. I know of one very successful professional woodworker who cuts all of his exposed through dovetails this way, yet they have all the earmarks of fine, hand-cut dovetails—pins that taper down to the width of a saw kerf and angles that are not dictated by the makers of router bits.

Cutting Pins with a Dado Head

If you have a good dado head for your table saw, preferably one that cuts dadoes with a nice smooth bottom, you can cut dovetail pins with it, as shown in *Cutting Pins with a Dado Head*. The best way to use this technique is to cut the pins first, then trace them onto the tail board to cut the tails. So begin by laying out the pins. They can be as delicate as you like.

Set up the dado head to a width not greater than the narrow side of the tail openings in the pin board, and adjust the depth of cut to the height of the pin baseline when the pin board is on end. Make a long extension fence for your miter gauge out of a piece of scrap, and screw it to the miter gauge. The fence should extend beyond the dado

head when the gauge is in the left slot *and* when it's in the right slot, because you'll be using the gauge in both slots.

Now adjust the miter gauge to the dovetail angle and cut the first side of all the tail openings in the pin board, as shown in the drawing. The long extension fence will support the stock where the dado head comes through, minimizing tear-out. Nevertheless, position the stock so the inside face is against the fence. This will ensure that any

CUTTING PINS WITH A DADO HEAD

Angle the miter gauge to cut one side of the tail openings, then angle the miter gauge in the opposite direction to cut the other side.

Miter gauge extension fence minimizes tear-out.

Set depth of cut to thickness of the tail piece.

Outside face of pin piece

Adjust miter gauge to the dovetail angle.

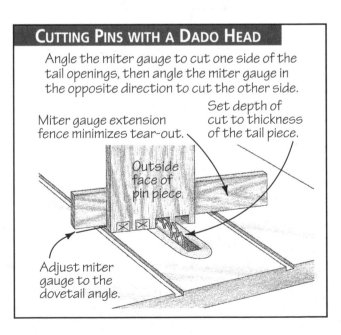

tear-out that you do get will be on the inside of the assembled joint, where it will show less. Hold the stock firmly against the fence by hand, and make just a single pass on the first side of the tail openings. You'll find it most convenient to make half of the cuts with the miter gauge on one side of the dado head and then switch to the other side when the stock begins to overhang the fence too far. Readjust the miter gauge to the dovetail angle in the opposite direction to cut the second side of the tail openings, and make additional passes as necessary to remove any remaining waste. With experience you'll be able to eyeball the pin locations as you cut them, without any prior layout.

If you discover that your dado head leaves an unacceptably ragged cut along the baseline, readjust the depth of cut slightly shallower so you can clean up the baseline with a chisel. To complete the joint, trace the pins onto the tail board and cut the tails by the conventional hand-tool methods described above, or with the aid of a band saw or scroll saw as described next.

Sawing Tails by Machine

For years, woodworkers with well-equipped shops have used band saws and scroll saws to speed up cutting tails. Most often they saw the angled sides by machine and then chop out the waste to the baseline with chisels. Making several additional saw cuts between the two side cuts makes the waste removal even easier. If the pin openings are uncommonly wide, you can even turn and saw along the baseline, removing most of the waste in one chunk before trimming to the baseline with a chisel.

The technique is straightforward, as shown in *Band-Sawing Tails,* and requires no explanation, but a couple of tips may help. First, keep in mind that these are straight cuts, not curves, so avoid narrow blades. I've had the best success with a ½-inch-wide band saw blade. Second, if you're not going to use the same blade for cutting curves, take the sharpness off the *sides* of the teeth by gently holding a Carborundum stone up to the sides of the blade while the saw is running. This will give you a markedly smoother cut.

Drilling Out Waste

If the only dovetails you've ever cut by hand were in fairly soft wood and had nice, big pin openings, you might not appreciate the advantage of

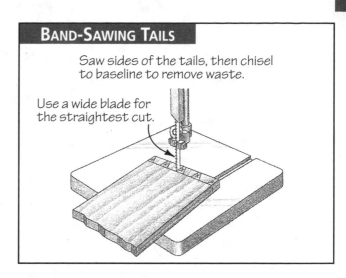

BAND-SAWING TAILS

Saw sides of the tails, then chisel to baseline to remove waste.

Use a wide blade for the straightest cut.

drilling out the waste. But if your stock is thick, the wood is hard, the pin openings are delicately proportioned, and there are a lot of them, then you'll understand why some woodworkers love this technique.

There are two secrets to making this technique work well. The first is to lay out the pin openings around the bit you intend to use, as shown in *Drilling Out Pin Openings/Pin-Opening Layout.* This not only ensures that the bit will fit but also ensures that after you've drilled the hole, the narrow part of the waste will be free to fall out. All that remains for you to do is chisel out the corners, which is easy because you've already sawed the sides of the openings.

The second secret is to use a Forstner bit. Since these bits are guided by their rim rather than by a brad point, you can position the bit to the layout lines accurately by eye.

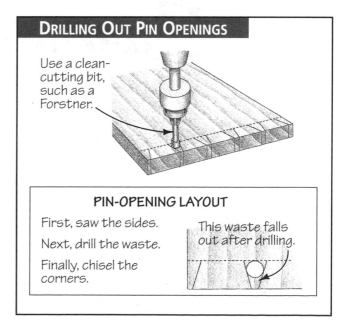

DRILLING OUT PIN OPENINGS

Use a clean-cutting bit, such as a Forstner.

PIN-OPENING LAYOUT

First, saw the sides.

Next, drill the waste.

Finally, chisel the corners.

This waste falls out after drilling.

4

SHAPING

*T*apered legs, molded and curved edges, and panel doors are no more difficult to make than good straight-and-square construction—but they're a leap ahead in appearance, giving your projects greater visual interest and less of a purely utilitarian look. And they're appropriate on both highly ornate designs and those with Shaker simplicity.

When I first started reaching beyond flat slabs of wood and boxlike shapes, I was quite surprised at the variety of techniques that would produce the same basic result. And I was surprised at how much I could do with the fairly modest tools and machines that I had. I expected, for example, that I would need a shaper to make really nice raised-panel doors and was surprised at how nice a door I could make with just my table saw. I expected that my router would limit me to dollhouse-sized moldings and was surprised at what I could achieve by building up larger profiles from smaller parts.

More important, I was surprised at how much these newly discovered shaping techniques improved the appearance of my projects and how much they revived my pleasure in woodworking. Now when I consider a new project, I look forward to the parts that challenge me to learn a new shaping technique.

TAPERING LEGS

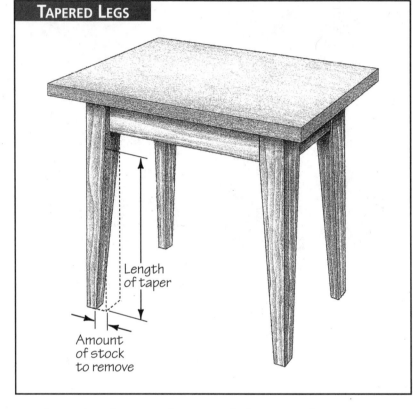

Length of taper

Amount of stock to remove

One of the most common design problems that a woodworker faces is making a leg that's thick enough to house the joinery at the apron yet doesn't look clunky or overengineered. The simple solution is tapering the leg. When a leg tapers, there's room enough at the top to house the tenons on the aprons, yet the rest of the leg appears more delicate. Tapering can make the difference between a leg that looks like it belongs on a dining table and one that belongs on a workbench, the difference between a table that looks like a gazelle and one that looks like a hippopotamus.

You can taper legs a variety of ways, using any of four different machines. An obvious and direct approach is to lay out the cut, saw to the line on the band saw,

then smooth the cut on the jointer or with a hand plane. But if you don't have a band saw, or want to avoid eyeballing your way down a line, you can taper legs quite efficiently and accurately with a table saw, a jointer, or a router table. Tapering with these tools is not more difficult than band-sawing, it's just a little less obvious because the tools are designed for straight and parallel cuts. My favorite technique happens to use the jointer, but each of the techniques mentioned here has its place.

When selecting stock for tapered legs, keep in mind that flat grain has a distinctly different appearance from edge grain. To my eye, a long, narrow shape like a leg looks best with fairly

CHOOSING STOCK FOR LEGS

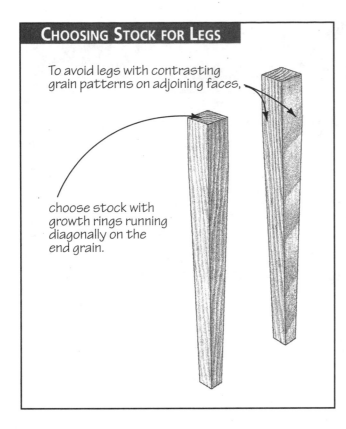

To avoid legs with contrasting grain patterns on adjoining faces,

choose stock with growth rings running diagonally on the end grain.

NOTE: *Before you start setting up for the taper cuts, make sure you have finished all your other work on the legs. You'll find it much easier to cut mortises and trim the legs to finished length while the stock is still straight, square, and uniform in width and thickness.*

Taper Layout

When the joinery and other shaping are complete, lay out the tapers on the legs. The easiest dimensions to use are the length of the taper and the amount of stock you want to remove, as shown in *Taper Layout*. Don't try to determine the number of degrees of taper. You can't do anything practical with that information.

Most legs are tapered on just two sides, the inside faces, as shown in *Tapered Legs*, though there may be occasions when you want to taper all four sides. Begin the layout by drawing lines square across the faces of the leg to indicate the tops of the tapers. On most designs these lines will be a fraction of an inch below where the aprons will go. Use a fairly soft lead for the marks because when you're done cutting the tapers, you'll have to sand or scrape off the marks. Some woodworkers mark the tops of the tapers with masking tape to avoid pencil marks on the leg. Next, mark off the amount of stock to remove at the bottom of the leg. Complete the layout by drawing the cut line between the two marks, as shown in *Taper Layout*.

Strictly speaking, the actual cut line is needed only if you intend to saw the taper on the band saw. The other tapering techniques require only a mark indicating the face to be tapered.

plain, parallel lines in the grain. I also find it most pleasing when adjoining faces of a leg are very similar, as shown in *Choosing Stock for Legs*. To keep the grain pattern simple and avoid big differences between adjoining faces, I usually choose stock with growth rings running diagonally on the ends of the legs. The appearance of this grain orientation is fairly plain. It avoids flamboyant face grain, horizontal lines across the legs, and the ray fleck found in oak and related species. For strength, and to avoid tear-out when planing, I try to choose straight-grained stock.

TAPER LAYOUT

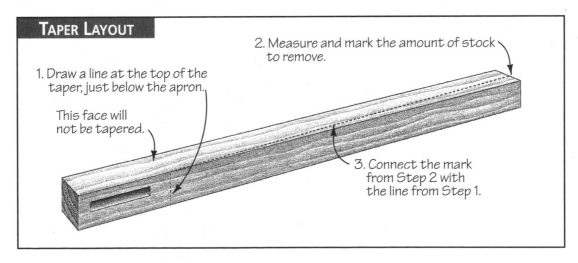

2. Measure and mark the amount of stock to remove.

1. Draw a line at the top of the taper, just below the apron.

This face will not be tapered.

3. Connect the mark from Step 2 with the line from Step 1.

TAPERING ON THE BAND SAW

Tapering a table leg on the band saw is about as simple as it gets. The only concern is near the top of the leg, where the tapering cut meets the untapered part of leg at a very low angle. When you try to start a band saw cut at this low angle, the blade tends to slide along the stock instead of biting in. But if you cut in the opposite direction so the cut ends at the low angle, the blade tends to jump out of the stock prematurely, leaving part of the taper uncut. For me, the little uncut ridge is the lesser evil. I start the cut at the foot, as shown in Step 1 on this page; then I plane off the uncut part of the taper when smoothing the sawed surfaces, as shown in Step 2. If you like, you can prevent the blade from jumping out by holding a piece of scrap against the side of the leg as shown in the bottom drawing of Step 1.

 Lay out the taper, then saw just outside the line.

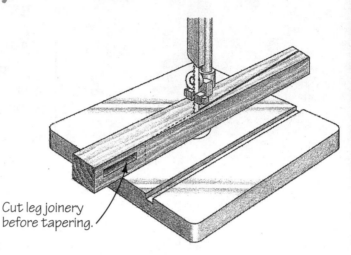

Cut leg joinery before tapering.

The blade will tend to jump out at the end of the cut. You can plane off the remainder when you smooth the sawed surfaces,

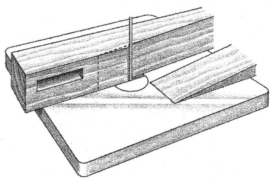

OR

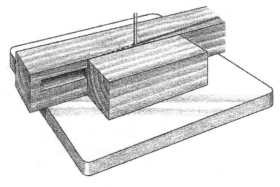

hold a block of scrap against the stock to prevent the blade from jumping out.

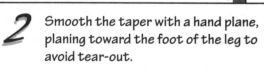 Smooth the taper with a hand plane, planing toward the foot of the leg to avoid tear-out.

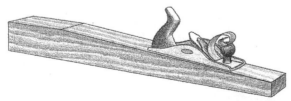

TAPERING ON THE JOINTER OR ROUTER TABLE

Some woodworkers consider tapering on the jointer a form of black magic. In practice, it's often the easiest and quickest way to taper a leg. I prefer it over other techniques whenever the amount of stock to remove is fairly little, say ⅝ inch or less.

The basic principle is this: When you start the cut with the top of the leg already resting on the outfeed table, the cutter will remove very little wood at the beginning of the cut. See *How the Jointer Tapers*. As the stock is fed forward, the cutter removes progressively more wood, until at the end it's removing the full depth of cut. Successive passes work the same way. Woodworkers who've never tried this technique often fear that lowering stock onto a running jointer cutter-head will result in phenomenal kickback; but the initial bite is so tiny, there's no kickback at all.

You do need to exercise caution, however, because you must remove or hold back the cutterhead guard to

HOW THE JOINTER TAPERS

At the beginning of a pass, the "bite" of the cutter is very small: less than 1/64" on a 20" taper with the depth of cut set to 1/8".

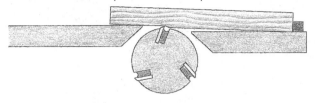

By mid-pass the cutter is removing ½ the depth of cut: 1/16".

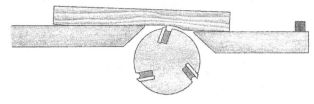

Only at the end of the pass is the cutter removing the full depth of cut.

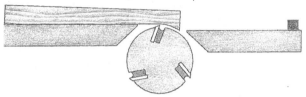

NOTE: Depth of cut is greatly exaggerated.

Repeated passes increase the taper.

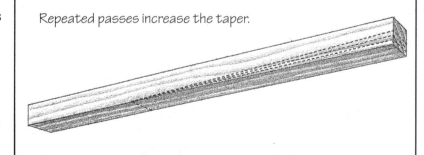

STEP-BY-STEP TAPERING ON THE JOINTER

1 Clamp starter block to the infeed table.

Adjust fence to expose only needed cutter width.

Length of taper

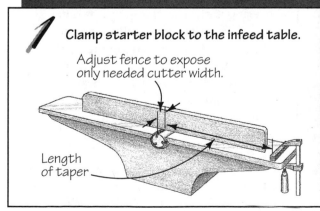

2 Place foot of leg against the starter block, then lower the stock onto running cutter-head. Feed forward to complete each pass.

Push block

Layout of taper

Cleat

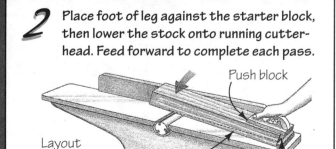

TAPERING LEGS

	BAND SAW	JOINTER	ROUTER TABLE	TABLE SAW
TOOLS REQUIRED	Band saw and hand plane	Jointer	Router table with shims or offset fence	Table saw and tapering jig
LAYOUT AND SETUP	Lay out each cut.	Lay out each cut.	Lay out each cut; fit shim or offset table.	Make or adjust jig.
STEPS	Saw, then plane smooth.	Multiple passes for each taper, then remove mill marks.	Multiple passes for each taper, then remove mill marks.	Saw, then plane smooth.
LIMITATIONS	None	None	Thickness of stock cannot exceed length of cutter.	Thickness of stock cannot exceed cut depth of saw.
BOTTOM LINE	Direct and intuitive but a bit laborious	Simple and fairly efficient; my first-choice technique	A good, safe technique for those without a jointer	Most efficient for large numbers of identical tapers

start the cuts. Jointer guards are designed to be easily removed because you have to take them off to cut rabbets. You can minimize the danger of the exposed cutter by covering it with the fence, exposing only enough of the cutter to taper the full width of the stock.

To ensure that each pass of the jointer begins at the same spot on the leg, clamp a starter block to the infeed table. The distance from the starter block to the center of the cutterhead should equal the length of the taper.

One writer I've come across advises that you divide the amount of stock to remove into a series of equal passes over the jointer. Either his jointer has a much better depth-of-cut scale than mine, or he's not very fussy about the finished dimensions of the taper. I can never get it to come out right. Instead, I set the jointer to remove ⅛ inch and cut all the tapers until less than ⅛ inch remains. Then I set the jointer to remove the remainder of the waste and finish all the legs.

Don't forget to plane or scrape away the cutter marks before applying your finish.

Tapering on the Router Table

If your legs are no thicker than the length of your longest, straight router bit, you can taper them on the router table. The procedure is the same as for tapering on the jointer—you just swing the stock horizontally into the router bit instead of lowering it onto the jointer cutterhead. Use an offset or shimmed outfeed fence as you would for jointing on the router table. (Plastic laminate applied with double-sided tape works well as a shim and is removable.) The only catch with a shimmed outfeed fence is that you can't adjust it to make the final pass at exactly the depth you want. You can either ignore the small discrepancy or else finish with a hand plane to the exact dimension when you clean up the cutter marks.

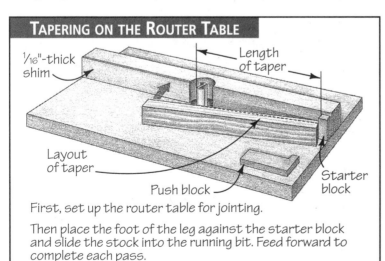

TAPERING ON THE ROUTER TABLE

1/16"-thick shim

Length of taper

Layout of taper

Push block

Starter block

First, set up the router table for jointing.

Then place the foot of the leg against the starter block and slide the stock into the running bit. Feed forward to complete each pass.

TAPERING ON THE TABLE SAW

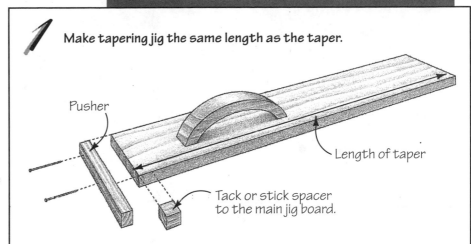

1 Make tapering jig the same length as the taper.

Pusher

Length of taper

Tack or stick spacer to the main jig board.

If you need to taper large numbers of legs or remove a lot of stock, or if you don't have a jointer or router table, the tool for tapering is the table saw. The secret to this technique is a jig. It holds the stock so the tapering cut is parallel to the rip fence. Such a jig can be very simple, made just for the job at hand, as shown in *Step-by-Step Tapering on the Table Saw,* or it can be fancy and adjustable like the one detailed in the "Adjustable Tapering Jig" chapter on page 256. Since the jig holds the stock so the tapering cut is parallel to the rip fence, you can adjust the rip fence to leave as much waste as you want for cleanup. One advantage of tapering on the table saw with a jig is that you can cut large numbers of identical tapers without laying them out on each piece.

If your legs require tapering on three or four sides, you'll need to adjust the setup after you've tapered the first two adjacent sides. Otherwise you won't remove any stock—the jig is set to remove a certain amount of stock and it will already have removed that amount. To make these cuts, double the thickness of the spacer after the first two tapers. Doubling the spacer adjusts the jig to the total amount of stock to be removed from the two opposite faces. Don't worry if this seems a bit confusing—it will all be quite clear once you have the jig and leg on the saw table in front of you.

The trick to using a tapering jig on the table saw is keeping the stock under control while keeping your fingers attached to your hands. Table legs are narrow, and you're passing two items, both a leg and a jig, between the blade and the fence. I find it comforting to have a jig that is at least 6 inches wide, so that I'm not working in a narrow canyon between the rip fence and the saw blade. Even though I rip on the right side of the blade, I taper

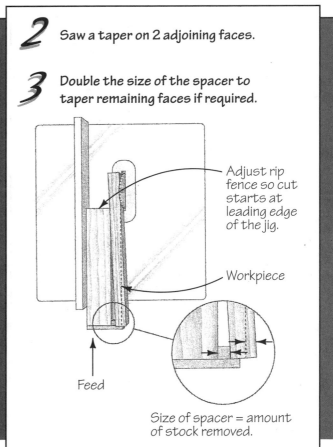

2 Saw a taper on 2 adjoining faces.

3 Double the size of the spacer to taper remaining faces if required.

Adjust rip fence so cut starts at leading edge of the jig.

Workpiece

Feed

Size of spacer = amount of stock removed.

stock on the left side of the blade. I can't explain why, it just feels right. A handle on the tapering jig helps to control the jig, allowing me to concentrate on holding the stock with a separate push stick.

All things considered, given a choice, I'd taper on the jointer. Yet I've tapered a lot of legs on the table saw and never had an accident.

SHAPING AND MOLDING

Moldings and molded edges and surfaces can change the whole personality of your projects, transforming their appearance from very utilitarian, almost mechanical, to more friendly and comfortable or even elegant and sophisticated. I like the way they add shadows that accentuate the main lines of my designs, protect users from sharp corners and edges, and protect corners and edges from wear and abuse. Even furniture as austere as that of the Shakers acquires a measure of warmth from tastefully shaped and molded edges.

BUILDING CLASSIC PROFILES

Simple circular arcs and flats form the classical shapes found in architecture and furniture.

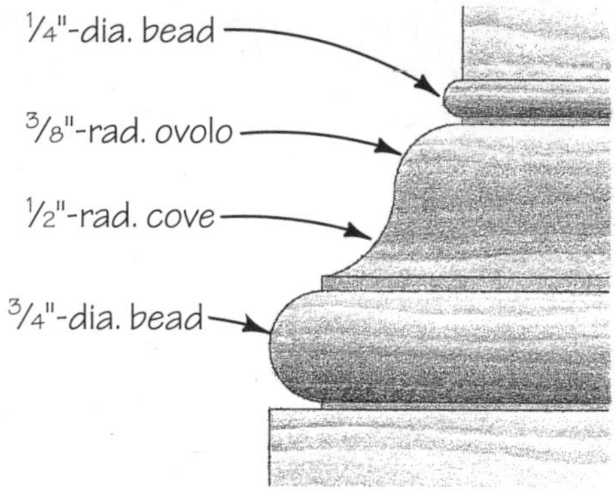

¼"-dia. bead

⅜"-rad. ovolo

½"-rad. cove

¾"-dia. bead

Assemble large moldings like this antique crown molding from separately shaped parts.

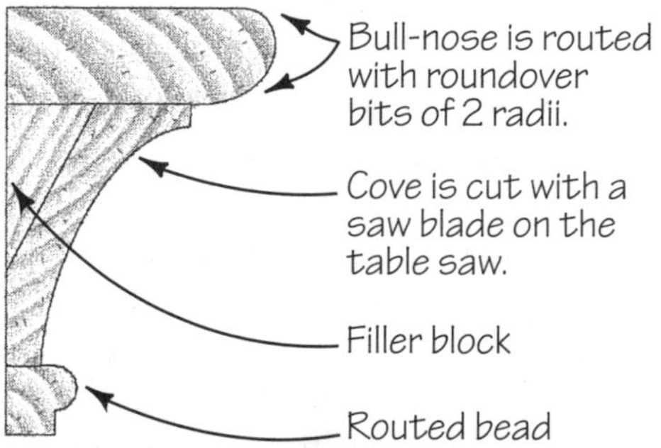

Bull-nose is routed with roundover bits of 2 radii.

Cove is cut with a saw blade on the table saw.

Filler block

Routed bead

The classic profiles found in furniture and architecture are combinations of simple cove, bead, and ovolo shapes. You can cut them in a series of passes, each with a different bit cutting just one element of the complex whole.

You can also build up large, complex shapes from smaller pieces of wood, each with a simple shape. This allows you to use smaller pieces of stock, to make moldings larger than the cutters your tools will handle, and to combine shapes made with different tools. For example, you can combine a large cove made on the table saw with beads cut on the router table to make a large crown molding.

You can shape and mold wood with a router, table-saw molding head, scratch stock, shaper, or hand plane, and you can even cut wide coves with an ordinary saw blade on the table saw. With so many alternatives, you can create tastefully decorated cabinetry and furniture in a wide variety of styles.

Each of these shaping tools has certain advantages. Router bits and shaper cutters are available in hundreds of profiles, and you can use the router bits either with a hand-held router or in a router table. The table-saw molding head has a more limited selection of cutter profiles, but they're less expensive than router bits. If you prefer hand tools, you can use a special type of hand plane with shaped cutting irons or use a scratch stock—just a piece of tool steel with a shape filed into the edge. The scratch stock scrapes the shape into the wood simply and directly and is capable of producing delicate shapes that no other tool can duplicate.

Of all these shaping tools, the two most frequently chosen by home-shop woodworkers are the

router and the table saw fitted with a molding head. While some woodworkers see the molding head as a poor man's poor substitute for the router, that attitude overlooks two big advantages: The molding head has a larger cutting arc than a router bit, which means it leaves shallower mill marks; and the molding head is ideally suited for shaping cuts near the middle of a board, as shown in *Machine Setups for Molding*. The drawing also gives some idea of the kinds of cuts that are possible with the router table and the table-saw molding head.

MACHINE SETUPS FOR MOLDING

Router bits require a single fence when shaping part of an edge (1) but separate infeed and outfeed fences when shaping the entire edge (2).

Table-saw molding head cutters require an auxiliary fence to house the unused part of the cutter when shaping an edge (3). To mold an entire edge, attach a piece of scrap to support the stock (4). The molding head is ideal for shaping cuts in the face of the stock (5).

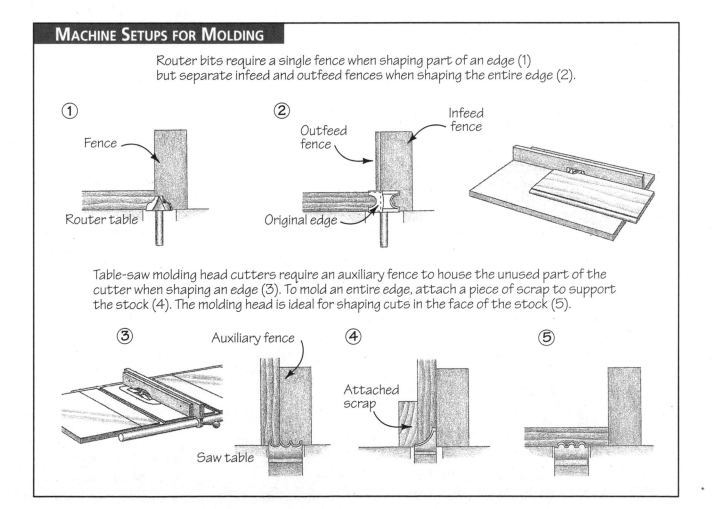

ROUTING MOLDINGS

Routers are strange beasts. They are manufactured as hand-held tools, but for shaping and molding they do their best work when they're mounted in a router table, pretending to be mini-shapers. With a router table, you'll avoid clamping stock to your bench to make it hold still, you'll find it easier to adjust the fence, you won't have to watch out for the cord during the cut, you won't gouge your wood by tipping the router, and on and on. Resort to hand-held routing only when the stock is too big to handle on the router table.

TECH TIP

PREVENTING TEAR-OUT: A router bit tears wood fibers, and even chunks, from your stock when the cutting forces are greater than the strength of the wood. There are three ways you can minimize the problem.

1. Sharpen the bit. This reduces the cutting forces.

2. Take a shallower cut.

3. When routing end grain, support the wood by clamping a piece of scrap at the end of the cut if you're hand-holding the router or by using a push block right at the cutting edge if you're routing on the router table.

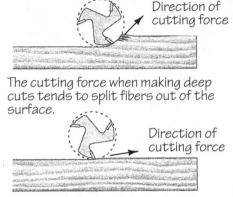

The cutting force when making deep cuts tends to split fibers out of the surface.

The cutting force of shallower cuts is more lengthwise to the stock; the uncut stock can better resist forces in this direction.

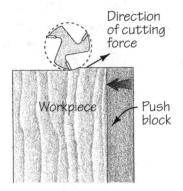

Provide support with a backup block or push block to prevent splintering at the end of an end-grain cut.

Router Table Techniques

Shaping moldings with a router is not difficult, but you can find yourself in some ticklish situations if you fail to think through what happens at each step along the way. For example, if you cut a bull-nose on the edge of your stock with a regular fence, you'll get a rude awakening when you get to the end of the cut. Since the bull-nose bit cuts away the entire edge of the stock, the finished edge won't touch the outfeed side of the fence. When you get to the end of the cut and there's no more stock to rest against the infeed fence, the stock will slip into the bit, sniping the end.

If you're in the habit of making successive cuts by raising the bit height rather than moving the fence, you'll have to rethink your procedures when you use certain molding bits. You can make successive cuts with the bit shown in *Machine Setups for Molding* on page 207, drawing number 1, by either raising the bit or moving the fence; but you can increase the depth of cut of the bit in drawing number 2 only by moving the fence.

A third way you can get caught napping is by finding that the only stock left for your moldings is too narrow to safely shape on the router table. Shaping stock less than 3 inches wide is unsafe because your hands come dangerously close to the cutter and because lightweight stock is more likely to vibrate and flutter, leaving a rough and wavy surface.

A handy trick for routing narrow moldings is to cut them on both edges of wider stock and then rip the two moldings apart. Another trick is to mold the edge of a board before cutting it narrower to make another part. For example if you intend to cut a 2-inch-wide stile from a 4-inch-wide board and will later need some 1½-inch-wide molding, mold the edge of the 4-inch-wide board before ripping the stile from the other edge.

The sequence in *Step-by-Step Router Table Shaping* assumes the most complex situation—a full edge cut, successive passes that require moving the fence, and narrow final dimensions. Some situations may not require all of the steps shown. If you need to shape adjoining edges, such as the sides and ends of a table, remember to shape the end-grain edges first.

Hand-Held Routing

Shaping and molding with a hand-held router is most convenient when you're working on the edge of a large piece like a tabletop, not when you're making narrow moldings that you'll apply to the project.

Bearing-guided bits may seem like a convenient way to guide a router, but I rarely use them. My biggest objection is that you can't make the cut in successive passes, first roughing out the shape and then finishing with a shallow cut to minimize tear-out. The only time I use a bearing-guided bit is when I don't have any alternative, such as shaping a curved edge.

When shaping long, straight edges like the edge of a dining table, guide the router with your router's edge guide. You can improve its performance by attaching a long auxiliary fence, as shown in *Edge Guide Fence* on page 210. You'll notice that the auxiliary fence is just like the fence for a router

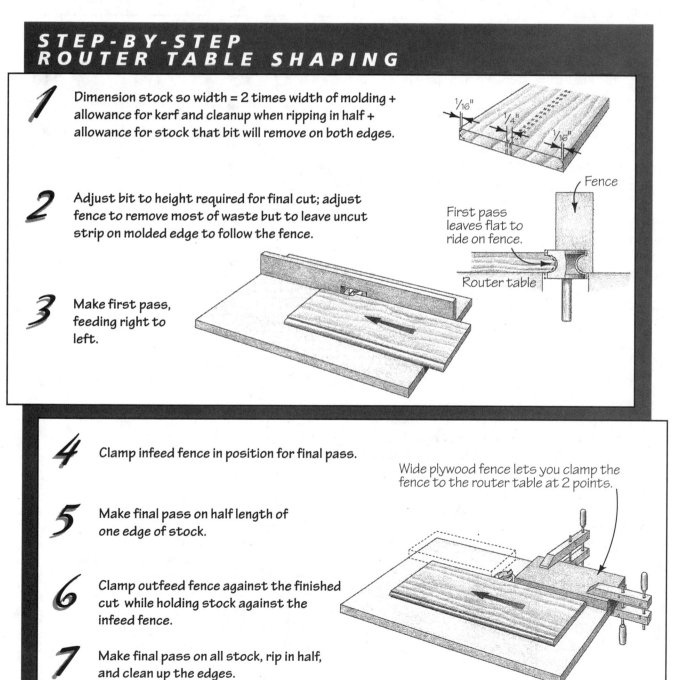

STEP-BY-STEP ROUTER TABLE SHAPING

1 Dimension stock so width = 2 times width of molding + allowance for kerf and cleanup when ripping in half + allowance for stock that bit will remove on both edges.

1/16"   1/4"   1/16"

2 Adjust bit to height required for final cut; adjust fence to remove most of waste but to leave uncut strip on molded edge to follow the fence.

Fence

First pass leaves flat to ride on fence.

Router table

3 Make first pass, feeding right to left.

4 Clamp infeed fence in position for final pass.

Wide plywood fence lets you clamp the fence to the router table at 2 points.

5 Make final pass on half length of one edge of stock.

6 Clamp outfeed fence against the finished cut while holding stock against the infeed fence.

7 Make final pass on all stock, rip in half, and clean up the edges.

table—so much so that I simply screw the router table fence to my router's edge guide.

Using the router table fence for hand-held routing is a good reminder that what works well with the router table usually works on a hand-held router as well:

▶ Rough out the cut, then make a separate pass that trims the rough cut to final shape.

▶ Feed the router so the bit tends to push the router away from the cut, not pull the router into the cut.

▶ Make sure the bit is sharp.

▶ Shape end grain before side grain. ●

A few other things to keep in mind when routing hand-held:

▶ Make sure your power cord won't jerk you to a stop halfway through your cut.

▶ Don't depend on the weight of the stock to keep it from moving during the cut; clamp it down.

▶ Hold the router firmly down on the stock—constantly guard against the router tipping.

▶ Make sure the bit is well away from the stock edge when you turn the router on or off, so it won't jerk the router when you turn it on or burn the edge as it coasts to a stop. ●

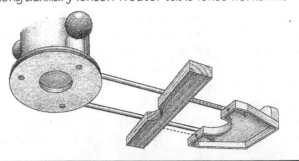

EDGE GUIDE FENCE

Improve your router's edge guide by attaching a long auxiliary fence. A router table fence works fine.

Bearing-guided bits are most useful when shaping a curved edge. To get a smooth molding, however, you must first smooth the edge that the bearing will follow.

SHAPERS

Forty years ago my shop teacher explained that a router was like a portable, hand-held shaper, and everybody got the idea. Today it seems more appropriate to explain that a shaper is like a stationary, heavy-duty, table-mounted router.

The advantage of a shaper over a big table-mounted router is primarily the large diameter of the spindle: A bigger spindle resists the flexing that causes rough cuts. If you wish that more powerful routers were available so you could make bigger cuts, give up the thought. The bigger cut would overwhelm the ½-inch shank on the bit.

Using a shaper is very much like using a router table but demands greater care because you're dealing with larger cuts and more horse-power. My advice for the woodworker considering a shaper:

• Don't even think about ½-inch spindle shapers—use a router table for small shapes.

• Look at ¾-inch and 1¼-inch spindle diameters. The 1-inch size has fewer cutters available.

• Interchangeable spindles are expensive and less rigid than solid assemblies. Buy a solid, larger spindle and cutters with the larger bore rather than interchangeable spindles and a mix of large and small bore cutters.

• If you don't think you have room for a shaper, find one with a spindle that can be lowered all the way below table height, and then use it as the outfeed table for your table saw.

TABLE-SAW MOLDING HEAD

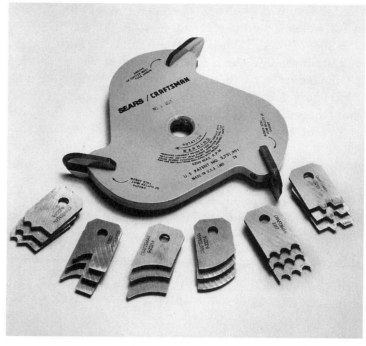

The table-saw molding head has several advantages over the router bit. For openers, it's bigger. Size, specifically diameter, is important because the larger cutting arc produces shallower mill marks, reducing the amount of sanding required. It's also important because the actual speed of the cutting edge changes very little from the largest-diameter portion of the shape to the smallest—both are about 50 to 60 miles per hour on a 5-inch-diameter molding head turning at 3,500 rpm. In comparison, a $\frac{5}{16}$-inch-radius bull-nose router bit turning

A table-saw molding head is inexpensive and can cut all of the basic shapes—beads, coves, ovolos—necessary for making the classic molding profiles.

STEP-BY-STEP TABLE SAW SHAPING

1 Prepare stock wide enough for 2 moldings + allowance for ripping them in half + allowance for stock that cutters will remove on both edges.

2 Attach scrap with hot-melt glue or double-sided tape to support stock after cutting away entire edge.

3 Adjust depth of cut to remove bulk of waste, but leave $\frac{1}{16}$" for final cleanup pass.

4 Make first pass on both edges, then raise the cutter to final shape and make the final pass.

5 Rip stock in half, and clean up the edges.

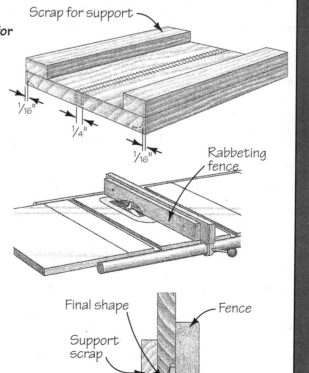

Scrap for support

$\frac{1}{16}$" $\frac{1}{4}$" $\frac{1}{16}$"

Rabbeting fence

Final shape   Fence

Support scrap

at 22,000 rpm has cutting edges that travel at 80 to 100 miles per hour at the large diameter but only 30 to 40 miles per hour at the smaller diameter. Trying to find the feed rate that gives the smoothest surface without burning is pretty difficult when one part of the cutter is moving more than twice as fast as another part.

A molding head on a table saw is also easier to adjust than a table-mounted router. Adjusting the depth of cut of a large beading bit between successive passes on the router table requires unclamping, moving, and reclamping the fence. The same adjustment with the molding head is a quick turn of the crank that adjusts cutter height.

A third advantage is the tilting arbor of the table saw, which allows you to make certain cuts with a molding head that are impossible with a

router table, like beading a corner at 45 degrees.

Also, since molding head cutters are made of high-speed steel, they take a sharper edge than carbide router bits. However, this can be both good and bad. If you're shaping a fussy wood that tears out easily, the sharpness possible with the molding head will give a cleaner cut. But high-speed steel also dulls faster, especially on wood like teak with grit in the cells. If you're shaping teak, a carbide router bit is the better choice.

The sequence in *Step-by-Step Table Saw Shaping* on page 211 shows how to make the most complicated cut you're likely to encounter—a full edge cut requiring multiple passes. You won't need the support piece if you're shaping only part of an edge, and you won't need to make multiple passes for shallow cuts.

TABLE SAW COVE CUTTING

The cove is the only curved shape that you can produce with a standard saw blade on the table saw. It's a simple operation: In a nutshell, the blade saws at an angle, partly sideways. The surfaces of these coves are rough and need considerable smoothing, but it's the only way to cut a large cove with home-shop machines. I should add that it works well; and as far as I can tell after using the technique for hundreds of feet of cove, it doesn't hurt either the saw or the blade.

A few things to note about table saw cove cutting:

▶ To get the smoothest cut, take very light passes and feed the stock slowly. I seldom raise the blade more than 1/16 inch for each pass.

▶ Plan ahead when you select stock for coves and when you lay out the coves on the stock. The figure of the grain within a cove depends on how the cove intersects the growth rings of the stock, as shown in *Laying Out Parts on Stock* on page 55.

▶ The center of the cut shifts as the blade is adjusted higher for successive passes. Don't readjust your fence after the first pass or two, thinking that you've set it up wrong. ●

To cut a cove, start by laying out a cross section of the molding you want to make. Drawing it on the end of the stock is awkward, so I usually do it on paper. You must draw the shape of the stock as well as the molding so that you can find the edge distance shown in Step 1 on the opposite page.

The key to the saw setup is a simple jig consisting of two parallel straightedges separated by the width of the cove. I make a pair of spacer blocks equal to the cove width and tape them between straight sticks of wood. With the height of the saw blade adjusted to the depth of the cove, place the jig over the blade. Then turn the jig so the blade teeth just touch the inner edges of the

TECH TIP   **BIG COVES FROM SMALL COVE CUTTERS:** I often use a molding head with 1-inch cove cutters instead of a saw blade for table saw cove cutting. Since the molding head lacks the sharp corners of saw teeth, it doesn't produce the score marks typical of coves cut with a saw blade.

straightedges. This is the correct angle for feeding the stock for your cove. Draw a line on the saw table along the inner edge of the near straightedge, then clamp a wooden fence to the saw table, parallel to the line but spaced away from the line by the "edge distance" shown on your layout.

With your fence in place, lower the blade so it's 1/16 inch above the table, and make the first pass. Raise the blade in increments of 1/16 inch or so for successive passes. When approaching the full depth of the cut, check the width of the cove after each blade adjustment—getting the width correct is usually far more important than getting the depth exactly as planned.

I've always found this technique to be a relaxed, safe, and easy operation. Just clamp the angled fence securely at both ends, take shallow cuts, keep in mind where the blade is when you can't see it, feed the stock with the kind of pusher you would use on a jointer (see Step 2 on page 203), and feed the stock slowly.

You can choose between two effective techniques for smoothing the cove. "Sanding Shapes" on page 114 explains a technique for shaping a foam sanding block to the curve of a cove. This is the method I prefer. I start with 80-grit sandpaper to remove the saw marks and progress to grits as fine as I feel are necessary for the particular project. You can also scrape the cove smooth with a curved hand scraper like the one shown in the photo on page 120.

STEP-BY-STEP COVE CUTTING

1 Lay out the cove on the end of the stock. Measure width, depth, and edge distance of cove cut.

2 Adjust saw blade height to the depth of the cove cut.

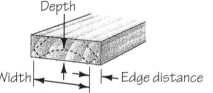
Depth
Width — Edge distance

3 Tape together 2 straight sticks and spacer blocks so sticks are separated by cove width.

4 Place sticks around blade, and turn so teeth at the surface of the table just touch the sticks.

5 Draw a line on the saw table along the inner edge of the near stick. Draw on tape if pencil won't mark the table.

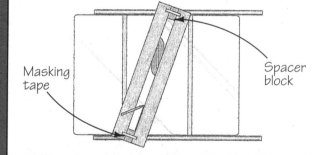
Masking tape
Spacer block

6 Clamp fence to the saw table parallel to the pencil line but "edge distance" away from it.

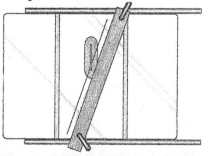

7 Lower the blade to a 1/16" cut, then cut the cove in successive passes of 1/16" each.

SCRATCH STOCK

A scratch stock is basically a hand scraper with a shape ground into the edge—it's that simple. You can hold the unadorned blade in your hands, but a simple wooden holder will help you guide it. The scratch stock works best for delicate shapes, and it's surprisingly fast and efficient at cutting them. It can cut shapes that would be impossible for a router bit. For example, the quirk (groove) alongside a bead can be very narrow if you cut it with a scratch stock; but it can't be much less than 1/16 inch wide if you rout it, because the tip of the bit profile would be too fragile.

Make the blade for your scratch stock from a piece of tool steel or other fairly hard steel (an old scraper, handsaw blade, or reciprocating saw blade) that's between 1/32 and 1/16 inch thick. File the shape that you want into an edge of the steel—I usually find it most convenient to cut the shape near a corner, as shown in *Making a Scratch Stock*. Hold the stock in a vise quite close to where you want to

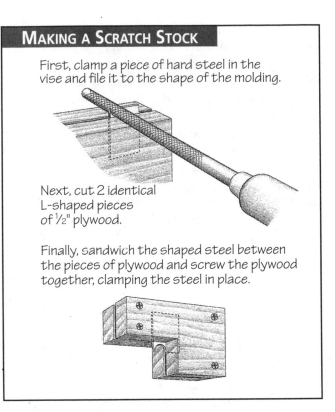

MAKING A SCRATCH STOCK

First, clamp a piece of hard steel in the vise and file it to the shape of the molding.

Next, cut 2 identical L-shaped pieces of 1/2" plywood.

Finally, sandwich the shaped steel between the pieces of plywood and screw the plywood together, clamping the steel in place.

Cutting a delicate bead with a scratch stock is as simple and straightforward as shaping and molding ever gets. The zero-dollar price tag even fits in the average woodworker's budget.

file the shape. The closer the vise holds the steel, the less it will vibrate as you file it. Use whatever shape of file works best for the profile you want. (Too many of my scratched beads are the same size as my chain saw file; I really ought to break down and buy some others.) Hold the file perpendicular to the blade as you shape the profile, at least as you approach the final shape.

If a little voice inside you says you'll create a better profile by filing to a line, blacken the face of the steel with a marking pen, then scratch the shape of the molding you want into the blackened surface. A scratch awl is the *proper* tool for this but doesn't work any better than a drywall screw.

The scratch stock body is simplicity itself: two L-shaped pieces of plywood screwed together with the blade clamped between them. One leg of the ell functions like a router edge guide to position the blade when scratching the shape.

To use the scratch stock, hold the fence against the edge of the stock with the body tilted slightly in the direction of the cut. Make long, even, unhurried strokes. You can cut on the pull or push stroke, or both. I use both since that uses both sides of the blade. When it no longer cuts like new, renew the edge with the file, the same way you made it. (One of the nice things about making your own tools is that the manufacturer is always available and sympathetic to your problems.)

HAND PLANING MOLDINGS

The moldings on fine Queen Anne antiques, or more rustic early American furniture, were not cut with routers or molding heads. They were shaped with wood-bodied hand molding planes. The metal successors to wooden molding planes are ingenious metal planes that accept a variety of differently shaped cutting irons. If your enjoyment of woodworking goes up when the amount of machinery between you and the wood goes down, buy a Stanley #45 on the used tool market, or get one of the more recent reproductions.

You won't learn to use one of these planes from a book—only from practice and experimentation. I found it easiest to begin the learning process by cutting grooves with one of the plane's narrower grooving cutters rather than jumping in with a big bead or ovolo cutter. I also found it necessary to learn on uniform, straight-grained wood. I learned on mahogany, but that was before the world's tropical rain forests were threatened as they are now.

The most versatile hand molding planes are the Stanley #45 and its more recent clones like the Record #405 shown here. The standard cutters include five sizes of bead and two sizes of ovolo. Additional cutters include a half-dozen sizes of flute plus sash and reeding cutters.

COMPARISON OF SHAPING AND MOLDING TECHNIQUES

	TOOLS NEEDED	ADVANTAGES	DISADVANTAGES	BEST APPLICATION
ROUTER TABLE	Router; router table bits	Wide choice of bits; easy setup; good control	Limited size of shapes	Edges and small complex shapes on maneuverable stock
HAND-HELD ROUTER	Router; edge guide bits	Wide choice of bits; no limit to stock size	Limited size of shapes; time-consuming to set up stock for cut	Edges of large stock like tabletops
TABLE-SAW MOLDING HEAD	Table saw; molding head with cutters	Economy; quality of cut; high feed rate	Limited shapes; special procedures needed for full edge cuts	Large quantities of molding in nonabrasive stock
SAW BLADE COVE CUTTING	Table saw; saw blade	Cuts wide coves with home-shop equipment	Requires extensive smoothing	Wide coves
SCRATCH STOCK	Scrap of hard steel; scrap of plywood; file	Economy; custom shapes; very fine quirks possible	Requires making tool; limited size of shapes	Delicate shapes on straight or curved edges

CUTTING CURVES

Curved edges on a tabletop or apron provide a welcome balance to the straight lines and square corners that dominate most furniture and architecture. An absence of sharp corners also makes edges more friendly and welcoming.

When you make something out of wood, it's usually easier to make it straight and square than to sculpt it into curves. The natural world, on the other hand, has very few straight lines or square corners. For variety in your projects, especially if you want an organic and natural appearance, introduce curves whenever they're easy to produce. You'll find that the edges of tabletops, aprons, valances, and other edges not involved in joinery are fairly easy to make into curves. You'll also find that curves along these edges are the most effective way to change the appearance of your projects because these are the edges that define the visible, outside shape.

You can choose from among three basic approaches to cutting a curve on the edge of a project part:

1. Draw the curve, saw to the drawn line, and smooth out the saw marks. This approach is the most versatile but is also the most labor-intensive.

2. Guide a router with a mechanical device like a circle trammel or ellipse trammel. This approach is very easy and very precise but is limited to circles, ellipses, and circular or elliptical arcs.

3. Duplicate an existing curve by guiding a router with a template. This usually requires that you make a template using one of the above approaches, unless you can *find* an appropriate template. You could, for example, use an existing tabletop as a template to make another just like it.

ROUTING ARCS AND CIRCLES

A circle trammel for a router makes the router into a wood-cutting compass. It's a simple jig, useful for much more than cutting out circles. I use mine more often for cutting arcs than for cutting whole circles. An obvious example is the curved bottom edge of a table apron. Less obvious examples are sweeping curves that consist of more than one circular arc, such as those shown in *Variations on Sweeping Curves* on page 19, and approximate ellipses, as described on page 21. Even if you have an ellipse trammel as described below, the approximate ellipse cut with a circle trammel is useful when you need a very elongated ellipse.

The adjustable trammel shown above and described in detail in the "Router Circle Trammel" chapter on page 285 is much handier than the one shown in *Simple Circle Trammel* on page 218 because it attaches quickly and easily to the router's edge guide rods. The simple version is more versatile, however, because you can easily make one that is enormously long.

You don't need to be an engineer or go through astronaut training to use a circle trammel, but things can still go wrong. You can avoid some unfortunate "learning experiences" by keeping the following in mind:

◗ Virtually all arcs and circles include portions where the router is going the right direction to minimize tear-out, and portions where it's going the wrong direction. Minimize tear-out by taking very shallow cuts.

◗ Use a plunge router rather than a conventional router. Even when you're cutting an arc and

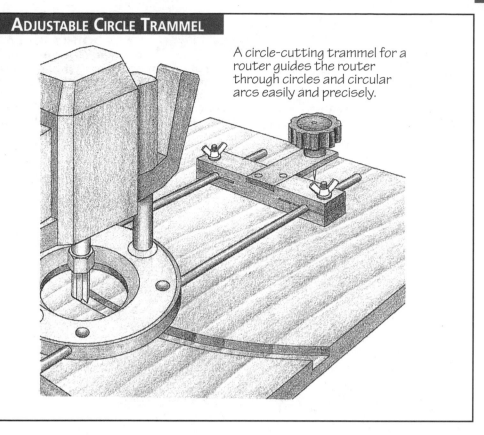

ADJUSTABLE CIRCLE TRAMMEL

A circle-cutting trammel for a router guides the router through circles and circular arcs easily and precisely.

can enter the stock from an edge, the plunge router makes it easier to rout successively deeper passes.

◗ A spiral upcut bit tears out the grain much less than a straight bit when cutting in the "wrong" direction.

◗ If the trammel pivots on a pin rather than on a nail or screw, hold it down during the cut—otherwise it will pop out and the router will plow a furrow across your stock. I designed the adjustable trammel with a knob rather than a wing nut for locking the pin so that I could comfortably hold the pin down during a cut.

◗ Successive passes sometimes leave score marks on the cut edge. To avoid having to sand them out, rout through the stock with the trammel set to cut a radius $\frac{1}{32}$ inch too large, then readjust the trammel and trim the stock to size in a single pass. ●

Normally you would rout a circle or arc from the back side of the stock, with the face down and the trammel pin sticking into the side that won't show. This has two advantages. The pin hole won't show, and any surface tear-out caused by a spiral upcut bit (usually minimal anyway) will be on the back side. In some cases, however, you may want to rout the circle or arc and then mold the edge using the trammel to guide the router. I prefer this to switching to a bearing-guided molding bit. Molding the edge with a trammel may require that you set up the trammel on the face side of the stock.

You can't rout from the face with the simple circle trammel if the pivot will leave a hole in the stock; but the adjustable circle trammel allows you to use a pivot block, as shown in the *Exploded View* for the router circle trammel on page 286. By sticking the pivot block to the face of the stock with double-sided tape, you can rout from the face without leaving a mark on the stock.

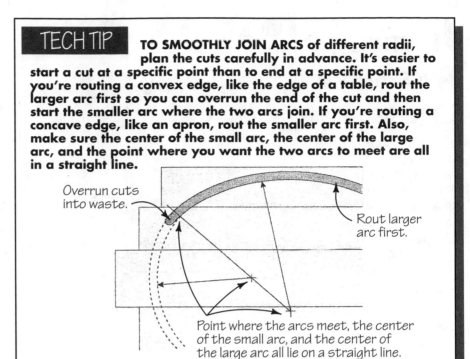

TECH TIP

TO SMOOTHLY JOIN ARCS of different radii, plan the cuts carefully in advance. It's easier to start a cut at a specific point than to end at a specific point. If you're routing a convex edge, like the edge of a table, rout the larger arc first so you can overrun the end of the cut and then start the smaller arc where the two arcs join. If you're routing a concave edge, like an apron, rout the smaller arc first. Also, make sure the center of the small arc, the center of the large arc, and the point where you want the two arcs to meet are all in a straight line.

Overrun cuts into waste.

Rout larger arc first.

Point where the arcs meet, the center of the small arc, and the center of the large arc all lie on a straight line.

SIMPLE CIRCLE TRAMMEL

First, replace your router subbase with a ¼" plywood trammel.

Next, pivot the trammel on the stock with a small nail or a screw with an unthreaded upper shank.

Finally, rout in a series of passes of increasing depth.

Measure the radius of the circle from the bit's cutting edge.

Trace bit opening and attachment screw holes from the router's subbase.

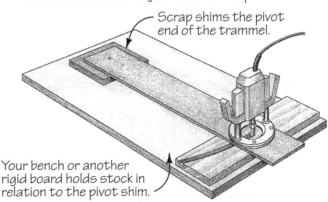

To rout large arcs on small stock, tack stock and scrap of same thickness to your bench or to particleboard.

Scrap shims the pivot end of the trammel.

Your bench or another rigid board holds stock in relation to the pivot shim.

ROUTING ELLIPSES

An ellipse trammel is not as widely useful as a circle trammel; but for cutting out elliptical table-tops, it is almost magical in its simplicity. Attach the trammel base, the part with the crisscross tracks, to the stock with screws or with double-sided tape. Then mark the holes in the trammel arm that you need for your particular ellipse size and proportions, as shown in *Step-by-Step Routing an Ellipse* on page 220. Fit the pivot slides to the arm, and rout the ellipse. The only mistake you might make is thinking that the jig is too complex to bother building. You'll find complete plans and instructions for the trammel in the "Ellipse (a.k.a. Oval) Trammel" chapter on page 290.

The ellipse trammel does have certain limitations imposed by the size of its parts. The length of the trammel arm limits the maximum size ellipse you can rout. Make it half the length of the largest ellipse you want to rout. Too long is cumbersome but doesn't limit you in any other way.

The base is more limiting, and you may want to make more than one size. The narrowest ellipse that you can make is about 14 inches wider than the length of the tracks—smaller bases allow narrower ellipses. But the *difference* between ellipse length and width is also limited by the length of the tracks—smaller bases mean less-elongated ellipses. If you scratch your head long enough, or play with one of these trammels long enough, you'll figure out that you can't rout an ellipse that is twice as long as it is wide, no matter what size you make the base. That may be a real limitation if you have in mind a very elongated hall table, but for dining tables or conference tables it doesn't matter: A very elongated elliptical table has ends that are too sharply curved to be useful.

An ellipse trammel is the easy way to cut out an oval. Set the jig to the length and width of the ellipse that you want, and it will guide the router with no further adjustment from you.

Using a Trammel

You will probably use an ellipse trammel more often for cutting elliptical tabletops than for any other furniture part. You will want to keep several things in mind when you do:

▸ Wax the pivot keys and the dovetail tracks of the trammel with paste furniture wax so they'll slide easily.

▸ There is sure to be at least a tiny bit of play in the fit of the keys in the track. Prevent that play from producing an irregular cut by holding the router toward the center of the stock as you rout counterclockwise.

▸ Routing will be easiest if you can rout the entire circumference of the ellipse without stopping to rearrange the stock on your bench. I usually set the tabletop up on sawhorses and screw the horses to the bottom of the stock if it's too light to stay put by itself.

▸ Plan ahead so you won't have to take your hands off the router to keep the power cord out of your way. I usually plug the router into an extension cord tied to a ceiling joist directly over the center of the stock. ●

STEP-BY-STEP
ROUTING AN ELLIPSE

 1 Screw trammel base to stock with tracks in line with the axes of the ellipse.

 2 Position router so the cutting edge of the bit just touches the end of the major axis, then mark the hole on the trammel arm directly over "crossroads" of the tracks on the base.

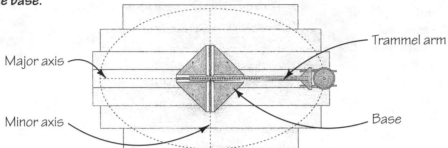

Major axis

Minor axis

Trammel arm

Base

3 Reposition router with bit at the end of the minor axis, then mark the hole at the "crossroads" of the tracks.

 4 Slide the pivots onto the tracks and fit them into marked holes.

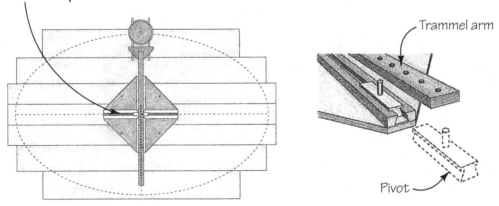

Trammel arm

Pivot

 **5** Rout counterclockwise in successively deeper passes.

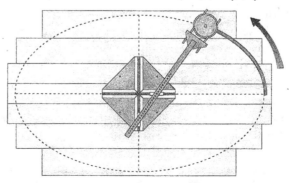

Sawing and Fairing Curves

There are no great secrets to sawing a curve. Lay out the curve using trammels or splines, as explained in "Circles and Arcs" on page 17, then saw along the line with a coping saw, saber saw, scroll saw, or band saw. Use the widest blade that will cut the tightest part of your curve—you'll find it easier to steer and less likely to break.

The fun starts *after* sawing the curve, when you notice a few humps and hollows—places where you left a little more or a little less stock for smoothing out the saw marks. *Fairing* a curve is the process of eliminating these humps and hollows so that the curve is pleasing to the eye. Remember this goal, pleasing to the eye, because you have no other tool to determine when a curve is fair.

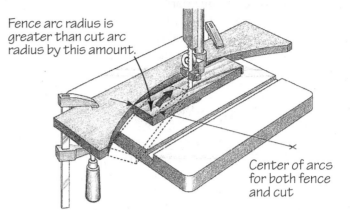

TECH TIP   **MAKE A CURVED FENCE to saw large numbers of arcs such as in table aprons. There's no need to lay out each individual arc on the stock. Cut the parts to uniform length before sawing the arcs, and note that this technique centers the curve along the length of the stock.**

Fence arc radius is greater than cut arc radius by this amount.

Center of arcs for both fence and cut

First, draw the part on paper, then draw curve of the fence through corners of the part using the same center for the arc.

Next, make a fence twice as long as the part, and clamp it to the band saw table in the position shown.

Finally, keep the stock against the fence while feeding it through the cut.

Judging Fairness

The best way to produce a fair curve is to lay it out with a spline, as described in "Free-Form Curves" on page 23, saw close to the line but leaving 1/32 to 1/16 inch to clean up, and then spokeshave or sand to the line. Unfortunately, two things can go wrong. First, the line that looked perfect on the uncut stock can look wrong when the waste is removed. This is a fact of life for which I have no explanation—all I know is that it happens to me fairly regularly. Fixing it means removing more stock until the curve is fair to the eye. Second, a shaving cut can go over the line, either by accident or because you needed to remove more stock in order to get a smooth surface. When that happens, the only way to salvage the piece is to blend the overcut into the curve. Once again, remove more stock until the curve is fair to the eye.

Judging fairness is tricky because the eye seems to delight in playing tricks on the brain. There are several ways that you can overcome the problem.

◗ Look at the curve from many different directions. The most useful views are from the ends, *both* ends; but don't neglect viewing the curve from the face of the stock, which is the way you will most likely see the curve after the project is finished.

◗ Look at the curve from a distance as well as from close up.

◗ Sight down the curve when the end of the stock is pointed toward a light, such as a window, as well as when the edge and the face are toward the light.

◗ Pay particular attention to areas of the curve that are a different color or texture from the rest. It is easy to mistakenly interpret the change in color or texture as unfairness.

◗ Ignore the grain when judging the curve. The irregular and sweeping curves of wood grain can cause optical illusions. If you think you've spotted unfairness when the grain is in full view, hold the stock so the grain is in shadow, and see if you can still find the unfairness. ●

You can also use your sense of touch to help in judging fairness. Use it to supplement your eye, not to replace it—your eye must remain the final judge. When running my fingers over a curve to detect unfairness, I find it helpful to close my eyes or at least to look away from the curve. Then when I think that my fingers have detected a hump or hollow that's not appropriate, I scrutinize the area carefully. The idea here is to allow the fingers full expression of their opinion while leaving the eye to judge that opinion.

Tools for Fairing

The tools that we normally associate with curved work—circular planes, spokeshaves, and sanding drums—have two serious built-in problems. First, they tend to reproduce their own shape, which is seldom the shape that we want; and second, the depth that they cut changes as the curve changes.

For example, if you adjust the sole of a circular plane for a convex curve with a 5-foot diameter, the plane will do a splendid job of giving your stock that curve. If you're making 5-foot-diameter wagon wheels while your router is at the repair shop, it's just the ticket. But the curves I'm most interested in fairing by hand have a continuously changing radius—I'll seldom want more than a few inches of the curve to have the same radius. If I use a circular plane, I'll have to change the setting after every couple of strokes.

The same is true for round-faced spokeshaves commonly used for concave edges—they work best reproducing their own curvature. The spokeshaves, whether round-faced or flat, also demonstrate the second problem: changing depth of cut. If you adjust a spokeshave to a good depth of cut on a 10-inch-radius concave curve, you'll find that it cuts too deeply on a shallower curve and too little or not at all on a deeper curve. The same thing happens on convex curves, whether you're using a flat-faced spokeshave or a block plane. Continuously changing curves require that you continuously readjust the depth of cut. On outside curves you can lessen the problem if you use a block plane with an adjustable mouth set very close to the blade, but you can't eliminate the problem.

The third common tool associated with curved work is the sanding drum. Its greatest weakness is its tendency to sand curves to its own shape, like

> **TECH TIP** **TEMPLATES ARE EASIER to judge for fairness than solid stock if you make them from material that has little or no grain pattern, like hardboard. The uniform color and texture and the lack of distracting grain figure allow you to concentrate on the shape of the curve.**

circular planes. The drums tend to produce lumpy edges whenever the curve in the stock is much greater than the drum itself.

With a great deal of practice and patience, you can get satisfactory results from any of these tools. But you can get better results with less practice and less patience using a sanding block that flexes in just one direction: lengthwise. My procedure has the following steps:

1. Lay out and saw the curve: close but not over the line.

2. Saw a piece of 5-ply plywood to 2 inches × 1 foot, with the grain in the surface veneers running lengthwise. I prefer lauan plywood because it's very uniform, is not too stiff, and has no hidden voids. You can only get 5-ply plywood in a limited range of thicknesses; my favorite is ⅜ inch.

3. Sand off the surface veneers, leaving a 3-ply plywood, with the new surface veneers running crosswise. I use a belt sander with an 80-grit belt. It's easy to tell when the surface veneer is gone because the black glue layer shows up. The resulting sanding block has good crosswise stiffness and good lengthwise flexibility.

4. Stick an abrasive to one of the surfaces. I use a strip from an 80-grit sanding belt for fairing curves and a strip from a 120-grit belt for smoothing. I usually stick it on with double-sided tape.

5. Bend the sanding "stick" to the presawn curve, holding it as tightly as you can to the curve with both hands, and work it back and forth, lengthwise, in short strokes.

I like this procedure because the "tool" springs naturally to a fair curve, it allows me to increase pressure over humps or on both sides of hollows, and it cuts fast enough to get the job done in reasonable time but slowly enough to keep me from overdoing it. I find it particularly effective for fairing hardboard templates quickly and easily.

TEMPLATE ROUTING

If you've read from the beginning of the chapter to here, you understand that I favor template routing over sawing and fairing solid stock. I find it much easier to cut and fair a curve on an inexpensive piece of bland hardboard or particleboard than on solid lumber, but "easier" is not the only advantage of the template.

A curve seldom occurs only once on a project. Most often a curved valance or apron is symmetrical. So by making a template for one half of the curve, you can turn the template over for cutting the other half with the assurance that the two halves will be identical. If you're shaping the edges of a tabletop, you probably don't need a template for more than one fourth of it. There's still another advantage to templates: It's easy to keep the curved edge of a ¼-inch-thick template square to the face when fairing—much easier than keeping the edge of a 1-inch-thick tabletop square. When you rout the tabletop, the router will keep the edge square for you.

The downside to template routing is putting up with the eccentricities of those itty-bitty bearings that I've complained about before. (See the list under "Bearing-guided router bits" on page 135.) You can minimize problems with these bearings by choosing a hard, uniform material for your template. You *must* avoid plywood with voids because the bearing is sure to deform the remaining veneers around a void, leaving you with a dent in your template. My usual choice of materials for templates is ¼-inch-thick tempered Masonite (hardboard). It's economical, uniform, reasonably durable, and easily shaped. On rare occasions in the past, I've needed a template that would stand up to heavy repeated use. I used ⅛-inch-thick aviation plywood with plastic laminate on both surfaces. But if I needed that many identical parts today, I would probably have them made at a shop with a computerized (CNC) router.

You can rout small, easily maneuvered parts with a template on a router table, or large shapes

TEMPLATE-ROUTING BITS

FLUSH-TRIMMING

Template same shape as stock; template under stock—allows routing directly on workbench.

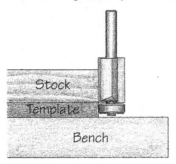

BEARING ON SHANK

Template same shape as stock; template over stock—requires blocking stock up from workbench.

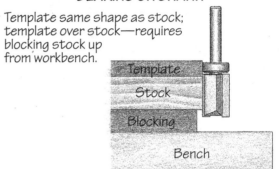

STRAIGHT BIT WITH TEMPLATE GUIDE

Template smaller than stock; template over stock—requires blocking stock up from workbench.

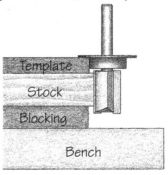

NOTE: *I don't like to use a template guide with a shop-made template, because of the added complication of making the template undersized; but I've used it on occasion to rout a curve and round-over the edge in a single pass with bits known as plunging roundover bits. If you try it, draw a complete, scaled cross section of the bit, the guide, the stock, and the template to make sure you get everything right.*

like tabletops holding the router by hand. The drawings *Template-Routing Bits* on page 223 and *Step-by-Step Template Routing* assume that the router is hand-held, but they show the table-mounted operation just as well if you turn the book upside down.

For either hand-held or table routing, saw and fair the template, as explained in "Sawing and Fairing Curves" on page 221, then fasten it securely to the stock. A little forethought here will help. If you prefer to nail or screw the template to the stock, think ahead about where the nails or screws will go. You want the nail or screw holes on the back side of the stock, you don't want their heads to scratch the surface of your router table, and you don't want a

hand-held router to bump into them. With three different bits to choose from, hand-held versus table-mounted routers, and templates that can go over or under the stock depending on the bit, you've got lots of arrangements to choose from. On the other hand, if you stick the template to the stock with double-sided tape, you don't have to worry about where nails or screws will be.

When sawing off the waste, be *very* careful that you don't saw into the template. If you don't have full confidence that you can saw within ⅟₁₆ inch of the template without nicking it, trace the template edge onto the stock and then remove the template for the sawing.

STEP-BY-STEP TEMPLATE ROUTING

1 Nail or tape the template to the stock.

2 Saw off waste, leaving ⅟₁₆" for router to clean up.

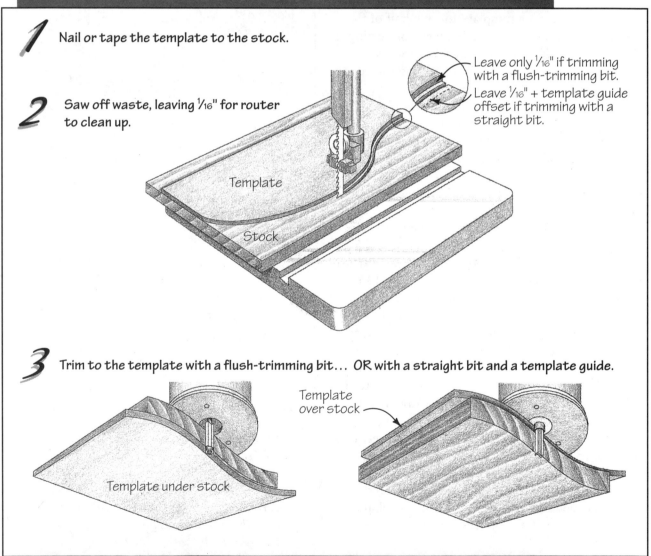

Leave only ⅟₁₆" if trimming with a flush-trimming bit.

Leave ⅟₁₆" + template guide offset if trimming with a straight bit.

Template

Stock

3 Trim to the template with a flush-trimming bit... OR with a straight bit and a template guide.

Template under stock

Template over stock

COMPARISON OF CURVE CUTTING TECHNIQUES

	ROUT WITH CIRCLE TRAMMEL	ROUT WITH ELLIPSE TRAMMEL	SAW CURVE AND FAIR WITH HAND TOOLS	ROUT WITH TEMPLATE
REQUIRED AIDS	Circle trammel	Ellipse trammel	None	Template
ADVANTAGES	Fast; precise; allows molding edge with same ease	Fast; precise; allows molding edge with same ease	Adaptable to any curve	Adaptable to any curve; fast after template is made
DISADVANTAGES	Makes only circles and circular arcs	Makes only ellipses and elliptical arcs	Time-consuming	Requires making template
BEST APPLICATIONS	Circles, circular arcs, combinations of arcs	Ellipses; elliptical arcs	Making templates	Free-form curves in solid stock

NOTE: *Install coping saw blades so that the saw cuts on the pull stroke, not the push stroke. That keeps much better tension on the blade. If you don't like coping saws, you've probably been using the common hardware-store variety. You can get a coping saw that's 10 times as good for only 2 or 3 times the price from mail-order woodworking tool suppliers.*

To make the router cut that trims off the remaining waste, clamp the stock solidly to your workbench. You don't want it to move during the cut. If the stock is small and you don't have bench dogs, wedge the stock, as shown in Step 1 on page 71. Adjust the bit so the bearing bears fully on the template and the cutting edge trims the entire edge of the stock. Feed the stock just fast enough to prevent burning, a speed that you can find only by burning a piece or two. It's easier to sand out a burn than to smooth a rough cut made by going too fast. Smooth the cut as necessary, using the flexible sanding stick described above in "Tools for Fairing" on page 222.

FRAME-AND-PANEL CONSTRUCTION

Long grain in rails keeps width of door stable when humidity changes.

Haunched tenon

Field

Bevel

Stile

Rail

Long grain in stiles keeps height of door stable when humidity changes.

Panel floats freely in frame's grooves, allowing for wood movement across the grain.

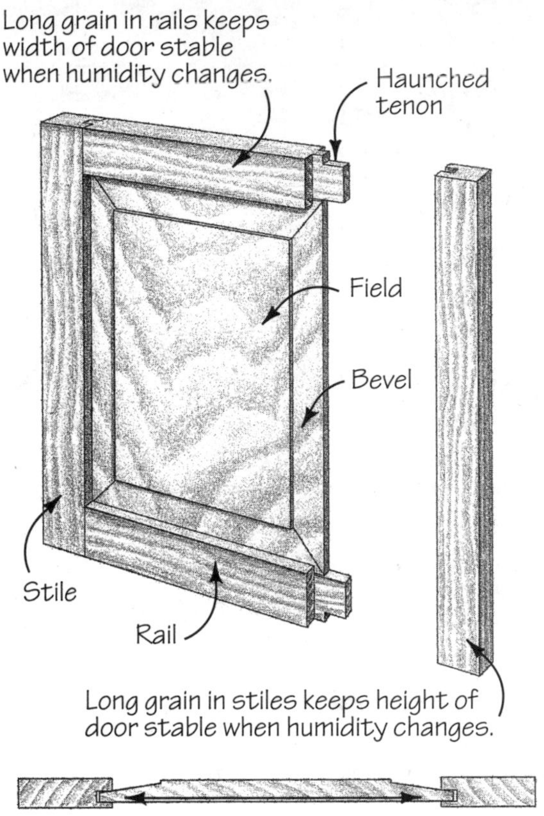

No basic construction technique conveys an aura of craftsmanship quite as well as framed panel construction. Folks react to the interplay of wood surfaces the way they react to delicate dovetails or graceful cabriole legs. Yet they're fairly straightforward to make if you choose a technique that suits your tools and preferences. I'm always rather amazed at the number of different ways, all of them good, that you can raise a panel.

Frame-and-panel construction was not invented out of boredom with flat slabs of wood. It was invented to accommodate the expansion of wood during humid weather and shrinkage during dry weather. The outside dimensions of the frame are stable because the rails

and stiles don't change in length, while the wide, solid-wood panel can expand into the frame grooves or can shrink without coming completely out of the grooves, as shown in *Anatomy of a Frame-and-Panel Door*.

Framed panels draw the eye—make sure you choose shapes for the frame edges and panel bevels that go well together. For example, make the frame edges square, beveled, or chamfered, as shown in *A Gallery of Frames and Panels*,

1, 2, 6, and 7, on pages 228–229, if the beveled edge of the panel will be straight and flat. And choose crisp, narrow panel bevels, as shown in 2, if the rest of the design for the project has clean, slender lines. More complex shapes, such as 4 and 5, look best on more elaborate projects that have molded shapes throughout.

You can make very attractive doors and cabinet sides by framing things other than raised panels. *A Gallery of Frames and Panels, 6,* shows a frame around a plywood panel. This avoids the panel-raising operation and concerns about panel expansion and contraction because the plywood is quite stable.

Multiple Panels and Panes on page 236 shows how to include glass in a door. This is a useful option for more than the obvious reason that it allows you to view what's inside the cabinet—it also makes a cabinet less imposing. For example, a small kitchen with wall cabinets over the counters will look much more spacious if the wall cabinet doors have glass in them instead of solid wood.

Other options available to you include framing pierced tin, as found in antique pie safes, and framing mounted artwork, like songbirds or botanical prints of herbs and spices.

Your design for a frame must include room in the grooves for the panel to expand from side to side. I usually allow ⅛ inch just for expansion for every 6 inches of panel width. For panels up to a foot wide, grooves ⅜ inch deep provide this room for expansion, plus room for shrinkage, and still hold the panel in place. If I'm building during a humid season, I size the panels so they fill all but ¹⁄₁₆ inch of that groove depth. During the dry time of year I make the panel narrower, filling the groove only halfway.

One further note about grooves: Keep in mind that the position of the grooves in the frame edge determines the position of the panel. For example, if the grooves are set too far to the front, the field will end up proud of the front surfaces of the frame. I don't like this appearance. To counteract it, I often use 5/4 (five-quarter) stock for the frames and then offset the panel grooves away from the front surface. This allows me to use a thicker panel and still have the field recessed. Some other ways to deal with the problem are shown in *Panel Appearance.*

Despite their aura of craftsmanship, framed panels are easy to make. The only techniques that are unique to frame-and-panel construction are raising the panel (creating a thin edge) and making cope-and-stick joints to join frames that have shaped edges. You can do the whole job with just a table saw and a sanding block; you can equip yourself with specialized panel-raising router bits and cope-and-stick bits; or, if you're feeling nostalgic for a nineteenth-century intimacy with the materials you're working with, you can do it all with hand tools.

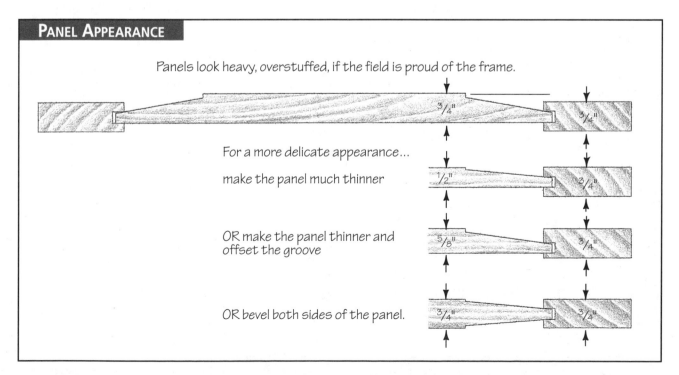

PANEL APPEARANCE

Panels look heavy, overstuffed, if the field is proud of the frame.

¾"   ¾"

For a more delicate appearance...

make the panel much thinner

½"   ¾"

OR make the panel thinner and offset the groove

⅝"   ¾"

OR bevel both sides of the panel.

¾"   ¾"

A Gallery of Frames and Panels

Frames and panels offer a rich array of both appearances and construction techniques, a few of which are shown here.

1 SINGLE-BEVEL PANEL, SQUARE FRAME EDGE

Frame and panel shaped with table saw or hand tools

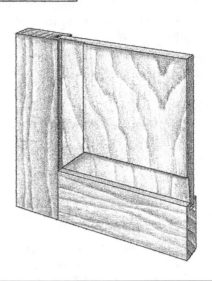

2 DOUBLE NARROW PANEL BEVELS, BEVELED FRAME EDGE

Frame and panel shaped with table saw

3 DOUBLE-BEVEL PANEL, ROUNDED FRAME EDGE

Frame shaped with table saw and router; panel shaped with table saw

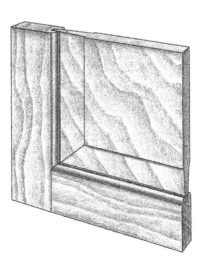

4 CURVED-BEVEL PANEL, COVED FRAME EDGE

Frame and panel shaped on router table

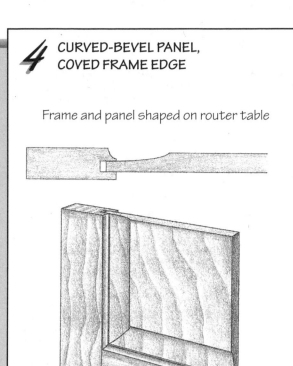

5 MULTISHAPED PANEL BEVEL, OGEE FRAME EDGE

Frame and panel shaped on router table

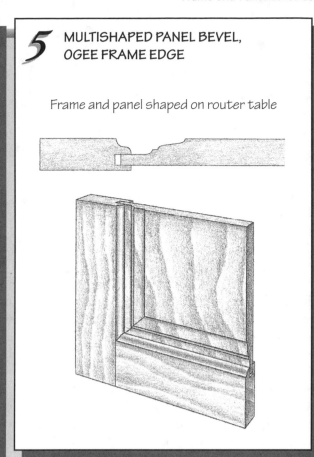

6 FLAT PANEL, CHAMFERED FRAME EDGE

Frame shaped with table saw or hand tools; plywood panel

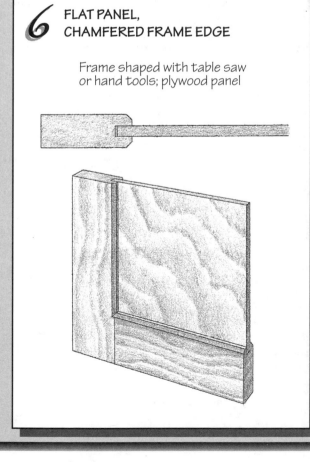

7 SINGLE-BEVEL PANEL, STOP-CHAMFERED FRAME EDGE

Frame chamfered with hand tools; panel shaped with table saw or hand tools

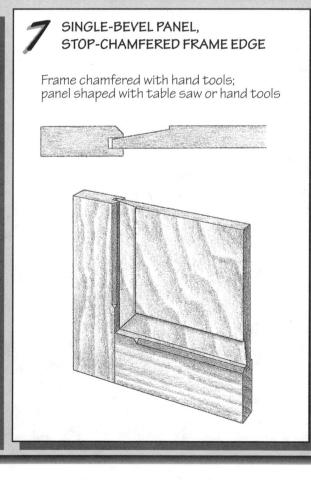

TABLE SAW TECHNIQUES

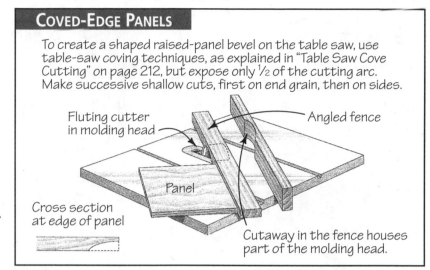

To create a shaped raised-panel bevel on the table saw, use table-saw coving techniques, as explained in "Table Saw Cove Cutting" on page 212, but expose only 1/2 of the cutting arc. Make successive shallow cuts, first on end grain, then on sides.

Fluting cutter in molding head

Angled fence

Panel

Cross section at edge of panel

Cutaway in the fence houses part of the molding head.

A table saw, with no special accessories, is quite sufficient to make a strong frame and an attractive panel. Join the corners of the frame with open mortise-and-tenon joints, as described in "Strong and Easy Mortise-and-Tenon Joints" on page 153. Cut the grooves in the frame members in two passes with a saw blade. Then raise the panel by sawing the bevel on the panel edges.

Raising panels on the table saw is a two-step process. First outline the field with shallow kerfs; then saw the bevels and sand or scrape them smooth.

Sanding the shallow step between the bevel and the field destroys its crisp appearance. To avoid this, I saw the step with my best crosscut blade and then keep abrasives away from it. The kerf is only about 1/8 inch deep, so the crosscut blade works well even when you're cutting parallel to the grain.

Use a rip blade for the bevel cuts. Its deep gullets clear the waste so the blade doesn't bog down, overheat, and burn the wood.

Smooth the bevels with sandpaper, a hand scraper, or a rabbet plane; and assemble the framed panel, as described in "Assembling Framed Panels" on the opposite page.

You can take other approaches to joining frames and shaping panels without getting involved with shapers or router tables. *Anatomy of a Frame-and-Panel Door* on page 226 shows a haunched mortise-and-tenon, the more traditional frame joint for raised-panel construction. Alternatives for raising panels include the clean, simple style shown in *A Gallery of Frames and Panels, 2,* on page 228, which you can shape with just the table saw and a saw blade; the shaped panel bevel cut with a table-saw molding head, as shown in *Coved-Edge Panels;* and the flat panel bevel made on your jointer, as shown in *Panel Raising on the Jointer.*

To raise a panel on the jointer, rig a rigid support to hold the panel at the required angle, then plane down the bevels in a series of passes.

FIRST PASS

FINAL PASS

Fence determines width of the bevel.

Depth of cut is depth of the step at the edge of the bevel.

Rig panel support to create the bevel angle.

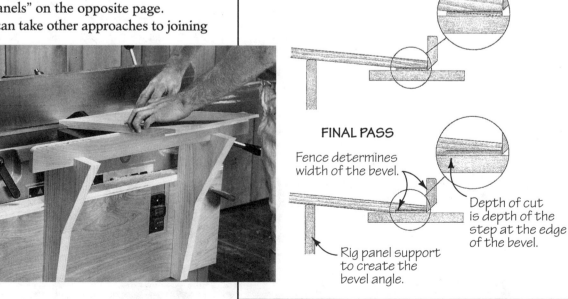

STEP-BY-STEP MAKING FRAMED PANELS ON THE TABLE SAW

1 Saw out the mortise-and-tenon; then groove the frame members with a dado cutter.

Depth of mortise matches width of tenon, not width of rail.

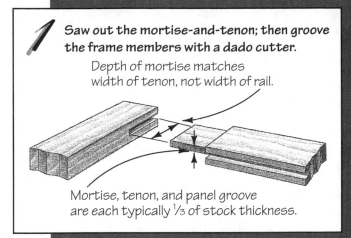

Mortise, tenon, and panel groove are each typically ⅓ of stock thickness.

2 Outline the raised panel field with shallow kerfs.

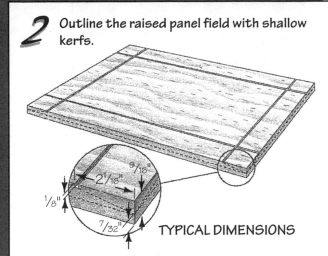

9/16"

2¹/₁₆"

1/8"

7/32"

TYPICAL DIMENSIONS

3 Tilt stock against a tall auxiliary fence and spacer to rip the bevels.

Saw end bevels first, then sides.

END VIEW

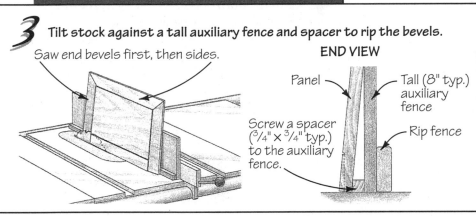

Panel

Tall (8" typ.) auxiliary fence

Screw a spacer (¾" × ¾" typ.) to the auxiliary fence.

Rip fence

*A*SSEMBLING FRAMED PANELS

Gluing a frame together around a panel can be nerve-wracking, but it's not difficult. You need to assemble the frame within the allowable open time for the glue but avoid gluing the panel into the groove. This would prevent wood movement and destroy the whole purpose of the framed panel.

To accomplish this, I finish and wax all my panels before assembling the frame. This prevents squeeze-out from bonding to the panel, and it ensures that my finish won't stick the panel in place.

A few other tricks and tips:

• Assemble the frame with liquid hide glue, which has a lengthy open time.

• Make sure the assembly is flat while the glue dries.

• When assembling separate-tenon frame joints, cut the mortises 1/16 inch longer than necessary. The little bit of leeway this allows in assembly helps get it all together quickly.

• Don't forget the panel. The first time I assembled a haunched mortise-and-tenon frame was under the watchful eye of the customer—my wife. After I swiftly and deftly applied the glue, assembled the frame, and clamped the whole, she asked with genuine innocence how the panel went in.

Router Techniques

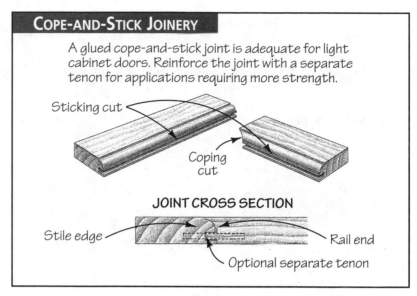

COPE-AND-STICK JOINERY

A glued cope-and-stick joint is adequate for light cabinet doors. Reinforce the joint with a separate tenon for applications requiring more strength.

Sticking cut

Coping cut

JOINT CROSS SECTION

Stile edge

Rail end

Optional separate tenon

Big, table-mounted routers and special panel-raising and cope-and-stick bits have one big advantage over the table saw techniques described above. That is their ability to cut the shaped bevels and frame edges shown in *A Gallery of Frames and Panels, 3, 4,* and 5 on pages 228–229.

Cope-and-stick joinery can produce very attractive results very simply. With this technique, you cope (shape) the ends of the rails so they conform to the sticking (the shape along the inner edge of the stiles). The two cuts are made with a matched pair of router bits, so the parts fit together snugly. The joint provides adequate strength for lightweight doors made from easily glued wood, such as a cherry hutch door. If you're using a wood that doesn't glue very well or you're making doors that need to be stronger, reinforce the cope-and-stick joint with a separate tenon, as explained in "Strong and Easy Mortise-and-Tenon Joints" on page 153.

Most woodworkers who rout cope-and-stick joints for their frames also raise their panels with the router, because the molded sticking goes well with the more shapely panel bevels that are possible with router techniques. But before you run out and spend a bushel of green money on a router bit that looks like a helicopter rotor, consider the following:

▶ You need a powerful router to swing these big bits.

▶ You'll need to limit the depth of cut on each pass. Even a ½-inch shank can flex slightly, giving a rough cut, if you try to remove more than ¹⁄₁₆ inch of hard wood at a time.

▶ Your router must have adjustable speed to keep these large-diameter bits within the safe tip speeds recommended by the manufacturers. ●

A workable alternative to the helicopter rotor is a vertical-style panel-raising bit that you can use on a router that doesn't have speed control. As shown in *Vertical Panel Raising,* these bits require a tall router table fence. They are not a perfect alternative to the horizontal bit, however; they have a greater tendency to leave mill marks.

If you envision making raised panel doors on a regular basis for many years, my advice is to save up for a shaper. The power, the larger spindle diameter, and the overall rigidity of a good shaper allow you to raise a panel in a single pass and still get glass-smooth cuts. You can start by saving yourself the considerable cost of a panel-raising router bit—raise your panels on the table saw for the time being.

The hands-on shop work of framing a panel on the router table is not difficult, but there are a

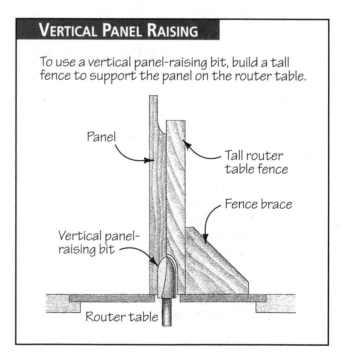

VERTICAL PANEL RAISING

To use a vertical panel-raising bit, build a tall fence to support the panel on the router table.

Panel

Tall router table fence

Fence brace

Vertical panel-raising bit

Router table

few tricks that will keep you out of difficult times. Coping the ends of the rails can be quite discouraging if you rip all of the rails to width before coping the ends. First, your stock can split at the end of the cross-grain cut; and second, the stock can creep along the miter gauge fence during the cut, giving your rails wavy ends. You can lick both problems and save time as well by coping the ends of wide boards and then ripping them to the width of your finished rails, as shown in *Step-by-Step Making Framed Panels on the Router Table.* I even glue up narrow stock if necessary to create these wide boards. The main advantage of the wide stock is that you can dispense with the miter gauge and guide the stock against the router table fence instead. Use a square-ended push stick to feed the stock. This prevents splitting as the trailing edge of the stock goes past the cutter.

Shaping the edges, or "sticking" the edges as some say, is pretty straightforward edge molding. But raising the panels can give you pause. Raise a few panels on a mild-mannered wood like pine or poplar before you tackle hard or difficult wood. Maple and cherry, for example, tend to burn. To get good, clean cuts, I hog off most of the

waste first, taking as much in a single pass as my machine will handle without bogging down. Then I shave off the last 1/32 inch at a fairly fast feed rate to prevent burning. It's also good to use cutters

STEP-BY-STEP MAKING FRAMED PANELS ON THE ROUTER TABLE

1 Cope the ends of the rails.

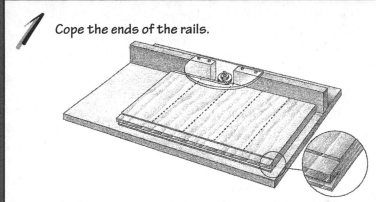

For safety and reduced tear-out, cut wide stock to length of rails, cope both ends, then rip into individual rails.

2 Shape the edges of the stiles and rails.

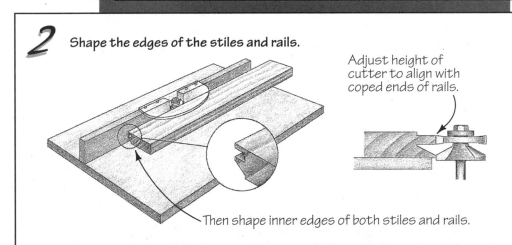

Adjust height of cutter to align with coped ends of rails.

Then shape inner edges of both stiles and rails.

3 Raise the panels.

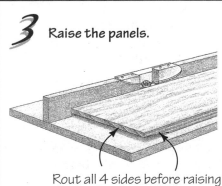

Hog out most of the waste.

Then clean up with shallow passes.

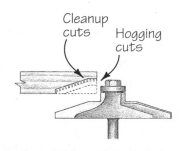

Cleanup cuts

Hogging cuts

Rout all 4 sides before raising the bit for the next pass.

that are sharp and clean to help prevent burning.

To raise a panel on the router table without a specialized panel-raising bit, make a tilted auxiliary table, as shown in *Bowl-Bit Panel Raising*. While a bowl bit is not the only kind of bit that you can use in this way, it gives a particularly nice shape and finish.

BOWL-BIT PANEL RAISING

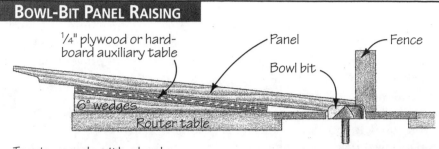

¼" plywood or hardboard auxiliary table — Panel — Fence — Bowl bit — 6° wedges — Router table

To raise panels with a bowl bit, or similar bits, build an angled auxiliary table to hold the panel at the angle of the panel bevel.

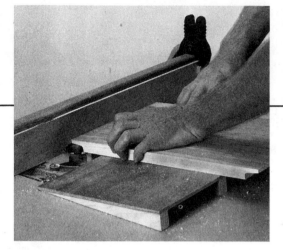

HAND TOOL TECHNIQUES

You don't need highly specialized planes to build a frame-and-panel door exclusively with hand tools, but you do need more than the basics. At a minimum, you need a plane for cutting grooves. This can be a plow plane, combination plane, or multiplane. Any of these will make the two different cuts you need. First, it will cut the grooves in the edges of the frame to hold the panel. Then it will cut a groove between the bevel and the field of the raised panel, allowing you to plane the bevel with a conventional bench plane. If you're one of the multitude of old-tool collectors, take a suitable plane off the display shelf, tune it up, and try it out. Even a halfway decent job of framing a raised panel with hand tools grants bragging rights far greater than the actual skill involved.

When working solely with hand tools, I cut

JOINING CHAMFERS

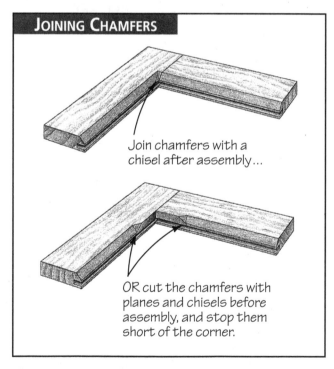

Join chamfers with a chisel after assembly...

OR cut the chamfers with planes and chisels before assembly, and stop them short of the corner.

the grooves first, then the mortise-and-tenon joints, because the groove is actually part of the mortise. (The chapter "Mortise-and-Tenon Joints" on page 152 provides instructions for hand cutting mortises and tenons.) I use the traditional haunched mortise-and-tenon, as shown here in Step 2; and

STEP-BY-STEP
MAKING FRAMED PANELS
WITH HAND TOOLS

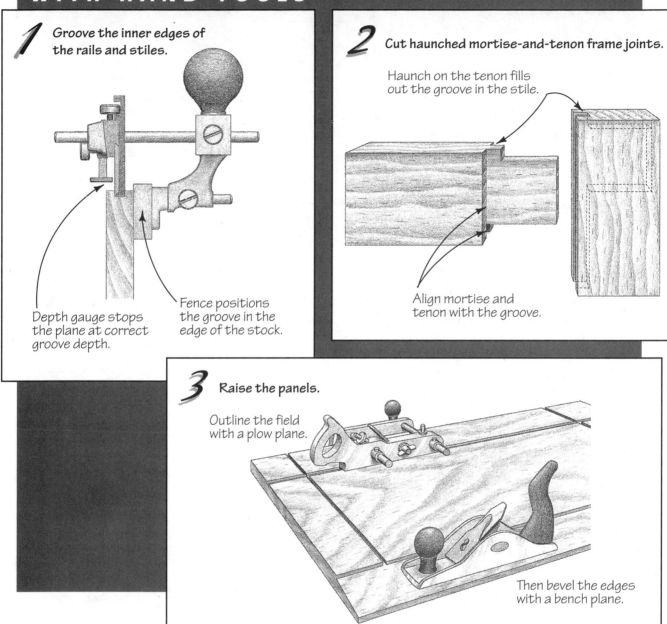

1 Groove the inner edges of the rails and stiles.

Depth gauge stops the plane at correct groove depth.

Fence positions the groove in the edge of the stock.

2 Cut haunched mortise-and-tenon frame joints.

Haunch on the tenon fills out the groove in the stile.

Align mortise and tenon with the groove.

3 Raise the panels.

Outline the field with a plow plane.

Then bevel the edges with a bench plane.

if I add additional shaping to the grooved edge, I use a stopped chamfer, as shown in *Joining Chamfers*.

Raising panels by hand is a two-step process, similar to raising panels on the table saw. First, outline the field with a groove. This will create a nice, crisp step between the field and the bevel and allow you to plane the bevel with an ordinary bench plane. If your plow plane doesn't have a spur to cut the wood fibers when planing across the grain, cut them with a sharp layout knife a few strokes ahead of the plow. Second, bevel the panel edges with either a smooth plane or a jack plane, stopping when the plane just reaches the bottom of the groove. Clean up the cross-grain cuts at the ends of the panel with a hand scraper. **Warning:** Hand-tool fever is both contagious and incurable. If you catch it, you'll eventually want old-fashioned panel-raising planes with skewed blades that give a smoother cross-grain surface.

BEYOND THE SINGLE-PANEL DOOR

Framing a single panel is just the beginning. Once you have some experience, you can apply the same techniques to framing multiple panels and to framing glass or other materials.

When designing the inner frame members for a multiple-panel door, make sure you use the strongest possible arrangement. For assemblies that are taller than they are wide, this means having the horizontal dividers go from stile to stile, as shown in *Multiple Panels and Panes*. This arrangement also makes cutting and assembling easier since the horizontal dividers will be the same length as the top and bottom rails.

You'll have to keep a few other things in mind if your frame will hold multiple panes of glass.

▶ The sticking has a rabbet instead of a groove, as shown in the drawing. After assembling the frame, install the glass with glazing compound or small strips of wood. Small brads are the traditional fasteners for these small strips, but I avoid the hammering by using hot-melt glue instead.

▶ Panes of glass will not change dimensions with changes of humidity but may change very slightly with changes of temperature. Allow about 1/16 inch of clearance on all four sides of the panes.

▶ The frame members between glass panes, called muntins, are usually very narrow. To shape them safely, use a push block with a coped edge, as shown in *Step-by-Step Shaping Muntins*.

▶ Assembly can be a nightmare if you don't plan ahead. Make a complete set of hardboard "panes" to hold the muntins in position during assembly. Cut the corners off these panes so they don't get glued in place by accident. ●

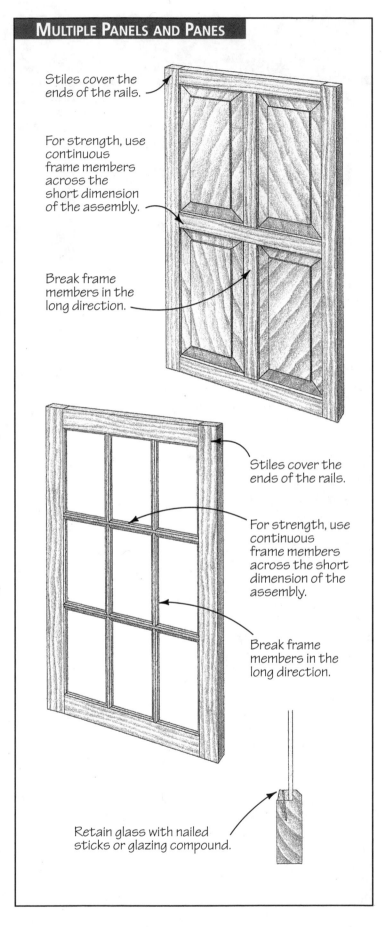

MULTIPLE PANELS AND PANES

Stiles cover the ends of the rails.

For strength, use continuous frame members across the short dimension of the assembly.

Break frame members in the long direction.

Stiles cover the ends of the rails.

For strength, use continuous frame members across the short dimension of the assembly.

Break frame members in the long direction.

Retain glass with nailed sticks or glazing compound.

STEP-BY-STEP SHAPING MUNTINS

1 Cope both ENDS of the muntin stock and one EDGE of the push block.

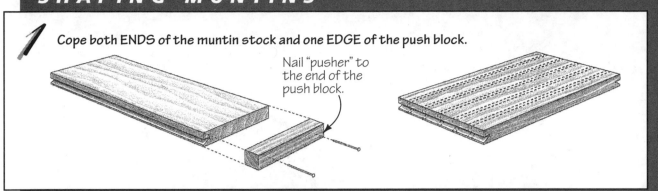

Nail "pusher" to the end of the push block.

2 Shape (stick) 1 edge of muntin stock, then rip muntin from stock.

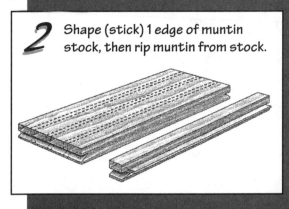

3 Fit muntin in push block to shape the second edge.

4 Repeat Steps 2 and 3.

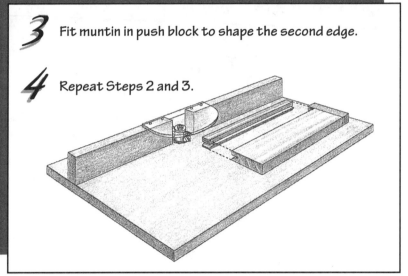

FRAME-AND-PANEL TECHNIQUES

	TABLE SAW TECHNIQUES	ROUTER TABLE OR SHAPER TECHNIQUES	HAND TOOL TECHNIQUES
TOOLS REQUIRED	Table saw with rip blade and crosscut blade; smoothing tool(s)	3-hp router; router table; cope-and-stick bits; panel-raising bit	Plow plane; smooth or jack plane (rabbet plane optional); mortising tools
BEST FRAME JOINTS TO USE	Open mortise-and-tenon	Cope-and-stick; separate tenon	Haunched mortise-and-tenon
STYLES OF PANEL PRODUCED	Flat, angular bevel; narrow coved edge	Angular or shaped, simple or complex	Flat, angular bevel
LABOR INTENSITY	Moderate; mostly in smoothing	Moderate with router table; low with shaper	High
BOTTOM LINE	No specialized investment, but limited shapes	Requires investment in special cutters; wide choice of shapes	Requires plow plane; limited shapes, but classic look

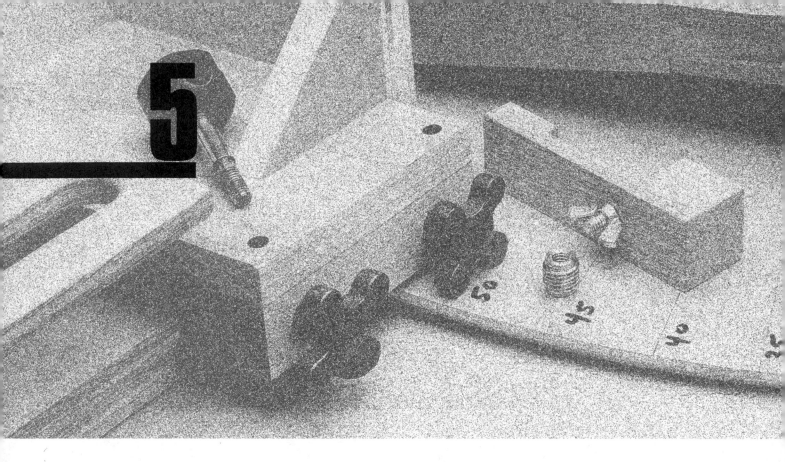

5

SHOP AIDS, JIGS, AND FIXTURES

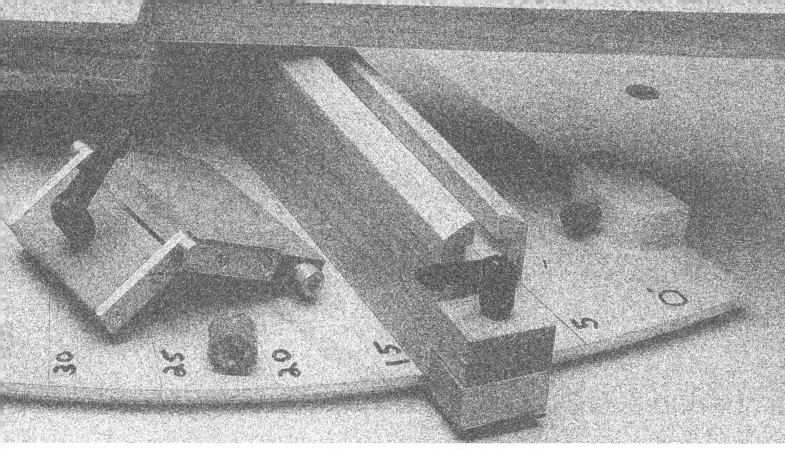

Somewhere, buried in some sofa-sized dictionary, there lie distinctions between jigs, fixtures, and shop aids. Let them lie—all three are tools to make your work in the shop easier and more pleasurable. Judge the tools you find here as you would any other. If they meet your needs, make them. If they don't, don't.

You'll find that these jigs are fairly basic in their function but are designed for yeoman service in the shop. That's because they're mine, and I'm a fairly harsh critic of my tools. I want them to work consistently well, and often, without a lot of baby-sitting, and to be pleasurable in use. The ones that I use most often are the "Adjustable Stop Block and Fence" (page 250), the "Crosscut Support" (page 298), and the "Router Circle Trammel" (page 285). A friend with fewer manufactured tools than I've accumulated puts the "Shop-Made Bar Clamps" (page 274) and the "Combination Mortise and Tenon Jig" (page 240) at the top of his list.

Since I'm fond of brass and nice hardwoods, I often use these materials in jigs that I use frequently, where I can enjoy them during my evenings in the shop. But if you want pure utility, use brass only when you need its machinability and self-lubricating properties; use cherry only when you need its strength and stability. You get the point.

COMBINATION MORTISE AND TENON JIG

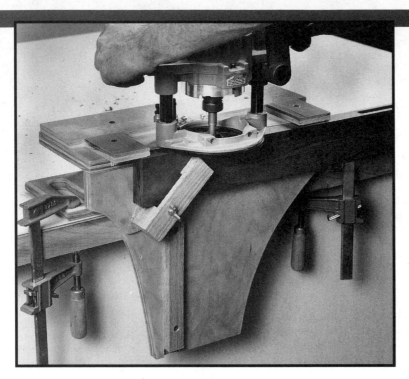

With this one, dual-function jig, you can saw tenons on the table saw and rout mortises with a plunge router.

Jigs for holding stock on end so you can saw a tenon on the table saw have been around for a long time. Some are better than others. For many years I used the heavy cast-iron Delta tenoning jig. Nobody can fault it for not being robust; but it has gotten more and more expensive over the years, and it *is* tiresome to use. When I couldn't figure out how to attach a toggle clamp to speed up clamping the stock, I decided it was time to make my own—and to make it less heavy to push back and forth. Then, when I realized that it could also function as a mortising jig, I was pleased. My

shop is a living example of the universal law that "stuff" accumulates to fill the available space; so having one jig perform the functions of two was too good to resist.

Detailed instructions for using the jig are found under "Cutting Tenons with a Tenoning Jig" on page 161 and "Routing Mortises" on page 154. The shop-made strap clamp that holds the stock for both mortising and tenoning is easily replaced with a toggle clamp if you use the jig regularly. For occasional use, the strap clamp is more than adequate and saves a bunch of money.

EXPLODED VIEW

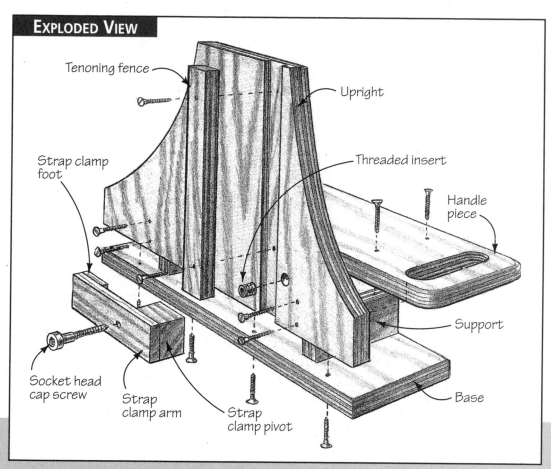

Tenoning fence

Upright

Strap clamp foot

Threaded insert

Handle piece

Socket head cap screw

Strap clamp arm

Strap clamp pivot

Support

Base

MATERIALS LIST

WOOD: Cut the parts for the strap clamp and tenoning fence from scraps of oak or cherry, and make the rest of the jig from ¾-inch-thick plywood or particleboard.

PART	QUANTITY	DESCRIPTION
Upright	1	¾" × 16" × 12"
Base	1	¾" × 6" × 16"
Handle piece	1	¾" × 5¼" × 18"
Supports	2	¾" × 2" × 5¼"
Tenoning fence	1	¾" × 1" × 10"
Strap clamp arm	1	⅜" × 1⅜" × 5"
Strap clamp pivot	1	1" × 1⅜" × 1⅜"
Strap clamp foot	1	¼" × 1⅜" × 1⅜"

HARDWARE

Drywall screws	as needed	#8 × 1⅝"
Drywall screws	as needed	#8 × 1"
Socket head cap screw	1	⁵⁄₁₆-18 × 1¾", ¼" hex-key socket. Part #SCS-256. Reid Tool Supply Co., 2265 Black Creek Road, Muskegon, MI 49444. (800) 253-0421.
Threaded insert	1	⁵⁄₁₆-18 for ½" hole. Part #EZ-14. Reid Tool Supply Co.

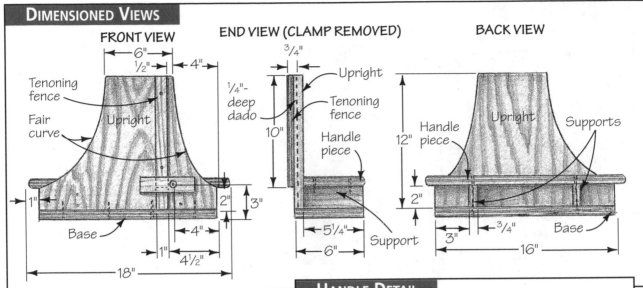

DIMENSIONED VIEWS

FRONT VIEW | END VIEW (CLAMP REMOVED) | BACK VIEW

CUT AND SHAPE THE JIG PARTS

1. Cut the base, handle piece, supports, and tenoning fence to the sizes given in the Materials List. Rough out the upright, too, but don't cut the curves yet.

2. Lay out the 1-inch-wide × ¼-inch-deep dado in the upright, as shown in the *Dimensioned Views*. Cut the dado with a dado cutter on the table saw or with a router and straight bit.

3. Cut the curves in the upright on the band saw. The exact shape of these curves isn't important.

4. Cutting out the handle slot in the front end of the handle is a two-step process. First, drill a 1-inch-diameter hole at each end of the handle slot, as shown in the *Handle Detail*. After drilling the holes, saw out the waste between them with a saber saw.

5. Round all the edges of the handle with a ¼-inch-radius roundover bit in a table-mounted router.

ASSEMBLE THE JIG

1. Drill and countersink two holes in the tenoning fence for #8 × 1-inch drywall screws, and screw the fence into the dado, as shown in the *Dimensioned Views*.

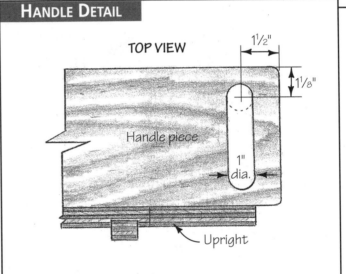

HANDLE DETAIL

TOP VIEW

2. Assemble the rest of the jig with glue and #8 × 1⅝-inch drywall screws. Drill pilot and countersink holes for each screw, and drive them all in place.

MAKE AND ATTACH THE STRAP CLAMP

1. Cut the strap clamp parts on the table saw to the sizes given in the Materials List. For safety, crosscut the parts from longer pieces of wood that have been cut to the proper thickness and width.

2. Drill a ⁵⁄₁₆-inch-diameter hole through the strap clamp arm where shown in the *Strap Clamp Layout*.

STRAP CLAMP LAYOUT

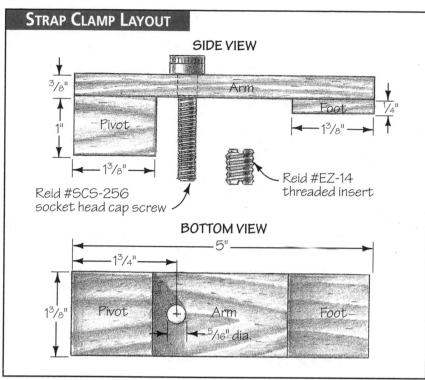

SIDE VIEW

$\frac{3}{8}$"

Arm

Foot

$\frac{1}{4}$"

1"

Pivot

$1\frac{3}{8}$"

$1\frac{3}{8}$"

Reid #SCS-256
socket head cap screw

Reid #EZ-14
threaded insert

BOTTOM VIEW

5"

$1\frac{3}{4}$"

$1\frac{3}{8}$"

Pivot

Arm

Foot

$\frac{5}{16}$" dia.

3. Glue and clamp the strap clamp foot and pivot to the strap clamp arm.

4. The strap clamp is bolted to a threaded insert in the upright. Drill a ½-inch-diameter hole for the threaded insert where shown in the *Dimensioned Views/Front View.* Screw the threaded insert in place, as shown in *Installing the Threaded Insert,* using a ⁵⁄₁₆-inch hex-head bolt, a matching nut, and a socket wrench. Screw the bolt partway into the threaded insert, and then lock the nut against the insert. Be careful to keep the insert straight as you turn it into the hole with the socket wrench.

INSTALLING THE THREADED INSERT

Screw the bolt into the threaded insert, and then lock the nut tightly against the top of the insert. Screw the insert into its hole by turning the bolt with a socket wrench. Be careful to keep the insert perpendicular to the surface of the upright.

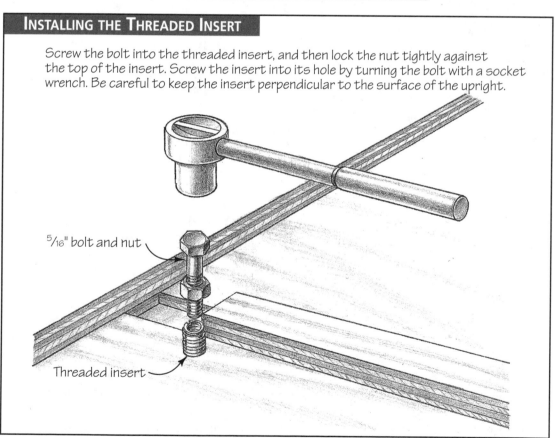

$\frac{5}{16}$" bolt and nut

Threaded insert

MARKING KNIFE

A well-designed marking knife is hard to find; but making one is an excellent introduction to knife making in general, because it's so simple.

You might group the tools in my shop into two categories. Some I like because they work well, but I'm not particularly attached to them. These are tools like my flat pry bar and my 25-foot tape. I wouldn't want to install a set of cabinets without them, but if I lost one, I'd only grumble at the inconvenience of replacing it. The second group of tools is different. These I like to use for the sheer joy of handling them—they're tools that my hands know and can manipulate without a second thought. One example is my marking knife.

A knife like this is surprisingly easy to make because it requires so little shaping of steel. All you need in materials is a length of high-carbon tool steel,

a few scraps of wood for the handle, and a length of brazing rod for rivets. The steel should be readily available from a local industrial supplier, or you can order a length from the source listed.

I've outlined a method that you can follow to make one without having to use any specialized metalworking equipment. The basic grinding and shaping are done on a drill press equipped with a grinding wheel, although a belt sander or even a bench grinder would do. The heat treatment is carried out with the aid of a propane torch. Feel free to modify the techniques to suit the tools you have at hand. Once the blade is ready, the scales that sandwich the blade to form the handle are epoxied and riveted in place.

EXPLODED VIEW

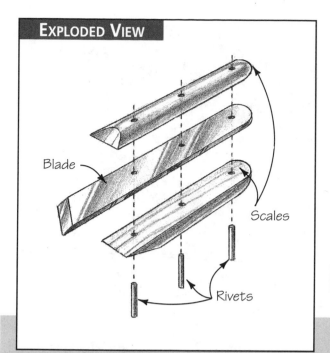

Blade

Scales

Rivets

DIMENSIONED VIEWS

FRONT VIEW

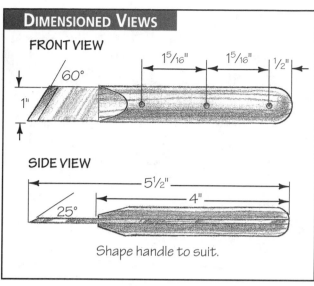

60°

1"

1⁵⁄₁₆"   1⁵⁄₁₆"   ½"

SIDE VIEW

25°

5½"

4"

Shape handle to suit.

MATERIALS LIST

MATERIALS: Use high-carbon tool steel for the blade, a dense hardwood for the scales, and brazing rod for the rivets.

PART	QUANTITY	DESCRIPTION
Scales	2	³⁄₈" × 1" × 4"
HARDWARE		
Blade High-carbon tool steel	1	³⁄₃₂" × 1" × 5½" Part #D-CGFS-1-1/2/16. Small Parts Inc., P.O. Box 381966, Miami FL 33238. (305) 751-0856.*
Rivets (cut from brazing rod)	3	⅛" dia. × ⅝". Part #D-ZRB–2-12. Small Parts Inc.

*Small Parts has a $15 minimum order, so get enough steel to make three knives, and you'll have some extra to play with.

CUT AND SHAPE THE KNIFE BLADE

1. Lay out the skew angle on the blade blank, as shown in the *Dimensioned Views/Front View.* Use a wide, felt-tipped marker to color the steel so you can see what you're doing; then scribe the line with the tip of an awl. Cut the blade to shape with a hacksaw. Even in its annealed (softened) state, tool steel is quite hard and will dull your saw blade in a hurry if you're not careful. Try to cut so there are at least three saw teeth in contact with the stock at all times. Don't put too much downward pressure

on the saw; a hacksaw has to be coaxed through the metal, not bullied. Push the saw with slow, full-length strokes, about one per second. Lift the blade slightly on the return to help keep it from overheating.

2. As shown in the top left photo on page 246, start grinding the bevel with a 100-grit grinding wheel chucked in your drill press. Build a tool rest to hold the blade at the proper angle, as shown in

Most drill presses have adjustable speed, allowing you to grind fast before you harden and temper the blade but then letting you slow down to avoid burning during final shaping.

The dimple raised by a center punch helps the drill bit get a bite into the metal surface. Without the dimple, the bit would tend to skate around and your hole would probably end up in the wrong place.

A Tool Rest for Grinding on the Drill Press. Which side of the blade you will bevel depends on whether you're right or left handed as well as your personal preference for marking. The blade in the photo on page 244 is for right-handed use. Take frequent breaks to let the blade cool as you grind. At no point should the blade be so hot you can't handle it.

Grind about two-thirds of the bevel, leaving a slight flat at the end of the blade, as shown in *How Far to Grind.* If you make the edge too thin now, it will be ruined during heat treatment.

3. Lay out the positions of the rivet holes on the blank. Mark the centers of the holes by dimpling the metal with a center punch, as shown in the top right photo on this page. Drill the ⅛-inch holes on the drill press. Be sure to clamp the blade down for safety. File off any burrs around the holes.

4. Grind the corners off the blade's handle end, as shown in the *Dimensioned Views* on page 245.

HOW FAR TO GRIND

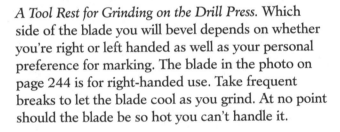

Stop grinding here before heat treatment.

Desired bevel

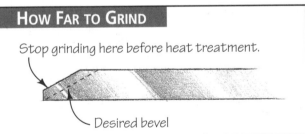

A TOOL REST FOR GRINDING ON THE DRILL PRESS

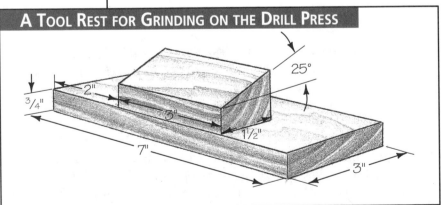

¾"

2"

3"

25°

1½"

7"

3"

HEAT TREAT THE BLADE

1. Polish both sides of the blade where it won't be covered by the scales. Do this the same way you would polish the back of a chisel or plane iron. See "Sharpening—An Overview" on page 25 for more details. This polishing is necessary so you can really see what's happening to the metal as you heat treat it.

2. Harden the blade. Heat treatment is a two-part process. First, you harden the blade so it will hold an edge. Then, since hardening also makes the steel very brittle, you take away some of that hardness to make the blade tougher, or less likely to chip. This is called tempering. To harden the blade, heat it until the first inch or so of the cutting end glows with a cherry red color, as shown in the photo on this page. Hold the blade at this temperature for two or three minutes to allow the heat to thoroughly penetrate the metal; then plunge the blade into a coffee can full of oil to quench it. This sudden cooling locks the molecular structure of the steel into a very hard matrix.

Note that there is probably as much controversy among blacksmiths about what fluid to use for quenching as there is among woodworkers about whether to cut dovetail pins or tails first. Some smiths like plain water; others prefer brine (saltwater); and still others favor a variety of oils, ranging from rendered lamb's fat to used 10W-30. Add to this controversy the fact that some steels are designed to be quenched in a specific fluid, and you've got a real dilemma. My advice is this: If you buy new steel, use whatever fluid the manufacturer recommends. If you make your tools from scrap metal for which you don't know what the manufacturer had in mind, use oil. Its cooling action is slower than that of water and thus is less likely to distort or crack your carefully shaped creation. I like olive oil, as it doesn't stink like motor oil does and isn't as much of a disaster should it spill.

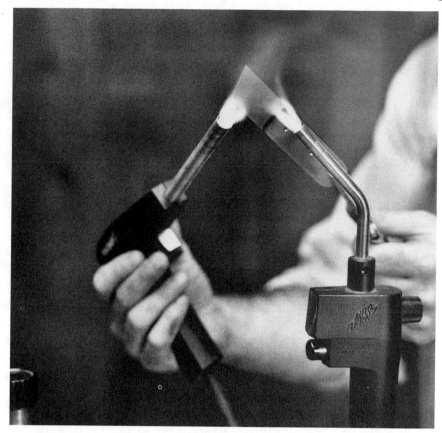

Holding steel at a glowing cherry red color for hardening is easier if two propane torches are used together. Arrange the gas cylinders so the flames overlap.

Work outside to avoid any danger of fire. I've never had the oil flame up as I quenched a tool, but the potential is there. What's more likely is a good quantity of smoke—not quite what my wife expects to see drifting up the staircase. Set up in the shade somewhere, preferably under a spreading chestnut tree, so you won't have to compete with the sunlight to see what color your blade is.

3. Temper the blade next. This is the tricky part. It involves heating the blade again, but only to a certain point—a little over 400 degrees. Too much heat and you'll take away too much hardness. Then

TECH TIP A CHARCOAL FIRE, FANNED WITH A HAIR DRYER, works well if you find you need more than propane-torch heat to get your blade to glow evenly. With either system, hold the blade in a pair of locking pliers to avoid toasting your fingers.

you'll have to harden the blade all over again. This may not seem like a big deal; but each time you heat and quench a piece of steel, you run the risk of having it warp or crack.

Polish away the oxides left from the hardening process. This isn't merely for cosmetic purposes. You need a clean, bright surface so you can actually see what you're doing. Heat the blade over the flame of a single propane torch, as shown in the photo on this page. As the blade heats, its surface will change colors. These hues are faint, but distinct, and are best viewed in dim light. I usually work in a dark corner of my shop when I'm tempering tools.

Each color represents a certain temperature. The first to appear will be a pale straw yellow; then full straw, dark straw, bronze, purple, and blue, with a number of mixed shades in between. Cutting tools should be tempered in the straw to bronze range, whereas tools like wrenches that must absorb a lot of shock should be heated further and will fall into the purple-blue range.

Patience is the key here. You want to heat the blade very slowly so you can control its temperature. The difference between just right and too hot is only a few degrees. Ideally, you want the entire blade to turn a single color all at once. For this knife, the color you're after is in the dark straw-bronze range. Once the proper color appears, continue moving the blade over the flame but raise it a few inches so it won't get any hotter. Hold the blade at temperature for 5 to 10 minutes to thoroughly temper it and then quench it again. Water will do this time, as there is little danger in the blade warping or cracking.

If you have trouble getting the colors to appear evenly, concentrate the heat toward the handle end of the blade. This way you'll be able to watch as the colors run out the blade toward the cutting edge. Quench the blade when the bevel starts to go bronze. It won't matter much if the rest of the blade is purple or blue.

This low-tech method of heat treatment has been practiced for hundreds of years. Like a lot of old technology, it requires a certain amount of skill—skill that takes practice to acquire. I recommend you try tempering some pieces of scrap steel before you start on your knife. No need to harden the pieces first, the colors will appear regardless. Just be sure to polish the steel well before beginning; the colors are much easier to see on a shiny surface.

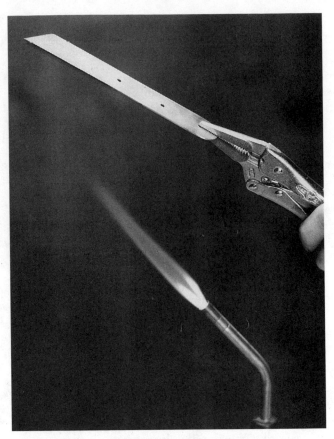

When tempering the blade, keep it moving 6 to 10 inches above the actual flame, turning it from side to side to keep the heat uniform. Linger over the area toward the handle end and move quickly out at the edge, the thinner bevel will heat faster than the rest of the blade.

ATTACH THE SCALES

1. Drill the scales for rivets. Attach one scale to the blade with double-faced tape. Drill ⅛-inch holes through the scale using the blade as a guide. Then tape the second scale to the blade and drill holes in it too. Mark the scales, so you know how they fit; then pull them off the blade and discard the tape.

2. Sand the sides of the blade with 220-grit sandpaper to remove any oxidation. Cut the rivets to size and set them aside. Mix up a batch of epoxy and apply it to both sides of the blade and the joining faces of the scales. For a really superior bond, sand the blade again right through the wet epoxy. This ensures a bond to steel, not to the oxide that begins to form immediately when bare steel is exposed to air. Messy? Yes indeed, but this

Flare the ends of the rivets with a ball peen hammer. Swing the hammer at a slight angle and try to strike the rivet slightly off center. Turn the knife as you go, so you can work the rivet from all sides.

final "wet" sanding does wonders for the quality of the joint.

Sandwich the blade between the two scales and insert the rivets into their holes for alignment. Make sure a little bit of each rivet sticks out on both sides. Clamp the scales lightly to the blade (or wrap it tightly with masking tape) and set the whole sticky works aside to cure.

3. When the epoxy has hardened, hold the knife on top of an anvil or other hard surface and peen the rivets over until they are flush with the faces of the scales, as shown in the photograph. File and sand the handle to a comfortable shape. Finish it with a penetrating oil finish.

4. Finish grinding the bevel. Be very careful not to let the blade get too hot. Remember those colors that appeared as you were tempering? The heat from grinding will produce them every bit as well as the torch did. Sharpen your new knife as you would a chisel.

ADJUSTABLE STOP BLOCK AND FENCE

A well-behaved stop block should move when you want it to and stay put when clamped. This one behaves.

Stop blocks come and go, and probably for good reason. I've seen lots of them in assorted shapes and sizes that never quite met my expectations. The catalog models that ride along the edge of your machine's fence lock solidly in place, but then they're in the way when you need to make a quick cutoff. And the kind that flip up out of the way are anything but solid. When you butt a piece of wood against them, they pivot away from the blade, destroying their setting.

This stop block gives you the best of both worlds—a solid stop that won't pivot and one that you can flip up out of your way. It consists of a lockable stop that slides along the top of a fence; but unlike others, the mating surfaces of the stop and the fence are beveled, so the stop wedges in place and can't pivot when you butt the stock against it. The flip-down stop arm is connected to the slide with two precision $3/16$-inch-thick leafed brass knife hinges. The wide spacing of the hinges keeps the arm aligned and without any play, while still allowing it to flip up easily. Fine adjustment bolts on the arm provide precise microadjustment.

There are a couple of things to consider before you begin making this stop. First, it is easiest to cut and shape the fence in two halves and then glue them

EXPLODED VIEW

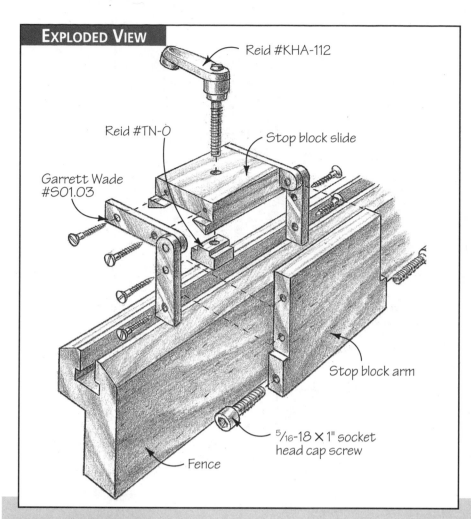

Reid #KHA-112

Reid #TN-0

Stop block slide

Garrett Wade #S01.03

Stop block arm

⁵⁄₁₆-18 × 1" socket head cap screw

Fence

together. And second, it is very important that the bevels on the fence match those on the stop block slide to provide perfect locking surfaces. Start by routing the grooves in the fence sides and stop block slide. Next, bevel the top edge of each half of the fence and the bottom edges of the slide. Cut the stop block arm to shape, and then drill all the holes. The fence can be made any length to fit any tool or jig you want. Make one for your table saw crosscut sled (like the ones shown in the "Crosscut Sleds" chapter on page 266), for your miter gauge, or for your router table.

MATERIALS LIST

WOOD: Use 4/4, straight-grained poplar, cherry, or mahogany for the fence. Use cherry for the stop block slide and arm.

PART	QUANTITY	DESCRIPTION
Fence sides	2	¾" × 2¾" × Variable*
Stop block slide	1	¾" × 1½" × 2⅝"
Stop block arm	1	½" × 2½" × 3"

HARDWARE

Knife hinges	2	Part #S01.03. Garret Wade, 161 Avenue of the Americas, New York, NY 10213. (800) 221-2942.
Socket head cap screws	2	⁵⁄₁₆-18 × 1"
Studded handle	1	Part #KHA-112. Reid Tool Supply Co., 2265 Black Creek Road, Muskegon, MI 49444. (800) 253-0421.
T-nut	1	Part #TN-0. Reid Tool Supply Co.

*Size for your needs.

FENCE LAYOUT

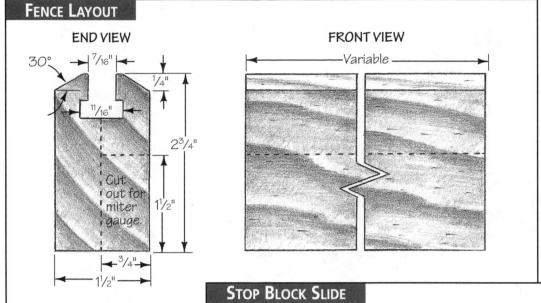

END VIEW

30°

$^7/_{16}$"

$^1/_4$"

$^{11}/_{16}$"

$2^3/_4$"

Cut out for miter gauge.

$1^1/_2$"

$^3/_4$"

$1^1/_2$"

FRONT VIEW

Variable

STOP BLOCK SLIDE

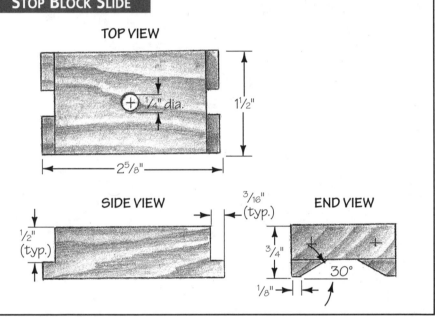

TOP VIEW

$^1/_4$" dia.

$1^1/_2$"

$2^5/_8$"

SIDE VIEW

$^1/_2$" (typ.)

$^3/_{16}$" (typ.)

END VIEW

$^3/_4$"

30°

$^1/_8$"

CUT THE GROOVES AND BEVELS

1. Prepare the stock. Cut the parts to the sizes given in the Materials List. Select clear, straight-grained stock well-adjusted to the humidity of your shop for the fence.

2. Lay out the grooves on the end of one fence piece and on the end of the stop block slide, following the dimensions shown in the *Groove and Bevel Layout*. Use a very sharp, fine-lined pencil and straightedge, because your layout needs to be precise.

3. Rout the grooves with a ¼-inch-diameter straight bit in a table-mounted router. Rout in the sequence shown in the *Groove Routing Sequence*. The grooves wider than ¼ inch need to be routed in two passes.

4. After routing the grooves, set your table saw blade at 30 degrees and bevel the stop block slide with the fence positioned to the right of the blade, as shown in the *Table Saw Bevel Setups*. Raise the blade until it just nips the bottom of the groove you routed in Step 3.

Next, reposition the fence and cut the bevel in the top of each fence side.

5. Glue and clamp the fence sides together, carefully aligning their top and bottom edges. Wipe off any squeeze-out in the slot.

6. For a really silky smooth sliding action you need to smooth out the saw marks from the bevel cuts on both the slide and the fence, but you dare not alter the fit between the mating surfaces. To achieve this, first stick self-adhesive sandpaper to the fence bevels and smooth the slide, then stick self-adhesive sandpaper to the slide and smooth the fence.

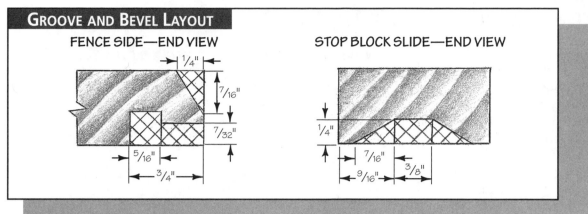

GROOVE AND BEVEL LAYOUT

FENCE SIDE—END VIEW

STOP BLOCK SLIDE—END VIEW

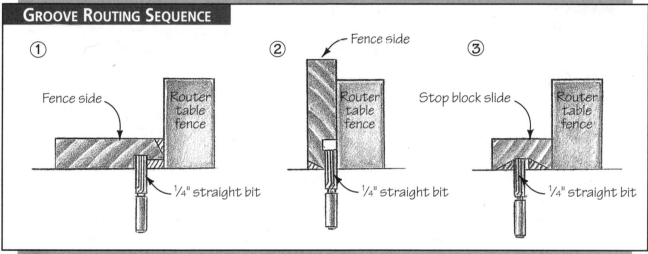

GROOVE ROUTING SEQUENCE

① Fence side — Router table fence — ¼" straight bit

② Fence side — Router table fence — ¼" straight bit

③ Stop block slide — Router table fence — ¼" straight bit

TABLE SAW BEVEL SETUPS

Stop block slide — Table saw fence — 30°

Table saw fence — Fence side — 30°

DRILL THE HOLES

1. Lay out and drill a ¼-inch-diameter stud hole centered in the top of the stop block slide. I find it's most accurate to do this on the drill press, but you can use a hand-held drill if necessary.

2. Next, lay out and drill the ⁹⁄₃₂-inch-diameter fine adjustment bolt holes on each end of

the stop block arm. Again, it's best to do this on the drill press. To keep the arm from tipping as you drill the hole, clamp it on end in the jaws of a hand screw. If you don't have a hand screw, clamp scraps of wood on each side of the arm with a C-clamp for support. Set the depth stop on the drill press to drill the holes 1⅛ inches deep.

CUT THE HINGE MORTISES

1. Both the stop block slide and stop block arm require ³⁄₁₆-inch-deep hinge mortises to accept the leaves of the knife hinges, as shown in the *Stop Block Slide/Side View* on page 252 and in *Stop Block Arm/Front View*. The secret to cutting small parts on the table saw is providing adequate support as you make the cuts. Make a support block from a 1-foot-long 2 × 4. Square the ends of the support block on the table saw.

2. Position the table saw fence for the cut and then fix the stop block arm to the support block with a strip of double-sided tape. The stop block arm should be upright, as shown in *Mortising the Arm*.

3. Next, cut the mortises in two passes. If you're using a standard ⅛-inch-thick blade, make the first pass, then put a ¹⁄₁₆-inch-thick shim between the fence and the support block and make a second pass to cut away the waste. A scrap of plastic laminate makes a perfect shim. You

could also make this cut with your dado blade, as shown in "Using Dado Cutters" on page 129.

4. Next, cut the mortises in the stop block slide. Stick a new piece of double-sided tape on the end of the support block and place the block flat on the saw table with its edge against the fence. Stick the stop block slide to the support block, as shown in *Mortising the Slide.*

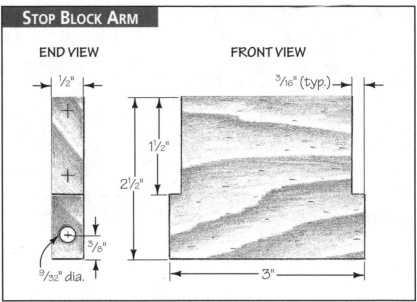

STOP BLOCK ARM

END VIEW — ½" — 1½" — 2½" — ³⁄₈" — ⁹⁄₃₂" dia.

FRONT VIEW — ³⁄₁₆" (typ.) — 3"

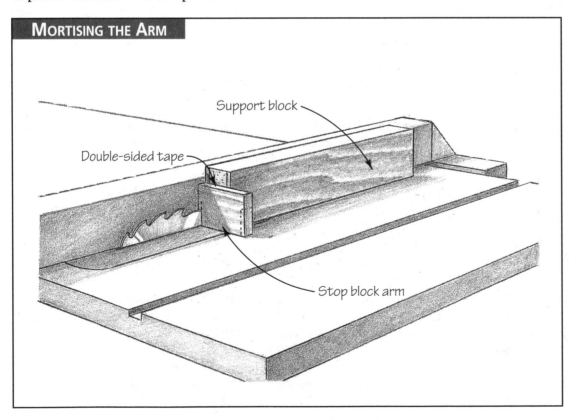

MORTISING THE ARM

Support block

Double-sided tape

Stop block arm

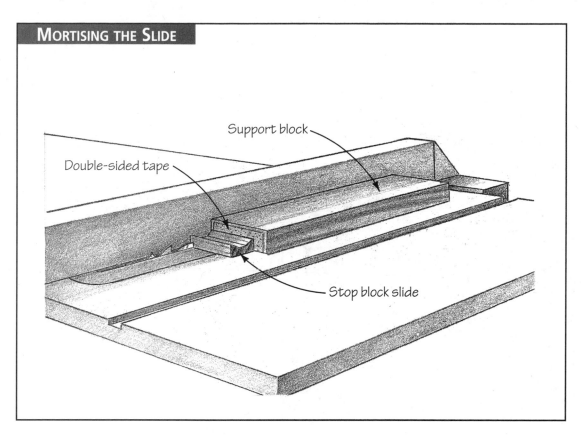

MORTISING THE SLIDE

Support block

Double-sided tape

Stop block slide

5. Again, cut each mortise in two passes. Hold the slide against the saw table with a scrap of wood as you make the cut. Next, put the 1/16-inch-thick shim you used earlier back between the fence and the support block; then cut away the waste.

INSTALL THE HARDWARE

1. Install the socket head cap screws into the stop block arm. Put the arm in a vise with the end of the arm about flush with the top edge of the vise and thread the holes. If you don't have a 5/16-18 tap, you can make one that will work okay on wood by filing three or four shallow grooves in the side of a 5/16-18 bolt. The grooves create notches in the threads, which then act as teeth to cut matching threads in the wood. The vise supports the stock as you tap the holes and keeps it from splitting.

2. Lay out and drill 5/64-inch-diameter pilot holes in the stop block slide for the knife hinge screws. Orient the hinges as shown in the *Exploded View* on page 251, and screw them in place. After attaching the hinges to the stop block slide, lay out the screw holes in the stop block arm, drill pilot holes, and drive the screws.

3. Put the studded handle through the top of the stop block slide and thread the T-nut onto it.

4. Slide the assembled stop block onto the end of the fence.

TECH TIP **SHIM THE HINGES** with heavy paper as necessary to get a fit that allows the arm to pivot easily but without play.

ADJUSTABLE TAPERING JIG

Unlike conventional taper jigs that adjust to a dimensioned angle, this one adjusts to dimensions that you're likely to know—the length of the taper and the amount of stock that you need to remove.

You're going to love making and using this jig. It looks enormously complex, but in fact it consists of just three major parts, and it's stone simple to make. Really! Forget about the intersecting dovetail tenons, the compound bevels, and weird angles; they'll just happen as a consequence of making some straightforward cuts. You shouldn't even look at the *Exploded View* on page 263 until the parts are cut. That's why I stuck it near the end of this project.

One word of caution about the construction, though: These parts are small, so you should be sure you use push sticks to guide the stock into your saw blade or router bit. And, before you start, ask your next-door neighbor to watch you make this project. You'll need testimony to prove that you made it yourself.

The jig is a good example of useful forethought at both the design and building stages. First, you'll notice as you read through the steps that the dovetails' dimensions let you shape all of the dovetails on all of the parts with a single setup. This required a bit of preliminary head scratching, but it was worth it because it ensured a perfectly matching fit.

Second, you'll notice that several parts have angled cuts, but you only have to set up and make one of them. Careful planning of the sequence of cuts allows you to cut the remaining angles as if they were parallel rips or square crosscuts.

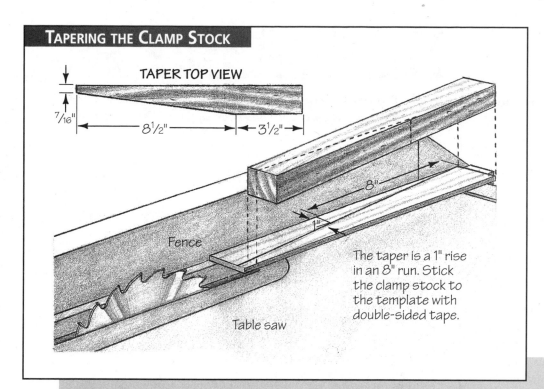

TAPERING THE CLAMP STOCK

TAPER TOP VIEW

7/16"

8½"

3½"

8"

1"

Fence

Table saw

The taper is a 1" rise in an 8" run. Stick the clamp stock to the template with double-sided tape.

MATERIALS LIST

WOOD: Use 8/4, straight-grained poplar, cherry, or maple.

PART	QUANTITY	DESCRIPTION
Beam stock	1	1½" × 4" × 46" to 60"*
Clamp stock	1	1½" × 1½" × 12"
Stop	1	1½" × 4" × 8"†
HARDWARE		
Brass stove bolt	1	¼-20 × 1⅝"
Wing nut	1	¼-20
Self-stick rule	1	6'. Part #08Y41. R-L Woodcraft, 210 Wood County Industrial Park, P. O. Box 1686, Parkersburg, WV 26102. (800) 225-1153.

* Includes an extra 8 inches for the stop.

† Cut from end of beam stock after dovetail is cut.

CUT AND SHAPE THE BEAM AND CLAMP STOCK

1. Cut the beam and clamp stock to the sizes given in the Materials List. Make the beam 48 inches long if you plan on tapering standard dining or occasional table legs. Make it longer if you have huntboard or standing-desk legs in your future. The length of the beam includes 8 inches extra, which you'll cut off later to make the stop.

2. Make a taper guide template for the clamp stock by laying out the taper on a scrap piece of thin plywood or hardboard at least 2 inches wide by about 14 inches long. (The single piece of clamp stock will become both the upper and lower halves of the clamp.) Run the taper layout line from one corner of the scrap at an angle of 1:8 (a 1-inch rise in an 8-inch run), as shown in *Tapering the Clamp Stock* on page 257.

3. Stick the clamp stock to the template with double-sided tape. The edge of the clamp stock should be aligned with the taper layout line.

4. Adjust the fence on your table saw to cut the stock to the dimensions shown in the *Taper Top View* on page 257, and rip the taper.

5. Rout the dovetails on the clamp stock and the beam. All the dovetail cuts are identical and can be made on a table-mounted router. First, chuck a 14-degree dovetail bit in the router and adjust the depth of cut to 7/16 inch. Next, adjust the router table fence so that 3/16 inch of the bit is exposed for the first pass. To avoid burning the stock or causing tear-out, I suggest making the cuts in three passes, increasing the bits exposure from 3/16 to 5/16 inch for the second pass and to 3/8 inch for the final pass. For clarity, however, I have shown the cuts being made in the clamp stock in one pass per side in *Step-by-Step Cutting Dovetail Tenons.* You'll just need to repeat the sequence three times. As you make the dovetails in the clamp stock, also rout the dovetail in the edge of the beam stock to produce the profile shown in the *Beam End View.*

As shown in the drawings, your clamp stock will end up having angles reminiscent of the Stealth Fighter,

STEP-BY-STEP CUTTING DOVETAIL TENONS

1 Position the clamp stock with the tapered edge facing up, as shown here. Guide the stock against a fence, as shown.

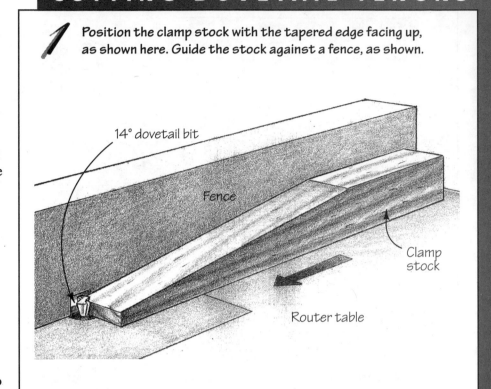

14° dovetail bit

Fence

Clamp stock

Router table

2 Turn the stock end-for-end with the same edge against the fence to make the second cut. The taper should be flat on the table, as shown here.

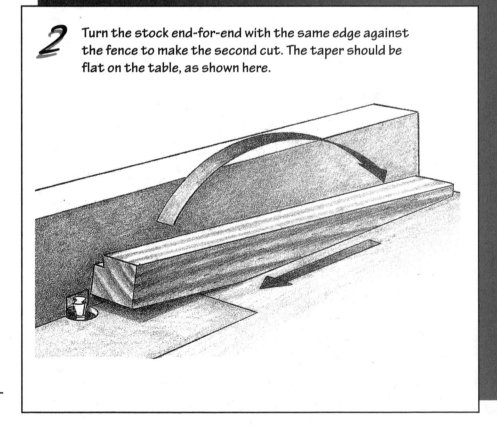

while your beam will have a simple long dovetail tenon running along its entire edge.

6. Lay out the bolt hole in the clamp stock, as shown in *Drilling the Bolt Hole* on page 260. Then chuck a ¼-inch-diameter bit in the drill press and bore the hole.

7. Lay out a centerline on the dovetail tenon on the tapered edge of the clamp stock. Carefully resaw the clamp stock on the band saw, as shown in *Resawing the Clamp Stock* on page 260.

3 Rotate the stock 180° so the side you just cut is facing away from the fence, and make the third cut.

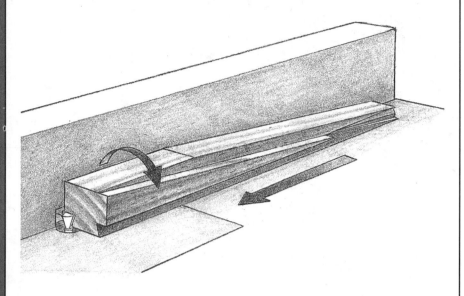

4 Reposition the clamp stop once more by turning end-for-end while keeping the same edge against the fence. Make the final cut.

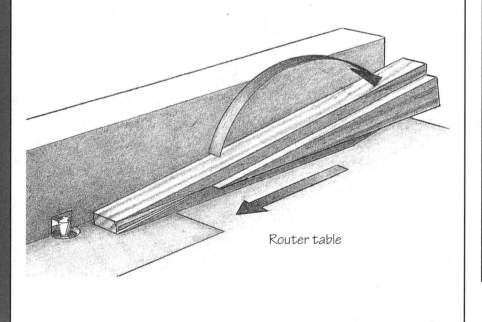

Router table

BEAM END VIEW

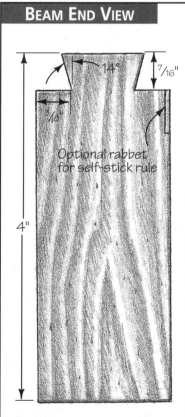

14°

7/16"

⅛

Optional rabbet for self-stick rule

4"

DRILLING THE BOLT HOLE

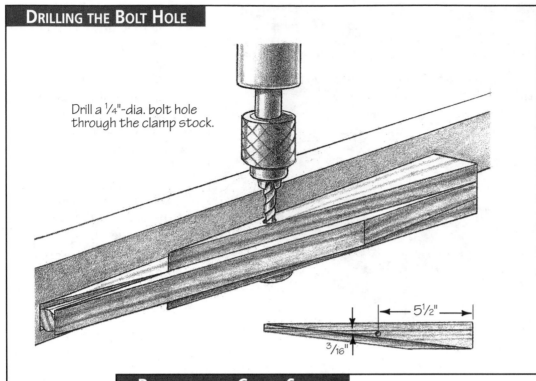

Drill a ¼"-dia. bolt hole through the clamp stock.

5½"

³⁄₁₆"

RESAWING THE CLAMP STOCK

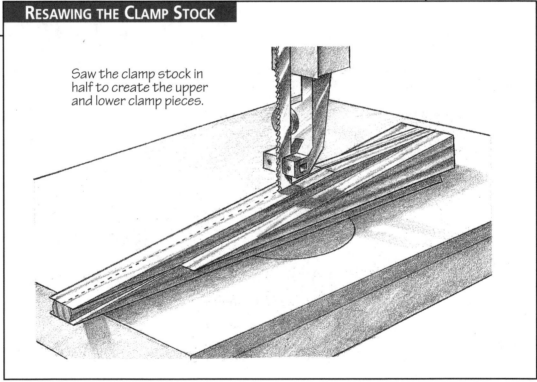

Saw the clamp stock in half to create the upper and lower clamp pieces.

8. Restack the clamp pieces so the dovetailed edges face inward, as shown in *Repositioning the Clamp Stock*, and clamp or tape them together. Countersink the lower half of the clamp for the head of the brass stove bolt, as shown in *Section A*. Use a countersink bit in the drill press so the hole ends up perpendicular.

Be careful at this stage; the drawing shows the favored lay out for right-handed woodworkers. If you're left-handed and prefer to rip on the table saw with the fence to the left of the blade, turn the stack upside down before countersinking for the bolt head. Otherwise, the wing nut on the jig will ride on the saw table.

REPOSITIONING THE CLAMP STOCK

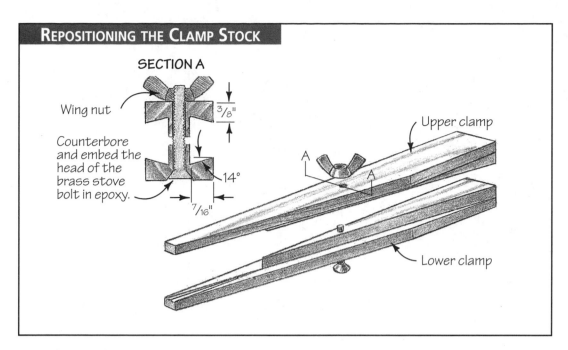

SECTION A

Wing nut

$3/8"$

Counterbore and embed the head of the brass stove bolt in epoxy.

$14°$

$7/16"$

Upper clamp

A   A

Lower clamp

CUT AND SHAPE THE STOP

1. Crosscut an 8-inch-long piece from the end of the beam stock. This short piece will become the stop, the remaining long piece is the beam.

2. Assemble the jig and screw the wing nut tight. Since the stop has not been trimmed to final shape, the assembly should look like the one in *Trimming the Stop's Dovetail* on page 262. Place the

beam against the table saw fence and adjust it to trim the stop, removing the shaded area shown in the drawing. Trim the stop and sand or plane away the saw marks.

3. Disassemble the jig and trim the dovetail tenon on the stop, as shown by the broken lines in *Trimming the Stop's Dovetail*. Since this trim cut is

TAPERING THE STOP

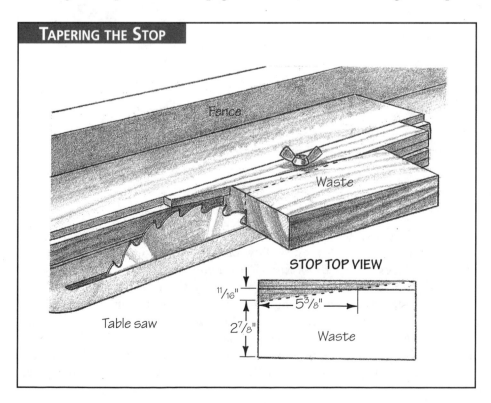

Fence

Waste

STOP TOP VIEW

$11/16"$

$5^3/8"$

$2^7/8"$

Table saw

Waste

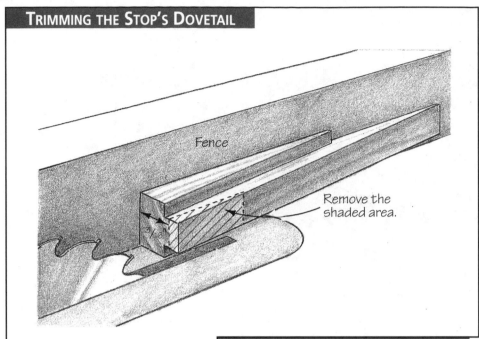

TRIMMING THE STOP'S DOVETAIL

Fence

Remove the shaded area.

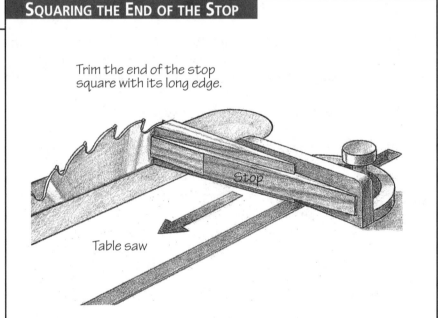

SQUARING THE END OF THE STOP

Trim the end of the stop square with its long edge.

Stop

Table saw

parallel to the trim cut that you just finished making, this cut is a simple rip, using the rip fence on the table saw. Guide the stock with a push stick as you make the cut.

4. Trim the end of the stop so it's square to the two trim cuts you've just finished. Use the miter gauge on the table saw, as shown in *Squaring the End of the Stop.* That completes the major shaping of the parts.

ADDING THE FINAL DETAILS

1. Begin the final detailing of the jig by sanding or planing the upper and lower clamp pieces so they're smooth and flush to the faces of the beam and stop. Assemble the jig; tighten the wing nut; and sand the top and bottom surfaces of the beam, clamp, and stop so they're flush.

2. You can install the self-stick rule directly to the beam, but for a more professional-looking

job that will better withstand abuse in the shop, rout a shallow rabbet for the rule, as shown in the *Beam End View* on page 259. Mark the location of the rule, then unclamp the jig. Chuck a straight bit in the table-mounted router (any diameter greater than ½ inch will do) and adjust the depth of cut to just a hair over the thickness of the rule. Adjust the router table fence to cut a rabbet in the beam a hair wider than the width of the rule; then

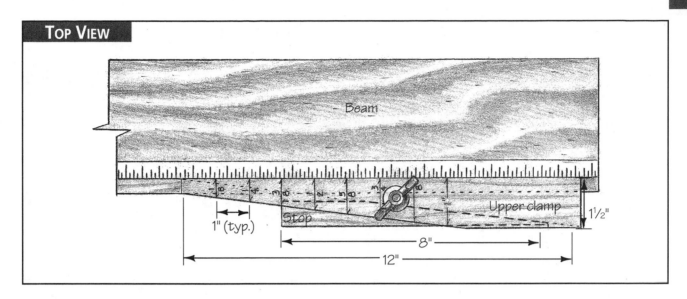

TOP VIEW

Beam

Stop

Upper clamp

1½"

1" (typ.)

8"

12"

rout the rabbet. Remove the paper backing from the rule and stick it in place in the rabbet, making sure the zero mark on the rule is flush with the leading end of the beam.

3. Lay out the taper depth indices that run across the upper clamp piece, as shown in the *Top View.* The lines fall in even, 1-inch increments,

starting from the front end of the clamp. Each mark represents a ⅛-inch difference in the amount of taper you will cut. Scribe the marks fairly deeply with a layout knife, ink the scribe marks with a felt-tipped pen, and sand the surface lightly. Pencil in the fractions, as shown in the *Top View.* At this point your jig should look like the one depicted in the *Exploded View.* It was a piece of cake, right?

(continued on page 265)

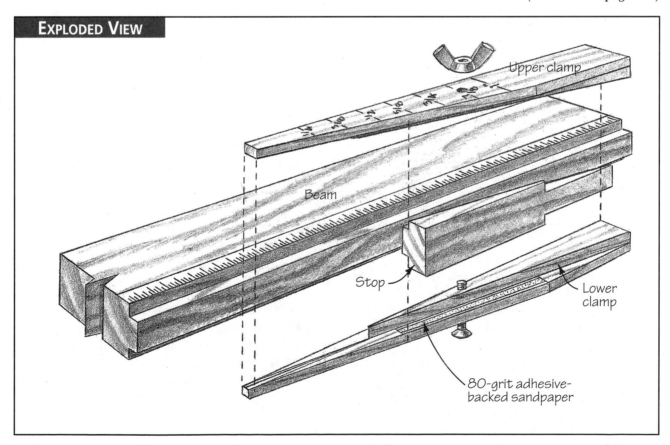

EXPLODED VIEW

Upper clamp

Beam

Stop

Lower clamp

80-grit adhesive-backed sandpaper

Using the Adjustable Tapering Jig

Using the jig is quite a pleasure. Adjustment is made in three simple steps. As an example, let's say you have a 1¾ × 1¾ × 26-inch leg to be attached to a 3-inch-wide apron. The plan calls for a 23-inch-long taper that cuts away ¾ inch of stock at the bottom of the leg.

1. Determine from the project plans (a) the length of the taper and (b) the amount of stock to remove. In this case 23 inches and ¾ inch, respectively.

Align the front of the stop with the index for the amount of stock to remove.

Stop

Align the index for the amount of stock to remove with the length of the taper on the beam rule.

Clamp

SAWING THE TAPER

Adjust the saw fence so the blade will begin the taper cut where required.

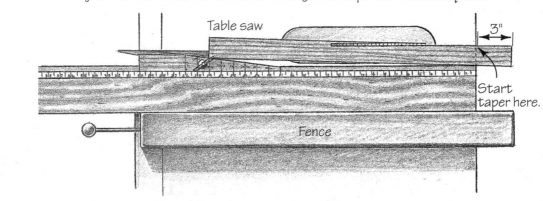

Table saw

3"

Start taper here.

Fence

2. Adjust the *stop* so its leading edge is opposite the index number that represents the amount of stock to remove, as shown in the upper drawing in *Adjusting the Stop*. In this case ¾ inch will be the amount of stock to remove.

3. Without moving the stop, slide the tapered *clamp* so this same index number aligns with the number on the rule that corresponds to the length of the taper, as shown in the lower drawing in *Adjusting the Stop*. In this case align it with the 23-inch mark.

4. Put the jig on the table saw with the leg in place, as shown in *Sawing the Taper*, and adjust the fence so the blade will cut into the wood 3 inches below the top of the leg.

5. Slide the jig along the fence to taper the leg.

4. In testing the jig, I found that even with the bolt tightened down there was a possibility that the stop could move. To solve the problem, I stuck two strips of adhesive-backed, 80-grit sandpaper under the angled portion of the dovetails on the upper and lower pieces, as indicated in the *Exploded View* on page 263. You should do the same. With the sandpaper in place you'll find that the clamp has more than enough holding power.

5. Finally, epoxy the stove bolt in place. Apply a buttering of epoxy to ½ inch of the threads of the bolt directly under the bolt head. Insert the bolt most of the way into the lower clamp piece, then dab additional epoxy paste into the counterbore under the bolt head. Push the bolt home, scrape off what squeezes out, and set it aside to cure.

When the epoxy is fully cured, sand off any remaining smears, file down the head of the brass stove bolt if it projects above the surface of the lower clamp piece, and apply a coat or two of polyurethane or other durable finish of your choice to all of the parts.

CROSSCUT SLEDS

This crosscut sled securely supports wide stock, and its pivoting fence locks at any angle between 0° and 60° for precise miters every time.

When it comes to accurate crosscutting of wide stock, a table saw and a crosscut sled are the best way to go. A miter gauge can't handle wide stock efficiently; and if you've read the chapter "Saws, Crosscutting, and Ripping" on page 92, you already know my feelings about the radial arm saw.

Plans for two sleds are included here. The first has a fence that adjusts to crosscut at angles from square to 60 degrees from square. I'll refer to this sled as the "angle" sled. The second has a fixed fence and a base that extends beyond the edge of the saw to a crosscut support of the type described on page 298. I'll refer to this sled as the "long" sled.

Using this long crosscut sled in combination with a table saw crosscut support lets you crosscut long boards without extra help.

ANGLE SLED

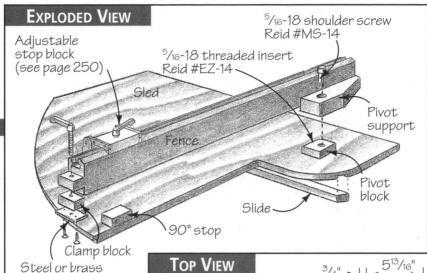

EXPLODED VIEW

Adjustable stop block (see page 250)

⁵⁄₁₆-18 threaded insert Reid #EZ-14

⁵⁄₁₆-18 shoulder screw Reid #MS-14

Sled

Fence

Pivot support

Pivot block

Slide

90° stop

Clamp block

Steel or brass clamp plate

The angle sled has a fence that will pivot and lock at whatever angle you choose, and the 25-inch-long fence provides ample support for most jobs. The best material for the base is nine-ply all-birch plywood. It's strong and stable.

You can find plans for the fence and adjustable stop block on page 250. The fence needs to be customized slightly to suit this jig, but that's all described below. You could replace this fence with a straight 2 × 4, but why not go first class?

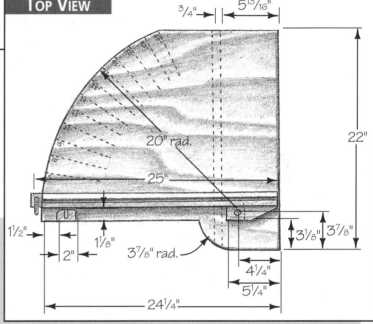

TOP VIEW

³⁄₄"   5¹³⁄₁₆"

20" rad.

25"

22"

1½"   1⅛"   2"

3⅞" rad.

3⅛"   3⅞"

4¼"

5¼"

24¼"

MATERIALS LIST

WOOD: Use nine-ply ½-inch plywood for the sled base and cherry or poplar for the other parts.

Part	Quantity	Description
Sled base*	1	½" × 22" × 24¼"
Pivot support	1	1" × 1½" × 5"
Pivot block	1	½" × 1⁷⁄₁₆" × 1¹¹⁄₁₆"
Clamp block	1	¾" × 1" × 1½"
90° stop	1	¾" × 1⅛" × 2"
Slide bar	1	¾" (approx.) × ⅜" × 22"

HARDWARE

Shoulder screw	1	⁵⁄₁₆-18. Part #MS-14. Reid Tool Supply Co., 2265 Black Creek Road, Muskegon, MI 49444. (800) 253-0421.
Threaded insert	1	⁵⁄₁₆-18. Part #EZ-14. Reid Tool Supply Co.
Stud-type adjustable handle	1	Part #KHA-116. Reid Tool Supply Co.
Steel or brass clamp plate	1	⅛" × 1¼" × 1½"
Socket-head cap screw	1	⁵⁄₁₆-18 × ⅞"

*Use quality nine-ply plywood for extra stability.

Cut and Shape the Parts for the Angle Sled

1. Cut the sled, pivot support, pivot block, clamp block, and 90-degree stop to the sizes given in the Materials List. Make the fence as described on pages 250–253. The fence should be 25 inches long, as shown in the *Top View* on page 267.

2. Lay out the angle on the pivot support, as shown in *Pivot Support Details/Top View.* Cut the angle on the band saw or with a saber saw and smooth the edge with a block plane or sandpaper.

3. Lay out the $^{11}/_{16}$-inch radius on the pivot block, as shown in *Pivot Block Details/Top View,* and cut the radius on the band saw or with a saber saw. Sand the radius smooth.

4. Lay out the large radius on the sled stock with a trammel and the small radius, with a compass.

5. Cut the back edge of the sled, as shown in the *Top View* on page 267. Set the table saw fence $18^1/_8$ inches from the blade and start the cut. When the blade is about 1 inch from the layout line of the small radius, carefully reverse direction and back the piece away from the blade while still keeping the stock tight against the fence.

6. Cut the sled's large and small radii on the band saw or with a saber saw. Use the same saw to continue the cut you made in Step 5. This will join it with the small radius cut and remove the waste. Sand all the edges smooth.

7. The underside of the large radius is rabbeted to accept the clamp plate, as shown in the *Exploded View* on page 267. To make this rabbet, clamp the sled, top down, to your workbench with the arc overhanging the edge of the bench. Smooth the saw marks from the curve and then cut the rabbet with a $^1/_4$-inch rabbeting bit in a router, as shown in *Cutting the Rabbet.*

8. Round the front corners of the 90-degree stop, as shown in the *Top View* on page 267, with a file and sandpaper.

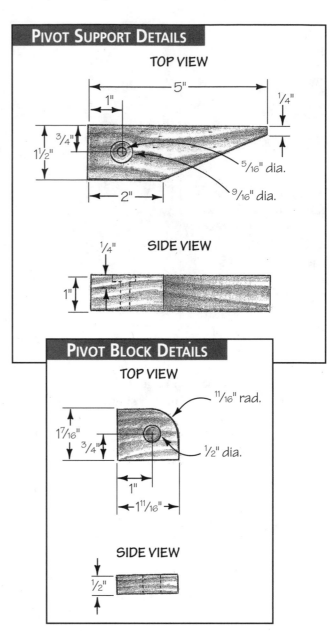

PIVOT SUPPORT DETAILS

TOP VIEW

5"
1"
$^3/_4$"
$1^1/_2$"
2"
$^1/_4$"
$^5/_{16}$" dia.
$^9/_{16}$" dia.

SIDE VIEW

$^1/_4$"
1"

PIVOT BLOCK DETAILS

TOP VIEW

$^{11}/_{16}$" rad.
$1^7/_{16}$"
$^3/_4$"
$^1/_2$" dia.
1"
$1^{11}/_{16}$"

SIDE VIEW

$^1/_2$"

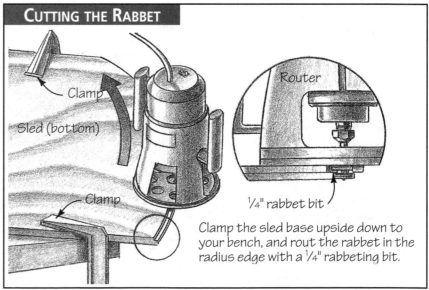

CUTTING THE RABBET

Clamp
Sled (bottom)
Clamp
Router
$^1/_4$" rabbet bit

Clamp the sled base upside down to your bench, and rout the rabbet in the radius edge with a $^1/_4$" rabbeting bit.

TAP THE 90-DEGREE STOP

1. Drill a 1-inch-deep $^9/_{32}$-inch-diameter hole for a cap screw, centering the hole in the front edge of the 90-degree stop, as shown in the *Top View* on page 267.

2. Put the 90-degree stop in a bench vise with the cap screw hole facing up. The vise supports the stock and keeps it from splitting as you thread the hole in the next step.

3. Thread the hole in the 90-degree stop with a socket-head cap screw that's been modified to work as a little tap. To modify it, file little notches at the tip of the screw, as shown in *Changing a Cap Screw into a Tap*. The notched threads act as teeth that cut threads in the wood. After cutting the notches, twist the socket-head cap crew a couple of turns into the hole with an Allen wrench. Then back it out, clean the waste from the threads, and turn it in some more. Repeat the process until the hole is completely threaded.

CHANGING A CAP SCREW INTO A TAP

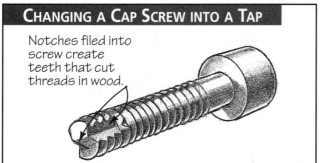

Notches filed into screw create teeth that cut threads in wood.

CUSTOMIZE THE FENCE

1. Lay out the little end extension or tongue on the side of the fence stock, as shown in *Fence Details*.

2. Make vertical cuts into the top and bottom edges of the fence stock to define the end of the extension, as shown in *Fence Details*. First, raise the blade to $^9/_{16}$ inch above the surface of the table to make the cut in the bottom edge of the fence stock. As shown in *Custom Cutting the Fence* on page 270, set the table saw fence so that the blade will just graze the layout line and guide the stock into the blade with a miter gauge.

3. Once you have made the first cut, turn the fence stock over, raise the blade to $1^3/_8$ inches above the surface of the table, and make the cut in the top edge of the fence stock.

4. The quickest and cleanest way to cut away the waste on the end of the fence is to clamp the fence in a bench vise and cut to the outside of the layout lines with a backsaw, as shown in *Trimming Waste with a Backsaw* on page 270. If you have a table saw tenoning jig, you can clamp the fence upright in the jig and cut away the waste on the table saw.

FENCE DETAILS

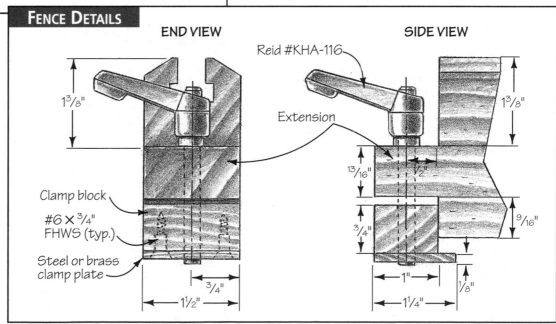

END VIEW

$1^3/_8$"

Clamp block

#6 × $^3/_4$" FHWS (typ.)

Steel or brass clamp plate

$^3/_4$"

$1^1/_2$"

SIDE VIEW

Reid #KHA-116

Extension

$1^3/_8$"

$^{13}/_{16}$"

$^1/_2$"

$^3/_4$"

$^9/_{16}$"

1"

$^1/_8$"

$1^1/_4$"

5. After cutting the tongue, drill a ¼-inch-diameter hole through it, as shown in the *Fence Details* on page 269. Use a drill press or drill guide to produce a clean, straight hole.

PREPARE THE CLAMP BLOCK AND CLAMP PLATE

1. Put the clamp plate stock in a vise and cut it to size with a hacksaw. File the ¼-inch-radius roundovers, as shown in the *Clamp Plate Detail,* and then relieve all the edges slightly with the file to take away the sharpness.

2. Bore the screw clearance holes in the plate for two #6 × ¾-inch wood screws, as shown in the *Clamp Plate Detail.* Drill the holes with a ⁵⁄₃₂-inch-diameter twist bit in a drill press. Recess the holes to accept the screw heads with a countersink bit. Countersink deeply enough so that the screw heads will be flush with the surface of the plate.

3. Hold the clamp plate against the bottom edge of the clamp block; mark the screw locations. Drill pilot holes for #6 screws with a ³⁄₃₂-inch-diameter bit. Screw the clamp plate to the clamp block.

4. Lay out the position of the bolt hole on the clamp plate, as shown in the *Clamp Plate Detail.* Put a ¹³⁄₆₄-inch-diameter (a machinist's #7) twist drill in the drill press and drill the bolt hole through both the clamp block and clamp plate. If you don't have a ¹³⁄₆₄-inch-diameter bit, you may be able to get away with using a ⁷⁄₃₂-inch-diameter bit.

5. Disassemble the clamp plate and clamp block. Thread the bolt hole in the clamp plate with a ¼-20 tap. For information on using a tap, see "Tech Tip" on page 287.

6. Enlarge the bolt hole in the clamp block to provide clearance for the bolt. Put a ¼-inch-diameter bit in the drill press and drill through the existing ¹³⁄₆₄-inch-diameter bolt hole.

7. Reassemble the clamp block and clamp plate, and bolt the unit in place on the fence.

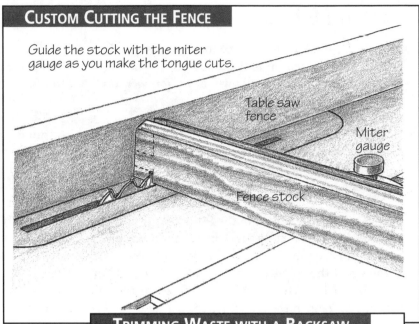

CUSTOM CUTTING THE FENCE

Guide the stock with the miter gauge as you make the tongue cuts.

Table saw fence

Miter gauge

Fence stock

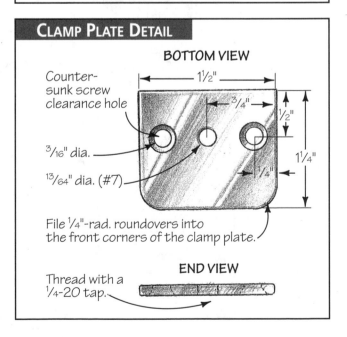

TRIMMING WASTE WITH A BACKSAW

Backsaw

Cut along the layout lines to remove the waste.

Fence

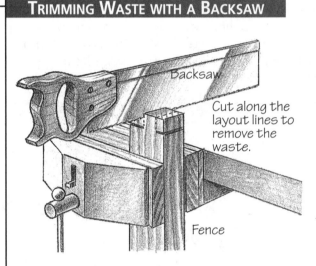

CLAMP PLATE DETAIL

BOTTOM VIEW

Counter-sunk screw clearance hole

1½"

¾"

½"

1¼"

¼"

³⁄₁₆" dia.

¹³⁄₆₄" dia. (#7)

File ¼"-rad. roundovers into the front corners of the clamp plate.

END VIEW

Thread with a ¼-20 tap.

ATTACH THE FENCE

1. Glue the pivot block to the sled, as shown in the *Top View* on page 267.

2. Drill a ½-inch-diameter pivot hole for the threaded insert in the pivot block, as shown in *Pivot Block Details/Top View* on page 268. Since the specified thread insert is ⁹/₁₆ inch long, drill all the way though the pivot block and into the sled below it by at least ⅛ inch.

3. Drill a clearance hole in the pivot support for the shoulder screw; then counterbore the support for the head. Bore the holes on the drill press with brad point bits, starting with a ¼-inch-deep ⁹/₁₆-inch-diameter counterbore. When the counterbore has been drilled, drill the ⁵/₁₆-inch-diameter clearance hole all the way through the stock.

4. When the shoulder screw hole has been drilled in the pivot support, glue the pivot support to the fence, as shown in *Fence and Pivot Assembly*.

5. Screw the threaded insert in place, as shown in *Installing the Threaded Insert*, using a ⁵/₁₆-inch hex-head bolt, matching nut, and socket wrench. Screw the bolt partway into the threaded insert and then lock the nut against the insert. Be careful to keep the insert straight as you turn it into the hole with the socket wrench. Turn the insert into the hole until the top of the insert is flush with the top surface of the pivot block.

6. When the insert is in place, bolt the pivot support and fence to the pivot block.

MAKE THE SLIDE BAR

1. The slide bar that guides the sled over the table saw via the miter groove is probably the most critical part of this jig. You need to produce a slide bar that slides in the miter gauge slot easily but without play.

First, rip a ⅜-inch-thick strip from a piece of 4/4 (four-quarter) hardwood. Guide the cut with a push stick if you still enjoy counting to ten on your fingers.

> **NOTE:** *If you plan on making the long sled on page 273 or other jigs that require a slide bar, make up a bunch of extra slide bar stock to save time later.*

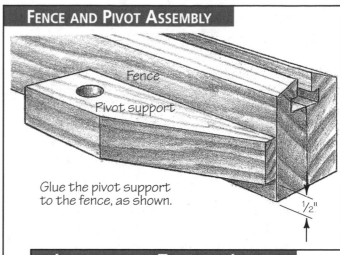

FENCE AND PIVOT ASSEMBLY

Fence

Pivot support

Glue the pivot support to the fence, as shown.

½"

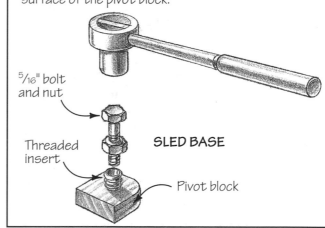

INSTALLING THE THREADED INSERT

To install the threaded insert, screw a bolt into the threaded insert and then lock the nut tightly against the top of the insert. Turning the bolt with a socket wrench will thread the insert into the wood. Be careful to keep the insert perpendicular to the surface of the pivot block.

⁵/₁₆" bolt and nut

Threaded insert

SLED BASE

Pivot block

2. Next, carefully measure the width of your table saw's miter gauge slot and then rip the ⅜-inch-thick slide bar stock slightly wider than that measurement. Most slots are around ¾ inch wide, so the ripped stock should be around ²⁵/₃₂ inch wide.

3. Now you have a choice. If you're good with a hand plane, set the longest plane you own to take off an onion-skin shaving, support the bar on a dead-flat surface, and plane the entire edge of the slide bar stock until the bar fits perfectly into your saw's miter gauge slot.

Your other choice is to glue a strip of 100-grit sandpaper to the edge of a straight ¾-inch-thick stick. With the bar stock on a flat surface, sand down the entire edge of the slide bar stock in broad strokes until the bar fits perfectly in the slot.

DADO THE SLED AND ATTACH THE SLIDE BAR

1. Since table saws come in several sizes and variations, you need to customize the position of the slide bar on the base of your sled. With your table saw unplugged, measure the distance from your table saw's blade to the miter slot to the left of the blade. Pencil this distance on the bottom of the sled.

2. Put a dado cutter in the table saw and space it to match the width of the slide bar. Plug in the saw, make a test cut in a piece of scrap plywood, and test the slide bar's fit in it. If necessary, add paper shims to the dado set to get a perfect fit (see "Using Dado Cutters" on page 129).

3. Position the table saw fence to the right of the dado cutter at the distance you marked on the bottom of the sled in Step 1 and cut the dado in the bottom of the sled, as shown in the *Top View* on page 267.

4. Glue the slide bar into its dado and wipe away any excess glue with a damp rag.

5. When the glue is dry, turn the sled over and give the slide bar and bottom a rubdown with paste wax. The wax will help it move more easily over the table saw. Be sure to buff away *all* the excess wax.

FINDING THE RIGHT ANGLE

1. An angle sled isn't much good if you can't quickly and easily adjust the angle of the fence, so you need to scribe some accurate angle settings on the sled. First, set the fence so it is exactly perpendicular to the blade side edge of the sled. To test the setting you need a truly straight piece of hardwood (check it with your most accurate straightedge) at least 4 inches wide and about 2 feet long. The long edges must be dead parallel.

Put the test piece against the sled's fence and crosscut about 6 inches from its end. Turn the cutoff over and butt the just-cut ends together, as shown in the photo on this page. If the fence is exactly perpendicular to the slide bar, the adjoining edges of the meeting pieces will still be straight across the cut. If not, readjust the cap screw in the

To check that the fence on a crosscut sled is holding the stock square, crosscut a parallel-edged board. Then, turn the cutoff over and butt it against its partner. If the resulting edge is straight, the fence is cutting square.

stop block slightly and try again until the fence is right. When it is, scribe a line on the sled base along the last 6 inches of the back edge of the fence (the clamp end) and label it "0°."

2. When the fence is at what I'll call true zero, or 0 degrees, place a square or drafting triangle against it to establish 90 degrees. Then place a straightedge against the square or triangle and clamp it in place. The straightedge should end up in the position shown in *Angles 0° to 45°*.

3. Next, put the edge of an adjustable triangle (I got mine at a local art supply store) against the straightedge, as shown in the drawing, and use it to adjust the fence in 5-degree increments from 0 to 45 degrees. Lock the fence in place and scribe a line like the 0-degree line at each increment along the back of the fence. To lay out the 50-, 55-, and 60-degree settings, rotate the adjustable triangle 180 degrees, as shown in *Angles 50° to 60°*.

4. To make the scribe lines clearer, trace over each one with a felt-tipped pen and then lightly sand over each scribe line. The sanding will remove the ink on the surface, leaving behind the ink within the scribe lines. Label each scribe line appropriately from 5 to 60 degrees. Assemble the clamp parts, as shown in the *Exploded View* on page 267, and you're done.

ANGLES 0° TO 45°

With the adjustable triangle in the position shown, adjust the fence in 5° increments from 0° to 45°, and scribe lines to indicate each increment.

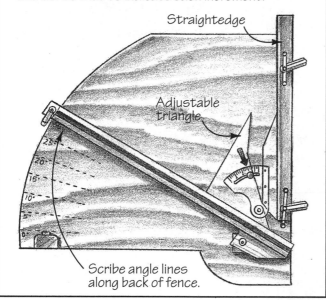

Straightedge

Adjustable triangle

Scribe angle lines along back of fence.

ANGLES 50° TO 60°

Rotate the adjustable triangle 180°, as shown, and scribe the angles from 50° to 60°.

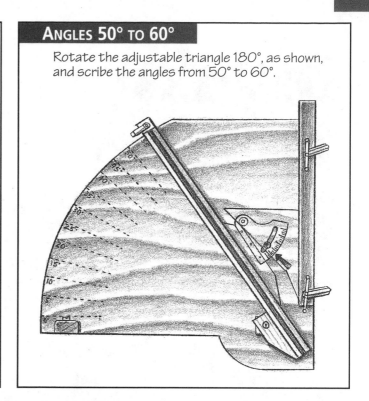

LONG SLED

LONG SLED EXPLODED VIEW

Drive this screw first, pivot the fence as necessary to square it, and then drive the other screws.

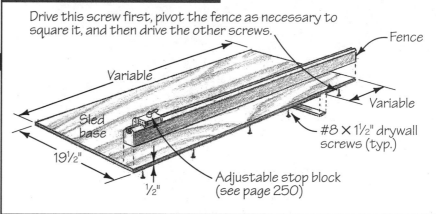

Variable

Fence

Variable

Sled base

19½"

½"

#8 × 1½" drywall screws (typ.)

Adjustable stop block (see page 250)

If you need to make clean, square cutoffs on long boards, make this simple crosscut sled. It has three main parts: a plywood base, a fence, and a slide bar. The sled is designed for use with the table saw crosscut support on page 298 and can safely support cutoffs up to 6 feet long. I used nine-ply ½-inch-thick plywood for the sled base for extra stability.

1. Cut the parts to size. As shown in the *Long Sled Exploded View,* the sled base is 19½ inches deep, but you need to customize the width so the sled will overhang the crosscut support slightly.

Cut the fence to equal the width of the sled and cut the slide bar to equal the sled's depth.

2. Fit a slide bar to the bottom of the sled base, as fully described in "Make the Slide Bar" on page 271 and "Dado the Sled and Attach the Slide Bar" on the opposite page.

3. Position the fence as shown in the *Long Sled Exploded View* and drive the screw closest to the blade edge of the jig.

4. Square the fence to the edge of the sled with a cabinet square and clamp it in place. Crosscut a hardwood board to test whether the fence is square, as described in Step 1 under "Finding the Right Angle" on the opposite page. When you are sure the fence is square, drive the other screws.

5. To help your sled move across the table saw more easily, turn it over and give the slide bar and bottom a good rubdown with paste wax. Buff off all the excess wax, and you're ready to go.

SHOP-MADE BAR CLAMPS

These inexpensive clamps are easy to use, and they help keep the stock flat during glue-ups.

Gluing stock on edge to create wide panels raises two concerns—creating tight joints, and keeping the assembled stock flat. These bar clamps get both jobs done without the need to add separate cauls. They're easy to make from scrap hardwood, and the cost is far less than that of any metal bar clamp I know of.

Each clamp is composed of two wooden "bars" held together with two machine bolts and wing nuts. You clamp your stock between the bars and then drive a wedge between one of the bolts and the edge of the stock to squeeze the boards together. The bolted bars function like cauls, keeping the assembly flat. Making the clamps is as simple as cutting the bars and

wedges and drilling the holes.

I make my clamps 42 inches long, to accommodate 36-inch-wide tabletops. But don't be afraid to make them longer. On the other hand, it would be silly and wasteful to make a bunch of 6-foot-long clamps if most of your projects require only 3-footers.

Finally, the thickness of stock you can clamp is determined by the length of the bolts and by how far you countersink them. The 5-inch bolts listed in the Materials List will let you clamp stock up to 1¾ inches thick. The wedges should be as thick as possible but no thicker than the stock being glued. Consider making wedges with a scrap from the stock you're gluing up.

EXPLODED VIEW

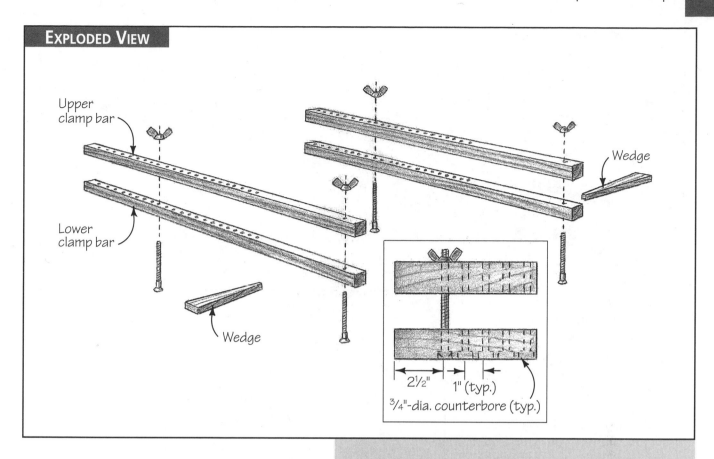

Upper clamp bar

Lower clamp bar

Wedge

Wedge

2½"   1" (typ.)

¾"-dia. counterbore (typ.)

MAKE THE CLAMP BARS

1. Cut the clamp bars to the sizes given in the Materials List, changing the length of the bars if you like.

2. Cut a template—from cardboard, Masonite, or plywood—that matches the length and width of the bars. Lay out the centerpoints of the bolt holes on the template, as shown in *Laying Out the Holes* on page 276, and drill a ³⁄₃₂-inch hole at each mark in the template.

3. Transfer the centerpoint marks for the bolt holes to each clamp bar with an awl.

4. Using a ¾-inch-diameter brad-point or Forstner bit, drill ³⁄₈-inch-deep counterbore holes for the bolt heads in half of your clamp bar pieces. These will become the lower clamp bars. Clamp a fence to the drill press table to center the stock under the bit, as shown in *Drilling the Holes* on page 276.

5. Drill ³⁄₈-inch-diameter bolt holes through all the bars. Guide the drill bit through the center-point of each counterbore hole in the lower clamp bars and through each centerpoint mark in the upper clamp bars.

MATERIALS LIST

WOOD: Make two bars for each clamp. Use any available hardwood.

PART	QUANTITY	DESCRIPTION
Clamp bars	2 per	1½" × 1½" × 42"
Wedge	1 per	⅝" × 1¼" × 8"

HARDWARE

Hex-head bolts	2 per	⁵⁄₁₆-18 × 5"
Wing nuts	2 per	⁵⁄₁₆-18

FINISH AND ASSEMBLE THE CLAMPS

1. Assemble the clamps by inserting the bolts into the lower, counterbored clamp bars and up through the upper clamp bars. Then spin a wing nut onto each bolt.

LAYING OUT THE HOLES

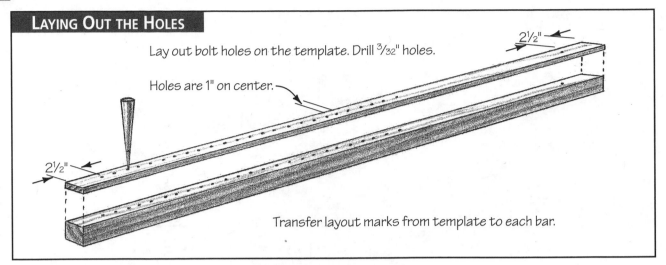

Lay out bolt holes on the template. Drill ³⁄₃₂" holes.

Holes are 1" on center.

2½"

2½"

Transfer layout marks from template to each bar.

2. Cut the stock for the wedges. Start with a rectangular blank, draw a diagonal line, and cut it on the band saw to produce two wedges, as shown in *Cutting the Wedges*.

3. To prevent the clamping bars from marring your glued-up stock, smooth the surfaces and soften the edges of each clamp bar and wedge with 180-grit sandpaper.

4. Wax the clamp bars with a heavy coating of paste wax to prevent squeezed-out glue from sticking to them.

DRILLING THE HOLES

Using a brad-point bit, drill ¾"-dia. counterbore holes at least ¼" deep in the bottom bars. Then drill the ³⁄₈" holes through all the bars.

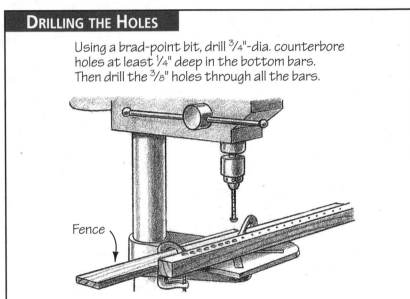

Fence

CUTTING THE WEDGES

Band-saw diagonally through a rectangular piece of scrap to produce a pair of wedges.

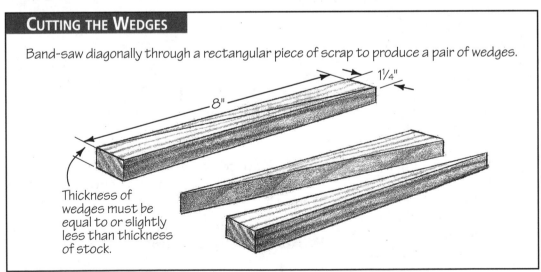

1¼"

8"

Thickness of wedges must be equal to or slightly less than thickness of stock.

Box Joint Jig

Mount this jig on your table saw's miter gauge to cut perfectly spaced box joints.

This no-nonsense jig for cutting box joints on the table saw has only three parts: a fixed fence, an adjustable fence, and a key. You simply screw it to your saw's miter gauge and go to work. The jig is set up to cut ¼-inch-thick fingers in ½-inch-thick stock using a ¼-inch-wide dado blade. If you plan on cutting thicker fingers, just cut wider slots in the fence and adjust the width of your dado blade. The distance between the slots must equal the thickness of each slot; i.e., ¼-inch-thick slots must have a ¼-inch distance between them while ½-inch-thick slots must have a ½-inch distance between them.

If you cut lots of box joints of var-ious sizes, it might be worth your time to make several adjustable fences with different finger spacings for your jig. Then you can bolt the appropriate fence in place and you're ready to go. For detailed information on using this jig, see "Making Box Joints" on page 174.

Cut and Shape the Fences

1. Cut the fixed fence and adjustable fence to the sizes given in the Materials List.

2. The fixed fence has two slotted bolt holes, which allow you to slide the adjustable fence back and forth. There are two ways to cut the slots.

It is easiest to rout the slots for the bolts with a plunge router and ¼-inch straight bit. Clamp the fixed fence to your workbench so the area to be slotted overhangs the edge of the bench. Lay out the beginning and end of the slot on the stock, adjust the router's edge guide to center the cut on the width of the stock, and let 'er rip. When the first slot has been cut, turn the stock around on the bench and lay out and rout the slot for the other bolt.

For the low-tech method, first, drill two ¼-inch-diameter holes in the stock, as shown in the *Fixed Fence—Front View*. Then cut out the stock between the holes with a saber saw or coping saw. Because saber saw blades are relatively wide, you will probably need to use the blade to chew away some of the stock after your initial cuts to produce slot edges that are tangent to the two holes.

3. As shown in the *Adjustable Fence—Front View*, the adjustable fence has two counterbored ¼-inch-diameter holes for the adjustment bolts. It's best to drill the hole and counterbore with a drill press, but careful drilling with a portable drill will work too. Drill the ¼-inch-deep counterbore first with a ⅝-inch spade bit. Then drill the ¼-inch-diameter hole.

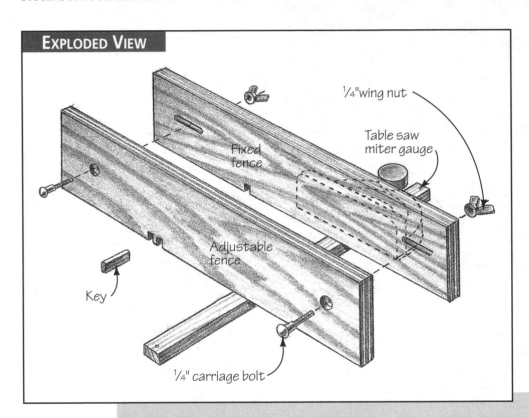

EXPLODED VIEW

¼"wing nut

Table saw miter gauge

Fixed fence

Adjustable fence

Key

¼" carriage bolt

MATERIALS LIST

WOOD: Use ¾-inch birch plywood for the fences and cherry or maple for the key.

PART	QUANTITY	DESCRIPTION
Adjustable fence	1	¾" × 4" × 18"
Fixed fence	1	¾" × 4" × 18"
Key	1	¼" × ½" × 1½"
HARDWARE		
Carriage bolts	2	¼-20 × 1¾"
Wing nuts	2	¼-20

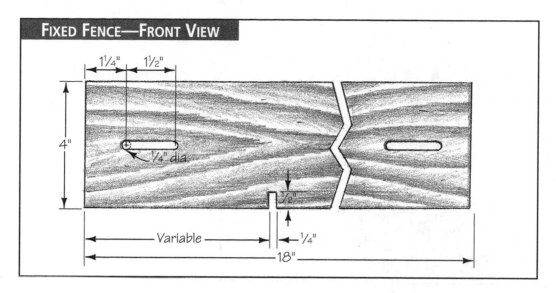

FIXED FENCE—FRONT VIEW

ASSEMBLE THE JIG

1. Assemble the fixed fence and adjustable fence, as shown in the *Exploded View*. Push the bolts through their holes and thread on the wing nuts.

2. Put your table saw's miter gauge in its slot to the left of the blade and hold the fence assembly against it, as shown in the *Exploded View*. Position the fence assembly so that it extends roughly 5 inches to the right of the blade. Then, holding the fence assembly firmly in place, drive two ¾-inch drywall screws through the holes in the miter gauge and into the back of the fixed fence.

CUT THE INDEXING SLOTS AND KEY

1. Put a ¼-inch-wide dado cutter on your table saw and raise it ½ inch above the surface of the table. Loosen the wing nuts on the jig and slide the adjustable fence ½ inch to the right (as viewed from the front). Tighten the wing nuts, turn the saw on, and push the jig into the blade to cut the key slot.

2. When the first slot has been cut, loosen the wing nuts and slide the adjustable fence back into its original position, ½ inch to the left. Tighten the wing nuts, turn the saw on, and push the jig into the blade to cut the second slot.

3. Next, cut the key to size; make it just wide enough to fit snugly into the slot and stay there without glue. In use, the key is often damaged or becomes worn, so it needs to be easily replaceable. Chamfer the top corners of the key with sandpaper to produce the shape shown in the *Exploded View*.

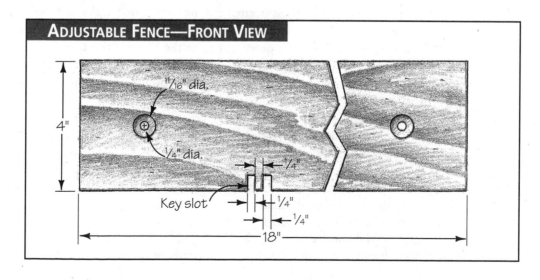

ADJUSTABLE FENCE—FRONT VIEW

RESAW FENCE FOR THE BAND SAW

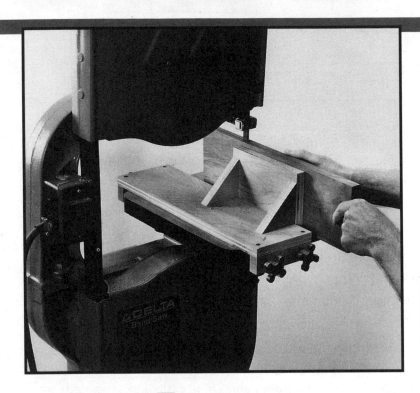

A resaw fence guides thick lumber as you saw it into thinner lumber. This one is easy to adjust to compensate for blade "lead."

This resaw fence has two distinctive features. First, the fence itself ends at the back of the blade so the stock won't bind against the blade if it cups after the cut. Second, it attaches with built-in clamps that hold it in place but still allow you to angle the fence to compensate for any tendency of the blade to "lead" the cut in one direction or the other. For more information on resawing with a band saw, see *Step-by-Step Resawing on the Band Saw* on page 79.

Before you plunge in, note that the correct length of the base and fence depend on the length of your band saw table and that the width of the lock blocks should match the thickness of your table.

CUT AND DRILL THE PARTS

1. Measure the length and thickness of your band saw table and the distance from the front edge of the table to the back of the blade. Cut the parts to the sizes given in the Materials List and the *Dimensioned Views/Front View* and *Side View*.

2. Drill ⅜-inch holes in the lock blocks, as shown in the drawings, and then drive ⁵⁄₁₆-inch T-nuts into the holes until the spurs bite securely into the wood.

3. Apply glue to the top edges of the lock blocks and clamp them to the ends of the base with the T-nuts toward the inside of the jig. Drill pilot holes and then screw the base to the blocks with 1¼-inch drywall screws.

4. Clamp the fence to the base and check that it's square to the base when clamped. Then drill pilot holes for three screws to hold the fence to the base. Note in the *Dimensioned Views/Side View* that the fence starts 1¾ inches from the front of the base. Apply glue to the edge of the base and then screw the fence to the base. Check again that the fence is square to the base. Screw and glue the angle blocks to the base and fence, flush with the ends of the fence.

5. Screw the studded knobs all the way through the T-nuts in the lock blocks and screw on the stud bumpers.

To use the fence, clamp it to the saw table parallel to the line of cut as explained in *Step-by-Step Compensating for Blade Lead* on page 80. Tighten all three clamps uniformly. To remove the jig when you're done, loosen only the rear clamp. That way you can reinstall the jig at the same "lead" angle by holding the front clamps against the table and tightening only the rear clamp.

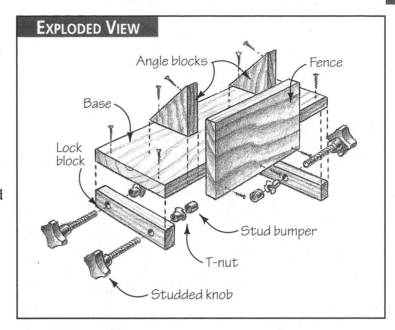

EXPLODED VIEW

Angle blocks
Fence
Base
Lock block
Stud bumper
T-nut
Studded knob

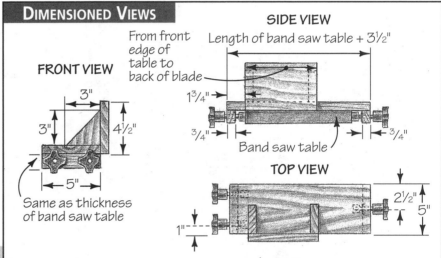

DIMENSIONED VIEWS

FRONT VIEW

3"
3"
4½"
5"

Same as thickness of band saw table

From front edge of table to back of blade

SIDE VIEW

Length of band saw table + 3½"
1¾"
¾"
¾"
Band saw table

TOP VIEW

1"
2½"
5"

Materials List

Wood: Use solid maple or cherry for the lock blocks and ¾-inch plywood for everything else.

Part	Quantity	Description
Base	1	¾" × 5" × variable
Fence	1	¾" × 4½" × variable
Angle blocks	2	¾" × 3" × 3"
Lock blocks	2	¾" × variable × 5"

Hardware		
T-nuts	3	⁵⁄₁₆-18
Studded knobs	3	⁵⁄₁₆-18 × 1¾". Part #KA-3. Reid Tool Supply Co., 2265 Black Creek Road, Muskegon, MI 49444. (800) 253-0421.
Stud bumpers	3	Part #FRB-202. Reid Tool Supply Co.

FRAME RESAW

An old-fashioned frame saw with a modern blade is the ideal solution to one of the home-shop woodworker's biggest problems: resawing thick stock to make thin project parts. Three-inch-deep kerfs from a table saw lighten the handwork and guide the frame saw.

Resawing a board by hand is so much easier than I anticipated that my biggest regret is not trying it sooner. By sawing 3 inches into both edges of the board on the table saw as shown in *Step-by-Step Resawing by Hand* on page 81, the amount of actual wood sawn by hand is greatly reduced. The table-saw kerfs also guide the frame-saw blade. By using a length of 1¼-inch-wide, 3 tooth-per-inch band-saw blade designed specifically for resawing, the effort required is not great. If you've priced thinner-than-standard lumber lately, you'll appreciate the economy too. Using mail-order prices from a recent catalog, I figure sawing 4/4 (four-quarter) lumber in half

pays me about 50 dollars an hour.

The saw is quite easy to make. The four wooden pieces are joined with mortises and tenons that are held together by tension on the blade. The blade is held in the frame with a piece of threaded rod and a wing nut on one end and a bolt on the other. I used pine for the handle and end because I had a piece handy; I used beech for the rails, but just about any stiff wood will do. I turned the handles on a lathe, but I'd be just as happy shaping them with a drawknife and wood rasp.

I might add that the saw looks pretty impressive when it's hanging on the shop wall.

MAKE THE FRAME

1. Cut the four pieces of the frame to the dimensions given in the Materials List.

2. Lay out the mortises. Measure along the length of both the handle and the end and draw a line across one face of each piece at the midpoint. Clamp the handle and end together with their centers aligned and lay out the mortises, as shown in *Joint Details*.

3. Drill and chisel the mortises, as explained in "Cutting Mortises by Hand" on page 157.

4. Drill the ½-inch bolt holes at the same time you're drilling out the mortises—they require the same size bit as the mortises.

5. Cut the tenons. Since the joints are held together by the tension on the blade, the fit of the tenons is not particularly critical. Saw them out with a tenoning jig if you're fastidious, or cut quick-and-dirty

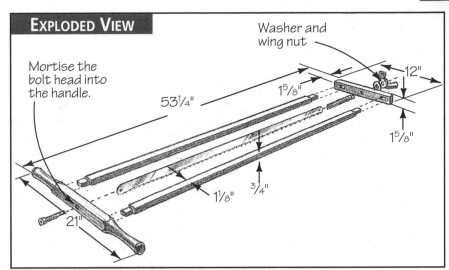

EXPLODED VIEW

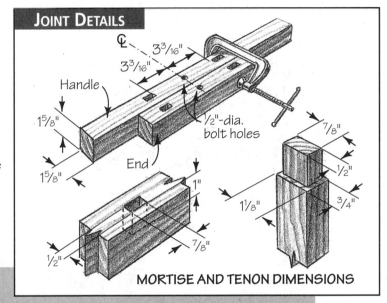

JOINT DETAILS

MORTISE AND TENON DIMENSIONS

MATERIALS LIST

WOOD: Use a hardwood for the rails and any wood you like for the handle and end.

PART	QUANTITY	DESCRIPTION
Rails	2	¾" × 1⅛" × 52"
Handle	1	1⅝" × 1⅝" × 21"
End	1	1⅝" × 1⅝" × 12"
HARDWARE		
Band-saw blade	1	3 tpi, 1¼" × 48". Olson Saw, 16 Stony Hill Road, Bethel CT 06801. (203) 792-8622.
Threaded rod	1	½" × 6"
Wing nut	1	½"
Washer	1	½"
Hex-head bolt	1	½" × 2½"
Machine screws	2	#10 × ¾"
Nuts	2	#10

HANDLE DETAIL

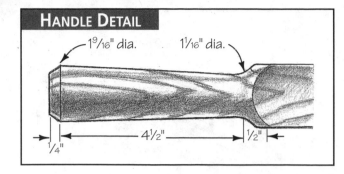

tenons as explained on page 165. It is important that you get the shoulders straight and square, so make sure your miter gauge fence is square to the bar when you saw the shoulders.

6. Round-over the edges of the rails with a ¼-inch roundover bit in a table-mounted router.

7. Turn (or carve) the handles to the shape shown in the *Handle Detail* or to whatever shape feels comfortable in your hands. The drawings show the handle shape I made. Shape the end piece, too, if you like.

BLADE-MOUNTING DETAIL

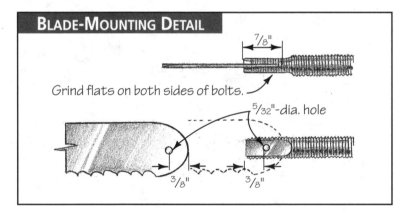

Grind flats on both sides of bolts.

⁵⁄₃₂"-dia. hole

FIT THE HARDWARE AND BLADE

1. If necessary, cut the length of the blade to 48 inches with a hacksaw. Drill a ⁵⁄₃₂-inch-diameter hole in both ends, as shown in the *Blade-Mounting Detail*. Round the corners of the blade as shown in the drawing to make them a little more friendly to be around. Either a file or a grinder will do the job.

2. Saw a kerf down the middle of both the bolt and the threaded rod, as shown in *Blade-Mounting Detail*. Then check that the frame-saw blade fits in the kerf. If necessary, you can spread the kerf a little bit by driving a cold chisel into the end.

3. File or grind the flats shown in the drawing onto the hex-head bolt and the threaded rod. Then drill ⁵⁄₃₂-inch holes through both pieces. Push the hex-head bolt through the hole in the handle and align the hacksaw kerf so the handle will be perpendicular to the blade. Trace around the bolt head; then remove the bolt from the hole and cut a mortise for the bolt head.

4. Assemble the threaded rod, washer, and wing nut through the hole in the frame end. Fit the rails into the mortises and then the handle onto the rails. Slide the blade into the hacksaw kerfs, align the holes, and insert the #10 × ¾-inch machine screws. Tighten the wing nut until the blade hums slightly when you pluck it.

ROUTER CIRCLE TRAMMEL

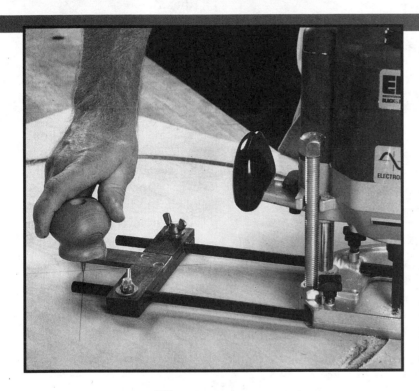

With a circle trammel, your router becomes a compass that cuts. It's an important enough jig to be worth making well.

Everybody who has used a router more than once or twice has cobbled together some means to rout a circle, usually with a lot of fuss and bother. Often these makeshift jigs are difficult to adjust or have parts that obscure your view when you try to plant the pivot point at the center of your circle. Routing circles and circular arcs is a frequent enough operation to warrant making a good, workable, and versatile jig that won't let you down. This one happens to be handsome as well.

The jig is solid enough to cut accurate, precise circles, and it lets you see exactly where you're placing the point. And you can either plant its sharp pivot point directly in the stock or reverse the point to expose a pivot pin that will fit a

block that is temporarily stuck to the stock. In both cases, a comfortable knob holds the pivot in position. The jig attaches to the edge-guide rods that come with most routers, or you can buy much longer rods from a hardware store to cut circles of practically unlimited diameter. By reversing the jig on the rods, you can cut circles with a diameter that is barely larger than the router base.

Not all routers are created equal, so the first step in building this jig is to customize the dimensions to fit your router. The spacing of the rod holes in the circle cutting jig must be exactly the same as the spacing of the rod holes in your router. The position of the holes above the work surface is also important.

If they're higher than the holes in your router, you won't be able to hold the router flat on the stock.

The pivot pin looks like a real piece of work, but it is actually simple to make with just a drill press and file. Both ends are filed to shape while the pin turns slowly in the drill press. Just be sure to file the cylindrical end first, so you won't be left trying to chuck the pointed end in the drill press.

CUSTOMIZE THE DIMENSIONS

1. Measure the spacing of the holes in your router—dimension "A" in *Dimensioned Views/Front View*—and then add 1⅞ inches to the spacing to get the overall length of the jig body, as shown. Measure the diameter of the rods, which is thediameter of the holes you'll drill.

EXPLODED VIEW

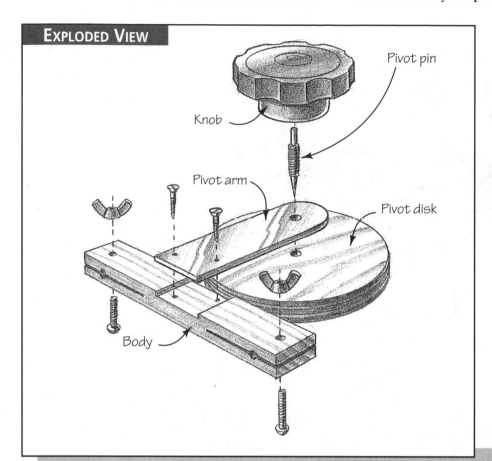

Pivot pin

Knob

Pivot arm

Pivot disk

Body

MATERIALS LIST

WOOD: The jig body should be a tough hardwood, such as oak.

PART	QUANTITY	DESCRIPTION
Body	1	¾" × 1" × 9" (approx.)
Pivot disk	1	¾" × 4" dia.
Knob stock (optional shop-made)	1	3" dia. × 2"

HARDWARE		
Pivot pin	1	⁵⁄₁₆-18 × 2⅛" threaded rod
Steel or brass pivot arm		³⁄₁₆" × 1⅛" × 4" heavy-duty mending plate, available from any well-stocked hardware store
Knob		Fluted plastic knob with ⁵⁄₁₆-18 threaded insert and through hole. Part #DK-120. Reid Tool Supply Co., 2265 Black Creek Road, Muskegon, MI 49444. (800) 253-0421.
Carriage bolt	2	⁵⁄₁₆" × 1¼"
Wing nuts	2	⁵⁄₁₆"
Roundhead wood screws	2	#6 × ⅝"

2. Measure the height to the center of the rod holes above the work surface. You may find it easiest to do if you install the rods and measure the clearance between the rods and the work surface, and then adding half the diameter of the rods. You will most likely find that this height is greater than ½ inch. If it is, everything is fine. If the height is less than ½ inch, you'll have to alter the position of the holes in the body to match this height. You can do this by lowering the position of the rod holes you drill from the recommended ½-inch height shown in the *Dimensioned Views/Front View.* Or you can file down the crowns of the carriage bolts or countersink the carriage bolts.

MAKE THE PIVOT ARM

1. Cut the pivot arm to the dimensions shown in the *Dimensioned Views/Top View* and *End View* with a hacksaw. Round the pivot end-corners with files or a grinder.

2. Lay out and drill the 9/64-inch-diameter screw shank holes in the body end of the arm and a 9/32-inch-diameter hole for the pivot pin (actually, a size F drill bit, which is slightly smaller, is better, but the 9/32-inch drill bit will work fine). Tap the pivot pin hole for the 5/16-18 threads of the pivot pin. If you don't have a 5/16-18 tap and can't get one locally, order one from Reid Tool Supply Co. when you order the knob (it's part #HSP-21196).

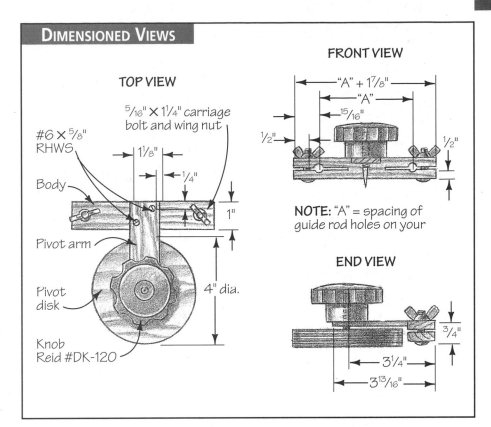

DIMENSIONED VIEWS

TOP VIEW

5/16" × 1¼" carriage bolt and wing nut

#6 × 5/8" RHWS

Body

Pivot arm

Pivot disk

Knob Reid #DK-120

1⅛"

¼"

1"

4" dia.

FRONT VIEW

"A" + 1⅞"

"A"

15/16"

½"

½"

NOTE: "A" = spacing of guide rod holes on your

END VIEW

¾"

3¼"

3¹³/16"

TECH TIP   **CUTTING THREADS: If you've never threaded a hole before, don't panic; mere mortals do it all the time. The secrets to success are four:**

1. Start with the right size hole, which you've already done.

2. Keep the tap perpendicular to the stock.

3. Lubricate the tap and hole with light machine oil.

4. Go slowly.

Begin by clamping the pivot arm securely in a vise or over the edge of your bench. Make sure it's level so it will be easier to keep the tap perpendicular. You can turn a tap with an open-end wrench but that makes it very difficult to avoid tilting the tap one way or another. To do the job right use a T-handle tap wrench. Oil the tap and the hole, place the tap in the top of the hole, check that it's perpendicular to the pivot arm, and begin turning slowly with slight downward pressure. After two or three full turns the slight downward pressure is no longer necessary; the tap will feed itself. Continue turning until the slightly tapered leading portion of the tap has passed all the way through the pivot arm, then back the tap out of the hole. If the tap sticks while backing it out, don't just apply more turning pressure. Instead, turn it in a half-turn or so to free the tap from metal debris and then continue backing it out. That's all there is to it. You're on your way to becoming a machinist.

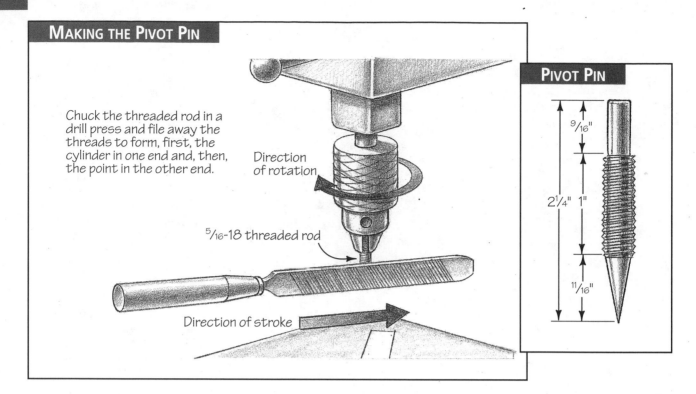

MAKING THE PIVOT PIN

Chuck the threaded rod in a drill press and file away the threads to form, first, the cylinder in one end and, then, the point in the other end.

Direction of rotation

⁵⁄₁₆-18 threaded rod

Direction of stroke

PIVOT PIN

⁹⁄₁₆"

2¼" 1"

¹¹⁄₁₆"

MACHINE THE PIVOT PIN

1. Using a hacksaw, cut the threaded rod to the length shown in *Pivot Pin* and then mark off the lengths of the cylinder and the point by filing a notch with a small triangular file.

2. Set your drill press to the slowest speed; then chuck the threaded rod in the drill press. Insert the rod only up to the end of what will be the pointed portion to avoid distorting the threads in the middle portion.

3. Turn on the drill press and, using light pressure, file down the threads on the cylindrical portion of the rod. Work against the rotation of the spinning rod, stroking the file as though the rod were not moving. Stroke the file from left to right with the file in front of the rod, as shown in *Making the Pivot Pin*. Proceed slowly as you get to the root of the threads, testing the diameter in a ¼-inch-diameter test hole drilled in a scrap of plywood. File until the cylinder fits the test hole easily, but without any play.

4. When the cylinder has been filed, reverse the rod in the chuck and file the point, using the same technique.

MAKE THE JIG BODY AND PIVOT DISK

1. Cut the jig body to thickness, width, and length. Lay out and drill the carriage bolt and rod holes, as shown in the *Dimensioned Views/Front View* on page 287. Then chisel snug-fitting recesses for the square portion of the carriage bolt shanks, so they won't split the hardwood when you clamp the wing nuts down tight.

2. Center the pivot arm on the top surface of the jig body and trace the arm's edges on the jig body. Adjust a marking gauge to the thickness of the pivot arm and use it to lay out the depth of the mortise for the arm. You can cut the mortises with multiple passes on the table saw, backing up the workpiece with your miter gauge, or with mallet and chisel.

3. Clamp the jig body in a tenoning jig to saw the slots that allow the jig body to clamp down on the rods. Use a thin-kerf blade, if you have one. The longer you make the kerfs, the less pressure you will need on the wing nuts to clamp the rods tightly, but try to leave at least 1¼ inches between the two slots in the middle of the jig body.

4. Drill pilot holes for the screws that hold the pivot arm to the jig body, then screw the arm in place. Insert the carriage bolts almost all the way into their holes, squirt a wee dab of silicone caulk under the carriage bolt heads, then screw the wing nuts down tight to seat the carriage bolts. The silicone will hold the bolts in place but still allow you to tap them out if you should need to. Thread the pivot point into the pivot arm and lock it in place by screwing the knob down over it.

5. The last step is to make the pivot disk. Ironically, it's too small in diameter to cut out with the trammel. Lay it out with a compass, bore the center hole to match the cylindrical end of the pivot point, and then cut out the perimeter with a coping saw or band saw.

Makin' It Fancy

Some of us see tools as purely utilitarian while others see them as at least a craft and perhaps an art form all their own. If you (like me) take particular pleasure in exceptionally well-made tools, this trammel offers an opportunity. To raise the trammel a notch above the purely utilitarian, turn the knob out of a dense hardwood with attractive curly, or perhaps bird's-eye, grain, then fit it with a threaded brass insert. If the knob is tall enough, house the unused end of the pivot pin in a deep blind hole instead of a through hole. To spice up the look of the jig body, you can use an attractive but fairly straight-grain piece of hardwood and chamfer all the edges. Make the pivot arm out of ¼-inch-thick brass that is the same width as the base of your knob. Jamestown Distributors (28 Narragansett Avenue, P.O. Box 348, Jamestown, RI 02835; 800-423-0030) can supply bronze carriage bolts and brass wing nuts.

SHOP-MADE KNOB

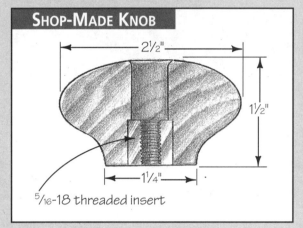

2½"

1½"

1¼"

5⁄16-18 threaded insert

ELLIPSE (A.K.A. OVAL) TRAMMEL

An ellipse trammel makes quick and easy work of routing out elliptical tabletops.

Of all the possible oval (or egg) shapes, the only one you can cut out with a mechanical guide, or trammel, is the true ellipse. That's fine with me, because I consider it the most handsome, by a wide margin. You don't need an ellipse trammel to produce an ellipse, of course. "Ellipses, a.k.a. Ovals" on page 20 gives a couple of alternatives. But the trammel makes it so easy that the work of making it is paid back after only a couple of uses. If you find that hard to believe, go back and reread the instructions for using the trammel in "Routing Ellipses" on page 219 and compare them with the alternative ways of cutting and smoothing curved shapes in the same chapter.

The jig as drawn here will make ellipses as narrow as 38 inches wide and as long as 9 feet. If you want smaller or larger ellipses, you'll find suggestions in "Routing Ellipses."

MAKE THE BASE

1. Cut the plywood base and the dovetail track to the dimensions given in the Materials List. Glue and screw the long and short tracks to the base, as shown in Step 1 on page 292. The short tracks will center the long track for you, but make sure the short tracks are also centered on the base. Pay attention to the screw placement, shown in the drawing, so you don't ruin a router bit by routing into a screw when you get to the next step.

2. Rout the dovetail slots in the center of the tracks. I prefer to rough out most of the waste with a ½-inch spiral upcut bit first and then trim the sides with a dovetail bit. This produces a smoother final cut. When making all three of these cuts—the rough cut and the two trim cuts—rout the short tracks and across the long track before routing the length of the long track—if you look at Step 2 on page 292, you'll see that this sequence is simply following the usual practice of routing end grain before long grain, to minimize splintering.

Don't try to trim both sides of the tracks with

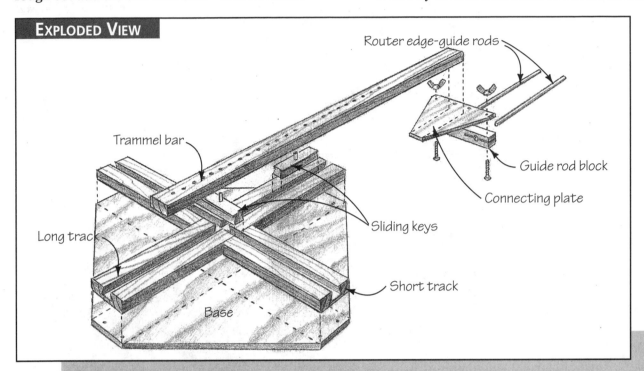

EXPLODED VIEW

Router edge-guide rods

Trammel bar

Guide rod block

Connecting plate

Long track

Sliding keys

Short track

Base

MATERIALS LIST

WOOD: Use a stable, close-grained wood such as cherry for the tracks and sliding keys. Use any reasonably strong wood for the trammel bar and plywood for the base and connecting plate.

PART	QUANTITY	DESCRIPTION
Base	1	½" × 23" × 23" plywood
Long track	1	¾" × 3" × 23"
Short track	2	¾" × 3" × 10"
Sliding key stock	1	¾" × 2" × 12"
Trammel bar	1	¾" × 1⅝" × 37"
Guide rod block	1	¾" × 1" × 6". Use leftover wood after making sliding keys.
Connecting plate	1	¼" × 4" × 6" plywood

HARDWARE		
Pivot pins	2	¼" × 1½" steel or brass rod
Drywall screws	as needed	#8 × 1"
Roundhead wood screws	4	#8 × ¾"
Stove bolts	2	¼" × 1½"
Washers	2	¼"
Wing nuts	2	¼"

STEP-BY-STEP
MAKING THE BASE

1 Glue and screw the tracks to the base.

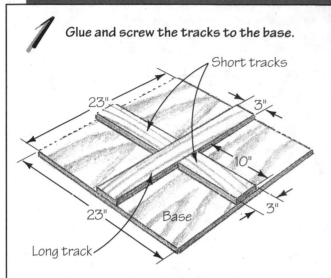

Short tracks

23"

3"

10"

23"

Base

3"

Long track

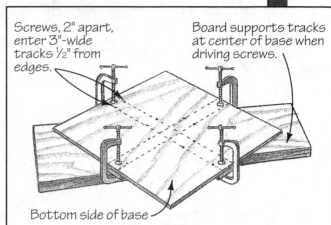

Screws, 2" apart, enter 3"-wide tracks ½" from edges.

Board supports tracks at center of base when driving screws.

Bottom side of base

2 Rout dovetail grooves in the tracks.

Rout ½" × ½" grooves centered in the tracks.

½"

½"

Widen the bottom of the grooves on one side with a 14° dovetail bit.

Keep downward pressure centered over tracks.

Then readjust the fence to widen the second side of the grooves.

½"

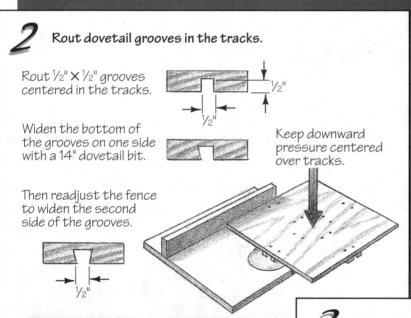

3 Saw off the corners of the base.

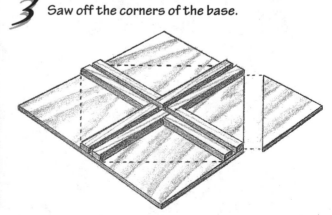

the same fence setting by turning the stock around and referencing the opposite edges of the base. Unless your base is absolutely, perfectly square you'll wind up with tracks of slightly different width or with a slight taper. Then your sliding keys won't fit right. Instead, trim one side of the groove, readjust the fence, and trim the other side of the groove, referencing the same two sides of the base for both trim cuts.

When you're finished, leave the bit in the router and don't change the height adjustment. You'll need the same setup to cut the sliding dovetail keys.

3. Saw off the corners of the base, as shown in Step 3. If you don't, the guide rod block will bump into the base when you're routing small ellipses. I cut off two adjacent corners with the aid of the miter gauge on the table saw; then I set the rip fence to saw off the remaining corners.

MAKE THE SLIDING KEYS

1. Your dovetail bit is already adjusted to the correct height in your router table. Adjust the fence so the bit will cut slightly *shallower* than shown in *Sliding Key Details*, then take a pass on both sides of the sliding key stock. Check the key stock against the tracks to see how much more you must remove; then readjust the fence to remove *less than half* of the excess. (Remember that you remove wood from *both* sides of the stock.) The key stock should now *almost* fit. Move the fence over again a very tiny amount, take another pass *on one side only*, and test

the fit. If it won't go, take a pass on the *other* side. Continue in this fashion until the key fits into the track, but with no play. If it fits but seems a bit too tight, wax both the track and the key with paste furniture wax before resorting to another cut.

2. Rip the dovetail key from the key stock, leaving a ⅛-inch-thick shoulder, as shown in *Sliding Key Details*. Then crosscut it into two 3½-inch-long keys.

3. Drill a ¼-inch-diameter hole in the center of each sliding key and epoxy the pivot pins into the holes.

MAKE THE TRAMMEL BAR

1. Cut the trammel bar, guide rod block, and connecting plate to the dimensions given in the Materials List. Drill a series of holes down the center of the trammel bar, as shown in *Trammel Bar Details* on page 294. Use either a drill press or a dowelling jig to make sure these holes are perpendicular to the stock.

2. Screw the connecting plate to the trammel bar and to the guide rod block with #8 × ¾-inch roundhead wood screws.

3. Assemble the trammel and mark the location of the guide rod holes on the guide rod block, as shown in *Trammel Bar Details*. Then unscrew the guide rod block from the connecting

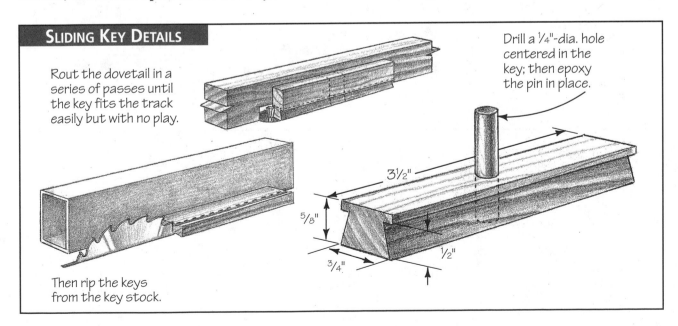

SLIDING KEY DETAILS

Rout the dovetail in a series of passes until the key fits the track easily but with no play.

Then rip the keys from the key stock.

Drill a ¼"-dia. hole centered in the key; then epoxy the pin in place.

3½"

5⁄8"

3⁄4"

1⁄2"

plate and drill the holes. If your router's guide rods have a metric diameter and you have bits only with inch dimensions, use the closest size you have, either slightly over or slightly under the size of the rods.

4. Screw the connecting plate back onto the guide rod block and lay out the stove bolt hole locations midway between the guide rod holes and the ends of the guide rod block. Drill the ¼-inch-diameter holes for the stove bolts and countersink them on the bottom of the guide rod block.

5. Unscrew the connecting plate once again. If the guide rods fit their holes snugly but slide

easily, saw two kerfs in the guide rod block, as shown in *Trammel Bar Details*. These kerfs should pass through the centers of the guide rod holes and extend ¾ inch beyond the holes. You can cut the kerfs with the guide rod block in a tenoning jig on the table saw, on the band saw, or by hand. If you had to use a slightly oversized or undersized bit for the guide rod holes, cut the entire bottom off of the guide rod block instead of sawing just kerfs. This will make attachment of the router to the jig a little less convenient; but once the wing nuts are tightened up, the assembly will be just as rigid.

Trim the corners off the connecting plate, as shown in the drawing, and reassemble the trammel bar.

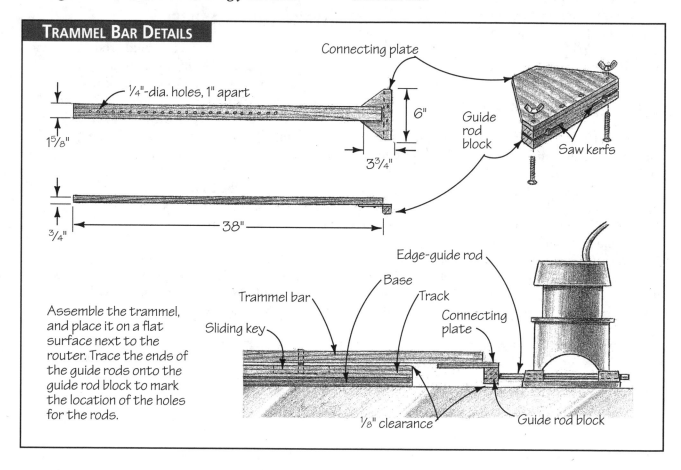

TRAMMEL BAR DETAILS

¼"-dia. holes, 1" apart

1⅝"

Connecting plate

6"

3¾"

Guide rod block

Saw kerfs

¾"

38"

Assemble the trammel, and place it on a flat surface next to the router. Trace the ends of the guide rods onto the guide rod block to mark the location of the holes for the rods.

Sliding key

Trammel bar

Base

Track

Edge-guide rod

Connecting plate

⅛" clearance

Guide rod block

COMPACT ROUTER TABLE

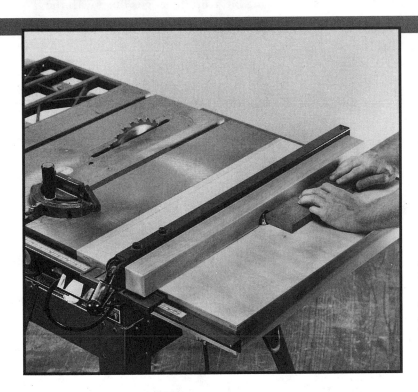

A router table that doubles as a table saw extension wing occupies space that is otherwise wasted and puts the rip fence to work on both machines.

A router table doubles the usefulness of a router by eliminating the need to clamp down stock and by making it possible to work on small pieces. You can have this increased utility without using up shop space by making a router table extension wing for your table saw. This arrangement also allows you to use the table saw rip fence for the router table. Add a thick wooden auxiliary fence to the side of the rip fence, as shown in the photo on this page.

You'll notice that the plan does not call for a separate router attachment insert in the router tabletop. I prefer the direct method of attaching the router because it avoids a potential source of unwanted movement. For changing bits,

I drop the entire router motor out of the router base, which I leave attached to the router table.

I've tried to make this design fit as many common table saws as possible, while still keeping it simple to make. Nevertheless, check the actual configuration of your saw before starting to build the table. You may need to modify the design to fit your saw. For example, check how your rip fence rails attach to the saw table and make sure you will be able to use the rails to help support the router table. Also, check that the router will not interfere with saw controls. You will certainly need to measure your saw table in order to determine the length of the top and long aprons.

MAKE THE TABLE

1. Cut the aprons, ribs, and cleat to the dimensions given in the Materials List.

2. Lay out the rib dados in the long aprons so the ribs will allow just enough room for your router base. Cut the dados ¼ inch deep × ¾ inch wide.

3. Cut the box joints on the ends of the aprons and assemble the aprons and ribs. I made these joints with ¼-inch-thick pins for maximum glue strength. (See "Making Box Joints" on page 174.)

4. Glue and screw the top to the rib and apron assembly. For a neat assembly, I suggest that you cut the top ¼ inch oversized; then, using a flush-trimming bit, trim the edges flush with the aprons after the glue is dry.

EXPLODED VIEW

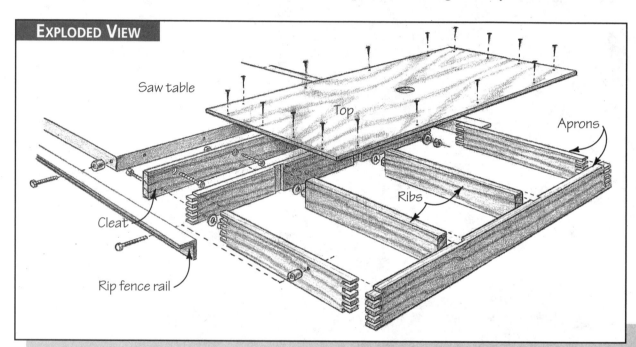

Saw table
Top
Aprons
Ribs
Cleat
Rip fence rail

MATERIALS LIST

WOOD: Use ¼-inch Baltic Birch plywood for the top and a stable hardwood like cherry for the other parts.

PART	QUANTITY	DESCRIPTION
Long apron	2	¾" × 2½" × saw table depth
Short apron	2	¾" × 2½" × 16"
Ribs	2	¾" × 2½" × 15"
Cleat	1	¾" × 2¾" × saw table depth
Top	1	¼" × 16" × saw table depth

HARDWARE

Mounting bolts	4	⁵⁄₁₆-18 × 1¼"
Mounting bolts	4	⁵⁄₁₆-18 × 2"
Nuts	8	⁵⁄₁₆-18
Flat washers	8	⁵⁄₁₆"
Lock washers	8	⁵⁄₁₆"
Wood screws	20	#6 × ¾"

ATTACH THE TABLE TO YOUR SAW

1. Remove the original extension wing from the saw. Clamp the cleat to the edge of the saw table and trace the extension wing bolt holes onto the cleat. You can position the cleat a whisker or two lower than the surface of the saw table, but not higher. Remove the cleat and drill ¹⁄₁₆-inch pilot holes through the cleat, centered on the bolt hole marks. Counterbore the opposite side of the cleat for the heads of the mounting bolts, then drill the shank holes for the bolts. Bolt the cleat to the saw table.

2. Clamp two straight-edged pieces of scrap to the saw table so they overhang where the router table will go, as shown in *Attachment Details*. Position one of them near the front edge of the saw and the other near the rear. Then clamp the router table to the bottom edges of the pieces of scrap, up tight against the cleat. This ensures that the router table will be exactly flush with the saw table. Drill ⁵⁄₁₆-inch holes through the long apron and cleat, and bolt the table to the cleat. Bolt the rip fence rails to the router table in the same way it is bolted to the saw table.

3. Remove the subbase from the base of your router and trace the mounting holes and the bit hole onto the router table top. Drill and countersink holes for the mounting screws. If you don't have a suitably large bit or hole saw to cut the router bit hole, drill a starter hole and cut out the bit hole with a saber saw. Mount the router base to the underside of the table. If you frequently switch back and forth between hand-held and table routing, consider buying an extra router base so you can leave one attached to the router table.

TOP VIEW

Space ribs to clear the router.

Router table length matches saw table.

16"

Cleat

Rip fence rails help support router table.

ATTACHMENT DETAILS

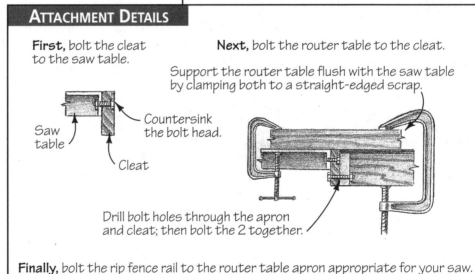

First, bolt the cleat to the saw table.

Saw table

Countersink the bolt head.

Cleat

Next, bolt the router table to the cleat.

Support the router table flush with the saw table by clamping both to a straight-edged scrap.

Drill bolt holes through the apron and cleat; then bolt the 2 together.

Finally, bolt the rip fence rail to the router table apron appropriate for your saw.

CROSSCUT SUPPORT

Stock support when crosscutting on the table saw is more than just a convenience; it helps you work safely and accurately. Since this support folds down when not in use, it works well in a home shop with limited space.

When I tell woodworkers that the most useful jig in my shop is my fold-down crosscut support, the response is predictable: "Your what?" They've never heard of such a jig. But it's a practical solution to one of the most common problems that woodworkers face: Supporting long stock when crosscutting on the table saw.

I think I know the reason why this jig, or something similar, is not in every book and magazine about woodworking: The design must change, sometimes quite a bit, to fit the wide variety of table saws on the market. But woodworkers are a pretty ingenious lot. Given the basic concept, I'm sure that the vast majority can figure out how to make the

idea work on their own saw. My guess is that you'll find it well worth your while to adapt the design and build it.

Adapting the Design

Your first step in adapting the design for your saw is determining the best way to hinge the support to the saw base. The drawings show T-hinges screwed to the saw base with sheet-metal screws. This works on quite a variety of saws. If it won't work on yours, consider fastening a separate hinge cleat to either the base or underside of the saw table.

Next, check that you will be able to access the saw's controls when the support is folded down. The control most likely to be in the way is the blade-tilt crank. You can change the attachment position or the spacing of the rails if you have an interference problem.

Finally, figure out the best overall length for the jig on your saw. As shown in the *Dimensioned Views/Front View* on page 300, the best support location is the same distance from the saw table edge as the blade. But on some saws, a jig that long will hit the floor when folded down, out of the way. When checking, be sure to measure from where the barrels of the hinges will be, since that's where the jig will pivot. If the best jig length for support will hit the floor, give up a little length.

MAKE THE SUPPORT

1. Cut the parts to the dimensions given in the Materials List (or as required by your adaptations) and chamfer the edges of the support bar.

2. Clamp the two rails together, side by side, with the ends flush. Hold the rails in their installed position under the saw table and mark the edge of the table on them. This will be the right edge of the latch bar. Lay out the left edge of the latch bar, which is also the right edge of the brace. Spread the rails apart and position the

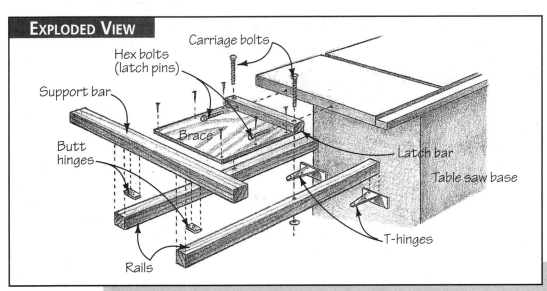

EXPLODED VIEW

MATERIALS LIST

WOOD: Use hardwood for the support frame and ¼-inch plywood for the brace.

PART	QUANTITY	DESCRIPTION
Rails	2	1½" × 1½" × variable
Latch bar	1	1½"* × 1½" × 12"
Support bar	1	1½"* × 2"† × 20"
Plywood brace	1	¼" × 12" × 15"

HARDWARE

Butt hinges	2	1½" with screws
T-hinges	2	3" with screws
Hex bolts	2	2½" × ¼"
Carriage bolts	2	3" × ¼" with nuts and washers
Drywall screws	6	#6 × 1"
Self-tapping sheet-metal screws	6	#10 × ½"

* Must match the thickness of the saw table.
† Must match the thickness of the saw table plus the thickness of the sled base.

brace on them. Glue and screw the brace in place, making sure the rails are parallel.

3. When the glue is dry, bolt the latch bar in place alongside the brace. Be sure to counterbore for the carriage bolt heads so they won't bump up your stock during crosscuts.

4. Lay out the hinge mortises on the support bar, as shown in *Hinge Details,* and chop the mortises so the hinge will be fully recessed in the support bar. This somewhat unconventional way of mounting the hinges is necessary so the support bar will be in full contact with the rails in both of its working positions. Install the hinges.

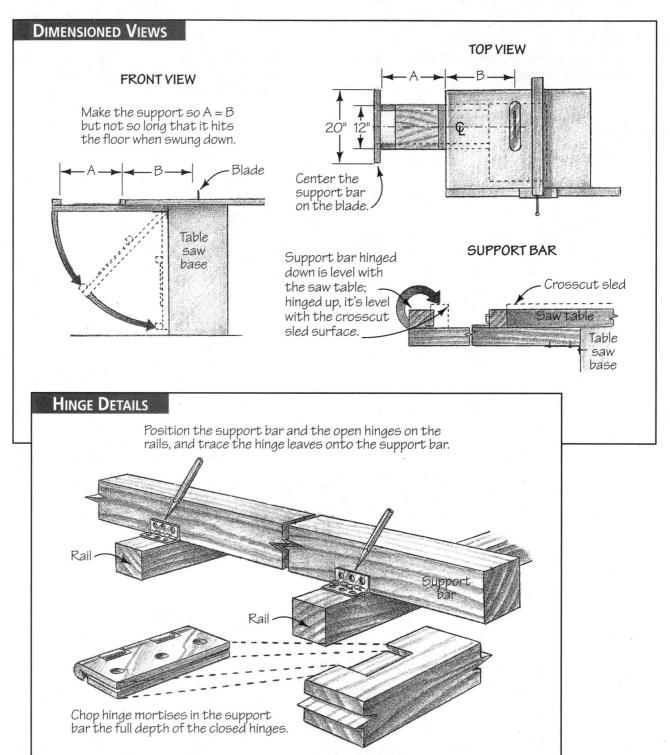

DIMENSIONED VIEWS

FRONT VIEW

Make the support so A = B but not so long that it hits the floor when swung down.

A   B   Blade

Table saw base

TOP VIEW

A   B

20"   12"

C L

Center the support bar on the blade.

SUPPORT BAR

Support bar hinged down is level with the saw table; hinged up, it's level with the crosscut sled surface.

Crosscut sled

Saw table

Table saw base

HINGE DETAILS

Position the support bar and the open hinges on the rails, and trace the hinge leaves onto the support bar.

Rail

Rail

Support bar

Chop hinge mortises in the support bar the full depth of the closed hinges.

INSTALL THE CROSSCUT SUPPORT

1. Screw the T-hinges to the bottoms of the rails, flush with the ends.

2. Clamp a pair of straight, stiff, pieces of lumber across the saw from the right edge of the saw table to approximately where the support bar will be on the left side. *Installing the Crosscut Support* shows 2 × 4s, but I've never seen a straight one. Use whatever is handy, long enough, and stiff enough to support the jig without bending—just make sure the bottom edge is straight. Clamp the jig to the bottom edge of the 2 × 4s, as shown in the drawing. Mark the centers of the T-hinge screw holes on the saw base with a center punch; then drill ⅛-inch holes in the saw base for the sheet metal screws. Screw the hinges in place.

3. Mark the ends of the latch bar on the edge of the saw table. Unclamp the jig from the 2 × 4s and let it swing down, but leave the 2 × 4s clamped to the saw table. Examine the saw table edge to find the best latch bolt locations. They should be at least an inch from the ends of the latch bar but not opposite any reinforcement ribs on the underside of the table. They should be about ½ inch down from the saw table surface. Drill ⅛-inch holes through the edge of the saw table at these locations.

4. Swing the jig back up and clamp it to the 2 × 4s; then mark the location of the ⅛-inch holes on the latch bar. Unclamp the jig and remove the 2 × 4s. Enlarge the holes in the table edge to ¼ inch and drill matching holes in the latch bar. You may need to unbolt the latch bar from the rails to drill these holes.

5. Use the hex bolts as latch pins by simply inserting them through the holes in the latch bar and into the holes in the edge of the saw table. There is no need for nuts on the ends. In fact, you may find that they work more easily if you saw off the threaded part and file the ends to a bullet shape. You could also replace both the latch bar and the latch pins with a couple of door bolts. If the support bar is not at quite the right height after you install the jig, don't try to change the T-hinge locations or the latch pins. Instead, either plane down or shim up the support bar. I shimmed mine up with low-friction tape so stock would slide more easily.

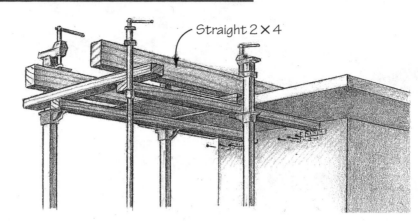

INSTALLING THE CROSSCUT SUPPORT

Straight 2 × 4

1. Screw T-hinges to rails.
2. Clamp straight 2 × 4s across saw table.
3. Clamp crosscut support to 2 × 4s.
4. Drill ⅛" holes in the saw base for sheet metal screws to hold T-hinges.
5. Screw hinges to the saw base.

INDEX

Note: Page references in *italic* indicate tables. **Boldface** references indicate photos and illustrations.